The IMPACT Coaching Guidebook

Discover Timeless Wisdom, Proven Coaching Strategies, and the Powerful Framework for Unleashing Your Full Potential

By

Chandan Lal Patary

From the Author of the books, The Scrum Master Guidebook, The Product Owner Guidebook, High-Performance Team Coaching Guidebook, The Innovation Blueprint and Master your Mind, Master your leadership

INDIA · SINGAPORE · MALAYSIA

ISBN 979-8-89961-799-7

Also, by Chandan Lal Patary

- *The Innovation Guidebook*

- *101 Enterprise Business Transformation Case Studies*

- *The Product Owner Guidebook: A Pragmatic Reference Manual for Maturing Product Coaching*

- *A Guidebook of Coaching High-Performance Team*

- *WE CAN LEAD: A Guidebook of Personal Leadership and Self-Coaching*

- *The Scrum Master Guidebook: A Reference for Obtaining Mastery*

- *The Agilist's Guidebook – A Reference for agile transformation*

- *50 Tools to Coach Your Way to Success*

- *Master your Mind, Master your Leadership*

Chandan Lal Patary: A Journey of Transformation, Knowledge, and Purpose

Chandan Lal Patary, based in Bangalore, Karnataka, India, is a seasoned transformation coach, technologist, and thought leader in enterprise agility, leadership, and innovation. He lives with his wife and two children and brings with him a diverse, two-decade-long journey filled with continuous learning, impactful leadership, and knowledge sharing.

Chandan began his professional life as an apprentice engineer in an electrical machine repair company and later transitioned into the software industry as a trainer. Over time, he grew into roles such as test engineer, developer, technical lead, project manager, program manager, global program manager, engineering manager, and finally into his current role as an enterprise agile transformation coach. His career trajectory is a testament to his adaptability, resilience, and lifelong learning mindset.

He has accumulated a rich tapestry of experience across various industries such as Retail Fashion, Oil & Gas, Banking, Healthcare, Aerospace, Building Automation, Power Automation, Consumer Electronics, and Industrial Automation. His work has spanned companies like GE Medical Systems, Honeywell, ABB, Société Générale, Royal Dutch Shell, Samsung, and H&M. He has collaborated with global teams from the USA, Germany, Sweden, China, Australia, Finland, Switzerland,

France, Poland, Korea, London, and the Netherlands—experiences that have sharpened his technical acumen and cross-cultural leadership skills.

Chandan holds a Bachelor of Engineering in Electrical Engineering from NIT Agartala (1998) and an Executive General Management Program certification from IIM Bangalore (2007). He is a certified PMP (2008), Green Belt holder (2005), Certified Scrum Master (2011), and SAFe Agilist (2017).

One of Chandan's most profound experiences was in product development. While working with GE Datex Ohmeda in Finland, he co-developed patient monitoring systems for critical care units, gaining deep insights into real-time systems and software architecture. Later, with Honeywell Aerospace, he helped deliver aviation software for cockpit systems used by Airbus and Boeing, including taking part in flight tests in Seattle—an unforgettable highlight of his engineering career.

He then joined ABB Power Automation in Sweden, where he worked on mission-critical industrial control systems. This role provided him deep insights into distributed Agile software development. His other key roles have spanned from managing large banking applications at Société Générale, oil & gas solutions at Shell, to driving omnichannel retail transformation at H&M.

Chandan stumbled into coaching in 2012 when a Head of Global Product Management in Finland recommended him for the role. What began as a suggestion turned into his life's mission: to facilitate enterprise-wide transformation through agility and leadership development.

As a transformation agent, Chandan has dedicated over a decade to studying Organizational Development, Business Agility, and the intersection of innovation, strategy, and people leadership. His work focuses on how these elements can accelerate organizational growth and create meaningful, lasting change.

Chandan is also a prolific author and educator. He has authored several best-selling books including:

1. ***The Agilist Guidebook – A Reference for Organizational Agile Transformation (2018),***

2. ***The Scrum Master Guidebook – A Reference for Obtaining Mastery (2019),***

3. ***We Can Lead – A Guidebook of Personal Leadership and Self-Coaching (2020),***

4. ***A Guidebook of Coaching High-performance team (2021),***

5. ***The Product Owner Guidebook (2022),***

6. ***101 Enterprise Business Transformation Case Studies (2023).***

7. ***Business Metamorphosis: 50 Tools to Coach Your Way to Success (2024)***

8. ***The Innovation Blueprint (2024)***

9. ***and Master Your Mind, Master Your Leadership (2025)***

His upcoming book, *The IMPACT Coaching Guidebook*, dives deep into his proprietary coaching framework, which blends timeless wisdom with modern strategies to guide leaders, teams, and organizations toward excellence.

Beyond books, Chandan has contributed over 1,000+ blogs on LinkedIn, authored seven free eBooks on SlideShare, and published more than 50 technical papers across domestic and international journals, including 21 on DZone. He has delivered 20+ talks at conferences and created 30+ public presentations. In recognition of his work, he received the PM World Journal Editor's Choice Award in 2017 for his paper on business agility through organizational transformation.

His ultimate goal? To build a "Body of Knowledge (BoK)" that can empower future leaders and change agents. His mission is rooted in sharing real-world discoveries, encouraging collaborative problem-solving, and creating guidebooks and tools that others can leverage.

Purpose: Share the research and practical experience I have gathered to help others overcome transformation challenges and build organizational strength.

Vision: To create a globally recognized knowledge ecosystem that supports enterprise transformation and leadership development.

Mission: To continuously document insights and results from real-world challenges and disseminate them through practical, accessible formats.

Join Chandan in his journey of knowledge, growth, and transformation. Learn more at: https://chandanpatary.com

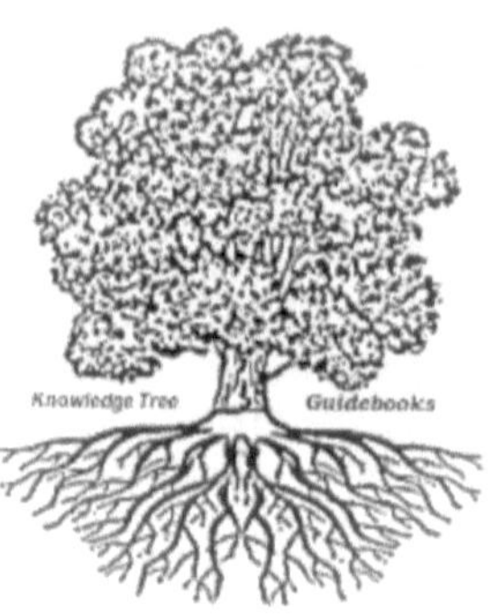

Acknowledgments

The contributions of numerous people have influenced this book. I want to thank everyone who offered feedback, shared tales, or offered suggestions. This book was inspired by all my friends and coworkers from both my current and past businesses. In order to write this book, I would like to thank all the Scrum masters, Agile coaches, and leaders with whom I have had contact or who I have interviewed. I would like to thank everyone of my fans and readers on social media for leaving me comments and suggestions so I can get better.

The wonderful people I have had the pleasure of getting to know and working with contributed to this book in a truly collaborative manner. It is an honor for me to work with such supportive coworkers. They offer motivation to write more effectively and pointers for doing study.

The hundreds of team members and clients that I have had the privilege of working with and listening to, coaching, advising, and learning from have allowed me to advance in my proficiency.

I would like to thank all my colleagues with whom I have discussed ideas and confirmed my knowledge. I appreciate the constant support and criticism from all 30,000+ of my LinkedIn contacts.

My sincere gratitude goes out to all the prior supervisors and mentors who have molded, supported, and encouraged my professional progress over the past two decades.

I am profoundly grateful for the valuable leadership lessons I have learned from remarkable individuals throughout my journey. Each mentor and colleague have contributed uniquely to my growth, imparting insights that have shaped my leadership philosophy. From understanding the importance of empathy to navigating complex challenges with resilience, these lessons have been instrumental in my professional development. I owe a debt of gratitude to each of them for the opportunities they provided and the wisdom they shared.

A heartfelt expression of gratitude extends to my beloved wife, children, and parents, who have been unwavering pillars of support throughout my endeavors. Their encouragement, love, and understanding have played an indispensable role in my ability to overcome challenges and achieve milestones. My wife's unwavering support has been my anchor, providing the strength needed to navigate the complexities of leadership. My children's boundless enthusiasm has infused joy into my journey, reminding me of the significance of passion and purpose. Lastly, my parents' guidance and wisdom have been a constant source of inspiration, instilling in me the values that guide my leadership approach.

Completing this task was not an individual achievement but a collective effort, and I am immensely grateful for the profound impact my family has had on my personal and professional growth. Their presence has touched every aspect of my life, making this accomplishment a shared success.

Contents

The Power of Coaching to Transform Leaders, Organizations, and Nations

A young boy sat in the dust of a crumbling empire, his future uncertain. Beside him stood a man whose eyes held the weight of a thousand plans. **"You will be a king,"** he declared—not as a wish, but as a certainty. That boy, Chandragupta Maurya, was nothing more than a street urchin at the time, yet he would rise to become the founder of one of the greatest dynasties in Indian history. His transformation was no accident—it was the result of relentless coaching from the brilliant strategist, Chanakya.

Across history, we find similar stories. A short, awkward soldier dismissed for his Corsican accent would go on to shake the very foundations of Europe—because he dared to learn, adapt, and be mentored. A penniless Scottish immigrant would rise to become one of the richest men in history—not through privilege, but through the guidance of a mentor who saw his potential. A company once at the peak of its industry would collapse under the weight of fear and hesitation, while another—on the verge of creative death—would rise again through visionary leadership.

These are not just stories of success. They are stories of transformation.

What turns an ordinary individual into an extraordinary leader? **The answer is coaching.**

The Coaching Effect: The Hidden Force Behind Greatness

Leadership is often painted as a lone journey—a single figure standing tall against all odds, charting an unshakable course to victory. But history tells a different story. Behind every great leader is a mentor, a coach, or a structured system of guidance that shapes their growth.

Napoleon Bonaparte, one of history's most brilliant military minds, was not simply born with strategic genius. He studied under master tacticians, absorbed their lessons, and refined his own methods. Andrew Carnegie, the steel magnate, credited his success to Thomas Scott, who taught him not only business but the art of leadership.

Even entire nations have been reshaped through coaching. Lee Kuan Yew took a struggling island and transformed it into one of the world's most prosperous nations through a vision fuelled by discipline, education, and structured mentorship. Swami Vivekananda did not just preach spiritual wisdom—he ignited the potential within millions, coaching a generation into self-belief and action.

Coaching is not a soft skill. It is the **single most powerful tool** for unlocking potential, driving transformation, and creating lasting impact.

The IMPACT Coaching Framework: A System for Transformational Leadership

Through the pages of this book, you will discover the **IMPACT Coaching Framework**, a model built upon real-world success stories, ancient wisdom, and modern behavioural science. It is not just a theory—it is a **proven methodology** that has guided leaders through crises, empowered businesses to thrive, and rebuilt entire communities from the ashes.

You will see how:

- History's greatest leaders—from Chandragupta Maurya to Marcus Aurelius—used coaching to refine their skills and navigate challenges.

- The world's most influential business minds, like Ed Catmull of Pixar, harnessed mentorship to fuel innovation and transformation.

- Companies, from Disney to struggling startups, have either thrived through structured coaching or crumbled in its absence.

- The wisdom of philosophers like Seneca, Confucius, and Rumi aligns with the principles of modern coaching, proving that the art of mentorship is timeless.

But most importantly, this book will challenge you to think about **your own leadership journey.**

This book will transform the way you think, lead, and grow yourself—and those around you—through the power of coaching

Your Journey Begins Now

The lessons within these chapters are not just stories—they are blueprints. The leaders you will read about were not born extraordinary; they became extraordinary through discipline, resilience, and mentorship. And if they could do it, **so can you.**

The only question that remains is: **Will you take action?**

You are not just a reader. **You are a leader in the making.**

The Science and Power of Coaching

Coaching is more than a process—it is a transformative journey that empowers individuals to unlock their full potential. It is not about generic motivation or feel-good exercises. It is a structured, science-backed approach that fosters real, lasting change. Coaching taps into the core principles of human psychology, neuroscience, and behavioral science to reshape the way people think, act, and grow.

Think of a time when you felt stuck—unsure of how to move forward, weighed down by doubts, or uncertain about the best path to take. This is where coaching becomes a catalyst for transformation. It provides clarity in the midst of confusion, structure amid chaos, and momentum where progress seems impossible. It bridges the gap between where individuals are and where they aspire to be.

At its heart, coaching is a dynamic partnership. The role of a coach is not to dictate solutions but to illuminate new perspectives, challenge limiting beliefs, and guide individuals toward breakthroughs. It is a process of self-discovery, where people learn to navigate their thoughts, emotions, and behaviors with greater awareness and control.

But why does coaching work? What makes it such a powerful force for change? The answer lies in the way it aligns with the fundamental mechanisms of human learning, behavior, and motivation.

Unlocking Self-Awareness and Emotional Intelligence

True transformation begins with self-awareness. It is the foundation of personal and professional success—the ability to recognize one's emotions, behaviors, and triggers. Yet, self-awareness is often clouded by habits, biases, and unconscious patterns.

A breakthrough study by psychologist Daniel Goleman found that emotional intelligence (EQ) contributes up to 90% of workplace success. People who understand their emotions and manage them effectively navigate relationships, challenges, and decisions with greater confidence and clarity.

Coaching acts as a mirror, reflecting hidden patterns that individuals might not see on their own. Through guided conversations, thought-provoking questions, and deep introspection, coaches help individuals uncover their strengths and weaknesses, empowering them to make more informed choices. With increased self-awareness, individuals shift from reactive to intentional living—taking control of their emotions, thoughts, and actions.

Rewiring the Brain: The Neuroscience of Coaching

The human brain is not fixed—it is constantly evolving and adapting, a phenomenon known as **neuroplasticity.** Every thought, experience, and habit strengthen or weakens neural connections. Coaching leverages this adaptability, helping individuals rewire their minds to break free from limiting beliefs and adopt new, empowering ways of thinking.

Research from the NeuroLeadership Institute reveals that coaching enhances neural pathways related to problem-solving, creativity, and emotional regulation. Over time, old mental roadblocks dissolve, replaced by fresh perspectives and strengthened cognitive flexibility.

Coaching conversations do not just inspire—they create physiological changes in the brain. With consistent coaching, individuals develop stronger neural connections that support confidence, resilience, and high-performance thinking.

The Strength-Based Approach: Fueling Success with Positive Psychology

Too often, personal development focuses on fixing weaknesses. Coaching takes a different approach—it amplifies **strengths.** Studies in positive psychology, pioneered by Martin Seligman, show that when people focus on what they naturally do well, they perform at higher levels, feel more engaged, and experience greater fulfillment.

A large-scale study by Clifton & Harter found that individuals who use their strengths daily are **six times more engaged at work and three times more likely to experience high life satisfaction.** Coaching helps people identify their unique talents and integrate them into their daily lives, shifting the focus from struggle to mastery.

By leaning into strengths, individuals create a cycle of motivation, confidence, and achievement—fueling momentum that propels them forward.

Goal Setting: Turning Vision into Reality

A dream without a plan remains a wish. Coaching transforms aspirations into **actionable, strategic steps** through the SMART goal framework—ensuring that goals are **Specific, Measurable, Achievable, Relevant, and Time-bound.**

Decades of research, including studies by psychologists Locke & Latham, confirm that individuals who set clear, challenging goals are significantly more likely to achieve them. However, goals alone are not enough—**the key lies in execution.**

A coach does not just help set goals; they break them down into manageable steps, create accountability, and ensure that progress stays on track. Each small success reinforces belief, turning possibility into reality.

Changing Habits, Changing Lives

Behavioral change is not easy. Habits are deeply ingrained, shaped by years of repetition and reinforcement. Breaking old patterns and building new ones requires more than willpower—it requires strategy.

Charles Duhigg, author of *The Power of Habit, explains that habits follow a cycle of* **cue, routine, and reward.** A 2009 study by Lally et al. found that on average, it takes **66 days** to form a new habit. Coaching makes this process manageable by **introducing habit-stacking techniques, structured repetition, and accountability.**

Rather than relying on discipline alone, coaching helps individuals design environments and routines that naturally support success. Over time, new behaviors become second nature—leading to lasting transformation.

Trust: The Foundation of Breakthroughs

Coaching is built on a foundation of **trust.** Without it, meaningful change is impossible. Trust allows individuals to open up, embrace vulnerability, and take the bold steps necessary for growth.

Studies in interpersonal psychology reveal that trust accelerates learning and progress. Research by Dr. John H. Zenger found that **trust accounts for 56% of coaching and leadership effectiveness.**

Coaches create this trust through empathy, active listening, and non-judgmental support. As trust deepens, individuals feel safe to challenge their limits, take risks, and push beyond their comfort zones—leading to profound breakthroughs.

The Power of Accountability

Commitment is easy—**follow-through is the challenge.** Research from the American Society of Training and Development (ASTD) shows that people are **65% more likely** to achieve their goals when they commit to someone, and **95% more likely** when they have regular check-ins.

Coaches provide **structured accountability,** ensuring that individuals stay committed to their goals. But accountability is not just about checking in—it is about **navigating setbacks, refining strategies, and keeping momentum alive.** When challenges arise, a coach ensures they do not derail progress but instead become learning opportunities.

Finding True Motivation

External motivation is fleeting. True, lasting change comes from within. **Self-Determination Theory,** developed by psychologists Edward Deci and Richard Ryan, shows that individuals are most motivated when they feel **autonomy, competence, and purpose.**

Coaching helps individuals uncover **what truly matters to them**—aligning their goals with their deepest values and passions. When aspirations are connected to a meaningful purpose, effort no longer feels like an obligation but a personal mission. This intrinsic drive creates **sustainable motivation and long-term success.**

The Science of Transformation

Coaching is not magic—it is a method grounded in psychology, neuroscience, and behavioral science. It works because it aligns with how humans naturally learn, grow, and change. Through self-awareness, neuroplasticity, strengths-based development, goal-setting, habit formation, trust, accountability, and intrinsic motivation, coaching provides a **clear roadmap to lasting transformation.**

The greatest potential lies **not in external circumstances, but within.** Coaching empowers individuals to tap into that potential, break through limitations, and create extraordinary results. With the right guidance, the path to growth is no longer uncertain—it becomes a journey of continuous evolution and achievement.

The pages ahead will explore this journey in depth—revealing the principles, techniques, and strategies that make coaching one of the most powerful forces for change.

Are you ready to transform your mindset, actions, and outcomes?

The journey begins now.

The Core Challenge We Aim to Transform

1. Self-Awareness & Identity

- What are my real strengths and blind spots—and how might ignoring them limit my growth or damage my relationships?

- Am I wearing a mask to fit in—and what is the cost of hiding my true self on my confidence and authenticity?

- What values truly define me—and if I do not act in alignment, how will that affect my clarity and decision-making?

- What emotions drive my choices—and if I stay unaware, how will that sabotage my leadership presence?

- What limiting belief am I still holding—and if I do not challenge it, how will it control my future?

2. Mental Agility & Mindset

- Do I view challenges as growth opportunities—or as threats—and if I do not shift this, how will it affect my resilience?

- What fears are shaping my decisions—and if I let them rule, what kind of life will I end up settling for?

- Do I over plan because I fear failure—and if I never act, what dreams will remain unlived?

- Is my perfectionism protecting me—or paralyzing me—and if I cling to it, what real progress am I sacrificing?

- How do I speak to myself when I fall—and if I stay self-critical, what will that do to my motivation and self-worth?

3. Purpose & Direction

- Am I pursuing goals that matter to me—or those that impress others—and if I do not align them, how long can I stay driven?

- What is my true purpose—and if I keep drifting without it, how will that drain my energy and direction?

- Am I chasing everything—or focusing on what matters—and if I do not prioritize, what will I actually accomplish?

- Do I celebrate progress—or keep chasing the next thing—and if I do not pause, how will I lose joy and momentum?

- Have I broken my vision into action—and if not, how will overwhelm stall my progress?

4. Action & Ownership

- What action have I been avoiding—and if I do not face it now, what will it cost me in the long run?

- Who or what keeps me accountable—and if I remain unaccountable, how likely am I to stay off course?

- Do I default to busyness instead of impact—and if I do not shift, how will that drain my time and energy?

- How do I respond to discomfort—and if I keep avoiding it, what confidence and growth am I missing?

- If I never start today, what will life look like a year from now—and how will I feel about that?

5. Relationships & Connection

- Do I ask for help when needed—or try to do it all alone—and if I do not shift, how will that limit my growth and trust?

- How well do I listen and communicate—and if I keep misaligning, how much trust and influence am I losing?

- Do I build others up—or lead from fear—and if I do not change, what kind of environment am I creating?

- Do I avoid hard conversations—and if I keep doing that, what unresolved issues will quietly grow?

- If I stay disconnected, how will I ever lead with depth and impact?

6. Growth & Transformation

- Am I evolving—or clinging to who I used to be—and if I resist change, how will I become irrelevant or stuck?

- What outdated habits or stories do I need to release—and if I do not let go, what transformation am I postponing?

- What is holding me back from bold moves—and if I do not act now, what regret might I carry later?

- Do I have inner peace—or just external success—and if I ignore this, what will it cost me emotionally?

- If I never fully transform, what version of myself will I be settling for?

The Impact of Coaching: Proven Benefits Across Business, Leadership, and Organizational Success:

1. Business & Leadership Coaching Impact

The Compelling ROI of Coaching: $7.90 for Every Dollar Invested. Let us talk numbers. A 2009 International Coach Federation (ICF) study revealed a remarkable average return on investment (ROI) of $7.90 for every single dollar spent on coaching. This is not just a marginal gain; it is a powerful testament to the profound financial impact coaching delivers for both individuals and the entire organization.

Leadership Development: The Top Priority, Powered by Coaching. In today's competitive landscape, effective leadership is paramount. The Human Capital Institute's 2016 report confirms this, with a significant 85% of organizations identifying leadership development as their number one priority. Coaching stands as a cornerstone of these initiatives, equipping leaders with the skills needed to excel in greater roles and navigate complex challenges with confidence.

Unleashing Human Potential: Coaching Drives Improved Performance. The impact of coaching is clearly seen in individual results. According to the 2016 ICF Global Coaching Study, an impressive 70% of individuals who received coaching reported improved work performance, and 60% experienced enhanced business management skills. Investing in coaching directly translates to a more productive and capable workforce.

2. Coaching for Employee Engagement and Satisfaction

Why Employees Stay: The Coaching Connection. Employee retention is a critical challenge. The ICF Global Coaching Study 2016 provides a compelling reason to invest in coaching: organizations with coaching programs saw a remarkable 48% improvement in keeping their talent. Coaching provides the very growth and development opportunities that employees seek, fostering a deeper connection and commitment to the organization's success.

The Engagement Equation: Coaching for a High-Performing Culture. Disengaged employees represent lost potential. Gallup's study highlights the power of engagement: highly engaged teams are significantly more productive (21%) and profitable (17%). Coaching plays a vital role in building this crucial engagement by nurturing trust, fuelling motivation, and developing the skills employees need to feel valued and contribute meaningfully.

3. Performance Improvement

Beyond Individual Growth: Coaching Elevates Team Performance. Why limit the benefits of coaching to individuals? A study in the International Journal of Coaching in Organizations demonstrates the profound impact of coaching on group dynamics, showing a significant 25% improvement in team performance. This underscores that coaching is a powerful tool for fostering collaboration, communication, and ultimately, collective success.

Thriving Individuals, Thriving Organizations: The Coaching Effect. The Human Capital Institute's 2019 report provides compelling evidence of the personal benefits of coaching. Employees who received coaching experienced a remarkable 61% increase in their personal productivity and a significant 53% rise in their job satisfaction. This highlights that investing in the individual through coaching not only boosts output but also cultivates a more engaged and satisfied workforce.

4. Coaching for Corporate Change and Transformation

The Change Challenge: 70% Failure Rate. Why do so many organizational change initiatives stumble? McKinsey & Company reveals a stark truth: a staggering 70% fail due to a lack of employee engagement and leadership buy-in. But there is a powerful solution...

Coaching: The Catalyst for Successful Change. Coaching is not just a nice-to-have; it is a critical lever for navigating change. It directly tackles the root causes of failure by overcoming resistance and fostering alignment among individuals and teams with new organizational goals.

Leadership Transformation: Coaching as the Engine. How do you equip leaders to steer through turbulent times? A 2019 Korn Ferry study confirms that coaching stands out as one of the most effective methods for leadership transformation. Leaders who embrace coaching become better equipped to not only manage change but to drive innovation and ignite inspiration within their teams

5. Coaching and Financial Performance

The Bottom Line Speaks Volumes: Coaching Drives Profitability. Why invest in coaching? The numbers provide a compelling answer. A 2014 PricewaterhouseCoopers (PwC) study found that organizations with structured coaching programs saw their profitability leap by a remarkable 25% over five years. This is not a coincidence; it is evidence of how coaching directly fuels enhanced financial success.

Leadership Development: A Direct Path to Financial Growth. Want to see a tangible impact on your financial performance? Research by Zenger & Folkman shows that organizations committed to leadership coaching experience a significant 22% increase in their financial results. This highlights a fundamental principle: investing in your leaders through coaching is a strategic imperative for driving financial growth.

6. The Neuroscience of Coaching

Lasting Change Starts in the Brain: The Coaching Advantage. Tired of fleeting improvements? Research from the NeuroLeadership Institute offers a powerful insight: coaching taps into neuroplasticity, the brain's inherent ability to rewire itself. This is not about quick fixes; it is about creating lasting behavioural change that sticks, whether you are aiming to sharpen decision-making, master your emotions, or conquer complex problems.

Emotional Intelligence: The Performance Multiplier, Enhanced by Coaching. The numbers speak for themselves. Talent Smart's research highlights that 90% of top performers excel in emotional intelligence (EQ), and those with higher EQ achieve up to 29% greater results than their counterparts. Because coaching often places a strong emphasis on developing and refining EQ, it emerges as an indispensable tool for unlocking and maximizing human potential.

7. Global Coaching Trends

- **Global Growth**: According to the **ICF Global Coaching Study**, the global coaching industry reached a **$15 billion market** in 2019, growing at a rate of **6.7% annually**. This shows how coaching has become a mainstream, essential tool for organizational and leadership development worldwide.

- **Industry Adoption**: **62% of Fortune 100 companies** reported using external coaches for leadership development, with coaching programs becoming an integral part of corporate development strategies. This reflects a widespread acceptance of coaching as a legitimate and necessary part of organizational growth.

8. Coaching for Well-being and Mental Health

- **Workplace Mental Health**: A **2020 report by Deloitte** found that **50% of employees** across various industries reported experiencing high levels of stress, with **mental health issues** costing companies an estimated **$1 trillion annually** in lost productivity. Coaching, especially focused on emotional intelligence and mental resilience, can be a powerful tool to mitigate stress and promote mental well-being.

- **Burnout Reduction**: According to a **Harvard Business Review** article, **executives who engage in regular coaching sessions** experience **lower levels of burnout** and higher levels of emotional resilience.

9. The Role of Coaching in Diversity and Inclusion

- **Diversity Coaching**: Research from the **Center for Talent Innovation** shows that organizations with diversity and inclusion coaching programs are more likely to retain and promote women and minorities in leadership positions, leading to better organizational outcomes.

- **Inclusion and Leadership**: The **2018 McKinsey Report** indicates that companies with higher levels of diversity are **35% more likely** to experience above-average financial returns. Coaching leaders on inclusivity and cultural competence can further drive positive organizational outcomes.

10. Coaching for Innovation and Creativity

- **Innovation Gains**: A **2017 study by PwC** showed that companies who actively invest in creativity and coaching for innovation saw a **20% increase in their innovation output**—this includes new product development, improved services, and disruptive business models.

- **Fostering Innovation**: According to **Harvard Business Review**, **coaching can help leaders foster a culture of creativity** by encouraging risk-taking, enhancing problem-solving abilities, and promoting cross-functional collaboration.

What You Will Read and Realize: Chapter by Chapter Transformation?

Chapter 1: The Foundation of Coaching Transformation

Embark on a journey of self-discovery in this chapter, where you will learn how true transformation originates from within. You will explore the IMPACT Coaching Framework as a guiding blueprint for your personal and professional evolution in a constantly evolving landscape. Understand the scientific foundation that makes this framework effective, fostering deep self-awareness, a strong sense of purpose, and the courage to act decisively. This chapter introduces the I-M-P-A-C-T model—Inspiration, Mindset, Purpose, Action, Connection, and Transformation—as your roadmap to conscious coaching. We will also examine the common hurdles encountered by coaches and young leaders, including the unseen internal forces that can impede their advancement. Through reflective exercises and practical advice, you will begin your coaching journey grounded in authenticity, emotional intelligence, and the empowering belief that transformation is not merely an end goal, but an integral part of your daily life and leadership.

Chapter 2: Timeless Coaching Wisdom and Global Philosophies

This chapter bridges the timeless wisdom of philosophers, spiritual leaders, and sages with the dynamic practices of modern coaching. Through the lives and teachings of luminaries like Swami Vivekananda, Marcus Aurelius, Rumi, Seneca, and Confucius, you will discover how inner mastery ignites profound outer impact. Journey through profound insights on resilience, self-leadership, and purpose, understanding that true greatness springs from stillness, reflection, and a life guided by core values. Through poetic narratives and grounded reflections, you will explore how enduring principles such as stoicism, spiritual alignment, self-inquiry, and mental discipline can profoundly deepen your coaching capacity. This chapter illuminates the powerful truth: effective leadership of others begins with a deep and unwavering ability to know, coach, and lead oneself with clarity, integrity, and conviction.

Chapter 3: Coaching in Action — Historical & Legendary Leaders.

This chapter reveals how the transformative power of coaching underpinned the success of history's greatest leaders. More than just warriors or kings, they were deeply influenced individuals who underwent profound personal growth before impacting the world. From Chanakya's mentorship of Chandragupta Maurya's strategic brilliance to Napoleon Bonaparte's visionary ambition, Zhuge Liang's spiritual strength, and Ernest Shackleton's unwavering resilience, we examine how coaching played a crucial role in pivotal leadership moments. Through compelling historical accounts, you will see how courage, clarity, mentorship, and perseverance, often fostered by coaching, shaped legendary figures, and their lasting legacies. You will also understand how coaching served as the silent catalyst for revolutions, peace missions, and nation-building, including Lee Kuan Yew's transformative leadership and Sierra Leone's post-war recovery. Ultimately, this chapter illuminates that leadership is not solely acquired through formal education but is forged in crisis, refined through adversity, and cultivated by coaching that identifies potential where others see only obstacles.

Chapter 4: The Modern Coaching Revolution

This chapter explores the profound impact of coaching in reshaping leadership across diverse fields—from boardrooms to creative studios and sports fields. Uncover the transformational journeys of modern visionaries such as Andrew Carnegie, Ed Catmull of Pixar, and Sir Alex Ferguson, each of whom applied coaching principles to spark innovation, restore trust, and build exceptional teams. Through examples ranging from Disney's digital rebirth to the leadership lessons embedded in The Social Network, you will see the IMPACT Coaching Framework at work in today's intricate and rapidly evolving world. This chapter also celebrates the unsung heroes of coaching—mentors who changed lives not through notoriety, but through unwavering presence, genuine empathy, and purposeful action. Whether leading through crisis or translating strategic visions into meaningful execution, you will learn how the modern coaching revolution is fundamentally about cultivating better humans—one insightful conversation, one transformative breakthrough at a time.

Chapter 5: Coaching the Future — Legacy, Children & Global Challenges

This chapter unveils how coaching can become the vital bridge connecting today's values with tomorrow's world. It transcends guiding adults through corporate objectives, focusing instead on nurturing the minds and hearts of children, empowering youth with purpose, and tackling our planet's most pressing challenges with clarity and courage. Through inspiring narratives of Dr. A.P.J. Abdul Kalam's enduring legacy, Jacinda Ardern's empathetic leadership, and real-world stories of youth transformation, you will witness how coaching can shape lives from their earliest years and leave an indelible mark. Explore how to coach future leaders not merely for success, but to serve with intention, innovate with vision, and stand resilient in the face of global adversity. Whether cultivating resilience, fostering emotional intelligence, or encouraging collaborative problem-solving, this chapter demonstrates how the IMPACT Coaching Framework can awaken the inherent potential in every child, ignite the next generation of changemakers, and help forge a world where leadership is defined by empathy, equity, and enduring purpose.

Why Should You Read This Book?

Imagine holding not just a book, but a personal transformation engine in your hands. A mirror reflecting your potential, a compass guiding your growth, and a detailed map charting your journey inward. From the very first chapter, are you ready to embark on a deeply personal exploration of transformation that begins within?

Whether you are a coach seeking deeper impact, a leader striving for greater influence, a teacher aiming to inspire, or simply an individual committed to your own evolution, what if this book offered more than just theories? What if it provided the clarity you seek, ignited your inherent purpose, and unveiled a renewed sense of boundless possibility?

Have you ever felt the quiet yet persistent call to lead with genuine heart, to serve with unwavering strength, and to transform not only your external world but the very essence of your inner being?

If so, what awaits you within these pages is the IMPACT Coaching Framework—not a collection of abstract ideas, but a vibrant, living roadmap built upon authentic human experiences, real emotions, and tangible, real-world applications.

Are you ready to journey through the corridors of time and across the tapestry of cultures?

To glean wisdom from the ancient insights of philosophers, the inspiring actions of legendary leaders, and the innovative approaches of modern-day visionaries?

Can you imagine learning how individuals like Marcus Aurelius, Swami Vivekananda, Chanakya, Sir Alex Ferguson, and Dr. A.P.J. Abdul Kalam weren't simply born into greatness, but were shaped by life's profound coaching, guided by insightful mentors, and forged in the intense heat of pivotal moments?

What if coaching was not just a fleeting trend, but a fundamental force capable of reshaping classrooms, transforming boardrooms, and even influencing the trajectory of entire nations?

Could it be the invisible yet powerful thread that weaves together resilience in the face of adversity, empathy in human connection, the spark of creativity, and the enduring power of legacy?

This book does not just aim to teach you how to guide others—it begins with the essential journey of learning how to effectively guide yourself.

Are you ready to elevate not just your skills but your entire perspective? Do you aspire to equip the next generation not just with tools, but with deeply rooted values, a compelling vision for the future, and an unyielding vitality? Do you yearn to leave a legacy that resonates not just in tangible achievements, but in the hearts and minds of the people you impact?

In a world clamouring for attention and riddled with complexity, what if you had a quiet guide, a personal mentor held within the pages of a book, offering sparks of profound insight?

And perhaps the most crucial question of all: shouldn't you read this book because our world doesn't just need more followers, but urgently requires conscious coaches, awakened leaders, and individuals who dare to step forward and make a real, lasting impact?

How I Found and Developed the IMPACT Coaching Framework: A Journey of Growth and Belief

For a decade, I, Chandan, have been privileged to witness a quiet revolution in the lives and leadership of individuals across diverse backgrounds and organizations, all through the lens of the IMPACT Coaching Framework. What if you could unlock a similar transformation within yourself and those you lead? This is not just theory; it is the story of real people, real breakthroughs, and the tangible power of a proven framework. Let me share glimpses of this journey with you...

I – Inspire Awareness & Identity: The Unveiling of Self Imagine Raj, a bright professional, hitting a wall despite his achievements, a stranger to his own true identity. Our work together became an exploration of his core—his strengths, values, passions. The revelation? He had been wearing his job title like a mask, obscuring the authentic leader within. Witnessing Raj shed that skin, embrace his unique style, and lead with genuine authenticity was a powerful testament: true leadership blossoms from the deep wellspring of self-knowledge.

M – Mindset & Mastery Shift: The Power of "Yet" The most profound shifts often begin with a change in perspective. Take Neha, a driven senior manager paralyzed by perfectionism and the fear of failure. Doubt was her constant companion, risk her sworn enemy. Through coaching, we did not just change her thoughts; we reframed her reality. Mistakes transformed from threats into invaluable teachers. The fear of failure receded, replaced by the thrill of new challenges. Her newfound confidence was not just visible; it was contagious, forging her into a far more impactful leader. This cemented my belief: a growth mindset is not just beneficial; it is foundational.

P – Purpose-Driven Goals & Strategy: The North Star of Intention Kunal, a brilliant entrepreneur brimming with ideas, felt adrift, his vision clouded by a lack of clear direction. Our focus became his "why"—what truly resonated beyond the bottom line. This unearthed purpose became his North Star, guiding the creation of specific, value-aligned goals. The result? Not just business growth, but a renewed sense of joy and passion that fuelled his every endeavour. This experience illuminated the undeniable power of purpose-driven action.

A – Action, Accountability & Adaptability: The Momentum of Progress The gap between intention and impact is often paved with inaction. Sameer, a talented tech professional, nursed a powerful idea for years, held captive by fear. We dismantled his grand vision into manageable steps, weaving in accountability through our sessions and a supportive mentorship network. He learned the power of the first imperfect step, igniting a snowball effect of momentum and adaptability. His project not only succeeded; it transformed Sameer into a staunch advocate for consistent, courageous action.

C – Connection & Collaborative Growth: The Strength of the We
Leadership is not a solo act; it is a symphony of connection. Rina, a capable team leader, struggled with communication and trust, hesitant to delegate or seek support, hindering both her growth and her team's potential. Our work focused on building bridges—improving her communication and fostering trust within her team. As Rina began to empower her members and actively solicit feedback, her leadership blossomed, and her team became a cohesive, high-performing unit. This underscored the vital role of collaboration and connection in strong leadership.

T – Transform & Thrive: The Art of Sustainable Impact Even success can feel like a cage. Arvind, a high-achieving executive, found himself burned out and stagnant despite his accomplishments. Our focus shifted to creating sustainable habits for long-term growth. He learned to manage his energy, prioritize well-being, and focus on enduring impact over short-term gains. Arvind's transformation was profound—a newfound balance, a deeper sense of purpose, and a conscious consideration of his lasting legacy. This final piece of the IMPACT puzzle revealed the crucial importance of not just achieving, but thriving.

My decade-long journey with the IMPACT Coaching Framework has been a front-row seat to profound and lasting change. From igniting self-awareness to cultivating a growth mindset, from setting purposeful goals to fostering collaborative growth and ultimately thriving, this framework is not just a theory; it is a catalyst for unlocking human potential. Every story of transformation fuels my passion, reminding me that coaching is not just about achieving success—it is about the powerful journey of becoming the most authentic and impactful version of ourselves, leaving a legacy that truly matters.

Chapter 1

The Foundation of Coaching Transformation

Where Real Change Begins

In today's fast-changing world, people are often searching for direction, clarity, and a deeper sense of purpose. Many young and emerging leaders struggle with questions about who they are, what they want, and how to move forward. This is where coaching becomes more than a helpful tool—it becomes a path to real transformation.

This opening chapter introduces the IMPACT Coaching Framework, a simple yet powerful model that helps individuals grow both personally and professionally. Whether you are a parent, teacher, leader, or mentor, this framework can guide you in helping others reach their full potential. But coaching is not just about giving advice or setting goals. It is about helping someone discover who they really are, shift the way they think, and take meaningful steps toward a better future.

True coaching begins with self-discovery. Before someone can lead others or chase big goals, they need to understand themselves. That means understanding their emotions, values, fears, and dreams. Many coaching methods jump straight to teaching or pushing for results. But lasting leadership begins when a person truly knows and accepts who they are. A good coach creates space for reflection, allowing individuals to meet themselves fully before offering guidance.

One of the biggest things that holds people back is fear. Children and young leaders especially need to be taught that fear is normal—and even useful. Instead of pretending fear does not exist, great coaches help them face it, understand it, and work through it. Confidence does not come from ignoring fear, but from learning to walk with it. This builds the kind of inner strength that leads to real, lasting courage.

Leadership is not a title or a destination. It is a way of living. It is about how we treat others, how we make decisions, and how we show up in everyday moments. Good coaching does not just focus on reaching big goals. It teaches people how to live the journey—with kindness, consistency, and purpose. By guiding children and young adults to find meaning in what they do, break down their dreams into small, achievable steps, and work together with others, we help them grow into leaders who make a real difference.

To begin this journey, self-awareness is essential. This means being honest with ourselves, even when it is uncomfortable. It means looking at our habits, beliefs, and emotional reactions, and asking tough questions. Tools like journaling or talking with a mentor can help with this process, but the most important part is the willingness to reflect and grow.

Changing how we think—our mindset—is also a key part of transformation. Many people are stuck because they believe they cannot change, or they are afraid to fail. But with the right support and simple techniques like visualization or shifting our inner dialogue, we can move from fear to confidence, and from hesitation to action. A strong mindset gives us the power to face challenges with more clarity and resilience.

Of course, knowing ourselves and thinking positively is not enough. We also need to take action. That is why goal-setting and accountability matter. By turning our purpose into clear steps, and tracking our progress, we build momentum. Small wins, celebrated regularly, keep us moving forward. When coaching includes clear goals, steady routines, and support from others, transformation becomes a lifestyle—not just a temporary boost.

Throughout this chapter, you will see how the six parts of the IMPACT Framework—Inspiration, Mindset, Purpose, Action, Connection, and Transformation—fit together to guide lasting growth. You will learn how coaching begins with reflection, builds through courage, and blossoms through action and connection. You will also discover how great coaches do not just help others reach success—they help them leave a legacy.

Coaching, at its best, is about helping people discover their own voice, believe in their strength, and build a life of purpose and service. As you read this chapter, think of it as an invitation to begin a new kind of coaching journey—one rooted in awareness, authenticity, and deep transformation.

Key Topics:

- **The Blueprint for Unshakable Growth in a World of Constant Change**

- **The IMPACT Framework: Unleashing Human Potential Through Conscious Coaching**

- **The Science Behind IMPACT: Why This Framework Delivers Consistent Results**

- **The IMPACT Coaching Framework: A Transformational Approach to Self-Coaching**

- **The I-M-P-A-C-T Coaching Framework: Empowering Leadership Through Mentorship**

- **Overcoming Challenges in Applying the IMPACT Coaching Framework**

- **The Silent Saboteurs: 6 Coaching Mistakes That Hold Young Leaders Back**

Story -1:

The Blueprint for Unshakable Growth in a World of Constant Change

The world is moving at an unforgiving pace. Change is no longer an occasional disruption; it is the very fabric of life. Those who rise above mediocrity and carve a path of excellence are not merely talented or lucky—they are intentional. They cultivate resilience, refine their thinking, and take purposeful action. They embrace transformation as a way of life.

This is where the IMPACT Framework comes alive. More than a structured approach, it is a philosophy—a proven method for achieving lasting personal and professional growth. Whether you are an executive navigating complexity, an entrepreneur pushing boundaries, a coach shaping lives, or an individual striving for excellence, IMPACT is the roadmap that leads to meaningful success.

Unlike conventional methods that address fragmented aspects of development, IMPACT weaves six fundamental elements—**Inspiration, Mindset, Purpose, Action, Connection, and Transformation**—into a seamless journey. It is not about short-term motivation; it is about rewiring thought patterns, strengthening resolve, and creating a legacy that endures.

Awakening the Self: The Power of Awareness and Identity

The journey begins with a question: **Who am I?** Before transformation can take root, self-awareness must be cultivated. Without it, people remain trapped in repetitive cycles, never realizing why success eludes them.

Mahatma Gandhi understood this deeply. Through relentless journaling and introspection, he uncovered his truth, clarifying his purpose in the fight for justice. His unwavering commitment to nonviolence was not a random decision; it was the outcome of profound self-inquiry.

To embark on a similar path, individuals must pause, reflect, and ask: *What are my values? What limiting beliefs hold me back? What version of myself do I need to become?*

Shifting the Mindset: The Art of Mastery

The mind is both a prison and a gateway—it all depends on how it is trained. Fear, self-doubt, and limiting beliefs are the invisible walls that keep people from realizing their full potential. Those who break free are not necessarily the strongest or the smartest; they are the ones who shift their mindset.

Nelson Mandela spent twenty-seven years in prison, but he did not allow his circumstances to define him. Instead of bitterness, he chose resilience. Instead of revenge, he chose reconciliation. His mindset shaped not just his life, but an entire nation.

This is the power of reframing. Instead of asking, *Can I do this?* the question must shift to, *how can I do this?* By embracing cognitive tools and visualization techniques, individuals can turn obstacles into stepping stones.

Fueling Purpose: The Compass for Long-Term Success

Goals without purpose are like a ship without a compass—directionless and vulnerable to the tides of circumstance. Many sets ambitious goals but abandon them when motivation fades. The ones who persist have something deeper—**purpose**.

Elon Musk did not build Tesla and SpaceX for profit alone. His vision to make humanity multi-planetary fuels his relentless pursuit of innovation. Purpose is the difference between working hard and working with conviction.

To align actions with purpose, individuals must ask: *What truly drives me? What impact do I want to create?* When goals stem from deep purpose, they become non-negotiable.

Taking Relentless Action: The Bridge Between Dreams and Reality

Vision without execution is an illusion. Many aspire, few act. It is not ambition that separates success from stagnation—it is **discipline**. Execution is the great equalizer.

Thomas Edison failed over 10,000 times before perfecting the light bulb. Each failure was not an end but a lesson, a step closer to success. He was not the most gifted, but he was the most relentless.

To sustain action, individuals must build discipline through structured habits, accountability systems, and adaptability. It is not about waiting for the perfect moment—it is about taking the next step, no matter how small.

The Power of Connection: Growth Through Collaboration

No one achieves greatness alone. The strongest leaders are those who build networks, seek mentors, and empower others. Growth flourishes in **connection**.

Warren Buffett attributes much of his success to his mentor, Benjamin Graham, who introduced him to the principles of value investing. This single relationship transformed Buffett's trajectory.

Seeking out mentors, joining peer groups, and fostering meaningful relationships accelerate personal and professional growth. Knowledge is amplified when shared, and success multiplies when built on collaboration.

Transformation: Thriving Beyond Success

True success is not just about reaching milestones; it is about **sustained evolution**. Those who thrive continuously learn, adapt, and give back. The highest form of leadership is not achievement—it is legacy.

Dr. APJ Abdul Kalam was more than a scientist; he was a mentor, a visionary who shaped India's future through education and inspiration. His success was not just in building missile programs but in empowering generations to dream beyond limitations.

Sustained transformation requires commitment to lifelong learning, consistent self-reflection, and the willingness to create impact beyond oneself. The goal is not just to succeed but to leave the world better than it was found.

Your Growth Story Starts Here: Are You Ready to Create Your Own IMPACT?

The IMPACT Framework is not just a model—it is a **movement**. It is a call to those who refuse to settle, to those who seek growth, purpose, and transformation. By embracing these six pillars, anyone can break past limitations, achieve the extraordinary, and leave a lasting legacy.

Transformation is not an event; it is a way of life. The question is not whether the IMPACT Framework works.

The real question is: **Are you ready to work the framework and create your own impact?**

Key challenges that individuals face in each area of the **IMPACT** framework and how coaching helps overcome them:

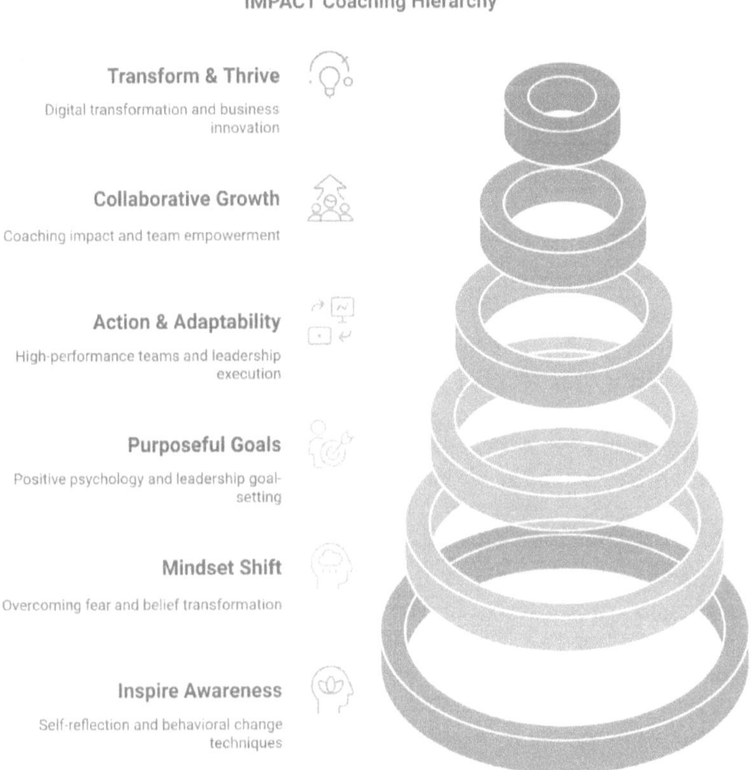

I - Inspire Awareness & Identity

Challenges related to self-awareness and leadership identity:

- **Lack of Clarity on Strengths & Weaknesses** – Struggling to identify what they excel at and where they need improvement.

- **Imposter Syndrome** – Feeling like a fraud despite achievements, leading to self-doubt.

- **Lack of Authentic Leadership Style** – Mimicking others rather than embracing a unique approach.

- **Emotional Blind Spots** – Difficulty recognizing how emotions impact decisions and actions.

- **Struggling with Core Values** – Unclear on personal values, leading to misalignment in choices.

- **Fear of Judgment** – Worrying too much about others' opinions, leading to hesitation.

- **Difficulty Receiving Feedback** – Feeling defensive or taking constructive criticism personally.

- **Confusion Between Identity and Role** – Defining oneself only by a job title rather than deeper qualities.

- **Unconscious Limiting Beliefs** – Holding onto internal narratives that restrict growth.

- **Resistance to Self-Reflection** – Avoiding introspection due to discomfort with facing personal truths.

How Coaching Helps: Coaching provides a mirror for self-reflection, helping individuals discover their identity, embrace their strengths, and develop emotional intelligence.

M - Mindset & Mastery Shift

Challenges related to mindset, confidence, and belief systems:

- **Fear of Failure** – Avoiding risks due to fear of making mistakes.

- **Negative Self-Talk** – Internal dialogue that reinforces self-doubt.

- **Fixed Mindset** – Believing that abilities and intelligence are static.

- **Perfectionism** – Struggling to take action due to an obsession with getting things "just right."

- **Fear of Change** – Resisting new opportunities due to uncertainty.

- **Overthinking & Analysis Paralysis** – Getting stuck in endless thinking without taking action.

- **Lack of Resilience** – Struggling to bounce back from setbacks.

- **External Validation Dependence** – Seeking approval before making decisions.

- **Comparing to Others** – Feeling inadequate by measuring success against others.

- **Procrastination Due to Fear of Judgment** – Delaying action out of fear of criticism.

How Coaching Helps: Coaching shifts individuals from a fixed mindset to a growth mindset, rewiring beliefs to embrace challenges, take risks, and build confidence.

P - Purpose-Driven Goals & Strategy

Challenges related to goal-setting, vision, and execution:

- **Unclear Goals** – Struggling to define what they truly want.

- **Lack of Direction** – Feeling lost or uncertain about their career or business path.

- **Setting Unrealistic Expectations** – Aiming too high too fast, leading to burnout.

- **Lack of Prioritization** – Trying to achieve too many things at once, leading to overwhelm.

- **No Action Plan** – Having big dreams but no roadmap to achieve them.

- **Failure to Track Progress** – Not measuring progress leads to loss of motivation.

- **Inability to Break Goals into Steps** – Feeling overwhelmed by the enormity of a goal.

- **Avoiding Commitment** – Hesitating to commit fully due to fear of failure.

- **Not Aligning Goals with Purpose** – Setting goals based on external expectations rather than personal values.

- **Giving Up Too Soon** – Quitting when results do not come immediately.

How Coaching Helps: Coaches help individuals create clear, achievable, and purpose-driven goals, breaking them into actionable steps while ensuring they stay aligned with their values.

A - Action, Accountability & Adaptability

Challenges related to execution, follow-through, and adaptability:

- **Lack of Accountability** – No one to ensure follow-through on commitments.

- **Procrastination & Lack of Discipline** – Struggling to maintain consistency in action.

- **Overwhelmed by Responsibilities** – Difficulty managing time and priorities effectively.

- **Fear of Taking the First Step** – Getting stuck in preparation mode instead of execution.

- **Inability to Adapt to Setbacks** – Struggling when plans do not go as expected.

- **Letting Emotions Disrupt Progress** – Allowing frustration or fear to halt progress.

- **Lack of Routine & Structure** – Struggling to create habits that support action.

- **Avoiding Difficult Tasks** – Prioritizing comfort over growth-driven tasks.

- **Inconsistent Motivation** – Losing drive when immediate results are not seen.

- **Waiting for the "Perfect Moment"** – Postponing action indefinitely.

How Coaching Helps: Coaches provide accountability, structure, and tools for execution, ensuring individuals stay committed, flexible, and proactive.

C - Connection & Collaborative Growth

Challenges related to networking, collaboration, and leadership influence:

- **Struggling to Build Meaningful Connections** – Difficulty forming authentic relationships.

- **Weak Communication Skills** – Struggling to express ideas effectively.

- **Lack of Trust in Teams** – Hesitation to delegate or rely on others.

- **Not Leveraging Mentors or Coaches** – Missing opportunities to learn from experienced individuals.

- **Fear of Public Speaking** – Anxiety around presenting ideas in front of others.

- **Feeling Isolated in Leadership** – Not having a support system for growth.

- **Conflict Avoidance** – Struggling to navigate difficult conversations.

- **Lack of Influence & Persuasion Skills** – Difficulty getting others to support their vision.

- **Networking Anxiety** – Feeling awkward or intimidated in professional settings.

- **Struggling to Inspire & Motivate Others** – Difficulty leading a team effectively.

How Coaching Helps: Coaching improves communication, leadership influence, and networking skills, helping individuals build strong relationships and lead with confidence.

T - Transform & Thrive

Challenges related to sustaining long-term transformation and growth:

- **Short-Term Focus** – Prioritizing immediate results over long-term success.

- **Burnout & Lack of Work-Life Balance** – Overworking without sustainable energy management.

- **Fear of Outgrowing Comfort Zones** – Resisting further challenges due to past success.

- **Lack of Consistency** – Failing to maintain positive habits long-term.

- **Relapsing into Old Patterns** – Falling back into unproductive behaviors.

- **Struggling with Self-Discipline** – Inability to sustain high-performance habits.

- **Avoiding Personal Growth** – Becoming stagnant and resistant to change.

- **Underestimating the Power of Reflection** – Not taking time to assess progress.

- **Lack of Adaptability in a Changing World** – Struggling to evolve with market and industry shifts.

- **Not Investing in Continuous Learning** – Thinking growth stops after one milestone.

How Coaching Helps: Coaches ensure lasting transformation by reinforcing new habits, sustaining motivation, and helping individuals embrace lifelong learning and adaptability.

The IMPACT framework is designed to **systematically address and overcome these challenges,** ensuring individuals:

- **Discover their identity and strengths (I)**

- **Develop a success-oriented mindset (M)**

- **Set and achieve meaningful goals (P)**
- **Stay committed to execution and adaptability (A)**
- **Build strong networks and leadership skills (C)**
- **Create lasting transformation and sustainable success (T)**

The IMPACT framework is a structured approach to coaching that focuses on transformational change, encompassing both personal and professional development. Let us break down each stage in more detail:

I - Inspire Awareness & Identity:

- **Core Focus:** This initial stage is all about self-discovery. It is about helping the client understand who they are, what drives them, and what their current reality is. It is about fostering self-reflection and building a strong foundation for growth.

- **Coaching Themes:** This stage draws heavily on self-reflection techniques, behavioral change models, and insights from neuroscience. It also incorporates the wisdom of figures like Aristotle, who emphasized self-knowledge as a cornerstone of leadership.

- **Key Elements:**

  o **Deep Dive into Values & Beliefs:** Exploring core values, identifying limiting beliefs, and understanding how this influence behavior.

  o **Behavioral Assessments:** Utilizing tools to understand behavioral styles, communication preferences, and strengths and weaknesses.

  o **Neuroscience Education:** Providing insights into how the brain works and how it impacts thoughts, emotions, and actions.

  o **Storytelling & Narrative:** Exploring personal narratives and identifying recurring patterns.

  o **Mindfulness & Self-Reflection Practices:** Developing practices to enhance self-awareness.

- **Example Questions:** *Who am I at my core? What are my values? What are my limiting beliefs? What are my strengths and weaknesses? What are the stories I tell myself about who I am?*

M - Mindset & Mastery Shift:

- **Core Focus:** This stage is about shifting mindsets and overcoming internal obstacles. It is about challenging limiting beliefs, fostering resilience, and cultivating a growth mindset.

- **Coaching Themes:** This stage draws upon principles of overcoming fear, transforming limiting beliefs, and cultivating optimism, inspired by figures like Nelson Mandela. It also incorporates tools like Neuro-Linguistic Programming (NLP) and Cognitive Behavioral Therapy (CBT).

- **Key Elements:**

  - **Identifying & Challenging Limiting Beliefs:** Uncovering and questioning beliefs that hold the client back.

  - **Reframing Negative Thoughts:** Developing techniques to reframe negative thoughts into more positive and empowering ones.

  - **Building Resilience:** Developing strategies to bounce back from setbacks and challenges.

  - **Cultivating Optimism:** Shifting focus towards possibilities and opportunities.

  - **Developing Self-Efficacy:** Building confidence in one's ability to achieve goals.

- **Example Questions:** *What fears are holding me back? What beliefs are limiting my potential? How can I reframe my challenges into opportunities? How can I cultivate a more optimistic outlook?*

P - Purpose-Driven Goals & Strategy:

- **Core Focus:** This stage is about clarifying purpose and setting meaningful goals. It is about developing a clear vision for the future and creating a strategic plan to achieve it.

- **Coaching Themes:** This stage utilizes principles of positive psychology, various coaching models, and leadership goal-setting strategies.

- **Key Elements:**

  - **Identifying Purpose & Passion:** Clarifying what truly matters to the client and aligning goals with their values.

  - **Setting SMART Goals:** Developing specific, measurable, achievable, relevant, and time-bound goals.

  - **Developing a Strategic Plan:** Creating a roadmap with clear steps and timelines.

  - **Prioritizing & Time Management:** Developing skills to manage time effectively and focus on key priorities.

  - **Visualization & Future Pacing:** Creating a clear mental picture of desired outcomes.

- **Example Questions:** *What is my purpose? What do I want to achieve? What are my SMART goals? What is my strategic plan? How will I measure my success?*

A - Action, Accountability & Adaptability:

- **Core Focus:** This stage is about putting the plan into action, staying accountable, and adapting to changing circumstances.

- **Coaching Themes:** This stage draws upon principles of high-performance teams, startup success stories, and effective leadership execution.

- **Key Elements:**

  - **Developing Action Plans:** Breaking down goals into smaller, manageable steps.

  - **Building Accountability Mechanisms:** Creating systems to track progress and stay on track.

  - **Developing Adaptability Skills:** Learning to adjust plans and strategies as needed.

- o **Overcoming Obstacles:** Developing strategies to navigate challenges and setbacks.

- o **Building Discipline & Consistency:** Cultivating habits that support goal achievement.

- **Example Questions:** *What are the key actions I need to take? How will I stay accountable? How will I adapt to challenges? What habits do I need to develop?*

C - Connection & Collaborative Growth:

- **Core Focus:** This stage emphasizes the importance of connection and collaboration. It is about building strong relationships, seeking mentorship, and empowering others.

- **Coaching Themes:** This stage draws upon the impact of coaching, mentorship principles, team empowerment strategies, and the collaborative leadership style of figures like Aristotle.

- **Key Elements:**

- o **Building Strong Relationships:** Developing skills in communication, empathy, and active listening.

- o **Seeking Mentorship & Support:** Identifying and building relationships with mentors and advisors.

- o **Empowering Others:** Developing skills in delegation, coaching, and feedback.

- o **Collaboration & Teamwork:** Building strong teams and fostering a collaborative environment.

- o **Networking & Community Building:** Expanding professional network and building connections.

- **Example Questions:** *How can I build stronger relationships? Who can I seek mentorship from? How can I empower others? How can I build a stronger team?*

T - Transform & Thrive:

- **Core Focus:** This final stage is about achieving lasting transformation and thriving in all areas of life.

- **Coaching Themes:** This stage draws upon principles of digital transformation, business coaching, innovation, and legacy building.

- **Key Elements:**

  - **Continuous Learning & Growth:** Developing a mindset of lifelong learning.

  - **Embracing Change & Innovation:** Developing skills in adaptability and innovation.

  - **Building a Legacy:** Defining what impact the client wants to make on the world.

  - **Giving Back & Contributing:** Finding ways to make a positive contribution to society.

  - **Living with Purpose & Fulfillment:** Achieving a sense of purpose and fulfillment in life.

- **Example Questions:** *How will I continue to grow and learn? How can I embrace change and innovation? What is my legacy? How can I make a positive impact?*

The IMPACT framework provides a comprehensive and structured approach to coaching, guiding clients through a journey of self-discovery, mindset shifts, goal setting, action planning, relationship building, and ultimately, transformation and thriving. It is designed to be flexible and adaptable to the specific needs of each client, whether they are an individual, a team, or an organization

Core Values & Principles of the IMPACT Coaching Framework

The **IMPACT** framework is built on a **strong foundation of values and guiding principles** that drive personal and professional transformation. These core values and principles serve as the **compass for self-coaching, leadership development, and continuous growth**.

Core Values of the IMPACT Framework

1. Integrity & Authenticity – *Lead with honesty and self-awareness*

Authentic leadership begins with staying true to oneself. Embracing both strengths and weaknesses without fear of judgment fosters genuine trust. True leaders make decisions that align with their values and ethical principles, inspiring others through integrity. Mahatma Gandhi embodied this by leading with truth and non-violence, proving that authenticity has the power to drive meaningful change.

2. Mastery & Continuous Growth – *Commit to lifelong learning*

Growth is an ongoing journey that requires continuous learning and self-improvement. True success is built by mastering skills, refining habits, and cultivating the right mindset over time. Every setback presents an opportunity for resilience, leading to breakthrough moments. Leonardo da Vinci exemplified this by relentlessly expanding his knowledge across disciplines, proving that lifelong learning is the foundation of greatness.

3. Purpose & Impact-Driven Leadership – *Align actions with meaning*

A clear sense of purpose drives motivation, guiding decisions with intention and clarity. True leadership is rooted in the desire to create impact beyond personal achievements, shaping a legacy that endures. Purpose-driven goals not only lead to success but also bring deep fulfillment. Nelson Mandela embodied this by dedicating his life to ending apartheid and uniting a divided nation, proving that purpose can overcome even the greatest obstacles.

4. Accountability & Ownership – *Take responsibility for actions and growth*

Growth occurs when individuals take full responsibility for their success, embracing both achievements and failures as stepping stones to progress. By owning challenges and setbacks, they develop resilience and adaptability, turning obstacles into opportunities for growth. Accountability plays a crucial role in ensuring commitment to goals, fostering discipline, and driving long-term success. A powerful example of this is Elon Musk, who exemplifies extreme ownership by setting high accountability standards for himself and his companies, relentlessly pursuing his vision despite setbacks.

5. Collaboration & Connection – *Success is built through relationships*

Growth flourishes when teamwork, mentorship, and shared learning become the foundation of success. Strong leaders empower those around them, cultivating a culture of support and innovation where ideas thrive. Embracing diverse perspectives enhances problem-solving and fuels creativity, leading to groundbreaking solutions. A remarkable example is Steve Jobs, who built Apple's success by fostering collaboration and assembling a team of top innovators, driving the company to revolutionize technology and design.

6. Transformation & Adaptability – *Embrace change as a catalyst for growth*

In a rapidly evolving world, flexibility and adaptability are essential for growth and success. True transformation occurs when individuals embrace change rather than resist it, turning challenges into opportunities. Innovation and reinvention are the keys to long-term success, allowing leaders to navigate uncertainty with confidence. Winston Churchill exemplified this during World War II, continuously adapting strategies to meet shifting realities, demonstrating resilience and strategic leadership in times of crisis.

Core Principles of the IMPACT Framework

- **Self-Awareness & Identity:** Know yourself before leading others.

- **Growth Mindset:** See challenges as opportunities, not barriers.

- **Purpose-Driven Action:** Align every step with meaningful goals.

- **Accountability & Ownership:** Take responsibility for results and progress.

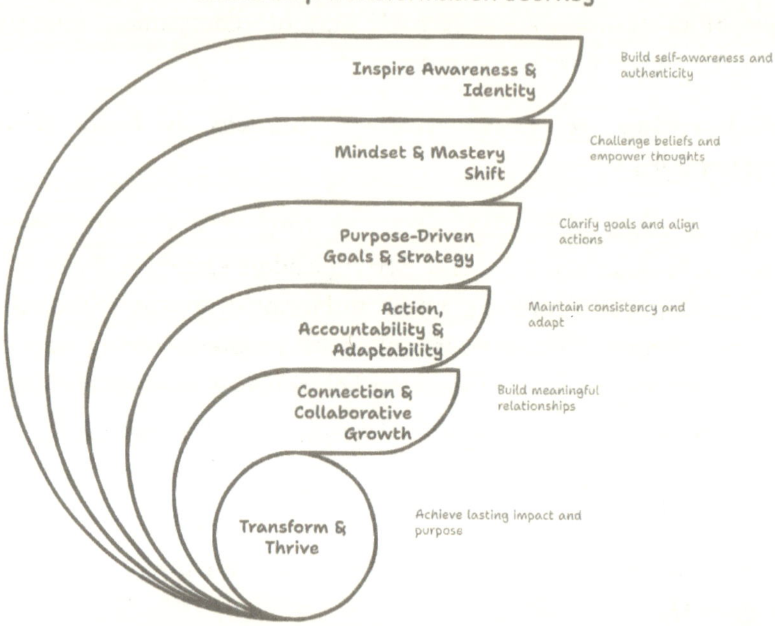

- **Collaborative Leadership:** Empower others and grow together.

- **Resilience & Adaptability:** Stay flexible in an ever-changing world.

- **Long-Term Legacy:** Strive for transformation beyond personal success.

Key Principles That Drive IMPACT Coaching

1. Self-Awareness & Identity (Know Yourself First)

Transformation starts with self-awareness, as reflection allows individuals to understand their thoughts, emotions, and actions. Embracing authenticity means recognizing personal strengths and values, leading to a more genuine leadership approach. Self-discovery is the foundation for continuous growth, helping individuals align their identity with their purpose. Tools like self-reflection exercises, journaling, and personality assessments such as StrengthsFinder and

360-degree feedback provide valuable insights, uncovering leadership styles and internal barriers to success.

2. Growth Mindset & Belief Rewiring (Change the Mind, Change the Outcome)

The brain has the incredible ability to rewire itself through consistent practice, making growth and transformation possible at any stage of life. By shifting perceptions and reframing limiting beliefs, individuals can reshape their reality and unlock new opportunities. Building emotional resilience strengthens mental toughness, allowing people to navigate challenges with confidence. Techniques like Cognitive Behavioral Therapy (CBT), Neuro-Linguistic Programming (NLP), and Mental Rehearsal help break negative thought patterns and replace them with empowering beliefs, fostering a mindset primed for success.

3. Purpose-Driven Action (Align Vision with Strategy)

Every great achievement begins with a clear intention. When purpose drives decisions, actions become more focused and meaningful. Strategic thinking ensures that goals are well-defined, leading to deliberate and effective execution. Visionary leadership, rooted in future-driven thinking, allows individuals to navigate uncertainty and create lasting impact. Tools like SMART Goals, OKRs (Objectives & Key Results), and Vision Boards serve as powerful frameworks to align daily actions with long-term aspirations, turning vision into reality.

4. Execution, Accountability & Adaptability (Move Beyond Planning to Action)

Success is built on the foundation of consistency—small, disciplined actions repeated daily lead to remarkable results. Ownership fosters a mindset of accountability, where individuals take full responsibility for their progress and outcomes. In a rapidly evolving world, agility becomes a superpower, enabling leaders to pivot and adapt without losing momentum. Tools like accountability partnerships, habit trackers, and milestone check-ins help maintain focus, while agility coaching ensures resilience in the face of change.

5. Connection & Collaborative Growth (Success is a Team Sport)

Innovation thrives when minds come together—collective intelligence harnesses the power of diverse perspectives to drive breakthrough ideas. True leadership is not about authority; it is about influence, inspiring and empowering others to create a ripple effect of impact. Mentorship accelerates growth, allowing individuals to learn from experienced leaders and avoid common pitfalls. Mastermind groups, team coaching, and leadership mentoring provide the support and guidance needed to expand influence, strengthen networks, and achieve greater success.

6. Transformation & Legacy (Create Impact Beyond Yourself)

Lifelong growth requires continuous learning—those who evolve stay ahead. True success is not just about personal achievement; it is about the impact you leave behind. Innovation ensures relevance in an ever-changing world. By embracing self-coaching, mentorship, and digital transformation, individuals can shape their future while building a lasting legacy that inspires others.

Applying These Values & Principles in Self-Coaching

- Regular self-reflection and journaling to strengthen self-awareness

- Practicing mindfulness and mindset-shifting techniques to break limiting beliefs

- Setting clear, purpose-driven goals and tracking progress with accountability partners

- Seeking mentorship and collaboration to accelerate learning and transformation

- Embracing change and uncertainty as opportunities for innovation and growth

IMPACT Coaching is more than a process; it's a partnership. It's about guiding others to unlock their true potential and become the leaders of their own lives.

Story -2:

The IMPACT Framework: Unleashing Human Potential Through Conscious Coaching

> **"Accountability breeds response-ability."**
>
> **– Stephen R. Covey**

The IMPACT Framework is a structured coaching model designed to help leaders, entrepreneurs, and organizations navigate the complex challenges that often hinder transformation and sustained success. By providing actionable strategies, it empowers individuals to overcome obstacles, develop stronger leadership, and create long-term impact.

One of the most significant challenges many professionals face is a lack of self-awareness and clarity in their identity. Doubts creep in, confidence wavers, and their true strengths remain unrecognized. The IMPACT Framework addresses this by fostering deep self-reflection. Through powerful tools like 360-degree feedback, journaling, and strengths assessments, individuals can uncover internal barriers, gain a clearer sense of identity, and develop the confidence needed for personal growth.

Another common struggle is the presence of limiting beliefs and fear of change. Fear of failure, imposter syndrome, and self-doubt can hold individuals back from taking bold action. Negative thought patterns hinder adaptability and discourage risk-taking. To counter this, the framework incorporates techniques such as Neuro-Linguistic Programming (NLP), Cognitive Behavioural Therapy (CBT), and belief transformation strategies. By shifting mindsets and reframing fears, it transforms hesitation into confidence, enabling individuals to embrace change with a growth-oriented perspective.

Without clear goals and a well-defined strategy, progress stagnates, and frustration sets in. Many people struggle to set and execute purpose-driven objectives, leading to wasted effort and lost momentum. The IMPACT Framework brings structure to ambition by introducing SMART goals, OKRs (Objectives and Key Results), and strategic roadmaps. These tools help align personal vision with execution, providing actionable steps, milestone tracking, and accountability mechanisms that ensure progress.

Even when goals are set, execution often falls short due to inconsistent discipline and a lack of accountability. Ambition alone is not enough—without structured follow-through, even the best intentions fail. The framework instils a culture of action and adaptability by implementing habit-tracking systems, peer accountability structures, and progress reviews. By integrating Agile principles, it ensures that individuals and teams can adjust to dynamic environments and maintain consistent execution.

Leadership is not just about personal achievement—it is about building strong teams and fostering collaboration. However, many leaders struggle to cultivate high-performance teams due to poor communication, lack of trust, and disengagement. The IMPACT Framework strengthens leadership influence by emphasizing active listening, conflict resolution, and team empowerment. Through coaching and mentoring techniques, it nurtures an environment of trust, collaboration, and shared growth.

Sustaining long-term success requires more than just achieving short-term wins. Many organizations and individuals experience initial success but struggle to maintain momentum. The absence of continuous learning, innovation, and a leadership legacy prevents long-term impact. The framework ensures lasting success by fostering a culture of continuous learning, future-proofing strategies, and innovation-driven transformation. By encouraging leaders to think beyond the present, it helps them create a legacy that endures.

This framework is particularly beneficial for leaders, executives, entrepreneurs, coaches, and teams seeking high performance, transformation, and long-term impact. It is a holistic, results-driven model that not only drives measurable growth but also strengthens leadership and sustains success in an ever-evolving business landscape. Through the integration of the right skills, tools, and methodologies, the

IMPACT Framework serves as a powerful guide for those who are ready to lead with confidence, execute with discipline, and leave a lasting mark on their organizations and industries.

Inspire Awareness & Identity (I)

Imagine inheriting a kingdom where the gates are closed, the people resistant to new ideas, their potential locked behind the bars of fixed beliefs. This was Microsoft before Satya Nadella. How did he unlock it? He did not issue commands; he cultivated a growth mindset, the belief in the boundless capacity for learning and development. He did not dictate self-awareness; he instilled it with tools like 360-degree feedback and strengths assessments, forcing a collective look inward at behaviour and impact.

The result? A cultural earthquake. Collaboration bloomed where silos once stood. Innovation, once a trickle, became a torrent. Employee engagement, the lifeblood of any organization, surged. This internal shift was not just about morale; it was the spark that ignited Microsoft's resurgence, fuelling its dominance in the cutting-edge realms of AI and cloud – a turnaround for the ages, born from a change in how people thought.

What if you could unlock this same transformative power in your own leadership? Where do your blind spots lie? How do others truly perceive your impact? The answer begins with a 360-degree feedback session – your opportunity to see yourself as others see you. Next, what daily ritual can you cultivate to shine a light on your actions and decisions? Daily self-reflection through journaling becomes your personal laboratory for growth, building self-awareness and emotional intelligence. Finally, what are the non-negotiable principles that guide your leadership? Defining your core leadership values and aligning them with your long-term vision provides the unwavering compass for authentic, purposeful, and consistent leadership.

Mindset & Mastery Shift (M)

Ever felt the weight of self-doubt despite your potential? Oprah Winfrey did. Early in her groundbreaking career, the internal battles were real, the limiting beliefs a heavy burden – a common experience for anyone striving for more, especially when challenging established norms.

How did she break free? Oprah turned inward, recognizing that true power begins within. She harnessed the transformative magic of visualization, mentally scripting her successes before they even unfolded, building an inner confidence that propelled her forward. She embraced neuro-linguistic programming (NLP), learning to reframe the negative narratives that held her back, effectively rewiring her responses to stress and uncertainty. And she incorporated the practical tools of cognitive behavioural therapy (CBT), dissecting her irrational fears, challenging their power, and replacing them with empowering beliefs.

The result? A media revolution led by a woman who dared to master her inner world. Oprah's story is not just about climbing the ladder; it is about building a new one entirely. It underscores a fundamental truth: leadership's true foundation lies not just in external skills, but in the unwavering command of our inner landscape. The inner work paved the way for unprecedented outer impact.

What if you could tap into this same wellspring of inner power? Are you aware of the subtle yet persistent patterns of your inner dialogue? When the whispers of "I'm not good enough" or "What if I fail?" surface, consciously meet them with affirmations that speak to your strength and potential: "I am capable," "I am ready." These affirmations are seeds of change, gradually rewiring your perception of challenges.

Have you explored the power of visualization? Before your next critical moment, take a few minutes to close your eyes and mentally walk through your success. See it, feel it, embody it. This mental rehearsal primes your brain for the outcome you desire.

Could small physical cues unlock powerful internal states? Explore NLP anchoring. Choose a simple physical action – a gentle press of your fingertips – and link it to a feeling of confidence through consistent visualization. Over time, this anchor can become an instant trigger for calm and empowerment in high-pressure situations.

Embrace these practices. They are the tools to dismantle the walls of fear and hesitation, replacing them with the unwavering foundation of courage and clarity – allowing your authentic leadership presence to emerge, strong and resonant, from the inside out.

Purpose-Driven Goals & Strategy (P)

Elon Musk did not just dream of a sustainable future; he engineered it. As the driving force behind Tesla and SpaceX, he faced a wall of scepticism and funding challenges, dismissed by many who doubted his audacious vision. But Musk's journey was not about blind faith; it was about a structured, strategic mindset that turned seemingly impossible goals into reality.

His approach? Bold vision coupled with relentless execution. He set long-term, world-altering objectives – accelerating the transition to sustainable energy and making humanity a multi-planetary species – and then meticulously reverse-engineered the steps to achieve them. To keep his team's laser-focused, he implemented the OKR framework, tracking progress with precision and ensuring unwavering alignment.

The results speak for themselves. Tesla did not just enter the electric vehicle market; it redefined it, pushing the boundaries of innovation and transforming how the world views transportation. SpaceX did not just dream of space travel; it revolutionized it, developing reusable rockets and dramatically lowering the cost of reaching for the stars. Elon Musk's story is a testament to the power of thinking big, planning strategically, and executing with unwavering determination.

Want to apply this same strategic power to your own leadership? Ground your inspiring vision in the practical reality of the SMART goal framework. Define objectives that are Specific, Measurable, Achievable, Relevant, and Time-bound. Then, implement the OKR system to track progress, maintain alignment, and drive accountability across your team or organization.

To transform your boldest ideas into tangible outcomes, master the art of reverse engineering. Start with your ultimate goal – your vision of success – and then meticulously work backward, identifying the critical milestones and steps required to reach it. This method turns lofty ambitions into a concrete, step-by-step roadmap, making even the most complex challenges navigable.

Action, Accountability & Adaptability (A)

When Jeff Bezos founded Amazon, the company initially faced significant challenges in scaling and executing efficiently. The lack of a clear execution roadmap and accountability measures made it difficult for teams to achieve their goals. Recognizing this issue, Bezos implemented data-driven accountability systems that allowed for precise tracking of progress and results. He introduced structured weekly progress reviews to keep everyone aligned and on track.

One of Bezos' key strategies was the creation of two-pizza teams—small, self-sufficient teams that could execute projects quickly and independently. This approach not only streamlined decision-making but also fostered a culture of agility, where teams were encouraged to experiment rapidly and pivot when necessary.

The results of these actions were transformative. Amazon grew into a global e-commerce and cloud computing giant, setting the standard for execution, accountability, and adaptability in the industry. Bezos' focus on execution and continuous innovation enabled Amazon to stay ahead of the curve and build an empire that reshaped the digital economy.

To apply Jeff Bezos' principles to your own leadership journey, start by utilizing habit-tracking tools like Trello or Notion. These tools can help you monitor your execution and keep you focused on the tasks that lead to success. Set clear milestones and track your progress consistently to ensure accountability and keep moving forward.

Establish peer accountability partnerships to maintain a sense of responsibility for your goals. Regular check-ins with a trusted colleague or mentor can help you stay committed, provide feedback, and push you to meet deadlines or expectations.

Finally, embrace Agile methodologies in your approach to problem-solving and execution. This allows you to stay adaptable and responsive to challenges, enabling you to pivot quickly when things do not go as planned. By adopting these strategies, you can create a framework for efficient execution, agility, and accountability in your leadership journey.

Connection & Collaborative Growth (C)

Indra Nooyi, as one of the first female CEOs of a global brand, faced the challenge of fostering inclusivity and collaboration within PepsiCo's diverse workforce. Her leadership was tested by resistance, particularly in a corporate culture that was not always supportive of her efforts to build a more inclusive environment.

To overcome these challenges, Nooyi took a personal and thoughtful approach. She wrote heartfelt letters to the parents of employees, thanking them for the role they played in shaping their children's careers. This gesture helped to build a deep trust and emotional connection with the workforce, as it demonstrated her genuine care and commitment to people. Furthermore, she implemented mentorship programs aimed at developing future leaders within the company, ensuring a steady pipeline of talent, and fostering a culture of growth and collaboration.

The results of Nooyi's actions were profound. PepsiCo experienced increased employee engagement, innovation, and long-term success under her leadership. By focusing on emotional connections and mentorship, she not only overcame initial resistance but also cultivated a thriving and forward-thinking organizational culture.

To apply the principles of strong leadership, start by strengthening your active listening skills. This is essential in building trust within your teams. When you actively listen, you make team members feel heard and valued, which fosters a deeper connection and encourages open communication. Next, implement mentorship and coaching programs to develop future leaders. By guiding individuals through their growth and leadership journey, you create a pipeline of capable leaders who can take on challenges and support the organization's long-term success. Finally, foster a culture of appreciation and recognition within your teams. When you acknowledge and celebrate achievements, no matter how small, you motivate people to collaborate more effectively and contribute their best work. This approach not only enhances teamwork but also creates an environment where everyone feels empowered and appreciated.

Transform & Thrive (T)

For Steve Jobs, being forced out of Apple was not a final chapter, but the catalyst for an extraordinary rebirth. Rather than dwelling in the past, he channelled his energy into a relentless pursuit of knowledge, becoming a student of design, philosophy, and the unfolding landscape of innovation. This period of intense personal growth was not a pause; it was the sharpening of his vision for Apple's future. His return marked not just a company revival, but a complete reimagining, restructuring Apple's long-term vision around the seamless fusion of innovation and user experience. Jobs' foresight, his ability to anticipate the next wave of technology, propelled Apple to unprecedented heights, transforming it into a global icon and solidifying his enduring legacy in technology and design.

To integrate the enduring lessons of Steve Jobs' leadership into your own path, prioritize continuous learning. Dedicate consistent time to expanding your knowledge through courses, reading, and mentorship, staying ahead of the curve in your field. Next, define your legacy blueprint. Articulate the long-term impact you aim to create, the mark you want to leave. This blueprint will provide unwavering focus and guide your strategic decisions. Finally, cultivate deliberate innovation strategies to ensure your lasting relevance. Embrace emerging technologies, foster a culture where creativity thrives, and consistently challenge the status quo to maintain a powerful competitive advantage.

> **"Efforts and courage are not enough without purpose and direction."**
>
> — *John F. Kennedy*

Here are three key learnings from *The IMPACT Framework: Transforming Leadership & Growth*:

- **Self-Awareness & Identity**: Developing a clear understanding of your strengths and weaknesses is essential for effective leadership. Tools like 360-degree feedback, journaling, and strengths assessments can help you uncover internal barriers and build the confidence necessary for personal growth. This self-awareness creates a solid foundation for leadership that aligns with your values and purpose.

- **Mindset Transformation**: Overcoming limiting beliefs and self-doubt is crucial for leadership success. Techniques like visualization, Neuro-Linguistic Programming (NLP), and Cognitive Behavioural Therapy (CBT) can shift your mindset from fear and hesitation to confidence and clarity. By managing your internal narrative and fostering a growth mindset, you can embrace challenges with a more resilient and adaptable approach.

- **Strategic Action & Accountability**: Execution is just as important as vision. Establishing clear goals, such as SMART goals and OKRs, and building accountability structures help ensure that your ambitions are turned into tangible results. Regular progress reviews, habit tracking, and leveraging Agile principles enable continuous learning, adaptability, and alignment with your long-term objectives. This disciplined approach drives sustainable growth and long-term success.

On Self-Awareness & Identity: *"Knowing others is intelligence; knowing yourself is true wisdom. Mastering others is strength; mastering yourself is true power."* **– Lao Tzu**

Story -3:

The Science Behind IMPACT: Why This Framework Delivers Consistent Results

> *"Change is not a threat; it is an opportunity. Survival is not the goal, transformative success is."*
>
> **— Seth Godin**

The **IMPACT** framework is not just a theory—it is a scientifically backed, real-world-proven methodology that enables deep and lasting transformation.

It systematically aligns human cognition, motivation, and execution strategies with established psychological and leadership principles. Let us explore why each component of this framework is designed to work—every time.

1. Inspire Awareness & Identity → The Science of Self-Perception

The Self-Perception Theory (Bem, 1972) suggests that people shape their identity based on their actions and experiences. When individuals begin to see themselves in a new light, they start behaving accordingly. This was evident in Shackleton's transformation from an explorer to a survival leader—by redefining his identity, he took full ownership of his new purpose.

Neuroscience confirms that visualizing oneself in a new role activates the same brain regions as actual experiences. This mental rehearsal strengthens neural pathways, making change feel more natural and reinforcing new behaviours.

For example, a struggling manager who believes they are "not leadership material" may subconsciously avoid responsibility, hesitate to speak up, and lack confidence. However, through coaching, once they start identifying as a leader, their actions align with this new identity. They take initiative, become more assertive, and step into leadership with confidence—transforming themselves from within.

2. Mindset & Mastery Shift → The Neuroscience of Fear & Confidence

Cognitive Behavioural Therapy (CBT) and Neuro-Linguistic Programming (NLP) demonstrate that fear can be rewired by forming new neural associations. The brain learns through repetition—when negative thoughts are challenged and reframed, fear is replaced with confidence. Research shows that reframing fear reduces amygdala activity (the brain's fear center) while strengthening the prefrontal cortex, responsible for rational thinking (Gross, 2002).

Fear often stems from past conditioning. By reprogramming their response to fear, individuals regain control. Shifting fear into excitement or opportunity transforms their emotional state, enhancing confidence and clarity.

For instance, an entrepreneur terrified of public speaking overcame their fear using coaching techniques like anchoring—linking a past moment of confidence to a simple physical action (such as pressing their fingers together). Over time, this association rewired their brain, enabling them to replace fear with self-assurance and deliver powerful presentations.

3. Purpose-Driven Goals & Strategy → The Psychology of Goal-Setting

The Goal-Setting Theory (Locke & Latham, 1990s) demonstrates that individuals with clear, specific, and challenging goals achieve significantly higher success than those with vague ambitions. Research also reveals that well-defined goals trigger dopamine release, boosting focus and motivation.

The brain thrives on clarity and direction. When abstract aspirations are replaced with structured, purpose-driven goals, motivation surges. Goals function like a mental GPS, steering individuals toward tangible progress.

For example, instead of the vague ambition, "I want to be a better leader," a coaching client refined their goal to: "Hold weekly strategy meetings with my team to drive innovation and collaboration." This shift transformed intention into measurable action, leading to real success.

4. Action, Accountability & Adaptability → Behavioral Psychology & Habit Formation

The Habit Loop Model (Duhigg, 2012) highlights that consistent action, reinforced by accountability, leads to lasting behavioural change. Research by the American Society of Training & Development (2018) found that individuals with an accountability system are 95% more likely to achieve their goals. Historical examples, like Shackleton's strict discipline and adaptability, underscore how structure and flexibility drive success in high-pressure situations.

Many fails at transformation because they depend solely on motivation, which is unreliable. Instead, structured accountability ensures follow-through, while adaptability helps individuals pivot when faced with challenges.

Take, for instance, a professional struggling with time management. By committing to a daily planning routine and weekly accountability check-ins with a coach, they saw rapid improvements in focus and productivity. The external accountability pushed them beyond excuses, turning intention into consistent action.

5. Connection & Collaborative Growth → The Science of Social Bonding & Leadership

Daniel Goleman's research on Emotional Intelligence (EI) proves that high-EI leaders foster trust, collaboration, and morale, driving superior team performance. Scientific studies also reveal that oxytocin, the "trust hormone," is released when people feel connected, enhancing cooperation and resilience (Harvard Business Review, 2017).

Transformation does not happen in isolation—strong leadership thrives on trust, delegation, and collaboration. When individuals shift from a solo mindset to a team-oriented approach, their effectiveness multiplies.

Consider a startup founder who initially micromanaged everything, leading to burnout. Through coaching, they learned to delegate, trust their team, and cultivate shared leadership. The result? Faster business growth, a highly engaged team, and a more sustainable leadership approach.

6. Transform & Thrive → The Long-Term Impact of Leadership Mastery

Scientific research on transformational leadership (Bass, 1985; Kouzes & Posner, 2007) highlights how visionary leaders drive lasting impact by fostering resilience, innovation, and continuous learning. Shackleton's leadership remains a global coaching model, proving that sustainable transformation is not about a single breakthrough—it is about cultivating mindsets and strategies that endure. When individuals learn to lead themselves first, they unlock limitless potential.

Take, for example, a mid-level executive who once hesitated to take initiative. Through consistent application of coaching principles, they gradually evolved into an industry thought leader, mentoring others and driving large-scale change. Their transformation was not instant—it was built over time, demonstrating the true power of leadership coaching.

Conclusion: The IMPACT Framework Is a Proven Blueprint for Transformation

The IMPACT framework is not just a theoretical concept—it is **backed by decades of psychological research, behavioral science, and real-world success stories.** Whether in extreme survival situations like Shackleton's expedition or modern leadership development, it works because it is deeply aligned with **how the human brain processes change, motivation, and resilience.**

Top Key Learnings for Coaches in Driving Transformation Through Coaching – With Quotes

1. **Identity Shaping is the Foundation of Change**

Help clients redefine their self-perception and align their actions with their new identity. Transformation starts when individuals see themselves differently.

- *"We are what we repeatedly do. Excellence, then, is not an act, but a habit."* — Aristotle

- *"Act as if what you do makes a difference. It does."* — William James

2. **Mindset Shifts Are Crucial for Overcoming Fear & Resistance**

Use cognitive techniques (like reframing and neuro-association) to help clients shift from fear-based thinking to confidence and opportunity-driven mindsets.

- *"Whether you think you can, or you think you can't—you're right."* — Henry Ford

- *"Fear is only as deep as the mind allows."* — Japanese Proverb

3. **Goal Clarity Drives Sustainable Progress**

Guide clients to set **specific, measurable, and purpose-driven goals** that translate abstract ambitions into actionable steps for real transformation.

- *"A goal properly set is halfway reached."* — Zig Ziglar

- *"You can't hit a target you cannot see, and you cannot see a target you do not have."* — Zig Ziglar

4. Accountability & Adaptability Ensure Lasting Change

Success depends on **consistent action, structured accountability, and the ability to adapt** when challenges arise. Coaches must create systems that reinforce progress.

- *"Discipline is the bridge between goals and accomplishment."* — Jim Rohn

- *"It is not the strongest of the species that survives, nor the most intelligent, but the one most responsive to change."* — Charles Darwin

5. Transformation is Strengthened Through Connection & Leadership

Emotional intelligence, trust-building, and collaboration accelerate growth. Coaches should help clients develop strong relationships, delegate effectively, and lead with impact.

- *"Alone we can do so little; together we can do so much."* — Helen Keller

- *"A leader is best when people barely know he exists; when his work is done, his aim fulfilled, they will say: we did it ourselves."* — Lao Tzu

Story 4:

The IMPACT Coaching Framework: A Transformational Approach to Self-Coaching

> **"The greatest coach you'll ever have is already within you—self-awareness is the spark, and purposeful action is the flame."**
>
> — *Inspired by the principles of the IMPACT Coaching Framework*

Why the IMPACT Framework Works

In an era defined by rapid change and relentless demands, personal and professional growth is not just a luxury—it is an essential cornerstone of success. The individuals who rise above challenges and achieve extraordinary results are those who continuously refine their thinking, embrace resilience, and take purposeful action.

The IMPACT Framework is a scientifically grounded, structured approach designed to facilitate meaningful transformation. Whether you are an executive, entrepreneur, coach, or someone striving for personal excellence, this framework serves as your roadmap to long-term success.

Unlike conventional coaching methods that address fragmented aspects of development, IMPACT integrates six fundamental pillars: **Inspiration, Mindset, Purpose, Action, Connection, and Transformation.** By embracing this holistic model, individuals can conquer self-doubt, build unwavering resilience, set purposeful goals, and craft a legacy that endures.

Let us delve deeper into why the IMPACT Framework is an indispensable tool for self-coaching and leadership mastery.

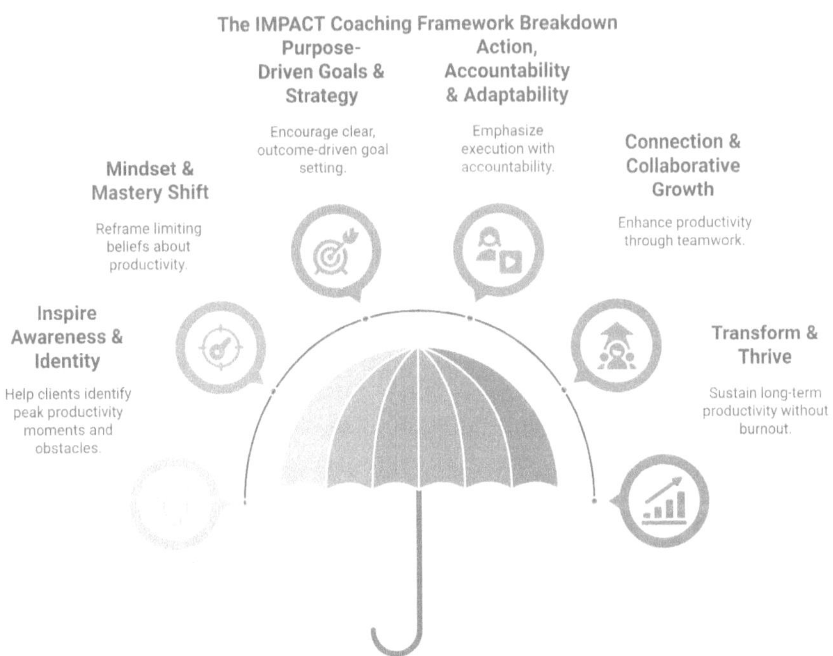

I - Inspire Awareness & Identity

Picture a traveller lost in a dense forest, wandering in circles without a map. No matter how determined they are, without direction, they remain stuck, endlessly retracing their steps. This is what life looks like without self-awareness—a cycle of habits, reactions, and choices made without understanding their deeper origins.

Self-awareness is the map that reveals who you truly are. It helps you recognize your strengths, acknowledge your weaknesses, and align your actions with your purpose. It is the foundation of personal growth, the starting point of transformation, and the key to intentional living. Without it, success can feel hollow, and decisions can lead to frustration rather than fulfilment.

Cultivating self-awareness requires deliberate effort. One of the most effective ways is through journaling. Writing down thoughts, experiences, and emotions helps uncover patterns that often go unnoticed in daily life. A simple yet powerful reflection question is: *What did I learn about myself today?* This small act of introspection creates clarity and deepens self-understanding.

Another transformative tool is 360-degree feedback. Seeking honest insights from colleagues, mentors, and trusted friends provides a mirror to both strengths and blind spots. Sometimes, others see the leadership qualities in us that we overlook. Their perspectives offer invaluable guidance for personal and professional growth.

Regular self-reflection is also essential. Taking a step back to ask questions like *Who am I as a leader? What values drive my decisions?* and *What beliefs might be limiting my growth?* creates the space for true self-discovery. These questions challenge assumptions, dismantle limiting beliefs, and pave the way for personal evolution.

Mahatma Gandhi's leadership was built on deep self-awareness. He did not wake up one day and decide to lead a movement; his philosophy of truth and nonviolence emerged from relentless self-reflection. Through journaling, meditation, and questioning his own values, he refined his principles and ensured that every action aligned with his greater purpose. His clarity was not just a personal strength—it became the force that inspired a nation and shaped a legacy.

The challenge today is to pause and reflect: *What is one belief I hold about myself that might be limiting my potential?* Awareness is the first step to transformation. The more you understand yourself, the more power you have to shape your future.

M - Mindset & Mastery Shift

Imagine standing at the edge of a deep canyon. On the other side is your full potential—everything you dream of becoming. But between you and that future lies an invisible gap. What is stopping you from crossing it? It is not your body—it is your mind.

Fear, self-doubt, and negative beliefs can feel like walls blocking your path. They make you think you are not good enough, or that you will never succeed. These thoughts do not come from the outside world—they live in your head.

This is where your mindset matters.

A fixed mindset says:

- "I can't do this."

- "I'm just not smart enough."

- "If I fail, I'll never recover."

It makes you believe that who you are today is all you will ever be. It shuts the door to growth before you even try.

A growth mindset, on the other hand, says:

- "I can learn from this."

- "I'm not there yet, but I'm improving."

- "Every challenge helps me grow."

People with a growth mindset do not fear mistakes—they learn from them. They use failure as a step toward success.

How Can You Build a Growth Mindset?

- Change your self-talk. Instead of saying *"I can't,"* ask *"How can I?"*

- Practice visualization. Picture yourself doing well—on the field, in class, or in life. Athletes and leaders use this tool to prepare their minds for success.

- Turn struggles into stepping stones. If something is hard, it does not mean you should quit—it means you are learning.

Nelson Mandela spent 27 years in prison. He had every reason to give up. But instead, he used that time to grow—reading, learning, and preparing to lead. When he was finally free, he did not seek revenge— he led a country with wisdom and peace. That is the power of a growth mindset.

Next time you catch yourself thinking something like *"I'm not good at this,"* stop and ask:

- "What can I learn here?"

- "How can I grow?"

Your mindset is the bridge. The more you believe in your ability to grow, the closer you get to your goals.

P - Purpose-Driven Goals & Strategy

Imagine climbing a mountain and reaching the top, only to find that the view is not what you expected. Many people work hard to achieve success, but they do not always stop to think if their goals truly match what they really want in life. They might reach their goals, but still feel empty inside because they were not focused on what truly matters to them.

To avoid this, it is important to know what success means to you personally. For some, success might be making money or having freedom. For others, it might be helping others or making a difference in the world. When you know what success means to you, you can focus on it and feel more fulfilled.

Once you know what success means to you, setting clear and realistic goals is the next step. It is important to break down big dreams into smaller, manageable goals. These goals should be specific, measurable, and achievable. This way, you can track your progress and stay motivated as you move forward.

But success is not just about checking off goals. It is about making sure those goals reflect your true values. For example, if being creative or helping others is important to you, your goals should include these things. When your work matches your values, it feels more meaningful. If your goals do not match your values, it can lead to frustration or burnout.

A good example of purpose-driven success is Elon Musk. He did not create companies like Tesla or SpaceX just to make money. His goal was to solve big problems, like climate change and space travel. For him, the mission is more important than the money. His success shows how having a clear purpose can help you keep going even when things are tough.

Ask yourself: Are your goals connected to your true purpose? If not, it might be time to rethink them. When your goals are meaningful to you, motivation becomes easier, and success will feel much more rewarding. Purpose-driven success does not just bring rewards—it brings a sense of meaning that lasts longer than any achievement.

A - Action, Accountability & Adaptability

Ambition alone does not lead to success—consistent execution does. Many people set inspiring goals but struggle to follow through due to a lack of discipline, accountability, and adaptability. The real challenge is not in dreaming big; it is in taking action every single day. Ideas remain ideas unless they are executed with persistence and precision.

Building discipline is the foundation of effective execution. Success is not about occasional bursts of effort but about small, consistent actions that compound over time. One of the most effective ways to maintain discipline is by using habit trackers. These tools measure progress, reinforce consistency, and create momentum, turning ambition into tangible results.

Accountability is another crucial factor in execution. It is easy to abandon a goal when no one is watching, but when individuals commit to an accountability group, hire a coach, or work with a mentor, they significantly increase their chances of following through. External accountability adds a layer of commitment that keeps people focused and motivated, even when challenges arise.

Adaptability is just as important as discipline and accountability. Obstacles and setbacks are inevitable, but the key to success lies in resilience. Those who embrace change, learn from failures, and pivot when necessary are the ones who keep moving forward, even in uncertain circumstances.

Thomas Edison's relentless execution exemplifies this mindset. He did not invent the light bulb in a single attempt; instead, he failed over 10,000 times. But rather than seeing these failures as defeats, he reframed them as steps toward progress. In his own words, *"I have not failed. I've just found 10,000 ways that won't work."* His discipline, accountability, and adaptability turned failure into one of history's greatest innovations.

The real question is: Are you consistently acting on your goals, or just setting them? Success does not come from merely planning or dreaming—it comes from daily execution. Focus on small, consistent actions that build momentum over time. Execution, not perfection, is what ultimately leads to meaningful results.

C - Connection & Collaborative Growth

Success is never a solo journey. The most impactful leaders and innovators did not thrive in isolation; they built strong relationships, sought mentorship, and embraced collaboration. No great achievement is ever the result of a single individual working alone—behind every success story is a network of mentors, peers, and supporters who provide guidance, challenge ideas, and inspire growth.

One of the most effective ways to strengthen personal and professional growth is by surrounding oneself with the right people. A strong network of mentors, coaches, and like-minded peers accelerates progress by offering insights, new perspectives, and constructive challenges. The right guidance can be the difference between struggling in uncertainty and moving forward with clarity and confidence.

Equally important is mastering the art of active listening. Growth is not just about speaking or asserting one's ideas—it is about deeply understanding others, learning from their experiences, and fostering meaningful connections. Leaders who listen attentively and engage in genuine conversations build trust, gain new perspectives, and create stronger collaborations.

True success is not just about personal achievement but about giving back. Those who empower others by sharing their knowledge, offering guidance, and creating opportunities contribute to a cycle of growth. Teaching not only strengthens one's own learning but also multiplies impact by helping others achieve their potential.

Warren Buffett's success is a testament to the power of mentorship. He credits much of his investment wisdom to his mentor, Benjamin Graham, who introduced him to the principles of value investing. Without Graham's guidance, Buffett might never have become one of the world's greatest investors. He understood that the best investment is not just financial—it is in learning, improving, and surrounding oneself with the right influences. As Buffett himself said, *"The best investment you can make is in yourself."*

The true challenge of growth lies in both seeking guidance and offering it. Every individual should ask: Who is guiding me? Who am I guiding? Growth flourishes when knowledge is shared, relationships are nurtured, and collaboration becomes the driving force behind success.

T - Transform & Thrive

Real success is not just about achieving goals; it is about continuous learning, adapting to change, and leaving a lasting impact. Those who make the greatest difference in the world do not simply reach personal milestones; they create a ripple effect by inspiring and empowering others to carry their vision forward.

Lifelong learning is the foundation of sustained growth. The world is constantly evolving, and those who embrace curiosity and adaptability remain relevant and influential. True leaders are not only focused on their own success but also on the legacy they leave behind. They mentor, teach, and uplift others, ensuring that their impact extends beyond their own lifetime. Leadership is not about personal accolades; it is about fostering the success of future generations.

Self-reflection and continuous improvement are essential for lasting influence. Those who regularly assess their progress, learn from their experiences, and refine their strategies build sustainable success. A true leader does not see setbacks as failures but as valuable lessons that shape the path forward.

Dr. APJ Abdul Kalam exemplified this philosophy. While he played a crucial role in advancing India's space and defense programs, his greatest contribution was in inspiring and mentoring young minds. His books, speeches, and personal interactions with students continue to guide future leaders long after his time. His vision was not confined to scientific achievements but extended to creating a culture of education, innovation, and national progress. He believed that dreams were the foundation of transformation, famously stating, "Dream, dream, dream. Dreams transform into thoughts, and thoughts result in action."

The true measure of success is not just in personal accomplishments but in the legacy one leaves behind. The question to ask oneself is not just whether goals are being achieved, but whether something meaningful and lasting is being built. Greatness is not about individual success—it is about empowering others to thrive and ensuring that the impact of one's work continues for generations to come.

Why Everyone Must Follow the IMPACT Framework

The IMPACT framework is a scientifically proven approach rooted in psychology, neuroscience, and coaching principles. It delivers measurable results by facilitating mindset shifts, leadership growth, and personal transformation. Designed to be adaptable to all roles—whether you are a CEO, entrepreneur, coach, or student—IMPACT provides a structured path to success. Unlike short-term motivation, it fosters sustainable change, ensuring long-term, meaningful transformation.

Final Thought: Are You Ready to Create Your Own IMPACT?

The IMPACT Coaching Framework is not just a model—it is a movement toward intentional, structured, and lasting transformation. By following these six pillars, you can break through limitations, achieve extraordinary success, and leave a meaningful legacy.

Here are the top key messages distilled from your comprehensive text on the IMPACT Coaching Framework:

1. *Holistic Transformation Requires More Than Motivation—It Needs a Framework*

In a world of constant change, sustainable personal and professional growth does not happen by accident. The IMPACT Framework provides a structured, scientifically grounded roadmap that goes beyond fragmented self-help tactics. By integrating Inspiration, Mindset, Purpose, Action, Connection, and Transformation, it equips individuals to lead with clarity, resilience, and purpose.

2. *Self-Awareness and Mindset Are the Gateways to Breakthrough Success*

Success begins within. Like a lost traveler without a map, individuals without self-awareness drift through life on autopilot. The framework's early pillars—Inspire (self-awareness) and Mindset shift—emphasize internal clarity and mental agility as the foundational steps to unlocking true potential and moving past invisible mental barriers.

3. *Legacy Is Built Through Action, Relationships, and Uplifting Others*

True success is not just about achieving goals—it is about consistent execution (Action), collaborative growth (Connection), and leaving a lasting legacy (Transformation). Figures like Edison, Mandela, and Dr. APJ Abdul Kalam exemplify that greatness is not just in personal milestones, but in the impact, they create for others and future generations.

Story - 5:

The I-M-P-A-C-T Coaching Framework: Empowering Leadership Through Mentorship

> **"Do what you can, with what you have, where you are."**
>
> *— Theodore Roosevelt*

The **I-M-P-A-C-T Coaching Framework** is designed to guide individuals through a journey of self-discovery, leadership development, and transformation. Below is an elaboration on each component of the framework, including the **steps** and **activities** involved in each stage.

I - Inspire Awareness & Identity: Who Am I as a Leader?

Purpose:

The goal of this phase is to help the individual discover their **authentic self,** reflect on their values, strengths, weaknesses, and their leadership style. It builds a foundation for self-awareness that is critical for growth.

Key Steps and Activities:

1. **Self-Reflection Journals:** Encourage the individual to keep a journal of thoughts, emotions, and reflections about their leadership experiences. This helps identify patterns and areas of strength or self-doubt.

2. **360-Degree Feedback:** Collect feedback from peers, colleagues, and subordinates. This comprehensive perspective allows the leader to assess how they are perceived and areas they may need to work on.

3. **Strengths and Values Assessment:** Conduct an assessment using tools like the **Gallup StrengthsFinder** or **VIA Character Strengths Survey** to help the individual identify their innate talents and values. Understanding these allows them to align their leadership with their core identity.

4. **Leadership Style Inventory:** Use a tool like the **Leadership Styles Inventory** to understand whether the person leans more toward democratic, autocratic, transformational, or servant leadership. This will help align their natural style with their aspirations.

5. **Vision-Mapping Exercise:** Create a vision board or engage in an exercise where the individual maps out their leadership journey, identifying milestones, strengths, weaknesses, and core principles.

M - Mindset & Mastery Shift: Shifting from Fear to Action

Purpose:

The goal of this phase is to help the individual shift their mindset from fear, self-doubt, and uncertainty to **empowerment** and **proactive action.** It involves transforming limiting beliefs and adopting a growth-oriented mindset.

Key Steps and Activities:

- **Mindset Awareness Exercise:** Begin by identifying limiting beliefs that are preventing growth. This could include thoughts like "I'm not good enough" or "I'm afraid of failure." Challenge these thoughts by asking, "Is this really true?" and replacing them with empowering beliefs.

- **Growth Mindset Training:** Teach the principles of the **growth mindset** as proposed by Carol Dweck. Conduct exercises where the individual reframes challenges as opportunities for growth rather than obstacles.

- **Visualizing Success:** Use guided visualization techniques where the individual imagines achieving their goals. This helps strengthen their belief in their abilities and increases motivation.

- **Resilience-Building Activities:** Introduce activities that encourage perseverance, such as meditation for stress reduction, or taking on small, manageable challenges that help build confidence and resilience over time.

- **Overcoming Fear with Action:** Encourage the individual to take small, courageous actions in situations that invoke fear. This could be public speaking, taking on a challenging project, or confronting difficult conversations—any action that leads to progress.

P - Purpose-Driven Goals & Strategy: Defining Clear Goals and Strategy

Purpose:

In this phase, the individual sets clear, **purpose-driven goals** that align with their personal vision and values. A strategic plan is created to ensure that the goals are actionable, measurable, and sustainable.

Key Steps and Activities:

1. **Goal-Setting Workshop:** Guide the individual through the **SMART Goals** framework (Specific, Measurable, Achievable, Relevant, Time-bound). This ensures that their goals are realistic, and aligned with their values.

2. **Vision to Action Mapping:** Take the vision created earlier and break it down into smaller, **actionable steps.** Map these steps on a timeline with milestones to track progress and accountability.

3. **Prioritization Exercise:** Use prioritization tools like the **Eisenhower Matrix** to help the individual focus on what is most important and urgent. This helps avoid overwhelm and ensures that the most impactful tasks are tackled first.

4. **Strategic Planning:** Work together to define a clear strategy that outlines **how** to achieve the goals. This includes understanding potential roadblocks, risks, and resources needed. Adjust strategies as needed to stay on track.

5. **Purpose Reflection:** Encourage the individual to reflect on the larger **purpose** behind each goal. This keeps motivation high and reminds them why they are pursuing these goals, helping them stay committed.

A - Action, Accountability & Adaptability: Turning Plans into Action

Purpose:

Action is the key to success. In this phase, the individual focuses on **execution,** creating accountability structures, and developing adaptability in the face of challenges.

Key Steps and Activities:

1. **Action Plan Development:** Break down the strategy into clear **daily, weekly, and monthly** tasks. The action plan should be specific, with clear deadlines, and identify who is responsible for each task.

2. **Accountability Partner:** Pair the individual with an accountability partner—someone who checks in on their progress regularly, challenges their excuses, and ensures they stay on track.

3. **Daily Check-Ins:** Establish a daily or weekly routine where the individual reviews their progress. This might involve setting aside time for reflection, reviewing completed tasks, and assessing challenges faced.

4. **Failure as Feedback:** Help the individual embrace mistakes and failures as **learning opportunities.** When setbacks happen, encourage them to reflect on the lessons learned and adapt their approach accordingly.

5. **Adaptability Drills:** Introduce **adaptability exercises,** such as handling unexpected change in a simulated environment, which helps the individual become comfortable with change and stay flexible under pressure.

C - Connection & Collaborative Growth: Building Networks and Teams

Purpose:

Success is built on relationships. In this phase, the focus is on **building meaningful connections** with mentors, peers, and a high-performing team. Collaborative growth accelerates success.

Key Steps and Activities:

1. **Networking Plan:** Help the individual develop a **networking plan** to build relationships with other leaders, mentors, and peers. Encourage them to attend industry events, online communities, or masterminds.

2. **Mentor Matching:** Connect the individual with relevant mentors who can provide advice, feedback, and guidance. This could involve regular one-on-one meetings or group mentorship.

3. **Team Empowerment:** Encourage the individual to foster an environment where their team feels empowered. This includes active listening, providing growth opportunities, and recognizing achievements.

4. **Collaboration Exercises:** Organize activities that encourage collaboration, such as **team-building exercises** or **brainstorming sessions.** This can help develop team cohesion and improve communication.

5. **Leadership Influence:** Teach the individual to build their **leadership influence** through trust, empathy, and positive reinforcement. Effective leaders know how to inspire and support their team to achieve shared goals.

T - Transform & Thrive: Becoming the Leader You Are Meant to Be

Purpose:

The final phase is about celebrating the transformation from where the individual started to who they have become. The goal is for them to feel confident and ready to take on even bigger challenges.

Key Steps and Activities:

1. **Celebrate Milestones:** Recognize and celebrate the individual's growth. Whether it is a promotion, a successful project completion, or overcoming a personal fear—acknowledging achievements helps reinforce positive behavior.

2. **Reflective Practice:** Set aside time for regular **self-reflection,** where the individual reviews their leadership journey. This helps them gain perspective on their progress and areas for continued growth.

3. **Vision for the Future:** Help the individual create a **vision for the next phase of their leadership** journey. Encourage them to set new goals that are bigger and more ambitious, continuing their growth cycle.

4. **Ongoing Learning:** Encourage a mindset of **continuous learning.** Help the individual create a personal development plan for further growth, which may include reading, additional coaching, or new leadership training.

5. **Mentor Others:** As the individual grows, encourage them to **pay it forward** by mentoring others. Becoming a mentor further solidifies their leadership identity and strengthens their legacy.

Conclusion:

The **I-M-P-A-C-T coaching framework** provides a structured and actionable roadmap for personal growth, leadership development, and success. Each phase—from increasing self-awareness and shifting mindset to setting purpose-driven goals and building lasting relationships—helps individuals move from uncertainty to confident leadership. Whether you are a coach or a leader looking to improve your leadership journey, these steps and activities provide a clear path for transformative growth.

The **I-M-P-A-C-T Coaching Framework** is a structured approach to leadership development, guiding individuals through a transformative journey of self-discovery, growth, and empowerment. Each phase—Inspire Awareness & Identity, Mindset & Mastery Shift, Purpose-Driven Goals & Strategy, Action, Accountability & Adaptability, Connection & Collaborative Growth, and Transform & Thrive—provides a clear path for individuals to become the leaders they are meant to be.

Here are some of the coaching questions that dive deeper into self-awareness, leadership transformation, and the application of the **I-M-P-**

A-C-T framework. These questions are designed to challenge thinking, provoke insights, and inspire meaningful action:

I - Inspire Awareness & Identity: Who Am I as a Leader?

1. If you were to describe your leadership essence in one word, what would it be, and why?

2. What hidden strengths have you yet to fully tap into, and how might they change the way you lead?

3. What leadership decisions have you made that you now regret? What have you learned from those moments, and how have they shaped your growth?

4. How do you see your leadership evolving in the next 3-5 years, and what specific identity shifts do you need to make now?

5. If you had to mentor yourself, what advice would you give your younger leadership self, and why?

M - Mindset & Mastery Shift: Shifting from Fear to Action

1. What is the cost of staying in your current comfort zone, and what opportunities would you unlock if you stepped into the discomfort of growth?

2. How do you view failure—do you see it as an opportunity for growth, or as something to avoid? How can you shift this perception?

3. What would it take for you to take massive, imperfect action today, even with the fear of failure?

4. When have you experienced a breakthrough in your leadership mindset? What made that shift possible, and how can you replicate it?

5. If fear was no longer a factor, what bold actions would you take to amplify your leadership?

P - Purpose-Driven Goals & Strategy: Defining Clear Goals and Strategy

1. How do your current goals align with your deeper sense of purpose and the legacy you wish to create? Are there any areas where they feel disconnected?

2. What would your ideal future look like if you were to accomplish your purpose-driven goals? How does that vision align with the needs of those you lead?

3. What would happen if you focused your energy on just one high-impact goal? What could you accomplish in the next 90 days if you gave it 100% of your attention?

4. How do you ensure that your strategy is flexible enough to adapt to unforeseen changes or challenges while staying aligned with your purpose?

5. What personal sacrifices are you willing to make in order to achieve your most important goal, and how will you ensure it is worth the investment?

A - Action, Accountability & Adaptability: Turning Plans into Action

1. What are the most significant roadblocks preventing you from executing your plan, and what is the first step you can take to remove them?

2. How can you intentionally create structures of accountability that not only keep you on track but also help you thrive under pressure?

3. When was the last time you pivoted a plan based on new information or feedback? What did you learn, and how can you apply that adaptability to future decisions?

4. How do you know when you are overthinking or under-executing? What systems can you put in place to ensure consistent action and results?

5. What is the one thing that, if you committed to it daily, would drastically accelerate your progress toward your goals?

C - Connection & Collaborative Growth: Building Networks and Teams

1. What impact would you have on your team if you fully embodied the values of trust, vulnerability, and collaboration? How would your leadership style shift?

2. How do you balance giving feedback with receiving it? How can you create an environment where feedback is mutual and supportive?

3. What types of relationships are you missing in your leadership journey, and who do you need to connect with to expand your influence and effectiveness?

4. How do you foster a sense of ownership and empowerment within your team, ensuring everyone feels like an integral part of the mission?

5. What legacy do you want to create with the people you collaborate with—how will you build that collaborative culture, and what specific actions will you take to nurture it?

T - Transform & Thrive: Becoming the Leader You Are Meant to Be

1. How do you measure your growth as a leader beyond tangible achievements, and how do you ensure that your leadership journey is one of continual transformation?

2. What is the most important habit or belief you need to cultivate to transition from a competent leader to an exceptional one?

3. How will you ensure that your leadership journey aligns with your deeper sense of purpose and the impact you want to have on others?

4. In what ways can you serve as a role model for others to inspire them to step into their potential? How are you actively building the next generation of leaders?

5. What legacy will you leave behind as a leader, and how do you want to be remembered by the people you have mentored, led, and worked alongside?

These are coaching questions push deeper introspection, challenging individuals to reflect on their purpose, take bold action, and embrace the vulnerability needed to evolve as a leader. They focus on long-term impact, both personally and for the people they lead, fostering a mindset of continuous growth and transformative leadership.

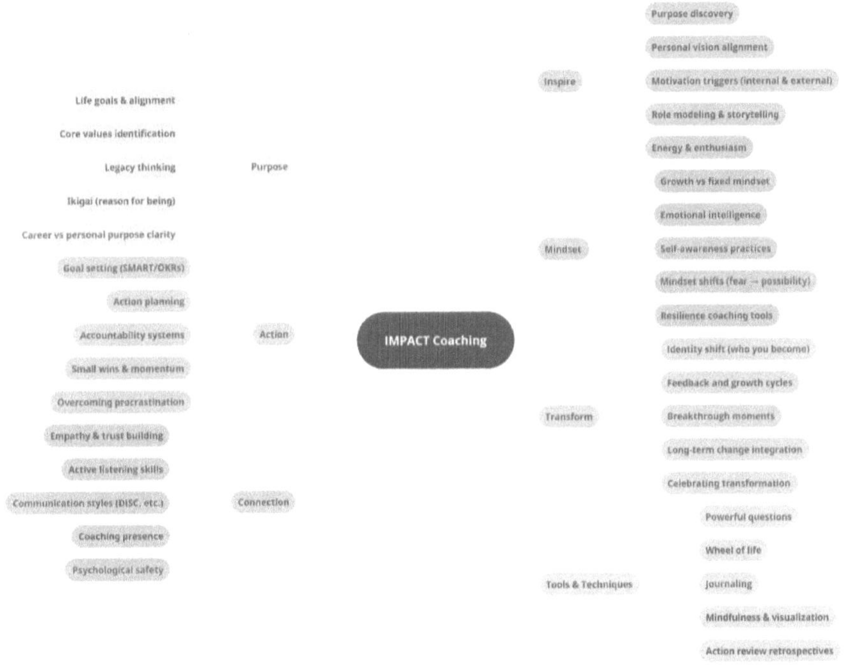

Key messages:

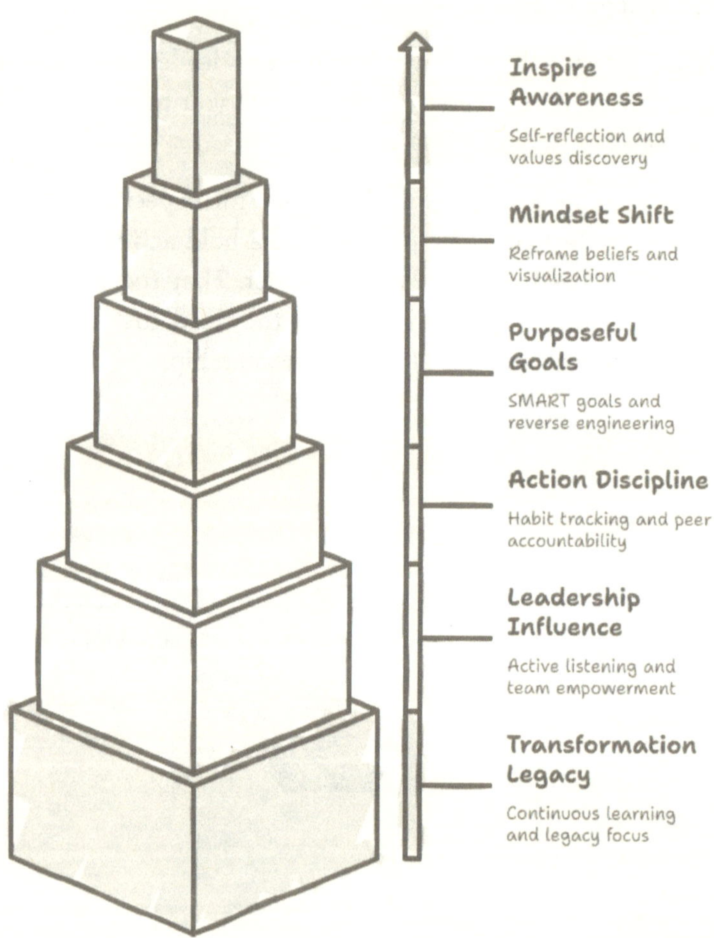

I - Inspire Awareness & Identity

An expert coach plays a vital role in helping other coaches develop self-awareness, which serves as the foundation for their growth and effectiveness. One of the most impactful ways to do this is by facilitating self-reflection exercises. These exercises encourage coaches to explore their unique coaching styles, values, and blind spots, allowing them to gain a deeper understanding of how they interact with their clients. By guiding them through this introspective process, an experienced coach helps them uncover both their strengths and areas that require further development.

In addition to self-reflection, using **360-degree feedback** can provide invaluable insights. By gathering perspectives from peers, clients, and other stakeholders, coaches receive a well-rounded view of their strengths and developmental opportunities. This process enables them to see themselves through multiple lenses, fostering a more comprehensive self-awareness.

Another powerful tool is guiding coaches in creating a **leadership identity statement**—a personal declaration that defines who they are as a coach and the impact they aim to create. This statement serves as a compass, helping them stay aligned with their values and coaching philosophy.

Through these approaches, an expert coach supports a coach's transformation by helping them recognize their **authentic coaching style**, whether it be directive, transformational, or servant leadership. This clarity allows them to refine their methods and become more intentional in their approach. Encouraging continuous introspection through journaling and debriefing after each coaching session further solidifies this growth, enabling them to track their progress and make necessary adjustments.

As Lao Tzu wisely said, *"To know others, you must first know yourself."* By fostering deep self-awareness, an expert coach equips other coaches with the tools to be more impactful, empathetic, and effective in their practice.

2. Mindset Transformation is Key to Overcoming Barriers

A great coach plays an important role in helping new coaches believe in themselves. Many new coaches feel unsure or have thoughts like, "I'm not good enough." Expert coaches help them see that these thoughts are not true and teach them to think more positively and confidently.

Through kind and helpful conversations, expert coaches create a safe space where new coaches can talk about their feelings and doubts. They help them understand the negative stories they tell themselves and show better, more encouraging ways to think.

To make this change stronger, expert coaches teach about the growth mindset. This means believing that your abilities and skills can grow with time and effort. They explain that the brain can change and improve when we practice, just like a muscle. This helps new coaches take on challenges and see mistakes as learning opportunities instead of failures.

One powerful way to build confidence is by practicing real-life situations through role-play. This could include how to talk to a client who does not want to listen, deal with difficult emotions, or stop feeling like they are not good enough (this is called "imposter syndrome"). These exercises help coaches stay calm, learn smart ways to handle things, and become more emotionally strong.

A big part of growing as a coach is moving away from trying to be perfect. Instead, new coaches learn to take small steps and improve a little every day. This helps them keep going, even if they make mistakes. Techniques like visualization (imagining success) and reframing (seeing problems in a better way) also help them become more confident and positive.

As Francis Chan once said:

"Our greatest fear should not be of failure, but of succeeding at things in life that don't really matter."

In the end, great coaches help others become strong, brave, and focused on what really matters—helping and guiding people with heart and purpose.

3. Clear, Purpose-Driven Goals Drive Meaningful Progress

A great coach helps new coaches set clear goals, stay true to their purpose, and track their progress as they grow. This starts with setting **SMART goals**—goals that are **Specific, Measurable, Achievable, Relevant, and Time-bound**. These kinds of goals give new coaches a clear path to follow, keeping them focused and motivated as they work toward success.

To help with this, expert coaches often hold **goal-setting workshops**. In these sessions, new coaches learn how to make a clear plan. They set small steps, decide what success looks like, and figure out what actions to take. Having a strong plan gives them confidence and helps them move forward one step at a time.

Besides goals, expert coaches also ask new coaches to write a **coaching philosophy statement**. This is a short message about their values, beliefs, and the kind of coach they want to be. It helps them stay true to themselves and show others what makes them different.

A big part of growing as a coach is finding the right **niche**—a special area they enjoy and are good at, like leadership coaching, agile coaching, or executive coaching. When coaches pick their niche, they can become experts, build trust, and attract the right clients.

Expert coaches also teach new coaches how to **track their progress**. They might keep a journal, ask clients for feedback, or do self-checks. This helps them see what is working well, what needs to improve, and how much impact they are making.

As the wise Lao Tzu once said:

"The journey of a thousand miles begins with one step."

By setting goals, writing their coaching philosophy, and tracking progress, new coaches take that important first step toward becoming amazing at what they do and making a real difference.

4. Accountability & Adaptability Ensure Sustainable Success

A great coach helps new coaches grow by teaching them how to stay strong during hard times, adapt to changes, and keep learning. One important way they do this is by being an **accountability partner—** someone who checks in, gives support, and makes sure the coach is following through on their goals. With regular talks and helpful feedback, expert coaches help new coaches stay focused and keep moving forward.

Sometimes, things do not go as planned. But instead of giving up, expert coaches help new coaches see problems as **lessons**, not failures. They talk about what went wrong, what can be learned, and how to bounce back stronger. This helps new coaches build **resilience**, or the strength to keep going even when things are tough.

To help new coaches think better and adapt quickly, expert coaches share **real-life examples and tricky situations**. They ask the new coach to think about how they would handle the problem, what choices they could make, and what is the right thing to do. This kind of practice builds **flexibility** and **smart decision-making**, which are important for dealing with all kinds of clients.

Great coaches also help build **peer coaching networks**—groups of coaches who learn from each other. These groups give support, share ideas, and help each other grow. It is like being part of a team that lifts each other up.

Another helpful habit expert coaches teach is **reflection**. This means looking back on what worked and what did not. New coaches might write in a journal, listen to recordings of their sessions, or do self-checks. This helps them see their strengths and what they can do better next time.

As Charles Darwin once said:

"It's not the strongest or smartest who survive, but the ones who can change."

By teaching responsibility, strength during challenges, the ability to adapt, and the habit of self-reflection, expert coaches help new coaches become successful, confident, and ready for anything.

5. Collaboration and Leadership Influence Magnify Impact

A great coach helps new coaches become confident, well-connected, and wise. One way they do this is by creating mentoring circles—small groups where experienced coaches and new ones share ideas, talk about challenges, and learn from each other. These groups are like learning families, where both old and new coaches grow together.

Expert coaches also help new coaches build their network. They encourage them to join coaching communities, attend events, and connect with others in the field. By meeting different people, new coaches learn about new trends, get ideas, and find chances to work with others. This helps them grow their career and stay up to date.

Another important thing expert coaches teach is how to influence others with trust. New coaches learn to listen carefully, be real, and connect deeply with their clients. When clients feel understood and supported, coaching becomes more powerful and helpful.

Expert coaches also guide new coaches to become thought leaders. This means writing articles, giving talks, or leading webinars to share their knowledge. When they do this, they become more respected, attract new clients, and help the whole coaching world grow.

Finally, great coaches encourage their mentees to give back by mentoring others. When new coaches teach someone else, they learn even more and help build a strong and kind coaching community. This way, coaching keeps improving and spreading.

As Lao Tzu once said:

"A leader is best when people barely know he exists. When his work is done, his aim fulfilled, they will say: we did it ourselves."

By mentoring, connecting, building trust, and sharing knowledge, expert coaches help new coaches become strong leaders who make a real difference in the world.

> **"It is not the mountain we conquer, but ourselves."**
>
> — *Sir Edmund Hillary*

Here are the top key messages distilled from the powerful content you shared, each highlighting a transformational pillar for developing coaches:

1. Inspire Self-Awareness & Identity

"To know others, you must first know yourself." — Lao Tzu

An expert coach's first and most profound gift is sparking self-awareness. Through guided introspection, 360° feedback, and leadership identity statements, they help developing coaches recognize who they are at their core. This awareness forms the foundation of authenticity, enabling coaches to lead with integrity, clarity, and purpose.

Core Impact: Coaches gain clarity on their unique voice, values, and coaching philosophy—empowering them to show up more intentionally and powerfully in every session.

2. Mindset Transformation Breaks Barriers

"Our greatest fear should not be of failure but of succeeding at things in life that don't really matter." — Francis Chan

Real transformation begins in the mind. Expert coaches challenge limiting beliefs, foster growth mindsets, and reframe failure as feedback. Through neuroscience-backed techniques like visualization, reframing, and role-playing, they build emotional resilience and coach confidence.

Core Impact: Coaches shift from perfectionism to progress, from fear to empowerment—ready to lead with courage and conviction.

3. Purpose-Driven Goals Ignite Forward Momentum

"The journey of a thousand miles begins with one step." — Lao Tzu

Transformation becomes tangible when guided by purpose-aligned, clear goals. Expert coaches support emerging leaders in crafting SMART goals, defining their coaching niche, and tracking impact through reflective practices. A personal coaching philosophy becomes their North Star.

Core Impact: With direction, structure, and a deep "why," coaches accelerate growth and consistently deliver meaningful results.

Story-6:

Overcoming Challenges in Applying the IMPACT Coaching Framework

> *"Knowing yourself is the beginning of all wisdom."*
>
> *– Aristotle*

Applying the IMPACT coaching framework requires deep self-awareness, a shift in mindset, and consistent action. However, many struggle with these transformations due to ingrained habits, fear of change, or a lack of clear direction. Below, we explore six common challenges and practical ways to overcome them.

1. The Challenge of Deep Self-Reflection

Self-awareness is the foundation of growth, yet many people struggle to pause and reflect on their true identity. In a world driven by deadlines and distractions, introspection often feels like a luxury. Moreover, looking inward can be uncomfortable—it requires facing fears, questioning long-held beliefs, and confronting personal limitations.

Consider a corporate leader battling imposter syndrome. Despite external success, they hesitate to examine their self-doubt, fearing it will expose their insecurities. Without this introspection, however, they remain trapped in uncertainty.

To cultivate self-awareness, start with structured reflection exercises like journaling or guided questions. Seeking feedback from trusted mentors or coaches can also provide valuable external perspectives. Most importantly, embracing discomfort as a natural part of growth allows for deeper transformation.

2. Overcoming Resistance to Change

Change, even, when necessary, often triggers resistance. Trusting the unknown can be difficult, and people tend to cling to familiarity, even when it no longer serves them. Uncertainty can feel riskier than staying in place.

An entrepreneur hesitant to pivot their business, despite shifting market trends, is a prime example. Fear of failure holds them back, even when inaction is the greater risk.

To navigate this, reframe fear as a learning opportunity—rather than focusing on what could go wrong, ask, **"What's the best that could happen?"** Small, experimental steps can make change feel more manageable. Visualization techniques—picturing success rather than failure—also help in rewiring fear-based thinking.

3. Finding Purpose and Avoiding Overwhelm

Many struggle to define a clear sense of purpose, often setting goals based on external pressures rather than internal values. The process of discovering one's true path can feel overwhelming, leading to stagnation.

A mid-career professional, for instance, might feel unfulfilled but uncertain about what direction to take. Without clarity, they remain stuck in indecision.

To overcome this, focus on passion, strengths, and impact—what activities bring fulfilment? Exploring different paths through small experiences (such as side projects or volunteering) can help clarify direction. It is also important to recognize that purpose evolves over time; what feels meaningful today may shift in the future, and that is okay.

4. The Struggle with Procrastination and Inconsistency

Inspiration without action leads nowhere, yet many fall into patterns of procrastination and inconsistency. They start with enthusiasm but quickly lose momentum, either due to a lack of accountability or because setbacks discourage them.

Consider someone determined to improve their health but constantly postponing workouts or diet changes. Despite knowing the benefits, they struggle to follow through.

The key is building accountability—whether through a mentor, a peer support system, or structured check-ins. Integrating new behaviours into existing routines (habit stacking) makes them easier to sustain; for example, listening to educational podcasts while commuting. Focusing on small, achievable wins also reinforces progress and builds motivation over time.

5. The Challenge of Finding the Right Support System

Growth rarely happens in isolation. However, many struggle to find mentors, coaches, or a supportive community, either due to lack of access or difficulty in asking for help. Some also fear vulnerability, worrying that seeking guidance makes them appear weak.

A new entrepreneur, for example, may feel isolated, unsure where to find mentorship that aligns with their vision. Without guidance, they risk making avoidable mistakes.

To overcome this, actively seek growth-oriented communities—networking groups, mastermind circles, or online forums provide valuable connections. Practicing giving before receiving—offering value to others before expecting mentorship—also fosters meaningful relationships. Above all, developing the courage to ask for help is a vital skill that accelerates progress.

6. Sustaining Growth Over Time

Many experience bursts of motivation but struggle to sustain long-term transformation. They start strong but, once the excitement fades, old habits resurface.

Someone embarking on a personal development journey might begin with enthusiasm, only to lose interest after a few months. Without consistency, their initial efforts do not translate into lasting change.

The solution is to make transformation a lifestyle, not a temporary phase. Integrating growth habits into daily routines ensures long-term impact. Regularly reviewing progress and adjusting strategies helps maintain momentum, while celebrating milestones reinforces motivation.

Final Thoughts: Turning Challenges into Strengths

Applying the IMPACT coaching framework is not about achieving perfection—it is about committing to continuous growth. Challenges like self-reflection, fear, lack of clarity, and inconsistency are common, but they can be overcome with intentional effort, structured action, and resilience.

The Key Takeaways? Transformation is not an event; it is an ongoing journey. By embracing self-awareness, taking small steps toward change, and building the right support system, anyone can create lasting impact in their personal and professional life.

Key actions:

- **Embrace Discomfort for Self-Reflection**:

  Self-awareness is crucial for growth, but it requires courage to face discomfort, question existing beliefs, and identify personal limitations. Reflection tools like journaling or seeking mentorship can catalyse deeper transformation.

- **Shift Your Mindset to Overcome Resistance to Change**:

  Fear of change can hold us back, but reframing it as an opportunity for learning and growth, and taking small steps toward action, can help mitigate that fear. Visualization of success rather than failure can be a powerful tool.

- **Consistency is Key to Sustaining Long-Term Growth**:

  Making transformation a lifestyle by integrating new habits into daily routines, seeking the right support systems, and maintaining consistency through regular reflection and celebration of small wins are essential for sustained progress.

> *"The only way to make sense out of change is to plunge into it, move with it, and join the dance."*
>
> **– Alan Watts**

Story-7:

The Silent Saboteurs: 6 Coaching Mistakes That Hold Young Leaders Back

> *"Children are not things to be molded, but people to be unfolded."*
>
> **— Jess Lair**

Before any child becomes a confident leader, they are first a curious observer. They notice when someone is left out. They ask why rules feel unfair. They feel deeply, even if they do not yet know how to name those feelings.

But this potential can be either nourished—or unintentionally shut down—by the kind of coaching they receive.

Coaching young minds into leadership is not just about giving advice. It is about shaping belief, identity, and resilience. And yet, many well-meaning coaches unknowingly fall into patterns that stifle rather than strengthen. Below are **six of the most common coaching mistakes** that can dim a child's inner light—and how we can avoid them.

1. Mistake: Teaching Before They've Discovered Themselves

One of the biggest missteps is jumping into instruction before the child has had a chance to understand who they are. True leadership begins with self-awareness, not checklists.

We often rush to guide, to shape, to Mold. But real growth happens when a child begins to see their own value—when they recognize their emotions, their reactions, and their sense of justice. Great coaching begins not with answers, but with space: space to reflect, to feel, to question.

- *Truth: Before you lead them, let them meet themselves.*

2. Mistake: Skipping Over Fear and Building Fake Confidence

"Be confident!" is a phrase thrown around easily. But children often carry quiet fears—of not fitting in, of not being good enough, of being wrong. Many adults avoid these fears, thinking positivity will cover the cracks.

But fear is not weakness. It is a doorway.

Children do not need blind encouragement—they need someone who sees their fear and teaches them how to walk through it. Real confidence is built not in the absence of fear, but in learning how to navigate it with courage.

- *Truth: Do not erase their fear. Help them befriend it.*

3. Mistake: Imposing Purpose Instead of Helping It Emerge

Coaches sometimes assume they know what is best: what a child should care about, what they should aim for. But true purpose is not assigned—it is discovered.

It arises when a child connects with something bigger than themselves. A cause. A question. A longing to help. When we let them explore what lights them up—and listen instead of leading—they find a reason to act that is deeply personal.

- *Truth: Do not give them a purpose. Guide them as they find their own.*

4. Mistake: Inspiring Big Dreams Without Teaching Daily Action

Many children are full of ideas and dreams—but no roadmap. Coaches often cheer on their aspirations without helping them break it down into steps. Dreams become dust when there is no direction.

Children must be shown that action matters more than ideas. That trying, failing, and showing up is where transformation happens. When we help them set real goals, take small steps, and stay accountable—they do not just dream. They **do**.

- *Truth: Every dream needs legs. Give them the shoes to walk it out.*

5. Mistake: Creating Stars Instead of Collaborators

A common coaching trap is praising only individual brilliance— raising stars instead of community-builders. This teaches children that leadership means being above others, rather than **with** them.

But the best young leaders are those who know how to listen, how to uplift, how to build teams. They do not lead with ego—they lead with empathy. And that begins when coaches encourage connection over competition.

- *Truth: Teach them to shine—but also to share the light.*

6. Mistake: Treating Leadership Like an Outcome Instead of a Way of Life

Too often, leadership is framed as a destination: a title, a medal, a stage. But if we only coach for achievements, we raise children who perform leadership, not **live** it.

Real leadership is woven into daily choices. Integrity. Kindness. Showing up. Speaking truth. It is not a one-time transformation—it is a lifestyle. Coaches who nurture this mindset prepare children not just for leadership roles, but for lives that lead with purpose wherever they go.

- *Truth: Do not coach them to reach a peak. Coach them to live the climb.*

The Deeper Lesson

Children do not need perfect coaches. They need *present* ones—who see them not as projects, but as people in progress.

When we avoid these six coaching traps, we give young leaders more than skills—we give them roots. We help them become individuals who lead not for praise, but for people. Not for power, but for change. And that kind of leadership does not end in childhood. It echoes for life.

Let us break down how the **IMPACT Framework** relates to each point:

1. I - Inspire: Self-Awareness and Reflection

The first mistake discussed in the text is "Teaching Before They've Discovered Themselves," highlighting the importance of self-awareness. In the **IMPACT Coaching Framework**, **Inspire** is about helping the coaches see their potential and purpose. Before a child can lead, they must first understand themselves—who they are, what they feel, and what drives them. This aligns with the truth that great coaching begins with creating space for reflection, where children discover their emotions, beliefs, and values before they are shaped by external instructions.

2. M - Mindset: Navigating Fear and Building True Confidence

The second mistake is "Skipping Over Fear and Building Fake Confidence," focusing on the need for children to confront their fears, not avoid them. In the **IMPACT Framework**, **Mindset** involves cultivating resilience, allowing individuals to understand and embrace challenges. True confidence is not about erasing fear but learning how to navigate through it. This mirrors the truth that children should be taught to befriend fear, as real growth happens when they learn to manage it, rather than avoid it.

3. P - Purpose: Guiding, Not Imposing

The third mistake highlights the danger of imposing a purpose instead of letting it emerge. This is directly related to the **Purpose** component of the **IMPACT Framework**, where coaching is about helping children connect with their internal motivations and guiding them to discover their own sense of purpose. Rather than imposing goals, great coaches help children identify what lights them up, their cause, and their deeper sense of meaning.

4. A - Action: Bridging Dreams to Reality

"Many children are full of ideas and dreams—but no roadmap," says the fourth mistake. In the **IMPACT Framework**, **Action** emphasizes the need to break down big goals into manageable steps. Children must be taught that taking action is the true measure of progress. Coaches should help them create a practical path to follow—breaking dreams into actionable steps and holding them accountable. This aligns with the truth that every dream needs legs, and children need the tools to act on their aspirations.

5. C - Collaboration: Encouraging Teamwork Over Individual Glory

The fifth mistake is about creating "stars" rather than collaborators, and teaching that leadership is about lifting others up. In the **IMPACT Framework**, **Collaboration** emphasizes the importance of working together to achieve common goals. Effective leadership is about teamwork, empathy, and collective success. Coaches should encourage children to develop collaborative skills—focusing on shared success rather than individual accolades.

6. T - Transformation: Leadership as a Way of Life

The sixth mistake—treating leadership as a one-time achievement rather than a lifestyle—aligns directly with the **Transformation** aspect of the **IMPACT Framework**. Leadership is not an endpoint; it is an ongoing journey. Great leaders consistently make choices that align with their values, showing integrity, kindness, and commitment in every action. Coaches should help children understand that leadership is about continual growth and service to others, not just titles or recognition.

7. Empowerment: Creating Present Coaches

The deeper lesson of the text is that children need coaches who are present, who see them as individuals in progress rather than finished products. This aligns with the **Empowerment** component of the **IMPACT Framework**, where coaches empower children to take ownership of their growth. By avoiding coaching traps and guiding children with empathy and patience, coaches can help them become leaders who act from a place of purpose and integrity, affecting change wherever they go.

In summary, the **IMPACT Coaching Framework** provides the structure for guiding children through each stage of their leadership journey. It focuses on **Inspiration, Mindset, Purpose, Action, Collaboration, Transformation**, and **Empowerment**—ensuring that children are not just taught leadership, but are nurtured to grow into empowered, purpose-driven leaders who can positively impact the world.

Here are the **key takeaways** from the text:

1. Leadership Begins with Self-Awareness

Before any child can become a confident leader, they must first discover who they are—what they feel, what drives them, and what their values are. Effective coaching creates space for children to reflect on their emotions and beliefs, fostering self-awareness before imposing instructions.

2. Fear Is Part of the Growth Process

Confidence is not about eliminating fear but learning how to navigate through it. Children should not be told to "just be confident," but instead coached on how to manage and embrace their fears, turning them into opportunities for growth and resilience.

3. Purpose Must Be Discovered, Not Assigned

True purpose arises from within, not from external imposition. Coaches should help children explore their passions, values, and motivations, guiding them as they uncover what drives them, instead of imposing a predetermined purpose upon them.

4. Action Turns Dreams into Reality

Having big dreams is important, but without actionable steps, those dreams remain out of reach. Coaches must help children break down their goals into manageable tasks, teaching them that consistent action and persistence are the key to transforming aspirations into accomplishments.

5. Leadership is About Collaboration, Not Individual Glory

True leadership is not about being the standout individual but about uplifting others and fostering teamwork. Coaches should encourage empathy, connection, and collaboration over individual accolades, teaching children that leadership is about building and leading together.

These takeaways focus on nurturing leadership as a journey of growth, resilience, and collaboration, rather than merely aiming for external achievements. They align with the **IMPACT Coaching Framework** in inspiring self-awareness, managing fear, discovering purpose, taking action, collaborating with others, and empowering individuals.

> *"The greatest good you can do for another is not just to share your riches but to reveal to them their own."*
>
> **— Benjamin Disraeli**

Case Study:

"The Phoenix Sprint: How Coaching Birthed a Thriving Team from the Ashes"

Let me share a story etched in my coaching journey – the tale of a software product team brimming with talent and ambition, yet tragically fractured and spiralling.

Their company's breakneck pace had bred chaos. Sprints were a frantic scramble, features shipped prematurely, and the very foundation of trust was crumbling. The clash between Amit, the driven Product Manager, and Raghav, the protective Engineering

Lead, had become a toxic forcefield, suffocating the entire team. Silence replaced open communication in standups, retros devolved into blame sessions, and morale plummeted to an alarming low.

Into this turbulent environment, I stepped – not as a fixer, but as a coach, armed with the IMPACT Coaching Framework. What unfolded was a remarkable rebirth.

1. **Igniting Self-Awareness (I):** Our initial sessions bypassed features and deadlines, delving into the core of who Amit and Raghav were. What fuelled their drive? What values anchored them? This introspective exploration sparked the breakthrough. Amit unearthed his relentless push for speed stemmed from a deep-seated fear of inadequacy in his new role. Raghav, conversely, resisted change out of a profound sense of responsibility to shield his team from burnout and technical debt. Seeing each other through the lens of their individual fears and values, rather than simply as opposing colleagues, was the first flicker of trust in the darkness.

2. **Cultivating a Growth Mindset (M):** I challenged their ingrained narratives. "What if your differences aren't liabilities, but untapped strengths?" I prompted. For Amit, the narrative shifted from "I must push to prove my worth" to "I can lead through alignment." For Raghav, it transformed from "Change is a threat" to "Change is an opportunity for growth." This fundamental mindset shift unlocked new possibilities, replacing the urge to win with a genuine desire to understand.

3. **Defining a Shared Purpose (P):** Together – Amit, Raghav, and the core team – we forged a unifying purpose: "Deliver exceptional value with pride, without sacrificing our well-being." This shared North Star began to dissolve the pervasive tension, providing a clear direction and transforming the product vision into a collective mission.

4. **Driving Action and Accountability (A):** This was not just theoretical. We moved into practical application, establishing clear

accountability rituals: weekly leadership check-ins, anonymous feedback channels, and a rotating facilitator for sprint retros. In a powerful display of vulnerability, Amit publicly acknowledged his past pressure tactics, and Raghav admitted his resistance to change had been too rigid. This openness created fertile ground for genuine transformation. Promises were not enough; they actively adapted. Amit began including Raghav in early roadmap discussions, and Raghav empowered his engineers with greater ownership. Small, consistent steps yielded significant shifts.

5. **Fostering Connection and Collaboration (C):** As trust deepened, so did the team's culture. Open communication resurfaced. They embraced experimentation, learned collectively from setbacks, and celebrated successes as a unified force. "Code & Coffee" Fridays emerged, a space for sharing ideas and code innovations. It was no longer "Amit's sprint" or "Raghav's team" – it was *their* shared mission.

6. **Transforming and Thriving (T):** By the quarter's end, the team did not just meet their OKRs; they surpassed them. Sprint velocity surged, bug counts plummeted by 40%, and, most importantly, the team rediscovered its vitality. Amit and Raghav, once adversaries in a power struggle, now mentor other cross-functional teams together, their transformation a powerful company-wide narrative. For me, this was a potent reminder of coaching's true potential – to unlock not just behavioural change, but fundamental shifts in identity, clarity, connection, and ultimately, legacy.

This is the transformative power of the IMPACT Coaching Framework – and why I firmly believe coaching is not a luxury; it is the essential pathway forward.

Key Actions to Take After Chapter 1

- **Start a Self-Awareness Journal** Begin the practice of reflecting daily on your thoughts, triggers, values, and emotional patterns. Each day, ask yourself, *who am I becoming* *as a coach? What drives me to keep pushing forward?* This ongoing reflection will give your insight into your growth journey and help you stay aligned with your purpose.

- **Identify Limiting Beliefs** Take a moment to write down 2-3 beliefs that may be holding you back. These could be thoughts like, *"I'm not experienced enough"* or *"Leaders shouldn't show vulnerability."* Once identified, reframe them into empowering beliefs. For example, transform *"I'm not experienced enough"* into *"I am learning and growing every day, and my experience is valuable."* Rewriting these beliefs helps you take ownership of your mindset and create new possibilities.

- **Craft Your Personal Leadership Purpose** Define why you want to coach or lead. This purpose should be short, clear, and deeply meaningful to you. It serves as a compass that guides your actions, decisions, and interactions with others. Make it a statement you can refer to often as you face challenges in your leadership journey.

- **Practice Mindset Shifts** Start noticing when you slip into fixed thinking patterns, such as fear of failure or perfectionism. When this happens, consciously choose a mindset that fosters growth: progress over perfection, curiosity over judgment. This shift will enable you to embrace challenges with an open and resilient attitude.

- **Design One Purpose-Driven Goal** Set one SMART (Specific, Measurable, Achievable, Relevant, Time-bound) goal that aligns with your coaching or leadership growth. This goal should be clear, actionable, and motivating. Track your progress and take time each week to reflect on how you are moving toward it. Regular reflection will keep you focused and energized as you advance.

- **Create a Space for Reflection in Others** In your next coaching conversation, intentionally ask more questions than you provide advice. Create a space where the person you are coaching can discover their own insights and solutions. This empowers them to think critically, take ownership, and find their own path forward.

- **Embrace Discomfort as Growth** Identify one area where you have been avoiding discomfort—this could be public speaking, receiving feedback, or asking for help. Choose one small, intentional step to face that discomfort. By stepping into uncomfortable situations, you will expand your comfort zone and grow as both a coach and a leader. Each small step will lead to greater confidence and resilience.

These actions will lay the foundation for your transformation as a coach and leader, setting you up for long-term growth and success. Take the time to engage deeply with these practices, as they will continuously shape and refine your approach to leadership.

Concluding Reflection:

What one action can you take this week to embody the Coaching qualities discussed in the chapter?

These questions can help facilitate deeper reflection and dialogue, encouraging individuals to connect their personal experiences with the principles outlined in the text

Core Message of Chapter 1:

True transformation begins with self-awareness. Before we can lead or coach others, we must first understand ourselves—our fears, values, dreams, and beliefs. The IMPACT Coaching Framework offers a powerful, human-centered path to growth by nurturing mindset, purpose, action, and connection. Real coaching is not about fixing people—it is about helping them find their voice, build inner courage, and take small, meaningful steps toward a life of impact and legacy.

Chapter 2

Timeless Coaching Wisdom and Global Philosophies

What if the secret to legendary leadership is not hidden in books or boardrooms—but waiting quietly inside you?

Real leadership does not come from titles or training programs. It is not inherited like an old watch or passed down like a family recipe. It is built. Slowly. Carefully. Inwardly. It is shaped in the still, honest moments when no one is watching. It is forged in the fires of doubt, purpose, courage, and hard-earned clarity.

From ancient thinkers like Confucius and Marcus Aurelius to spiritual guides like Rumi and Vivekananda, voices from across time all echo one truth: before you can lead the world, you must first lead yourself.

This chapter is your invitation into that journey—not a sprint to success, but a deeper exploration of who you are beneath the noise. It begins with quiet but powerful questions. Who are you when the spotlight fades? What do you stand for when everything around you shake? What inner strength do you call on when you have fallen—again and again?

Inside these pages, you will not find surface-level motivation. You will find something more meaningful: the raw truths of leadership that many overlook. That purpose is not just a nice idea—it is the breath that keeps you moving when energy runs dry. That failure, as painful as it feels, is your clearest teacher. That taking responsibility—owning your story—is what gives you true power. That we grow faster and stronger when we grow together. That integrity, when your values and your actions match, makes you unshakable. And that real legacy lives not in applause, but in the small, brave choices you make every single day.

Through stories and wisdom, we will walk beside great minds who lived this inner truth. Napoleon Hill, who decoded the psychology of success. Marcus Aurelius, the Roman emperor who found peace in chaos. Rumi, whose poetry still lights the path of transformation. Al-Farabi, who united wisdom with leadership. And Vivekananda, whose fearless voice stirred the soul of a nation.

What connects them? One clear message: your outer impact begins with inner work.

So, whether you are a coach guiding others, a leader shaping a team, or simply someone hungry for deeper meaning, this chapter offers you more than insight. It offers you a mirror. And a compass. A call not to control others, but to become conscious of yourself. Not to chase titles, but to live from your essence. Not to wait for the world to change—but to become the change from the inside out.

This is where your true leadership begins. Let us begin the journey.

Key Topics:

- **Coaching for Greatness: Vivekananda's Philosophy in Action**

- **Stoic Leadership: How Seneca's Wisdom Aligns with the IMPACT Framework**

- **Rumi's Path to Transformation: Timeless Coaching Lessons for Modern Success**

- **Al-Farabi – The Leadership and Wisdom Coach**

- **The Emperor Who Coached Himself: Marcus Aurelius and the Art of Leadership**

- **How Confucius's Philosophy Aligns with Modern Leadership and Personal Growth**

- **The Hidden Code of Success: How Napoleon Hill's Philosophy Mirrors the IMPACT Framework**

Story-8:

Coaching for Greatness: Vivekananda's Philosophy in Action

> **"You have to grow from the inside out. None can teach you, none can make you spiritual. There is no other teacher but your own soul."**
>
> **- Swami Vivekananda**

You know, coaching is not just about giving advice or telling someone what to do. It's so much deeper than that—it's about awakening a person's hidden potential, challenging their self-imposed limits, and helping them transform into who they're truly meant to be.

When I think about this, one name that immediately comes to mind is Swami Vivekananda.

He wasn't just a spiritual leader; to me, he was the ultimate coach—a mentor, a guide, a real catalyst for greatness.

Through his powerful teachings, his inspiring speeches, and even just through the way he interacted with people, he shaped minds, built unshakable confidence, and helped countless individuals realize what they were truly capable of.

If we look at it through the lens of today's coaching principles, Swami Vivekananda's life is a masterclass in what it means to be a transformational coach.

1. A Coach Who Helped People Discover Their True Identity

You know, it is heartbreaking when you realize how many people go through life never truly knowing who they are.

Swami Vivekananda understood this so deeply. He believed that real success—*true* success—starts with self-discovery.

I want to share a story that really stayed with me.

One day, a young man, visibly frustrated and lost, came up to Swamiji. His voice trembled as he said,

"I feel so lost. I do not know what to do with my life."

Swami Vivekananda did not rush to answer. He just looked at him—*really* looked at him—with this intense, piercing kindness.

Then he asked, very simply,

"Tell me, what are you passionate about?"

The young man stood there, confused. After a long pause, he admitted,

"I don't know..."

And that's when Vivekananda smiled—a knowing, almost compassionate smile—and said,

"That is the real problem. It is not that you lack ability. It is that you have not discovered yourself yet."

You see, he was not the kind of guide who would simply hand over answers. No, he asked the kind of questions that *pulled the answers out of you.*

Because a truly great coach does not tell you who you are—they help you *remember* it, *discover* it, for yourself.

And here is a powerful question we all need to sit with:

Who am I—beyond my job, beyond my responsibilities, beyond my fears? What is the unique light I am meant to bring into this world?

2. A Coach Who Built an Unbreakable Mindset

You know, Swami Vivekananda understood something so deeply, something that most of us wrestle with all our lives:

The biggest enemy of success is not a lack of talent. It is not bad luck.

It is fear.

It is that little voice of self-doubt that whispers, *"You can't."*

And Swamiji made it his mission to coach people to build an unbreakable mindset—one so strong that no storm, no challenge, no defeat could ever break them.

There is this moment that gives me chills every time I think about it.

He stood before a group of young men—men who felt small, defeated—and he thundered,

"You are lions, not sheep! But you have been told you are weak. And that is why you live in fear. RISE! Strength is life; weakness is death!"

He did not accept excuses. He did not let people hide behind their fears.

He called them out. He *called* them *up*.

He challenged them to face their struggles head-on, to stop shrinking themselves, and to turn their pain into unstoppable power.

And it makes me wonder—

How often do we hold ourselves back because of fear?

And what could we become... if we dared to replace that fear with unstoppable confidence?

3. A Coach Who Set Purposeful Goals for His Nation

You know, Swami Vivekananda's vision was never just about personal success.

He was after something much, much bigger.

He coached people to lift their eyes beyond their own gain—and to live for a higher purpose.

One story that truly inspires me is his journey to Chicago, to speak at the Parliament of Religions.

Imagine this: a young man, far from home, standing on the world stage with one burning mission in his heart—to elevate India's spirit and dignity before the entire world.

He did not just show up and hope for the best.

No, he prepared like a warrior.

He studied Western thought, refined his understanding, mastered the art of speaking to foreign minds without losing his own soul.

Every single moment of preparation was fuelled by purpose—not ego.

And when he finally stood to speak...

He did not roar with anger.

He did not plead for sympathy.

He moved hearts—with wisdom, with clarity, with *purpose*.

In that one moment, he made India's voice echo across the world.

It makes me think—

Are our goals just about us? Or are they about something bigger, something that leaves a mark long after we are gone?

Because the truth is...

The most extraordinary success stories?

They belong to those who chase missions far greater than themselves.

4. A Coach Who Taught Adaptability & Resilience

When I think about resilience... I think about Swami Vivekananda.

He was not handed success. He *earned* it—through storms most of us cannot even imagine.

When he first arrived in America, he had *nothing*.

No money.

No contacts.

No support.

He slept on park benches.

He faced open racism.

People turned him away.

And yet... he never gave up.

Did he complain? Did he break down and quit?

No.

He *adapted.*

He studied Western philosophy.

He reshaped his message—without ever compromising who he was.

He spoke with such authenticity, such brilliance, that eventually... he won their hearts.

Not by pretending to be someone else, but by standing even taller in his own truth.

And it makes me wonder—

When life throws its hardest challenges at us... do we sit down and complain?

Or do we rise, adapt, and let those very challenges shape us into something stronger?

Because the truth is:

Obstacles do not break strong people. They forge them.

5. A Coach Who Built a Strong Network

You know, one thing I have realized is...

Great leaders never walk alone.

They do not just work harder—they build stronger alliances.

And Swami Vivekananda lived this truth so powerfully.

He did not just gather crowds of followers.

No.

He attracted *thinkers, scholars, reformers*—people with minds on fire and hearts aligned with a bigger purpose.

He was not just creating a moment.

He was building a *movement.*

He mentored leaders, inspired educators, and fuelled visionaries who carried his mission forward long after he was gone.

Because he knew—one voice can start a ripple, but many voices together? They can move oceans.

It makes me reflect deeply—

Who do I surround myself with?

Are the people in my circle lifting me higher—or holding me back?

Because the truth is...

Success is not just about personal strength.

It is built on powerful, purpose-driven networks.

6. A Coach Who Created a Legacy of Transformation

You know, Swami Vivekananda did not just change *one* life.

He transformed *millions*.

He founded the Ramakrishna Mission—not just to preach—but to *serve*, to *heal*, to *uplift humanity*.

And even today, that mission still breathes life into communities across the world.

His spirit?

It did not stop with his lifetime.

It ignited the hearts of freedom fighters like Subhas Chandra Bose, who saw in Vivekananda not just a spiritual leader—but a *source of unstoppable inspiration*.

His words shaped an entire generation's mindset—fuelling dreams of freedom, courage, and greatness.

And it really makes me ask myself—and I ask you too:

True success isn't just about what you achieve.

It is about the lives you touch.

What legacy are you building?

Whose lives are you lighting up by just being you?

Because Swami Vivekananda was more than a speaker.

More than a monk.

He was a *model coach for our world today*—

A leader who did not just talk about change...

He *awakened* it.

He *lived* it.

He *breathed* it into others, until they became powerful beyond what they had ever imagined.

Want to lead like him? Ask yourself:

- **Identity:** *Do I truly know who I am?*
- **Mindset:** *Do I let fear control me, or do I cultivate strength?*
- **Purpose:** *Are my goals meaningful and impactful?*
- **Adaptability:** *Do I resist change, or do I use it to grow?*
- **Connections:** *Am I surrounding myself with the right people?*
- **Transformation:** *Am I leaving behind a legacy that matters?*

Swami Vivekananda was not just a **spiritual leader**—he was a **coach who empowered the world**.

I – The Search for Identity: A Boy Who Questioned Everything

The young boy sat quietly by the banks of the Ganges, his eyes tracing the endless flow of the river.

The evening sky blazed crimson, but inside him... a storm raged.

"Who am I?"

"Why am I here?"

The questions gnawed at his soul, refusing to let him rest.

This boy—Narendranath Datta, who the world would one day know as Swami Vivekananda—was no ordinary child.

While others around him accepted traditions without question, he *dared* to challenge them.

He was not satisfied with rituals or empty words.

He would look into the eyes of scholars, priests, even revered elders, and ask the piercing question:

"Have you seen God?"

Silence.

Avoidance.

No answers that could satisfy the fire burning inside him.

Until one day... he met Ramakrishna Paramahamsa.

A simple man.

A saint whose humility concealed a profound truth.

When Narendra asked him the same question, Ramakrishna looked at him with unwavering eyes and said:

"Yes. I have seen Him. Just as clearly as I see you."

That one moment...

It cracked open something deep within Narendra's soul.

His search was no longer about books or arguments.

He had found what he was truly seeking: *Purpose.*

A life not of blind acceptance—but of discovery, truth, and awakening others.

And when I think about it, I realize—

Modern leadership is not about knowing all the answers.

It is about asking the right questions.

The ones that refuse to let you sleep until you become the person you were born to be.

So, I ask you—

What questions keep you awake at night?

Because somewhere in those questions...

is the beginning of your true impact.

M – The Struggle and the Mindset Shift: Lessons from Hunger and Despair

The streets of India were harsh...

Unforgiving.

Dust clung stubbornly to his worn-out robes as Swami Vivekananda walked, barefoot and determined, from village to village.

Days would pass without a proper meal.

The gnawing pain of hunger was a constant companion.

But his spirit?

Unshaken. Unbreakable.

One night...

A furious storm tore through the skies.

Swami Vivekananda, exhausted and soaked to the bone, found shelter in the crumbling ruins of an abandoned temple.

The roof leaked.

The walls groaned under the assault of the wind.

The rain slashed in like icy knives, and the cold bit into his very bones.

It would have been easy—so easy—to surrender to despair.

To curse fate. To question why he was enduring such suffering.

But in that darkest moment, a thought struck him with the force of lightning:

"If this is what I endure for a night... what about the millions who sleep hungry, who face storms like this every single day of their lives?"

That night... in the howling darkness, he made a vow.

His mission would not just be about personal enlightenment.

It would be about the *awakening* and *upliftment* of an entire people.

He would train his mind to endure hardship.

He would build a spirit too strong to be broken by storms, hunger, or fear.

And he would devote his life to a cause greater than himself.

And as I share this, I cannot help but wonder—

Modern Leadership is not built in comfort.

It is forged in adversity.

So, let me ask you:

When the storms come... when the nights get cold and lonely...

Do you let them break you—or do you let them build you?

Because that choice... that moment... defines everything that comes after.

P – The Goal That Changed the World: A Monk Among Scholars

Imagine it...

The grand hall of the Parliament of Religions, Chicago, 1893.

It was packed—overflowing—with scholars, priests, theologians from every corner of the world.

Most of them had come with one goal:

To prove that their faith, their ideology, was the greatest.

And then...

There stood a young monk.

A simple figure in saffron robes.

No wealthy sponsors.

No powerful allies.

No grand title before his name.

Only a mission burning fiercely in his heart.

He waited silently... patiently... as speaker after speaker took the stage.

And then—his moment came.

He stepped forward, calm yet powerful.

He looked out at the sea of faces...

Took a deep breath...

And uttered five words that would shake the very soul of the gathering:

"Sisters and Brothers of America..."

For a heartbeat, there was silence.

And then—

An eruption.

A thunderous wave of applause, rising and crashing like a mighty tide through the hall.

Because in that one moment, he was not just representing Hinduism.

He was not just representing India.

He was embodying something far greater—

Unity. Compassion. Global Brotherhood.

You see, Swami Vivekananda did not speak to divide.

He spoke to unite.

He did not fight for superiority.

He fought for oneness.

And that day...

He did not just speak.

He *moved* the world.

Modern Leadership Insight:

Great leaders do not just chase goals for fame, money, or pride.

They chase *missions that matter*.

So, let me ask you—

Are your ambitions fuelled by ego... or are they ignited by impact?

What kind of legacy are you building?

A – Adaptability & Execution: Navigating a Foreign Land

Swami Vivekananda stepped into a world that was unlike anything he had ever known—the Western world.

It was a place of scepticism, where every move he made was scrutinized.

The newspapers mocked him.

The streets whispered doubts.

Resources? Almost non-existent.

Yet... did he retreat? Did he run back to what was familiar, to what was comfortable?

No.

Instead, he adapted.

He did not simply learn English. He learned the language of logic, reason, and science. He studied Western philosophy, engaged with the sharpest minds, and refined his message until it spoke not just to one, but to all.

He did not try to force his beliefs upon anyone. He did not raise walls.

He built bridges.

He found common ground. He did not see the cultural gap as a barrier. He saw it as an opportunity to connect, to share ideas, to create understanding where there was none.

And in doing so, he won hearts and minds, not through aggression, but through wisdom and empathy.

Modern Leadership Insight:

The world around us is changing faster than ever. The question is not whether we will face change—it is how we respond to it.

Are you resisting change, or are you learning how to thrive in it?

Are you focused on building walls or creating bridges?

C – The Power of Connections: Allies Who Strengthened His Mission

Swami Vivekananda did not walk this path alone.

Behind every powerful movement, there are unseen hands, quiet supporters, and trusted allies.

Take J.J. Goodwin, for instance. A devoted stenographer who documented every word Swami Vivekananda spoke—preserving his teachings for generations to come.

And then there was Josephine MacLeod—an American philanthropist who believed so deeply in his mission, she funded it, without hesitation.

But these were just two of many. Swami Vivekananda's journey was shaped by a network of incredible individuals—scholars, thinkers, reformers—people who shared his vision, who believed in his mission, and who carried his message forward long after his time had passed.

His genius was not just in his teachings, but in his ability to *connect*. To inspire. To unite.

And that is why his movement did not fade. It *grew*. It multiplied. It resonated, not just with one man, but with countless hearts, across nations.

Modern Leadership Insight:

No leader rises alone.

Behind every great achievement, there is a circle of supporters, mentors, and collaborators who help amplify your vision.

So, I ask you—

Who are the people in your life who lift you up?

Are you surrounding yourself with those who elevate your vision and help you scale your mission?

T – Transformation & Legacy: Awakening a Nation

When Swami Vivekananda returned to India, he was not just a monk anymore—he was a force of transformation.

The man who had once roamed the streets of India in search of meaning now stood tall as a beacon of strength, purpose, and unwavering conviction.

He looked at his countrymen and saw weakness, fear, and despair. But he did not accept it. He challenged them. He called them to rise, to stand tall.

"Arise, awake, and stop not till the goal is reached," he said, his voice a thunderclap that echoed in the hearts of generations.

These words were not just an instruction—they were a call to action. A rallying cry for leaders, for freedom fighters, for visionaries who would reshape a nation.

Swami Vivekananda founded the Ramakrishna Mission, a movement that continues to educate, uplift, and serve millions to this day. His impact is not confined to pages of history books—it lives in the actions of countless people, in the movements he inspired, and in the revolutions he sparked.

Modern Leadership Insight:

True leadership is not about what you achieve in your lifetime—it is about what you leave behind. It is about creating something that continues to grow, evolve, and serve long after you are gone.

So, I ask you—

What will your legacy be?

Will your work endure? Will your vision ignite change that lives on for generations to come?

The IMPACT Framework in Your Life

Swami Vivekananda's story is **not just history—it is a blueprint** for modern leadership, success, and self-mastery.

Success is not just about hard work—it is about having a clear framework to guide your journey. The IMPACT Framework helps individuals and organizations unlock their full potential by focusing on six key areas:

- Identity: Understanding your unique strengths and purpose is the foundation of success. What truly drives you? When you align your actions with your core values, you create authenticity and impact.

- Mindset: Resilience is the key to overcoming adversity. How do you handle setbacks? The difference between success and failure often comes down to mental toughness and the ability to learn from challenges.

- Purposeful Goals: Goals without meaning lead to burnout. Are your ambitions aligned with impact? Purpose-driven goals provide clarity and motivation, ensuring that every step moves you closer to a greater mission.

- Adaptability: The world is constantly evolving—are you growing with it? Success requires learning, pivoting, and embracing change rather than resisting it. Adaptability separates those who thrive from those who fade away.

- Connections: No one succeeds alone. Who are your allies? Strong relationships—whether in business, leadership, or personal growth—create opportunities, support systems, and long-term success.

- Transformation: True success is about leaving a legacy. What impact will you leave behind? The greatest leaders focus not just on personal achievements but on creating meaningful change that outlives them.

Your Call to Action

The real question is not whether this framework works—it is how you will use it to shape your own journey. What steps will you take today to build a future of purpose, adaptability, and impact?

For coaches, Swami Vivekananda's story offers powerful lessons that can be applied to help coachees unlock their potential and achieve meaningful transformation. Here are the top coaching insights from his life that can be turned into action:

1. Help Coachees Discover Their True Identity

So many of us wander through life, feeling like we are just going through the motions, never quite connected to who we truly are. In both life and work, many struggle because they do not have a deep understanding of their own strengths, values, or purpose. They seek answers outside of themselves, but the truth is—*the answers lie within*.

As a coach, our job is not to provide answers. It is to guide people on a journey of self-discovery, helping them uncover the vast potential already residing within them. It is not about giving them the road map—it is about helping them *create* it.

One of the most powerful ways to ignite this self-awareness is by asking the right questions. Deep, reflective questions that stir the soul. Questions like, "Who are you beyond your job?" or "What would you do if there were no limitations, no barriers to your success?"

These are not just questions—they are keys that unlock new possibilities. They push individuals to look beyond their current situation and open their minds to the future they never imagined. They create space for transformation.

Additionally, using tools like personality assessments or strengths-based coaching can reveal so much about a person's natural abilities. These insights help people align their goals with their true self—reminding them of their unique gifts and potential.

When we focus on self-awareness, we empower others to take ownership of their own destiny. It helps them make informed decisions, build unshakable confidence, and move toward a life and career that truly fulfil them.

Coaching Insight:

You cannot unlock someone else's potential if they do not know their own. As a coach, your role is to guide them on the path of self-discovery, allowing them to step into their true power.

2. Develop an Unbreakable Mindset

Many of us get stuck because of fear and self-doubt. We let these emotions dictate what we can or cannot do, often stopping us from trying new things or stepping into unknown territory. But this is where Swami Vivekananda, a visionary leader and thinker, teaches us something profound. He did not see problems as barriers; he saw them as opportunities to grow, to challenge ourselves, and to become more than we ever thought we could be.

Just like Swami Vivekananda, a coach or mentor is there to help us shift our mindset. When we fail, it is easy to believe we are not good enough. But the truth is, failure is not the end. It is merely a stepping stone—a lesson that moves us forward. A great coach reminds us of this: every mistake, every setback, is a chance to learn, adapt, and emerge stronger.

One of the most powerful tools a coach uses is positive self-talk. It is as simple as saying to ourselves, "I can do this" or "Every challenge is an opportunity for growth." In those moments, when we feel uncertain or weak, these words can shift our energy and attitude. The more we repeat them, the more we start to believe them, and soon enough, we can face challenges with a mindset that fuels resilience.

But there is more. Coaches know that real growth happens when we take small, brave steps. It does not matter how small they are; what matters is that we take them. Each time we push beyond our comfort zone and succeed—even in little things—we build our confidence. And every small win reminds us that we are capable of more than we realize.

This cycle of courage and success grows, and before we know it, we are embracing bigger challenges with a strong belief in ourselves. We begin to trust that we are more powerful than we ever thought possible.

Coaching Insight:

Growth does not happen overnight, but with each step, you become stronger, braver, and more capable of facing the unknown. Are you ready to take that first step?

3. Set Purpose-Driven Goals

Swami Vivekananda's journey was not just about personal growth—it was about igniting a flame of purpose that could light up the world. His influence spread far beyond the individual; it was deeply connected to a higher mission. He understood that when people align their goals with something meaningful, they unlock a reservoir of motivation and resilience that keeps them moving forward, no matter the obstacle.

As a coach, one of the most powerful things you can do is help someone shift their focus from "what" they want to achieve to "why" it matters. Instead of just asking, "What are your goals?" you dive deeper— "Why does this goal matter to you?" This shift transforms a goal from a task into a calling. When individuals understand the deeper purpose behind their goals, they are better equipped to stay committed, even during the hardest times. The "why" provides clarity and strengthens their resolve.

True fulfilment comes not from personal success alone, but from how that success serves a greater mission. Coaches can help people recognize how their growth contributes to something larger—whether it is making a difference in their community, advancing their industry, or leaving a legacy for future generations. When goals are tied to a greater purpose, resilience becomes almost second nature, and setbacks are seen not as failures, but as stepping stones leading toward something profoundly meaningful.

Coaching Insight:

When you connect your goals to a greater purpose, challenges become opportunities to build something that lasts. What is the bigger "why" behind your goals, and how does it inspire you to keep moving forward?

4. Teach Adaptability & Resilience

Swami Vivekananda's life was filled with obstacles—poverty, cultural differences, and harsh criticism—but he did not allow these challenges to define him. Instead, he embraced them as opportunities to grow. He continuously adapted his approach, kept learning, and never gave up on his mission to inspire the world. His resilience and flexibility were key to sharing his message, and they continue to inspire millions today.

What can we learn from Swami Vivekananda's example? One of the most powerful lessons is the importance of having a growth mindset—the belief that we can improve through effort, learning, and perseverance. Coaches and mentors play a crucial role in helping people develop this mindset. They encourage individuals to embrace change, see challenges as opportunities, and recognize that growth often comes from the most difficult experiences.

Instead of viewing setbacks as failures, we can reframe them as steps on the path to success. A good coach helps clients shift their perspective by asking questions like, **"What can you learn from this?"** instead of focusing on the negative aspects of failure. Coaches may also use tools like scenario planning, where individuals imagine and prepare for potential challenges in the future, or encourage reflective journaling. Writing down thoughts, feelings, and experiences allows us to reflect, track our progress, and identify strategies for moving forward more effectively.

When we learn to adapt, we do not just survive challenges—we thrive because of them. With each obstacle overcome, our belief in ourselves grows stronger, and we realize that our potential for growth is limitless. Every challenge becomes a stepping stone, not a roadblock.

Coaching Insight:

Challenges are not barriers—they are opportunities to grow. How can you reframe your setbacks as learning experiences, and how can you use them to push yourself further?

5. Build Strong Networks and Support Systems

Swami Vivekananda's success was not solely due to his intellect or determination—it was also the result of the meaningful relationships he nurtured. He understood that his mission could only reach its full potential through collaboration with scholars, patrons, and devoted followers. His ability to connect with the right people amplified his message, allowing his teachings to transcend borders and inspire people worldwide. His legacy shows us that no great leader achieves success in isolation—collaboration and mentorship are the cornerstones of lasting impact.

For coaches, this insight is crucial. It underscores the importance of teaching coachees how to build and nurture meaningful connections. Coaches can encourage individuals to actively seek mentors, advisors, and like-minded peers who can provide new perspectives, offer guidance, and open doors to opportunities. A strong network is not just about receiving—it is also about giving. It serves as a support system, offering encouragement, accountability, and insight, especially during challenging times.

Coaches can help individuals shift their mindset from competition to collaboration, emphasizing that success is not about individual achievements, but about creating a shared impact. Networking should not be viewed as a transactional activity; instead, it should be seen as an opportunity to exchange knowledge, contribute to the growth of others, and collectively work toward greater goals.

By fostering an ecosystem of support and collaboration, individuals can break past their own limitations, leverage collective wisdom, and create a far greater influence than they ever could on their own.

Coaching Insight:

Success is often amplified by those you surround yourself with. Who are the people that can help you grow, and how can you contribute to their growth in return?

6. Create a Legacy of Transformation

Swami Vivekananda's legacy endures because his mission was not just about personal success—it was about creating a profound and lasting impact on society. His teachings continue to inspire people around the world, proving that true leadership is measured not by what one achieves, but by the positive influence one leaves behind. A leader's true role goes beyond achieving personal goals; it is about shaping a future that benefits others and elevates society as a whole.

For coaches, this offers a valuable lesson: to guide individuals in thinking beyond immediate success and focusing on their long-term impact. Coaches can encourage coachees to reflect on questions like, ***"How will your work impact others beyond yourself?"*** These reflective questions help foster a purpose-driven mindset. Crafting a personal mission statement that extends beyond personal gain ensures that an individual's work remains meaningful and resilient, even in the face of challenges.

One of the most powerful ways to leave a lasting legacy is through mentorship. Coaching does not just focus on immediate success—it empowers individuals to pass on their knowledge, mentor others, and help build future leaders. When coachees recognize the value of guiding and uplifting others, it creates a ripple effect of transformation that extends far beyond their own accomplishments.

As a coach, one of the greatest gifts you can give is not just helping someone succeed in the present but equipping them with the tools and mindset to inspire and empower others, ensuring their impact resonates for generations to come.

Coaching Insight:

True leadership lies in the legacy you leave behind. How will your work shape the future, and how will you help others create their own legacies?

> **"Arise, awake, and stop not till the goal is reached."**
>
> *- Swami Vivekananda*

Final Coaching Challenge:

Ask coachees: *If Swami Vivekananda were coaching you today, what would he challenge you to change in your mindset, actions, or goals?*

Here are key messages a reader can take away from this powerful narrative about Swami Vivekananda as a transformative coach and leader:

1. Discover Your True Identity

"Who are you beyond your job, your responsibilities, and your fears?"

Swami Vivekananda believed that real success begins with self-awareness. He did not give people answers—he asked questions that stirred introspection. Every reader is invited to embark on this inner quest: to uncover their passions, strengths, and values. Only when you know yourself can you lead yourself and others effectively.

2. Build an Unbreakable Mindset

"You are lions, not sheep."

Fear and self-doubt keep most people from fulfilling their potential. Swami Vivekananda's legacy shows us that courage is not the absence of fear, but the decision to rise above it. Readers are reminded that mindset is a muscle—one that must be trained with resilience, reflection, and self-belief.

3. Set Goals That Serve a Higher Purpose

"Are your goals only about success—or also about significance?"

Swami Vivekananda aligned his personal mission with a larger vision—uplifting a nation. He spoke not to impress, but to impact. This challenges readers to look beyond personal gain and ask: How can my goals serve others, inspire change, and create a ripple effect of positive influence?

4. Embrace Adaptability and Growth

"Strong people are not those who never fall, but those who rise every time."

His journey in the West showed immense adaptability. Whether you are facing a career change, life challenge, or cultural shift, your ability to pivot and evolve determines your progress. Leaders are not rigid—they are resilient learners.

5. Build Powerful Connections and Leave a Legacy

"No mission is successful alone. Strong networks lead to strong impact."

Vivekananda surrounded himself with thinkers, reformers, and believers who amplified his mission. He did not just influence during his time—his legacy still lives. This reminds readers that true success is measured not by what you achieve alone, but by the lives you empower and the movements you spark.

Story-9:

Stoic Leadership: How Seneca's Wisdom Aligns with the IMPACT Framework?

> **"While we teach, we learn."**
>
> *— Seneca*

Lucius Annaeus Seneca, commonly known as **Seneca the Younger,** was a Roman philosopher, statesman, playwright, and one of the most influential figures in **Stoic philosophy.** His teachings have stood the test of time, offering profound insights into **resilience, self-mastery, leadership, and emotional control.** As an advisor to Emperor Nero, Seneca navigated the complexities of political power while championing wisdom and virtue. His writings, particularly his letters and essays, continue to serve as timeless guides for those seeking clarity, strength, and purpose in life.

Resilience and the Power of Endurance

Seneca firmly believed that **life is filled with challenges, setbacks, and hardships,** but rather than resisting them, one should embrace them as opportunities for growth. He personally endured exile, political downfall, and betrayal—yet he remained composed and steadfast in his principles. For him, **true strength lies not in avoiding adversity but in developing the resilience to withstand it.** His philosophy has inspired countless leaders, entrepreneurs, and individuals to **view difficulties as stepping stones to greatness** rather than as obstacles.

Modern leadership and personal development coaching heavily draw from Seneca's ideas on resilience. **CEOs, athletes, and high-performing professionals** who face immense pressure apply his teachings to stay composed in crises. His wisdom is particularly relevant in today's fast-paced world, where resilience is crucial for navigating uncertainty and change.

Emotional Mastery and Self-Control

One of Seneca's most powerful lessons is the importance of **emotional discipline.** He emphasized that emotions—whether fear, anger, or anxiety—should not control our actions. Instead, he encouraged individuals to develop **self-awareness, detach from negative emotions, and respond rationally rather than impulsively.** His famous quote, *"We suffer more in imagination than in reality,"* highlights how much of our distress comes not from actual events but from the stories we tell ourselves.

By practicing **daily reflection and self-examination,** Seneca believed that people could **gain mastery over their thoughts and emotions.** He often recommended journaling as a method to process emotions and develop rational thinking. Today, many personal development experts, psychologists, and executive coaches advocate **mindfulness techniques, cognitive behavioral therapy (CBT), and self-reflection exercises**—practices that echo Seneca's teachings on emotional mastery.

Wisdom in Leadership and Decision-Making

As an advisor to Emperor Nero, Seneca played a crucial role in shaping political decisions, though he later distanced himself from Nero's tyranny. His writings on **moral integrity, ethical leadership, and rational governance** remain highly relevant to modern-day leaders. His book *On the Shortness of Life reminds individuals—whether in leadership or personal life—to* **use their time wisely and focus on meaningful pursuits.**

Many leaders, entrepreneurs, and decision-makers today turn to **Stoic principles** when facing complex challenges. The ability to make **calm, rational, and ethical decisions under pressure** is a key characteristic of great leadership. By integrating Seneca's wisdom, leaders can balance ambition with **moral responsibility,** ensuring that their success is not built on compromise but on lasting impact.

Minimalism and Detachment from Materialism

Despite his wealth, Seneca lived simply and practiced **minimalism,** believing that **true happiness comes not from external possessions**

but from inner contentment. He warned against the dangers of excessive ambition and materialism, arguing that those who constantly chase wealth or status often end up feeling empty. His teachings inspired later movements in minimalism, **mindfulness, and financial independence,** emphasizing the importance of focusing on what truly matters—**personal growth, relationships, and purpose.**

Today, many financial experts and life coaches use Seneca's principles to help individuals **prioritize experiences over material possessions, manage wealth wisely, and cultivate a sense of fulfillment beyond monetary success.** His timeless wisdom serves as a powerful reminder that **happiness is an internal state, not an external achievement.**

Facing Mortality and Living with Purpose

One of Seneca's most profound teachings is the **acceptance of mortality.** He believed that **embracing the inevitability of death helps people live more fully and intentionally.** Instead of fearing the end of life, he encouraged individuals to use this awareness as motivation to make **meaningful choices, focus on personal growth, and leave a lasting legacy.**

His letters on death and impermanence continue to inspire those struggling with **fear, anxiety, or regret.** Many **psychologists, end-of-life coaches, and mental health experts** reference Seneca's wisdom to help people **find peace in uncertainty** and appreciate each moment with greater depth and gratitude.

The Lasting Impact of Seneca's Teachings

Seneca's Stoic philosophy has left a profound mark on **modern coaching, leadership, and personal development.** His principles of **resilience, self-discipline, emotional mastery, and purpose-driven living** continue to guide individuals toward excellence.

His teachings are particularly valuable for:

- **Leaders & Entrepreneurs** – To develop mental toughness, clarity, and ethical decision-making

- **Students & Lifelong Learners** – To cultivate focus, discipline, and a love for knowledge

- **Coaches & Mentors** – To integrate Stoic principles into leadership and self-improvement coaching

- **Personal Growth Enthusiasts** – To achieve emotional mastery, embrace simplicity, and live with intention

Seneca's **timeless wisdom** remains as relevant today as it was over two thousand years ago. Whether applied in leadership, personal growth, or emotional well-being, his insights continue to **transform mindsets, shape leaders, and inspire people to live with purpose and wisdom.** As he famously said,

"Luck is what happens when preparation meets opportunity."

By following his teachings, individuals can cultivate **resilience, clarity, and excellence,** ultimately leading more fulfilled and impactful lives.

Aligning Seneca's Coaching Philosophy with the IMPACT Coaching Framework

Seneca's Stoic wisdom aligns deeply with the principles of the **IMPACT Coaching Framework,** both emphasizing self-awareness, resilience, action, and long-term transformation. While Seneca's philosophy was rooted in **self-mastery, ethical leadership, and endurance,** the IMPACT framework provides a **structured, actionable coaching model** that applies these timeless lessons to modern leadership and personal development. Below is how each element of IMPACT resonates with Seneca's coaching and life philosophy:

1. I - Inspire Awareness & Identity → The Power of Self-Reflection (Seneca's Core Teaching)

What if the key to wisdom was not about knowing more but about understanding yourself better?

Seneca, the great Stoic philosopher, believed that true mastery begins with self-awareness. He did not just preach wisdom—he lived it, practicing deep reflection, questioning his own beliefs, and journaling daily to sharpen his mind. To him, life was not about reaching a final state of knowledge but about constantly refining how we think and act.

"As long as you live, keep learning how to live," he famously said. These words were not just advice—they were a challenge. A challenge to look inward, to examine every decision, and to question the thoughts that shape our actions.

This philosophy aligns with the Inspire Awareness & Identity pillar of the IMPACT framework. Just as Seneca urged people to reflect and grow, this pillar pushes individuals to explore their values and break free from self-imposed limits. Tools like journaling and self-assessment—core to Seneca's own practice—help individuals gain clarity and align with their true potential.

Imagine a leader struggling with tough decisions, second-guessing every move. What if, instead of feeling stuck, they took five minutes each night to write down their thoughts, reflect on their choices, and challenge their assumptions? Over time, this simple habit could sharpen their judgment, build confidence, and transform them into a decisive, visionary leader.

The question is—are you willing to take a deeper look at yourself?

2. M - Mindset & Mastery Shift → Overcoming Fear & Emotional Mastery (Seneca's Resilience Principle)

What if I told you that most of your struggles exist only in your mind?

The room is silent, yet it roars inside his head. A hundred eyes stare, or at least, it feels that way. His shirt clings to his back, damp with nervous sweat. The air is thick, carrying the faint scent of coffee and paper—things that should be familiar, comforting, yet feel foreign in this moment. His throat tightens. His hands are ice-cold, yet somehow burning. The microphone in his grip feels heavier than it should. The words he had rehearsed over and over now seem to scatter like dry leaves in the wind.

But nothing is actually happening. No one in the audience is leaning forward in judgment. No one is waiting for him to fail. The fear is real, but the danger is not.

Seneca, the Stoic philosopher, knew this well. "We suffer more in imagination than in reality," he said. The mind builds illusions, crafting shadows where there is only light. But just as the mind creates fear, it can unmake it.

By shifting his focus, by breathing deeply, by grounding himself in the present—the warmth of the stage lights, the steady rhythm of his own voice—he reclaims control. The fear does not disappear. It transforms. It becomes energy. It sharpens his presence. It fuels his words.

The mind is both the cage and the key. The question is, will you set yourself free?

3. P - Purpose-Driven Goals & Strategy → Living with Intention (Seneca's Lesson on Purpose)

What if you woke up one day and realized you had spent years chasing things that did not matter?

The days slip by, each one blending into the next. Meetings, emails, endless scrolling—busyness disguised as progress. A man sits at his desk late at night, exhausted but unsatisfied. He has worked hard, but for what? The weight of unfulfilled purpose settles in his chest like a stone.

Seneca warned against this kind of life. In *On the Shortness of Life*, he argued that time is not truly short—it is simply wasted on distractions. The real tragedy is not that life ends too soon, but that we fail to use it wisely. He urged people to focus on what truly matters, to cut away the trivial, and to live with direction.

The same wisdom applies today. Defining clear goals—whether in life or business—is not just helpful; it is essential. A startup founder who sets a strong vision avoids the trap of chasing short-term gains. With a clear purpose, every decision moves the company toward long-term impact. Tools like SMART goals and OKRs bring Seneca's philosophy into action, ensuring that effort is spent on what truly matters.

Life is not short. But without purpose, it can feel that way. The question is, are you spending your time or truly investing it?

4. A - Action, Accountability & Adaptability → The Stoic Art of Taking Control

What if your greatest ideas never became more than thoughts?

A man sits at his desk, lost in planning. His notebook is filled with strategies, his mind brimming with ambition. He has read every leadership book, attended every seminar, yet his goals remain distant. He tells himself he will start tomorrow. But tomorrow turns into next week, next month, next year. The pages of his plans gather dust while time quietly slips away.

Seneca saw this all too clearly. "It is not that we have a short time to live, but that we waste much of it," he wrote. Thinking, planning, and learning are valuable—but without action, they are meaningless. Legacy is not built on ideas alone, but on the steps taken to bring them to life.

Execution is everything. A corporate leader struggling with procrastination does not need more theories; they need movement. By eliminating distractions, setting clear priorities, and staying accountable to a mentor or team, they shift from passive thinking to active doing. Tools like habit trackers and resilience exercises reinforce commitment, ensuring progress is made—not just imagined.

The difference between a dreamer and a doer is simple: action. The question is, will you start today or let another tomorrow slip away?

5. C - Connection & Collaborative Growth → Leadership & Mentorship (Seneca's Teachings on Relationships)

What if the key to your success was not what you achieved alone, but what you helped others achieve?

A manager watches his team from the corner of the room. Deadlines loom, yet motivation is slipping. Some employees seem disengaged, others hesitant to speak up. He wonders if he should push harder, demand more. But then he remembers the leaders who once guided him—not with orders, but with wisdom, support, and trust.

Seneca understood this deeply. In his *Letters to Lucilius*, he did not just offer advice—he built a legacy of mentorship. He believed that true leadership was not about control, but about lifting others up. Knowledge, when shared, multiplies. Strength, when given, empowers. A great leader does not demand obedience; they cultivate growth.

A manager struggling with team motivation does not need stricter rules—he needs connection. By embracing mentorship, he creates a culture where employees feel valued, heard, and inspired. Coaching sessions replace rigid commands. Wisdom is exchanged, not imposed. As trust builds, so does motivation.

Leadership is not about standing above others—it is about standing beside them. The question is, will you lead alone, or will you bring others with you?

6. T - Transform & Thrive → Leaving a Lasting Legacy (Seneca's Philosophy on Mortality & Impact)

What if you only had a year left to live?

Would you still worry about trivial problems? Would you chase temporary success, or would you focus on something greater—something that lasts?

Seneca believed that true wisdom comes from facing mortality, not fearing it. "You are dying every day," he reminded us, not to spread fear, but to inspire urgency. Life is not endless, and time wasted can never be reclaimed. Yet, those who accept this truth live differently. They choose depth over distraction, impact over impulse. They do not just chase success; they build something that endures.

A retiring executive stands at a crossroads. The accolades, the promotions, the numbers—they once mattered, but now, something deeper calls. Instead of clinging to past achievements, he chooses to give back. He mentors young leaders, documents hard-earned lessons, and ensures his wisdom outlives him. Much like Seneca's letters, his legacy is not in what he owned, but in the knowledge and inspiration he leaves behind.

Life is not measured by how long we live, but by what we leave behind. The question is, when time runs out, what will your legacy be?

Conclusion: Why Seneca's Coaching Approach & IMPACT are Perfectly Aligned

Imagine if Seneca were coaching leaders today.

He would not offer empty motivation or quick-fix strategies. Instead, he would challenge them to think deeply, to strip away illusions, and to lead with wisdom and purpose. He would remind them that true growth begins with self-awareness, that fear is an obstacle created by the mind, and that success without meaning is no success at all.

His philosophy aligns perfectly with modern coaching. The IMPACT Framework reflects the very principles he lived by—mindset shifts to break limiting beliefs, purpose-driven goals that align with values, resilience in the face of adversity, and mentorship that lifts others up. He would teach that leadership is not about control, but influence. That action, not theory, shapes destiny. That legacy is built not through wealth or titles, but through the wisdom we pass on.

If Seneca were here today, he would not ask what you have achieved—he would ask what impact you have made. And more importantly, what kind of life you are truly living. The question is, are you leading with purpose, or simply going through the motions?

Step-by-Step Guide to Applying the IMPACT Framework

1. I - Inspire Awareness & Identity

To apply this practice, start with daily self-reflection. Spend around 10 to 15 minutes each day writing in a journal. Use this time to think deeply about your strengths, values, and leadership style. Ask yourself questions like, "Who am I as a leader?" and "What are my strengths and where do I need to grow?" This simple habit builds self-awareness over time.

In addition to journaling, take a strengths assessment such as CliftonStrengths or the VIA Character Strengths survey. These tools can help you discover what makes you unique and where your natural talents lie.

You should also seek feedback from others. A 360-degree review from colleagues, peers, or mentors can give you valuable insights about how others see you. This outside perspective often reveals blind spots and areas for improvement that you may not notice on your own.

For example, Rahul, a mid-level manager, often felt like he was not good enough—a feeling known as imposter syndrome. By practicing self-reflection and asking for feedback, he discovered that his real strength was solving complex problems, not trying to control every small detail. With this new awareness, he began to delegate tasks more effectively and became a more confident, capable leader.

2. M - Mindset & Mastery Shift

Start by identifying limiting beliefs—write down fears and self-doubts, then actively reframe them into empowering beliefs. This shift in mindset lays the foundation for confidence and resilience. Incorporate daily affirmations and visualization by spending five minutes each morning affirming your growth mindset. For example, say: *"I am capable of leading with confidence."*

Make growth a habit by changing your response to mistakes. Instead of self-criticism, ask: *"What did I learn?"* This simple shift fosters continuous improvement.

Example: Priya, a startup founder, initially feared failure. Through consistent mindset work, she began reframing setbacks as learning opportunities. This new perspective empowered her to take bold risks, ultimately leading to her startup securing its first major investment.

3. P - Purpose-Driven Goals & Strategy

Start by defining your vision—write down your long-term goals and clarify why they matter. A strong "why" fuels commitment and direction. Break this vision into actionable steps using SMART goals, ensuring they are specific, measurable, achievable, relevant, and time-bound.

For instance, instead of a vague goal like "I want to improve communication," reframe it as "I will give feedback to my team weekly." The OKR (Objectives and Key Results) framework can further enhance goal alignment, helping track progress with clear milestones.

Example: Arjun, a software developer, aspired to transition into leadership. By setting SMART goals and actively seeking mentorship opportunities, he systematically developed the necessary skills and mindset. Within a year, he successfully stepped into a team lead role.

4. A - Action, Accountability & Adaptability

Establish an accountability system by scheduling weekly check-ins with a coach, mentor, or peer group. This structure keeps you committed and motivated. Strengthen resilience by celebrating micro-wins—small daily progress matters more than striving for perfection.

Embrace adaptability by recognizing when a strategy is not working and pivoting instead of quitting. The ability to adjust course ensures continuous improvement and long-term success.

Example: Meera, a sales executive, consistently tracked her progress with an accountability partner. By analysing market feedback and refining her sales approach, she increased her client conversions by 30%.

5. C - Connection & Collaborative Growth

Seek a mentor who has successfully navigated the path you aspire to follow. Their insights and experiences can accelerate your growth. Practice active listening in meetings—focus on truly understanding others before responding to foster stronger collaboration.

Create a culture of constructive feedback by both giving and receiving it openly. Honest, growth-oriented feedback strengthens professional relationships and enhances team performance.

Example: Ananya, a product manager, balanced mentoring junior employees while seeking guidance from senior leaders. This dual approach expanded her leadership influence and fast-tracked her promotion.

6. T - Transform & Thrive

Make regular reflection a habit—set aside time each month to evaluate progress, identify growth areas, and realign with your vision. Shift to legacy thinking by asking, "How can I create a lasting impact beyond my personal success?" This mindset fosters purpose-driven leadership.

Commit to lifelong learning by staying curious—read books, take courses, and engage in continuous self-improvement. Expanding knowledge keeps you adaptable and innovative.

Example: Vikram, a senior executive, shifted from focusing solely on career success to mentoring upcoming leaders. This strengthened his leadership influence and cultivated a culture of growth within his organization.

Final Thought: Your Personal IMPACT Plan

Action Steps to Apply Right Now:

- Choose **one area** from the IMPACT framework to focus on this week.

- Set **one clear, small goal** to implement in your daily routine.

- Find an **accountability partner** or mentor to support your journey.

Transformation happens **one step at a time.** By applying these practical steps, you will not only enhance your own performance but also **create meaningful impact in your work and leadership**

> **"It is not that we are given a short life, but we make it short, and we are not ill-supplied but wasteful of it."**
>
> – Seneca, *On the Shortness of Life*

Here are the five Key Takeaways:

1. ***Resilience and Endurance****: Seneca emphasizes embracing challenges and hardships as opportunities for growth. His teachings on resilience, especially in the face of adversity, align with modern leadership coaching, encouraging individuals to view difficulties as stepping stones to success rather than obstacles.*

2. ***Emotional Mastery and Self-Control****: Seneca advocates for emotional discipline, urging people to detach from negative emotions and respond rationally. His focus on mastering one's emotions through self-reflection and journaling resonates with modern practices such as mindfulness and cognitive behavioural therapy (CBT).*

3. ***Purpose-Driven Leadership and Decision-Making****: Seneca's wisdom on ethical leadership and wise decision-making emphasizes*

the importance of moral integrity, time management, and living with purpose. His teachings encourage leaders to focus on meaningful pursuits and make decisions with a sense of responsibility.

4. ***Minimalism and Detachment from Materialism***: Despite his wealth, Seneca practiced minimalism, valuing inner contentment over material possessions. His teachings warn against excessive ambition and materialism, promoting personal growth, relationships, and purpose as the true sources of happiness.

5. ***Living with Purpose and Mortality Awareness***: Seneca believed that embracing mortality motivates individuals to live more fully and intentionally. His teachings encourage people to focus on what truly matters in life, create meaningful legacies, and live with a sense of urgency, knowing that time is finite.

Story-10:

Rumi's Path to Transformation: Timeless Coaching Lessons for Modern Success

> **"Try not to resist the changes that come your way. Instead, let life live through you."**
>
> *– Rumi*

Jalal al-Din Muhammad Rumi, known simply as Rumi, was more than just a poet—he was a guide, a teacher, and a spiritual coach whose wisdom transcended time.

Born in 1207 in present-day Afghanistan, Rumi's journey took him through Persia and into the heart of the Sufi tradition, where he became one of the most influential mystics of all time.

His words did not merely express emotions; they awakened the soul, guiding people toward profound self-awareness, love, and transformation.

At the center of Rumi's coaching philosophy was the belief that true change comes from within.

He did not tell people what to do—he invited them to explore their deepest selves.

Through his poetry, he posed questions that made individuals reflect on their fears, desires, and the illusions that held them back. His verses were not just written words but mirrors that forced people to see their true potential.

One of his most famous lines, *"You were born with wings, why prefer to crawl through life?"* was not merely poetic; it was a call to action, urging people to break free from self-imposed limitations.

Rumi's approach to coaching emphasized emotional intelligence. He understood that transformation could not happen without embracing emotions fully—joy, sorrow, longing, and love.

He guided people to move beyond surface-level happiness and dig deeper into their own hearts.

He believed that pain was not an obstacle but a teacher. "The wound is the place where the light enters you," he wrote, teaching that struggle and suffering were pathways to enlightenment and growth.

One of the most profound aspects of Rumi's coaching was his emphasis on love—not just romantic love but divine and self-love. He believed that the ultimate transformation occurred when a person dissolved their ego and surrendered to love's power. His relationship with his spiritual companion, Shams of Tabriz, was a testament to the idea that true coaching and mentorship come from deep, soul-level connections. Shams challenged Rumi's intellectual knowledge and pushed him into a state of deep emotional and spiritual awakening. This transformation led Rumi to create the Masnavi, a collection of teachings that continues to inspire millions today.

His methods align with modern coaching principles in remarkable ways. His focus on **self-awareness** mirrors mindfulness techniques, his belief in **embracing challenges** aligns with growth mindset strategies, and his **use of storytelling and metaphor** serves as a powerful tool for guiding people toward change. His whirling dervish practice, a form of meditative movement, was a physical embodiment of his belief that transformation happens when one loses themselves in something greater.

Even centuries later, Rumi's coaching continues to impact leaders, creatives, and seekers of wisdom.

His teachings guide individuals through personal struggles, helping them navigate emotional barriers and discover their highest potential.

Whether through poetry, philosophy, or spiritual practice, Rumi remains one of history's greatest emotional and spiritual coaches, proving that true transformation begins not in the outside world, but within the soul.

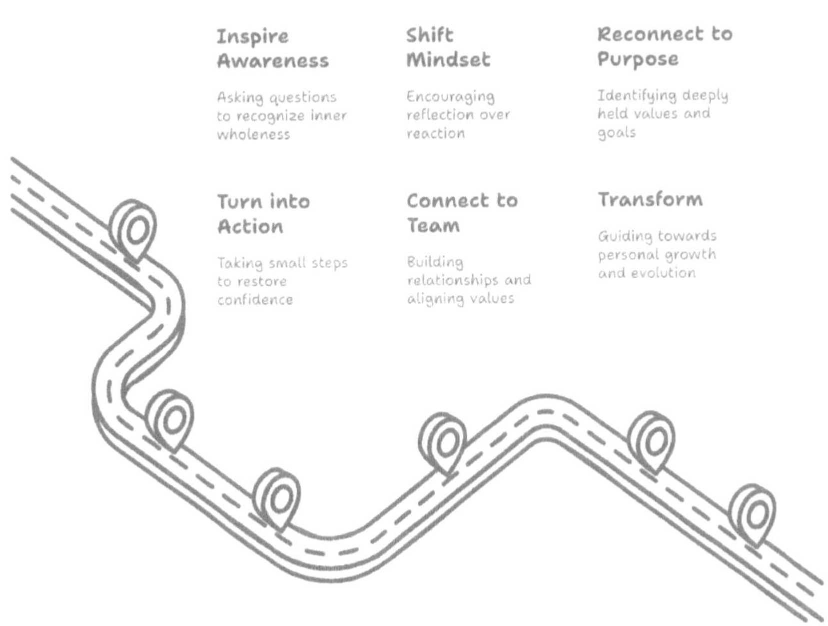

Rumi's coaching philosophy aligns closely with the **IMPACT** framework, as his teachings and guidance touched on each of its core elements in profound ways. His wisdom, conveyed through poetry, philosophy, and spiritual mentorship, naturally reflected the transformative principles of coaching. Here's how Rumi's approach aligns with the **IMPACT** framework:

1. Inspire Awareness & Identity

Rumi's poetry and teachings were rooted in **self-awareness and identity discovery.** He urged people to look inward, question their beliefs, and recognize their divine potential.

His famous words, *"Don't grieve. Anything you lose comes round in another form,"* guided individuals to redefine their struggles and see their identity beyond temporary setbacks.

Much like Shackleton embraced his new purpose as a survival leader, Rumi helped his followers awaken to their true selves and embrace their spiritual journey.

2. Mindset & Mastery Shift

A key aspect of Rumi's coaching was **shifting from fear and limitation to love and mastery.** He believed that fear was an illusion and that embracing uncertainty was the key to transformation.

His advice, *"Try not to resist the changes that come your way. Instead, let life live through you,"* is a direct call for a **mindset shift**—one that moves from control and resistance to flow and mastery.

Just as Shackleton turned fear into action, Rumi encouraged his followers to transform suffering into wisdom, making his approach a timeless coaching model for overcoming doubt and embracing potential.

3. Purpose-Driven Goals & Strategy

Rumi did not just encourage people to dream—he provided a **roadmap to enlightenment and transformation.**

His structured teachings in the *Masnavi* served as a guide for those seeking wisdom, much like a purpose-driven strategy.

He emphasized that true fulfillment comes from aligning one's actions with a higher purpose. *"Let yourself be silently drawn by the strange pull of what you really love,"* he advised, helping people align their personal and professional journeys with their core values, just as Shackleton redefined success for survival.

4. Action, Accountability & Adaptability

While Rumi's teachings were spiritual, they were not passive. He emphasized **taking action and being accountable for one's growth.** His whirling dervish practice was not just a ritual—it was a form of active meditation, a physical commitment to transformation. He reminded his followers that merely contemplating change was not enough; one had to step forward and embrace it. His coaching, like Shackleton's leadership, instilled resilience, and adaptability, pushing people to move beyond thought into decisive action.

5. Connection & Collaborative Growth

One of Rumi's greatest lessons was about **love, relationships, and interconnectedness.** His relationship with Shams of Tabriz was a deep coaching dynamic—Shams challenged Rumi, guiding him toward greater self-discovery.

His teachings constantly emphasized the power of human connection: *"Be a lamp, or a lifeboat, or a ladder. Help someone's soul heal. Walk out of your house like a shepherd."*

His words encouraged mentorship, leadership, and the **collective growth of communities,** mirroring the leadership and teamwork principles seen in Shackleton's journey.

6. Transform & Thrive

Rumi's ultimate goal was not just personal growth but **complete transformation.** He believed in breaking free from old patterns, embracing new wisdom, and thriving in every aspect of life.

His quote, *"Don't be satisfied with stories, how things have gone with others. Unfold your own myth,"* is a direct challenge for individuals to take ownership of their transformation and not live in the shadows of others.

Just as Shackleton's strategies became a global coaching model, Rumi's teachings continue to guide millions toward self-mastery and leadership.

Conclusion: Rumi's Legacy Through IMPACT Coaching

Rumi's coaching philosophy and the **IMPACT** framework share the same foundation—transformation through awareness, mindset shifts, purpose-driven action, accountability, collaboration, and ultimately, personal mastery.

His poetic wisdom serves as a timeless guide for anyone looking to navigate uncertainty, overcome fear, and lead with both heart and strategy. His teachings prove that transformation is not just an external journey but an internal evolution—one that, when fully embraced, leads individuals to thrive at the highest level.

Major Learnings from Rumi's Coaching Philosophy

Rumi's life and teachings offer profound lessons for modern coaches seeking to enhance their coaching journey.

His transformational approach—rooted in self-awareness, emotional intelligence, and purposeful action—aligns with the principles of effective coaching today. Here are the major takeaways that modern-day coaches can integrate into their practice:

1. Self-Awareness is the Foundation of Transformation

Rumi taught that deep, lasting transformation begins with self-awareness. His philosophy encouraged individuals to **look inward, confront their fears, and embrace their true nature.** Modern coaches can apply this by helping clients develop self-awareness before setting goals. Encouraging reflection, journaling, or mindfulness exercises can allow clients to **discover limiting beliefs and redefine their self-perception** before taking action.

Key Lesson for Coaches: Start with deep self-inquiry. Help clients explore their inner world before guiding them toward external success.

2. Mindset Shifts are Essential for Growth

One of Rumi's core teachings was the **importance of shifting from fear to love, from doubt to faith, and from stagnation to**

movement. He believed that fear and resistance were illusions, and true wisdom came from embracing change. Similarly, modern coaches must help their clients reframe their struggles, **turn fear into motivation,** and **develop a mindset that welcomes challenges as growth opportunities.**

Key Lesson for Coaches: Focus on mindset transformation. Help clients shift their beliefs so they see challenges as stepping stones to success.

3. Purpose-Driven Coaching Leads to Sustainable Change

Rumi did not just inspire people with poetic wisdom—he provided a roadmap for enlightenment and purposeful living. He emphasized aligning life with **a deeper purpose rather than chasing external validation.** Today, coaches must guide clients to define success on their own terms, setting goals that align with their values and vision rather than societal expectations.

Key Lesson for Coaches: Help clients define their purpose and set meaningful, aligned goals to ensure lasting motivation and fulfillment.

4. Action, Accountability, and Adaptability Drive Results

While Rumi's teachings were spiritual, they were also action-driven. He encouraged **movement, discipline, and accountability**—whether through the whirling dervish practice or deep contemplation followed by action. Modern coaches can apply this by holding clients accountable, ensuring they take **consistent steps toward their goals,** and helping them stay adaptable in the face of change.

Key Lesson for Coaches: Inspire action. Transformation does not happen through words alone—it requires commitment, adaptability, and perseverance.

5. Connection and Mentorship are Powerful Tools

Rumi's deep connection with his mentor, Shams of Tabriz, was a turning point in his transformation. This highlights the **importance of strong coaching relationships** built on trust, challenge, and encouragement. Modern coaches must cultivate meaningful connections with clients, creating a safe yet growth-oriented environment where clients feel supported yet challenged to push beyond their limits.

Key Lesson for Coaches: Coaching is not just about guidance—it is about building trust, deep connections, and empowering clients to grow through collaboration.

6. Transformation is an Ongoing Journey

Rumi emphasized that transformation is not a one-time event but a **continuous process of self-discovery, change, and mastery.** Coaches today must remind clients that setbacks are part of growth, and evolving into one's best self takes time, patience, and commitment. Encouraging a **long-term growth mindset** ensures that transformation lasts beyond the coaching engagement.

Key Lesson for Coaches: Teach clients that transformation is a lifelong journey. Foster resilience so they continue evolving beyond coaching sessions.

Rumi's Teachings as a Timeless Coaching Model:

Rumi's coaching philosophy, though spiritual in nature, is deeply practical and aligns with modern coaching methodologies. His approach to **self-awareness, mindset shifts, purpose-driven action, accountability, collaboration, and lifelong transformation** provides a blueprint for coaches looking to make a lasting impact. By integrating these principles, modern-day coaches can guide clients not just toward success, but toward **a life of purpose, mastery, and fulfillment.**

> **"Don't get lost in your pain, know that one day your pain will become your cure."**
>
> *– Rumi*

5 key learnings:

1. Self-Awareness is the Starting Point for Transformation

Key Message: Rumi taught that deep transformation begins with looking inward.

Modern coaches must guide clients to explore their inner fears, beliefs, and truths before setting goals.

Practical Takeaway: Encourage reflection, journaling, and mindfulness to uncover self-limiting beliefs.

2. Mindset Shifts Fuel Growth

Key Message: Rumi believed that fear is an illusion and true change happens by embracing uncertainty with love.

Coaches should help clients reframe resistance as opportunity and shift from limitation to possibility.

Practical Takeaway: Support mindset changes from fear → faith, doubt → trust, and stagnation → movement.

3. Purpose is the Anchor for Sustainable Change

Key Message: Rumi aligned action with higher purpose. He believed true fulfillment comes from following the heart, not societal standards.

Coaches can help clients define what truly matters to them.

Practical Takeaway: Clarify core values and align goals with personal purpose for lasting motivation.

4. Action, Accountability & Adaptability are Non-Negotiable

Key Message: Rumi's teachings were not just about wisdom—they were about living it.

He emphasized disciplined action (e.g., whirling dervishes) and personal responsibility.

Practical Takeaway: Set action plans, track progress, and coach adaptability during change.

5. Deep Connection is the Heart of Transformation

Key Message: Rumi's relationship with Shams was a coaching masterpiece—built on trust, challenge, and love.

Modern coaching thrives on meaningful, soul-level connections that spark growth.

Practical Takeaway: Build a safe space that balances compassion and challenge to unlock client potential.

Example: Transforming Fear into Purpose through Coaching Conversations

During a leadership coaching session with one of my clients — a senior product manager struggling with self-doubt about leading a new cross-functional initiative — I used the Rumi-inspired approach to guide her transformation.

Step 1: Inner Exploration Before Goal Setting

Instead of jumping straight into KPIs or strategies, I invited her to pause and reflect. Through journaling prompts like *"What are you afraid of?"* and mindfulness exercises, she unearthed a core belief: "I'm not strategic enough to lead innovation." This self-limiting thought had silently shaped her confidence for years.

Step 2: Mindset Shift from Fear to Faith

I shared Rumi's idea that *"The wound is the place where the Light enters you."* This opened a new perspective. We reframed her fear as an indicator of growth. Together, we shifted her thinking from *"What if I fail?"* to *"What if this challenge is the path to becoming a better leader?"*

Step 3: Purpose Anchoring

We worked to align her leadership goals with her personal values—creativity, autonomy, and team growth. Rather than chasing external validation, her focus became: *"How can I create a space where innovation thrives through people?"*

Step 4: Action, Accountability & Adaptability

We created a clear, agile plan with weekly check-ins. She practiced presenting her ideas, sought feedback, and adapted based on real-time outcomes—showing remarkable resilience through ambiguity.

Step 5: Deep Connection & Trust

Throughout this journey, the coaching space was sacred—open, honest, and filled with both challenge and compassion. Like Rumi and Shams, our conversations stirred something deeper than just professional development: a return to self-belief and authentic leadership.

Result:

She not only led the initiative successfully but also earned recognition for fostering a psychologically safe and innovative team culture.

This transformation was not just about skills. It was about **awakening inner wisdom**, trusting the journey, and leading from within—just as Rumi would teach.

Story-11:

Al-Farabi (c. 872-950 AD) – The Leadership and Wisdom Coach

> **"The virtuous city is the one whose purpose is to help its people achieve happiness."**
>
> *– Al-Farabi, The Virtuous City*

Al-Farabi, often referred to as the "Second Teacher" after Aristotle, was one of the greatest philosophers, scholars, and visionaries of the Islamic Golden Age.

He was not just a thinker but a guide, shaping the intellectual and leadership landscape of his time. His writings on ethics, governance, and personal mastery laid the foundation for coaching rulers, scholars, and leaders in wisdom, strategic thinking, and the pursuit of knowledge.

His Coaching Philosophy and Methods

Ethical Leadership & Virtuous Governance Al-Farabi believed that a great leader must be a philosopher-king—someone who leads not through power alone, but through wisdom and moral integrity. He coached rulers to develop ethical leadership by aligning personal virtue with governance, ensuring that decisions served the well-being of society rather than personal ambition.

Strategic Thinking & Decision-Making Much like modern executive coaching, Al-Farabi emphasized critical thinking and strategic decision-making. He guided scholars and statesmen to analyze complex problems through reason and logic, encouraging them to seek long-term solutions rather than short-term gains. His concept of a "perfect city" mirrored today's leadership models that promote vision-driven organizations with clear values and ethical frameworks.

The Pursuit of Knowledge & Self-Mastery for Al-Farabi, knowledge was not just about accumulating facts but about refining the soul and developing intellectual and emotional intelligence. He coached his students to cultivate lifelong learning, self-reflection, and the ability to question assumptions—a key component in modern coaching aimed at mindset transformation.

Impact and Lasting Legacy

Al-Farabi's coaching and intellectual contributions shaped Islamic philosophy, influencing later thinkers such as Avicenna and Maimonides. His leadership principles resonate even today, as modern coaches adopt his ideas on wisdom-driven leadership, ethical decision-making, and the integration of knowledge with personal growth.

His timeless teachings offer invaluable lessons for today's leaders, showing that true success is not just about power or achievement, but about developing wisdom, integrity, and a deep sense of responsibility for the greater good.

Al-Farabi's Contributions to Mankind: The Legacy of a Mastermind

Al-Farabi (c. 872–950 AD) was more than just a philosopher—he was a visionary whose contributions shaped human civilization across multiple disciplines, influencing leadership, ethics, governance, psychology, and the sciences. His intellectual legacy helped bridge Eastern and Western thought, laying the foundation for both Islamic and European Renaissance philosophies.

1. Pioneer of Political Philosophy & Leadership

Al-Farabi's vision of leadership was revolutionary. In his famous work *The Virtuous City (Al-Madina al-Fadila)*, he outlined what makes an ideal leader—one who rules not by power but by wisdom, ethics, and virtue. He compared this to Plato's *Republic*, advocating that a just society thrives when governed by philosopher-kings who prioritize the well-being of their people. His theories directly influenced governance models and ethical leadership principles that are relevant even today.

2. A Bridge Between Ancient Greek and Islamic Thought

Al-Farabi was instrumental in preserving and expanding upon the works of Aristotle and Plato. He did not merely translate their texts—he refined and built upon their philosophies, making them more accessible to the Islamic world and beyond. His commentaries were later studied by European scholars, playing a key role in the rediscovery of classical knowledge during the Renaissance.

3. Development of Logical and Scientific Thought

Often called "The Second Teacher" (after Aristotle), Al-Farabi was a pioneer in logic, laying the groundwork for rational thinking in science and philosophy. He classified knowledge into different disciplines, influencing later thinkers such as Avicenna (Ibn Sina) and Thomas Aquinas. His contributions helped shape the scientific method, emphasizing empirical observation and logical reasoning.

4. Contributions to Psychology and Emotional Intelligence

Long before the modern era, Al-Farabi explored human emotions, cognition, and intelligence. He believed that intellectual and emotional mastery were essential for both personal and societal transformation. His teachings align with today's coaching principles, where self-awareness, mindset shifts, and emotional intelligence are key drivers of success.

5. Advancements in Music and Its Psychological Effects

Al-Farabi was not just a philosopher—he was also a musician and scientist. His book *The Great Book of Music (Kitab al-Musiqa al-Kabir)* explored how music influences human emotions and cognitive states. He studied the mathematical principles behind sound and the healing properties of music, insights that are now used in modern music therapy.

6. A Universal Approach to Knowledge and Wisdom

Unlike many scholars of his time, Al-Farabi believed in an interdisciplinary approach. He saw philosophy, science, ethics, and leadership as interconnected. His holistic vision encouraged scholars to seek knowledge across multiple fields, shaping the Renaissance ideal of a well-rounded, intellectually curious individual.

Al-Farabi's Lasting Impact on Humanity

Al-Farabi's teachings continue to influence modern thought in leadership, education, governance, psychology, and philosophy. His emphasis on wisdom-driven leadership, ethical governance, and intellectual growth offers timeless lessons that are still applicable today. His work reminds us that true progress comes not just from acquiring knowledge, but from applying it with wisdom, ethics, and a commitment to human flourishing.

Al-Farabi's Coaching Approach Through the Lens of the IMPACT Framework

His approach to leadership and personal transformation aligns remarkably well with modern coaching frameworks, particularly the **IMPACT Coaching Framework,** which focuses **on self-awareness, mindset shifts, purpose-driven goals, execution, collaboration, and long-term transformation.**

Let us explore **how Al-Farabi's coaching approach aligns with the IMPACT model, supported by examples and their potential coaching outcomes.**

1. I - Inspire Awareness & Identity → Self-Reflection & Wisdom

Al-Farabi's philosophy places self-awareness at the core of wisdom and effective leadership. He believed that true mastery in any field begins with an individual's deep understanding of their identity, strengths, and moral values. Without this foundational self-knowledge, a leader may struggle to make sound decisions, inspire others, or navigate challenges with clarity and purpose.

In a coaching context, this principle can be applied to business executives who find themselves struggling with decision-making under pressure. When stress mounts, they may react impulsively or second-guess their choices, leading to inconsistent leadership. Through structured self-reflection exercises such as journaling, self-assessments, and guided introspection, a coach can help them uncover their natural leadership style, identify emotional triggers, and align their decision-making with their core values.

As the executive develops greater self-awareness, they cultivate emotional intelligence, allowing them to regulate their responses and make thoughtful, value-driven decisions. Their newfound clarity brings consistency to their leadership, which in turn fosters trust and engagement within their team. Employees respond positively to leaders who demonstrate authenticity and stability, creating a work environment where motivation, collaboration, and confidence thrive. Ultimately, by mastering self-awareness, the executive not only enhances their own leadership effectiveness but also contributes to a culture of integrity and resilience within their organization.

2. M - Mindset & Mastery Shift → Intellectual & Emotional Mastery

Al-Farabi's philosophy underscores the importance of mastering logic, emotions, and reasoning as the foundation for personal and intellectual growth. He believed that fear, uncertainty, and impulsive reactions could be controlled through disciplined thinking, continuous learning, and self-awareness. By applying these principles, individuals can cultivate a growth mindset—one that embraces challenges as opportunities rather than obstacles.

In a coaching scenario, this approach is particularly valuable for leaders and entrepreneurs facing self-doubt. Consider a startup founder who is paralyzed by the fear of failure, convinced that they are not capable of building a successful company. Their mindset, shaped by past experiences and limiting beliefs, holds them back from taking bold steps forward. Through coaching that integrates Cognitive Behavioral Therapy (CBT) and Neuro-Linguistic Programming (NLP), they begin to reframe their perspective. Instead of seeing failure as a definitive end, they learn to view it as an essential part of growth and innovation.

By challenging negative thought patterns and replacing them with constructive beliefs, the entrepreneur gradually shifts from a fear-driven mindset to one centered on opportunities and resilience. This transformation is not just internal; it also impacts how they lead their team. They begin to take calculated risks, encourage innovation, and create an environment where setbacks are seen as learning experiences rather than failures. As a result, their startup thrives, fuelled by a culture of adaptability, continuous improvement, and confidence in overcoming challenges.

3. P - Purpose-Driven Goals & Strategy → Leadership for a Virtuous Society

Al-Farabi, in *The Virtuous City*, emphasized that true leadership must be rooted in a purpose that transcends personal ambition. He argued that great leaders do not merely seek power or success for themselves but rather dedicate their efforts to long-term goals that align with ethical principles and the greater good of society. Leadership, in his philosophy, is a moral responsibility—one that requires vision, integrity, and a commitment to creating lasting impact.

This concept is highly relevant in leadership coaching, especially for corporate leaders who may feel disconnected from their work or uninspired by the daily demands of their role. A leader in such a situation might struggle with motivation, feeling as though their efforts lack deeper meaning. Through coaching, they embark on a journey of self-discovery, reflecting on their core values and aspirations. Rather than focusing solely on performance metrics or financial targets, they begin to explore how they can drive meaningful change within their organization.

For some, this might mean fostering a culture of innovation where employees feel encouraged to experiment, take risks, and push boundaries. For others, it could involve championing sustainability initiatives that contribute to long-term environmental and social impact. By aligning their leadership with a higher purpose, they reignite their sense of motivation and begin making decisions driven by values rather than short-term gains.

As this transformation unfolds, the effects extend beyond the leader. Employees notice the shift in leadership style and become more engaged, inspired by a leader who has a clear vision and a sense of mission. The organization, in turn, benefits from a renewed sense of direction, where long-term sustainability and ethical considerations become the foundation for success. Through this values-driven leadership, the leader not only achieves personal fulfilment but also leaves a legacy that continues to shape the organization long into the future.

4. A - Action, Accountability & Adaptability → Practical Wisdom & Execution

Al-Farabi emphasized that true leadership extends beyond philosophical understanding and self-awareness; it demands the practical application of wisdom. He believed that leaders must not only comprehend ethical principles but also integrate them into their governance, decision-making, and problem-solving processes. For him, knowledge without execution was incomplete—wisdom had to be lived and practiced, not just contemplated.

This philosophy is highly relevant in leadership coaching, where many individuals struggle to turn their insights into tangible results. Consider a team manager who continuously delays implementing a new business strategy due to fear of failure. Despite possessing the necessary knowledge and skills, their hesitation prevents them from taking decisive action. Through coaching, they learn to break this cycle by setting clear and structured SMART goals—objectives that are specific, measurable, achievable, relevant, and time-bound. Additionally, they commit to weekly accountability check-ins, ensuring steady progress and reinforcing their commitment. By embracing an agile mindset, they become more comfortable with change, viewing adaptation as a strength rather than a risk.

As a result, the manager begins to move beyond procrastination, making deliberate and confident choices that drive progress. Their newfound decisiveness has a ripple effect on their team, inspiring a culture of proactivity and adaptability. With a leader who is willing to take action, the team responds in kind, fostering innovation and efficiency within the organization. Over time, the shift from hesitation to execution transforms not just the manager's leadership approach, but the overall effectiveness and resilience of the company itself.

5. C - Connection & Collaborative Growth → The Power of Mentorship & Learning Communities

Al-Farabi believed that learning and growth should never occur in isolation. For him, knowledge flourished best in an environment of mentorship, intellectual collaboration, and shared wisdom. He championed the idea that sustainable progress comes from collective learning, where individuals support and challenge each other to expand their understanding. His philosophy emphasized that great leaders do not merely accumulate knowledge for themselves but actively create communities that exchange ideas, refine perspectives, and push innovation forward.

In leadership coaching, this approach plays a crucial role in developing strong, connected teams. Imagine a new leader who struggles to build meaningful relationships with their team. Despite their expertise, they find it difficult to engage employees, creating a gap in trust and collaboration. Through coaching, they come to understand the power of mentorship and peer learning. They begin fostering a culture where employees learn from one another, implementing structured peer-learning groups that encourage open discussion and knowledge-sharing. They also practice active listening and refine their feedback techniques, ensuring that communication becomes a two-way process rather than a top-down directive.

As a result, the leader not only strengthens their own leadership skills but also builds a robust support system within the organization. Employees feel valued and empowered, knowing their contributions matter. This shift leads to higher engagement, better retention, and a workplace where individuals continuously grow together. Over time, the organization transforms into a thriving ecosystem of innovation and improvement, where learning becomes a shared journey rather than an isolated pursuit.

6. T - Transform & Thrive → Lifelong Learning & Lasting Impact

Al-Farabi emphasized that learning and transformation are lifelong pursuits. He believed that wisdom is not defined by reaching a final destination but by the continuous evolution of thought, action, and impact. True knowledge, in his view, is dynamic—always growing, refining, and expanding its influence beyond the individual. He advocated for a philosophy where leaders do not merely accumulate success for themselves but use their experience and insights to shape the world around them, ensuring that their contributions extend far beyond their own lifetime.

In leadership coaching, this principle is particularly relevant for high-performing executives who have already achieved significant career success but now seek something more meaningful. Consider an executive who has climbed the corporate ladder, built a strong reputation, and mastered their field. Despite their accomplishments, they feel a sense of incompleteness, wondering how they can leave a lasting impact. Through coaching, they are encouraged to think beyond personal success and shift their focus toward legacy-building.

They may begin by mentoring emerging leaders, passing down their knowledge and experience to shape the next generation. Some may choose to write a book, distilling their insights into a resource that continues to inspire long after they have moved on. Others might launch initiatives, such as leadership development programs or social impact projects, that transform industries or communities.

As they embark on this journey, their mindset shifts from individual achievement to collective progress. They find fulfilment not just in personal victories but in knowing that their transformation has contributed to the growth of others. Their legacy becomes one of empowerment, ensuring that wisdom, leadership, and innovation continue to thrive long after their direct influence has faded.

Final Thoughts: Why Al-Farabi's Coaching Model Still Matters Today

Al-Farabi's teachings on **self-awareness, mindset shifts, leadership with purpose, execution, collaboration, and continuous growth** make his approach a **timeless coaching model.** His philosophy aligns seamlessly with the **IMPACT Coaching Framework**, proving that wisdom from centuries ago is still highly relevant in modern coaching.

By integrating Al-Farabi's timeless principles with the IMPACT framework, coaches can go beyond conventional leadership strategies. They can develop transformational leaders who prioritize long-term vision over fleeting wins. They can help individuals master their emotions, fostering resilience and mental clarity in the face of challenges.

Leadership is not just about individual achievement—it is about guiding organizations toward ethical, purpose-driven decision-making. It is about creating mentorship-driven cultures, where knowledge is shared, and learning never stops.

Most importantly, it is about leaving a lasting impact. True leaders do not just chase success; they create legacies that inspire future generations.

The question is—how will you use your leadership to shape the future?

Coaching takeaways: True transformation happens when wisdom meets action. Like Al-Farabi, great coaches do not just provide knowledge—they **empower individuals to think deeply, act wisely, and lead with purpose.**

Key Practical Steps Individuals Can Take to Create Impact at Work

Individuals can apply practical steps to **elevate their contribution, influence, and impact in the workplace.** Below are actionable steps that align with **the IMPACT Framework** to create a meaningful difference at work.

1. Inspire Awareness & Identity → Develop Self-Awareness

Imagine standing in front of a mirror—not just any mirror, but one that reflects not only your appearance but also your strengths, fears, and the impact you have on others. This is the kind of deep self-reflection that great leaders embrace.

To truly grow, you must take a step back and understand who you are as a leader. Start by keeping a journal, gathering honest feedback from others, or using self-assessment tools. These will help you see patterns in your behavior—what you do well and where you struggle.

Ask yourself:

- What are my greatest strengths, and how do they help my team?

- What fears or habits are holding me back from my full potential?

- How do others see me as a leader? Do they find me inspiring, supportive, or distant?

But knowing yourself is only the beginning. The next step is alignment—making sure that your daily actions reflect your core values and larger purpose. If you believe in fairness, do your decisions reflect it? If you value creativity, do you encourage it in your team? When actions and values align, leadership becomes more natural, confident, and powerful.

What Happens When You Do This?

- You gain a clearer sense of who you are and where you are headed.

- You build confidence because you understand your strengths and use them wisely.

- You make better decisions, knowing they align with your values and long-term goals.

The question is—are you shaping your leadership journey with intention, or are you letting circumstances define it for you?

2. Mindset & Mastery Shift → Reframe Challenges as Growth Opportunities

Picture yourself standing before an audience, heart pounding, convinced that you are not a great public speaker. But what if that belief isn't the truth—just a mental roadblock you have built over time? Limiting beliefs are like invisible chains, holding you back from your full potential. The good news? You can break free.

The first step is to challenge these beliefs. Instead of saying, *"I'm not good at public speaking,"* shift your mindset to *"I can improve with practice."* This small change in perspective opens the door to growth.

Next, embrace learning and feedback. The best leaders are not those who never fail—they are the ones who learn from every setback. When faced with a challenge, ask yourself:

- *What can I learn from this situation?*

- *How can I turn this obstacle into an opportunity?*

Building emotional resilience is just as important. Practices like meditation, mindfulness, or gratitude help you stay calm under pressure and navigate challenges with a clear mind.

What Happens When You Shift Your Mindset?

- You become more resilient and adaptable in tough situations.

- You develop stronger problem-solving skills, turning setbacks into stepping stones.

- You gain confidence in handling workplace challenges, no longer held back by fear.

The truth is, growth is not about avoiding failure—it is about learning how to rise every time you fall. Are you ready to see challenges as opportunities instead of obstacles?

3. Purpose-Driven Goals & Strategy → Align Daily Work with Long-Term Vision

Imagine waking up every morning with a clear sense of purpose, knowing exactly what steps to take toward your goals. No more feeling stuck or overwhelmed—just focused, intentional progress. This level of clarity does not happen by chance. It is built through smart goal-setting and strategic planning.

The first step is to set SMART goals—specific, measurable, achievable, relevant, and time-bound. Instead of saying, *"I want to be a better leader,"* define it: *"I will complete a leadership course and mentor two team members within the next six months."*

Next, prioritize high-impact tasks using the Eisenhower Matrix—a simple tool that helps you separate urgent tasks from important ones. By focusing on what truly matters, you avoid distractions and make steady progress.

To keep your vision alive, create a vision board or success roadmap—a visual reminder of where you are headed. Whether it is a leadership position, a new business venture, or a personal milestone, seeing your goals daily keeps motivation high.

Finally, track your progress and adjust when needed. Success is not about rigid plans—it is about adapting and improving along the way.

What Happens When You Do This?

- You gain a clear direction in your career and personal growth.

- You feel more motivated and productive, knowing your actions have purpose.

- You master time management, focusing on what truly moves the needle.

The future is not something you wait for—it is something you create. Are you ready to take control of your success?

4. Action, Accountability & Adaptability → Execute & Stay Consistent

Think of a mountain climber standing at the base of a towering peak. The journey ahead looks overwhelming, but instead of freezing in fear, they take one step forward—then another. Success is not about waiting for the perfect moment; it is about taking consistent, intentional action every day.

The first step is to ditch the perfection trap. Many people delay action, waiting for ideal conditions. But progress comes from small, steady steps toward big goals. Instead of saying, *"I'll start when I'm ready,"* shift to *"What's one thing I can do today to move forward?"*

To stay on track, build accountability systems—whether through peer check-ins, mentors, or digital trackers. Knowing that someone (or something) is monitoring your progress boosts commitment and keeps momentum alive.

Adaptability is also key. Change is inevitable, and the most successful people anticipate challenges rather than fear them. When obstacles arise, ask:

- *What is stopping me from taking action right now?*

- *How can I turn this challenge into an opportunity?*

What Happens When You Take Action?

- You become more productive and efficient, no longer stuck in hesitation.

- You gain credibility as a leader, showing reliability and initiative.

- You develop greater agility, easily adapting to workplace changes.

Momentum is built through action, not waiting. What is the first step you will take today?

5. **Connection & Collaborative Growth → Build Influence & Team Impact**

Picture a workplace where ideas flow freely, where teammates trust each other, and where leaders uplift instead of command. Success is not just about individual talent—it is about building strong relationships that drive collaboration and growth.

The first step is active listening and empathy. Instead of waiting for your turn to speak, truly hear what others are saying. Watch body language, ask thoughtful questions, and acknowledge emotions. A simple *"I understand how you feel"* can turn a conversation into a connection.

Next, seek mentorship. The best leaders are also learners. Whether through formal mentorship or informal conversations, surrounding yourself with experienced voices helps you avoid mistakes and accelerate growth.

But leadership is not just about learning—it is about teaching. Share your knowledge, support your team's success, and empower others to step into their full potential. A culture of trust and collaboration starts with leaders who invest in their people.

What Happens When You Prioritize Relationships?

- You build a strong professional network, increasing influence and career opportunities.

- Your team becomes more engaged, trusting, and effective in their work.

- You sharpen your leadership and communication skills, making a lasting impact.

Leadership is not about standing alone—it is about lifting others up. Who will you invest in today?

6. Transform & Thrive → Create Sustainable Impact

Imagine walking into a library filled with the wisdom of the greatest minds in history. Every book holds a lesson, every conversation a new perspective. Growth is not something that happens by chance—it is a habit, a mindset, a daily commitment to learning.

Start by feeding your mind. Read books that challenge your thinking, listen to podcasts that expand your knowledge, and engage in training programs that sharpen your skills. The most successful leaders never stop learning.

But knowledge alone is not enough. Reflection is key. Ask yourself:

- *What is working well in my career?*

- *What skills should I develop to stay ahead?*

- *How can I leave a lasting impact at work?*

Growth is not just about climbing the career ladder—it is about aligning your work with a bigger purpose. Whether through leadership, mentorship, or innovation, true fulfilment comes from creating something that outlasts you.

What Happens When You Commit to Growth?

- You unlock long-term career success and leadership opportunities.

- You make a meaningful impact on your organization and colleagues.

- You build a life of continuous self-improvement and purpose.

Success is not a destination; it is a journey of learning and evolving. What is the next step in your growth?

By applying these **practical self-coaching steps,** individuals can transform their **mindset, performance, and leadership presence,** leading to **greater impact, recognition, and career growth** at work

> **"Excellence of the soul comes from the perfection of reason and character."**
>
> *– Al-Farabi*

Key take aways:

1. *Wisdom is Timeless — Coaching Rooted in Self-Awareness Creates Legacy*

Al-Farabi's ancient insights into self-awareness remain the bedrock of transformational leadership. Just as he urged deep reflection, modern leaders must know who they are to align actions with purpose.

Takeaway: Leadership starts with knowing yourself—true impact begins when identity and intention are aligned.

2. Mindset Shapes Reality — Reframe Challenges to Unlock Growth

Al-Farabi believed in developing the inner world to transform the outer. In today's context, this translates to shifting limiting beliefs into learning mindsets.

Takeaway: Obstacles are not barriers—they are invitations to grow. Leaders rise when they change how they see setbacks.

3. Purpose Drives Performance — Align Daily Work to a Bigger Vision

Al-Farabi emphasized purposeful leadership for societal harmony. Today's leaders must go beyond tasks to design lives and teams around long-term vision and meaning.

Takeaway: Do not just work harder—work with clarity. When your strategy is rooted in purpose, your impact multiplies.

4. Action with Accountability Builds Trust and Agility

Wisdom, to Al-Farabi, was only powerful when acted upon. The same holds today—small, consistent action backed by accountability is what creates real progress.

Takeaway: Execution beats perfection. Take one meaningful step daily and hold yourself to a higher standard.

5. Collective Growth is True Leadership — Lift Others as You Climb

Al-Farabi valued ethical, collaborative communities. Leaders today must model mentorship, empathy, and shared success.

Takeaway: Great leadership is never solo. Your influence grows exponentially when you empower others to thrive.

Final Reflection:

"True transformation happens when wisdom meets action."

Like Al-Farabi, let your leadership be a blend of deep thought and courageous execution. Do not just lead for today—build a legacy that inspires generations.

Legacy in Motion: Coaching a Senior Leader Through Al-Farabi's Lens

When Rajeev, a senior executive overseeing a complex digital transformation, first came to me, he was not lacking in vision or intelligence. What he was lacking—though he did not know it at the time—was alignment. His strategies were sound, but his energy was scattered. There were silos within teams, mounting resistance from peers, and a quiet erosion of his confidence.

We did not begin with quick wins.

We began with stillness.

I invited him to pause the noise, just long enough to hear himself think. "What's really going on inside you?" I asked. It was then he confessed something powerful:

"I feel like I'm leading out of fear... trying to control outcomes, not inspire people."

That moment cracked something open.

Self-Awareness as the Starting Line

Inspired by **Al-Farabi**, whose teachings placed self-awareness at the core of wise leadership, we explored Rajeev's inner landscape—his values, fears, blind spots, and hopes. He began to realize he was operating from an outdated internal script. Leadership, for him, had become a performance, not a purpose.

We began a ritual: weekly reflection sessions—no strategy talk, just space to listen to himself. Over time, he grew less reactive and more anchored. He was no longer leading from fear. He was leading from intent.

Seeing Resistance Differently

As Rajeev began to stabilize inwardly, his outer world started making more sense. Where he once saw resistance, he now saw uncertainty. Where he assumed defiance, he recognized fear.

"They're not pushing back against me," he reflected, *"they're protecting what they understand."*

This reframing, rooted in Al-Farabi's belief that *inner transformation precedes outer harmony*, allowed him to shift his tone—from defensive to curious. He began hosting dialogues, not briefings. Conversations replaced commands.

Purpose Over Pressure

With clarity returning, we turned to strategy—but through a very different lens. Instead of asking, *"How do I hit the next milestone?"* Rajeev asked, *"What legacy do I want to leave through this transformation?"*

He crafted a vision not of systems or structures—but of **culture**.

"I want this to be a place where innovation feels safe and shared ownership is real."

This was no longer a project. It became a movement.

He invited his teams to create their own purpose statements, mapping their daily work to a shared vision. Ownership, once missing, began to emerge organically.

From Intention to Action

But as Al-Farabi taught—*wisdom without action is like a flame never lit.* We built accountability into Rajeev's leadership rhythm. Weekly syncs that connected vision to delivery. Learning logs to capture reflection. Peer reviews to keep momentum honest.

He stopped chasing perfection. He started building trust.

Progress was not linear—but it was real. Teams felt the difference. And so did he.

Empowering Others to Rise

The final shift was the most profound. Rajeev let go of the belief that he had to carry everything. He stepped back just enough to let someone else step forward—a rising leader who had once doubted his voice, now empowered to co-lead.

That act of trust changed everything. Culture shifted. Ownership spread. A legacy was seeded.

"Leadership isn't about control anymore," Rajeev said in our last session.

"It's about creating the space where others can find their own strength."

A Closing Reflection

Al-Farabi believed the greatest leaders build harmony by aligning the soul with higher purpose. Coaching Rajeev reminded me that transformation is never just about KPIs, roadmaps, or tools. It is about courage—the courage to face yourself, rewrite your story, and lead from that renewed truth.

Rajeev did not just lead change.

He *became* the change.

And that is the real legacy.

Story-12:

The Emperor Who Coached Himself: Marcus Aurelius and the Art of Leadership

> **"You have power over your mind — not outside events. Realize this, and you will find strength."**
>
> **- Marcus Aurelius**

The night was cold. The torches flickered against the stone walls of his chamber as Marcus Aurelius dipped his quill into the ink. The weight of the empire pressed on his shoulders—another war, another betrayal, another outbreak of the plague. He could have cursed fate, collapsed under the burden. Instead, he wrote.

"If you are troubled by external things, it is not they that disturb you, but your judgment of them. And it is in your power to wipe out that judgment now."

He was not just an emperor—he was his own coach. In the silence of the night, with no one to guide him but his thoughts, he held himself accountable. He questioned his own fears, dissected his weaknesses, and coached himself into resilience.

The Coach of a Collapsing Empire

The world around him was unravelling. Barbarians threatened Rome's borders. A plague ravaged the cities, claiming thousands of lives each day. Inside the palace, whispers of betrayal slithered through the halls.

A lesser ruler would have panicked, lashed out, or retreated into indulgence. But Marcus Aurelius believed in something greater than himself. He saw his life not as a privilege, but as a duty—to serve, to guide, to leave the world better than he found it.

He could not afford the luxury of despair. **Instead, he transformed his struggles into his greatest coaching lessons.**

Integrity & Authenticity – The Emperor Who Refused to Be a God

Most emperors declared themselves divine, wrapping themselves in gold, demanding worship. Marcus Aurelius did the opposite.

His robes were simple. His meals were modest. He walked among his soldiers, sharing their burdens instead of commanding from a throne.

One night, a trusted advisor suggested he declare himself a god, as other rulers had done. **"The people will revere you more,"** the man urged.

Marcus looked at him, calm but unwavering. **"If I must lie to be respected, then I am not worthy of respect."**

His truthfulness, his refusal to deceive, made him a leader people could trust—not out of fear, but out of admiration.

Coaching Lesson: True leaders do not demand trust. They earn it by being authentic, by standing firm in their values even when deceit seems easier.

Mastery & Continuous Growth – The Journals of a Reluctant Emperor

Marcus never wanted to be emperor. He was a philosopher at heart, drawn to wisdom, not war. But fate chose him, and he refused to shrink from responsibility.

Every night, after the empire's affairs had been settled, he wrote.

He questioned himself: *Did I act justly today? Did I allow anger to cloud my judgment?*

He wrote not to impress, but to improve. Not to instruct others, but to refine himself.

Even at the height of power, he remained a student. He read. He studied. He sought out teachers—**because he knew that the moment a leader stops learning, they begin to decline.**

Coaching Lesson: The best leaders are perpetual students. Growth is not a destination—it is a daily practice.

Purpose & Impact-Driven Leadership – A Plague, a Choice, and an Emperor Who Stayed

When the Antonine Plague struck Rome, panic spread faster than the disease. **The rich fled to the countryside. The Senate locked themselves away.**

Advisors begged Marcus to leave.

"Your life is too important," they pleaded.

But Marcus Aurelius stayed.

He walked through the streets, overseeing aid efforts. He funded hospitals, redistributed resources, and ensured that Rome's poorest were not abandoned.

At night, he sat with the sick, offering comfort where medicine failed. He did not see himself as above the suffering—**he saw himself as responsible for it.**

Coaching Lesson: Leadership is not about self-preservation. It is about standing firm when others flee. True leaders put their mission above their comfort.

Accountability & Ownership – No Excuses, Only Action

One evening, a senator arrived at the palace, fuming.

"The war is not my fault," he argued. **"It was the general's mistake."**

Marcus listened; his face unreadable. Then, he said softly, **"The empire does not have the luxury of blaming others. Fix it."**

No excuses. No shifting of responsibility.

Marcus knew that great leaders take ownership—not just of their successes, but of their failures. If his empire suffered, he suffered. If mistakes were made, he corrected them.

Coaching Lesson: Leaders do not point fingers. They take responsibility and solve problems instead of complaining about them.

Collaboration & Connection – The Emperor Who Listened

Unlike other rulers, Marcus did not surround himself with yes-men. He sought out diverse perspectives, even from those who disagreed with him.

His court was filled with scholars, generals, merchants—people who saw the world differently. He understood that **wisdom was not found in one voice, but in many.**

One day, a commander questioned his strategy in battle. The court fell silent, expecting Marcus to rebuke him. Instead, Marcus asked, **"What would you do differently?"**

The commander laid out his plan.

Marcus listened. He thought. And then, to everyone's shock, he changed his mind.

Coaching Lesson: The strongest leaders are not those who dominate conversations, but those who listen, learn, and adapt.

Transformation & Adaptability – The Obstacle Is the Way

One of Marcus' most famous lines would later inspire generations:

"The impediment to action advances action. What stands in the way becomes the way."

He lived by this.

War? A chance to practice patience.

Plague? A chance to serve his people.

Betrayal? A chance to test his wisdom.

Nothing broke him—because he **saw every hardship as fuel for growth**.

Coaching Lesson: Struggles are not roadblocks. They are stepping stones. The obstacle in front of you is not stopping you—it is shaping you.

Final Lesson – The Emperor's Last Words

On his deathbed, Marcus Aurelius did not weep. He did not fear. He called his son, his advisors, his generals.

"Do not mourn me," he told them. **"Live by virtue. Do what is right. Lead wisely."**

Even in death, he was coaching.

Even in his final moments, he was teaching.

Coaching Lesson: A leader's true impact is not measured by titles or statues—but by the principles they leave behind.

Marcus Aurelius & The IMPACT Framework – A Timeless Coaching Blueprint

- **Integrity & Authenticity** → He led with truth, refusing to deceive for power.

- **Mastery & Continuous Growth** → He coached himself daily, always striving to improve.

- **Purpose & Impact-Driven Leadership** → He saw leadership as a duty, not a privilege.

- **Accountability & Ownership** → He took responsibility for everything under his rule.

- **Collaboration & Connection** → He valued diverse perspectives and sought wisdom from all.

- **Transformation & Adaptability** → He embraced hardship as a tool for growth.

Marcus Aurelius did not just lead an empire—**he coached a civilization.** His wisdom remains, not in the ruins of Rome, but in the hearts of those who seek to lead with courage, wisdom, and purpose.

Coaching Lessons from Marcus Aurelius: A Masterclass in Leadership & Resilience

Marcus Aurelius was not just a ruler—he was a **coach in the purest sense**. He guided an empire not through force, but through wisdom, self-discipline, and an unwavering commitment to self-improvement. His life offers a **masterclass for modern coaches**, revealing powerful lessons on how to **develop others, overcome obstacles, and create lasting transformation**.

Below are key coaching takeaways from his story, mapped to the **IMPACT Framework**, showing how coaches can **apply his wisdom to guide individuals and teams toward success.**

I – Integrity & Authenticity: Coaching Begins with Truth

While other emperors shrouded themselves in myths of divinity, Marcus Aurelius chose to stand firmly in the realm of reality. He never allowed himself to be elevated beyond the status of a man. His leadership was not built on illusion or grandeur; it was rooted in the truth of his actions. There were no golden statues in his honour, no demands for blind obedience. His leadership spoke through integrity and example, not through pomp or pretense. Marcus knew that true respect is not something one can command—it must be earned, and it is earned through authentic actions that reflect unwavering values.

This same principle lies at the heart of great coaching. Authenticity is the cornerstone of trust. A coach who speaks only words without living them cannot inspire true transformation. To bring about lasting change, a coach must embody the principles they teach, leading by example. Similarly, clients must confront their own truths, unshielded by the comforts of illusion. It is not about striving for perfection; it is about embracing honest self-awareness. Growth starts when we face ourselves, both our strengths and weaknesses, with an open mind and heart.

Ask yourself: *What truths about yourself are you avoiding? What might change if you confronted them?* It is only when we acknowledge our reality, without distortion, that we can begin to transform.

To build authenticity and trust with clients, create a safe space where they can explore their fears and insecurities without fear of judgment. Challenge them to align their actions with their core values, just as Marcus refused to rule through deception. Growth is not found in hiding flaws or pretending to be perfect—it is found in accepting those flaws, using them as stepping stones toward becoming a better, more genuine version of ourselves.

M – Mastery & Continuous Growth: Coaching is a journey, not a Destination

Even in the height of his power as the ruler of Rome, Marcus Aurelius remained deeply committed to the idea of learning and self-improvement. Despite the constant demands of leadership, he understood that true mastery did not come from titles or accolades—it came from continuous self-reflection and growth. Long after the Senate had adjourned and the streets of Rome had fallen into silence, Marcus would sit alone with his journal. There, in the stillness of the night, he would reflect on his actions, his thoughts, and even his failures. He held himself accountable—not to others, but to his own deeply held principles. It was in these quiet moments that he shaped his character and deepened his wisdom. For Marcus, mastery was not a destination, but a lifelong practice.

This same mindset is essential for any great coach. Coaching is not about having all the answers or offering quick fixes. It is about the willingness to evolve, to learn, and to grow alongside your clients. Just as Marcus used his journal as a tool for self-discovery and refinement, a coach must guide their clients to develop habits that foster transformation.

To cultivate continuous growth, encourage your clients to create a space for daily reflection. A coaching journal, much like Marcus's, becomes a record of insights, challenges, and lessons learned. These small moments of introspection lead to profound change over time. It is not about the grand gestures or dramatic shifts—it is about embracing micro-improvements. Those little actions, taken daily, compound over time and build mastery.

The path to success is rarely marked by a single defining moment. It is instead shaped by quiet, consistent commitments to getting better. So, ask yourself and your clients: *What daily habit will make you 1% better tomorrow?*

P – Purpose & Impact-Driven Leadership: Coaching for Meaningful Change

When a deadly plague descended upon Rome, panic spread faster than the disease itself. People fled the city in droves, desperate to escape the terror that gripped the streets. But Marcus Aurelius, the Emperor, chose a different path. In the face of immense fear and chaos, he did not retreat to the safety of his palace. Instead, he remained in the heart of the crisis, standing by his people. He walked among the sick and suffering, ensuring that aid was given, decisions were made, and that

Rome did not descend into chaos and despair. He did not act out of a desire for power or control; his actions were rooted in an unwavering sense of purpose. Marcus understood that true leadership was not about personal safety or prestige; it was about being of service, especially in the most difficult moments.

A great coach embodies this same principle of service and purpose. True coaching is not about individual accolades or achievements; it is about aligning one's ambitions with a deeper mission that transcends the self. A coach should encourage individuals to consider the broader impact of their actions, pushing them to think beyond personal gain and towards how their growth and success can serve others.

Ask yourself: *What legacy do you want to create? How does your work contribute to something bigger than yourself?* True fulfilment does not come from achieving personal success alone—it comes from making a difference that extends beyond you.

To coach with impact, it is essential to help clients define their "why" before setting any goals. Encouraging them to shift their mindset from personal ambition to collective growth will help them see the far-reaching effects of their leadership. Success is not just about climbing higher; it is about lifting others as you rise. Great leaders do not just ascend—they bring others with them, ensuring that their journey has a lasting and positive impact on the world around them.

A – Accountability & Ownership: No Victim Mindset in Coaching

Marcus believed that responsibility was non-negotiable. When a senator tried to shift blame for a military failure, he refused to entertain excuses. His response was sharp and direct: **"The empire does not have the luxury of blaming others. Fix it."** He understood that progress comes from taking ownership, not from deflecting responsibility.

This principle is just as crucial in coaching. Growth happens when clients take full responsibility for their actions, mistakes, and progress. A coach's role is to hold them accountable, ensuring they do not fall into the trap of excuses. Instead of allowing self-pity, a coach should ask,

"What part of this situation do you control? What will you do differently next time?" These questions shift the focus from problems to solutions, fostering real transformation.

To make this shift actionable, coaches should implement **accountability check-ins**, where clients commit to specific actions and report back on their execution. When setbacks occur, they should be reframed—not as failures, but as **valuable data for improvement**. This approach ensures continuous learning and lasting growth.

C – Collaboration & Connection: Coaching is a Two-Way Dialogue

Marcus Aurelius understood that true wisdom did not come from surrounding himself with people who merely agreed with him. Unlike other emperors who silenced opposition, he actively sought out dissenting opinions, knowing that diverse perspectives led to better decisions. He believed that real strength came from listening, not just leading.

This mindset is essential in coaching. Great coaching is not about handing out advice—it is about listening deeply and guiding clients toward their own insights. The best solutions do not come from the coach; they come from the client's own understanding and problem-solving. A coach should challenge them with questions like, "What perspective are you missing? Who else can offer insight?" This pushes them to think beyond their usual patterns and seek broader wisdom.

To apply this in practice, coaches should encourage clients to seek mentorship, feedback, and collaboration rather than isolating themselves. Instead of giving direct answers, coaches should use powerful questions to guide clients toward their own breakthroughs—helping them think, grow, and take ownership of their solutions.

T – Transformation & Adaptability: Coaching Resilience Through Challenges

Marcus Aurelius saw obstacles not as barriers but as stepping stones to greatness. Every challenge, every hardship, was an opportunity to grow stronger. Where others saw failure, he saw lessons. To him, adversity was not something to fear—it was the very thing that shaped character and sharpened the mind.

This philosophy is a cornerstone of effective coaching. Resilience is not about avoiding hardship; it is about learning from it. A great coach helps clients reframe setbacks, not as signs of failure, but as necessary steps toward transformation. Instead of letting obstacles discourage them, clients should ask, "How is this challenge shaping me? What skill or mindset is it forcing me to develop?"

To make this shift, coaches can teach Marcus' reframing technique—viewing every difficulty as a training ground for personal growth. Clients should also develop a personal philosophy for resilience—a guiding belief system that keeps them steady in the face of adversity. When setbacks come, they will not break. Instead, they will adapt, grow, and emerge even stronger.

Final Coaching Lesson: The True Measure of a Coach

As Marcus Aurelius lay on his deathbed, he did not cling to power or seek praise. There were no elaborate speeches, no desperate attempts to cement his legacy. Instead, his final words were simple, yet profound:

"Do not mourn me. Live by virtue. Do what is right. Lead wisely."

Even in his last moments, he was not thinking of himself—he was still teaching, still guiding, still coaching.

The true measure of a coach is not found in the words they speak but, in the transformation, **they ignite in others.** It is not about their own success but the **ripple effect of their wisdom.** A great coach does not seek recognition. Instead, they empower others to grow, to lead, and to carry the lessons forward.

In the end, the greatest coaches disappear—but their impact lives on forever in those they have shaped.

Marcus Aurelius & The IMPACT Framework – A Coaching Guide for Lasting Transformation

- **Integrity & Authenticity** → Coaches must embody what they teach.

- **Mastery & Continuous Growth** → A great coach is always a student.

- **Purpose-Driven Leadership** → Coaching must connect to a deeper mission.

- **Accountability & Ownership** → No excuses. Take responsibility for growth.

- **Collaboration & Connection** → Coaching is a dialogue, not a monologue.

- **Transformation & Adaptability** → Challenges are stepping stones, not barriers.

Marcus Aurelius did not just **lead an empire—he coached an entire civilization.** His lessons are a **blueprint for modern coaches**, showing how to develop others, inspire resilience, and cultivate wisdom that lasts.

> **"If you are distressed by anything external, the pain is not due to the thing itself, but to your estimate of it; and this you have the power to revoke at any moment."**
>
> **- Marcus Aurelius**

Key take aways:

1. Lead from the Inside Out: Self-Coaching Builds Inner Strength

Marcus Aurelius did not wait for guidance from others—he became his own coach. Through nightly reflections and brutally honest journaling, he confronted his fears and flaws. He cultivated self-awareness not to appear perfect, but to grow wiser and act with clarity.

Learning:

True leadership begins with self-coaching. Before leading others, lead your own mind. Reflection is not indulgence—it is the crucible of character.

2. Integrity Over Image: Trust Is Earned Through Authenticity

While other emperors sought worship, Marcus chose humility. He refused divine titles and instead modeled a life of simplicity, honesty, and shared burden. His truthfulness—even when pressured to deceive—earned him enduring trust.

Learning:

Authenticity is the currency of leadership. When leaders walk their talk and stand by their values, trust follows naturally.

3. Responsibility Is Power: Own It All, Blame Nothing

When Rome faltered, Marcus did not point fingers—he pointed inward. Whether it was war, plague, or betrayal, he never excused failure. He acted, adapted, and held himself fully accountable.

Learning:

Great leaders do not escape responsibility—they embrace it. Accountability is not a burden—it is the source of their strength and credibility.

4. Wisdom Requires Many Voices: Listen to Understand, Not to Win

Instead of demanding loyalty or blind agreement, Marcus surrounded himself with diverse perspectives. He even changed strategy when convinced by better ideas, showing strength in humility.

Learning:

Leaders grow when they listen. Coaching is not about controlling the conversation—it is about co-creating wisdom through dialogue.

5. Obstacles Are the Way: Resilience is a Leadership Superpower

To Marcus, hardship was not a detour—it was the path. Every challenge, from plague to betrayal, was an opportunity to practice courage, patience, and compassion. He saw adversity as the forge of greatness.

Learning:

Coaches and leaders alike must train themselves—and others—to see difficulty as fuel. The obstacle does not stop the path. It becomes the path.

From Breakdown to Breakthrough: How a Product Team Transformed Using Inner Leadership Principles

At a global retail tech company, the **Product Catalyst Team** was struggling. They were responsible for launching a new omnichannel inventory engine—crucial for customer experience—but deadlines were slipping, team morale was low, and finger-pointing had replaced collaboration.

That is when I was brought in to coach the Head of Product, **Anika**, and her leadership triad: the Engineering Manager, Design Lead, and Data PM. The turnaround began not with tools or frameworks—but with mindset.

1. Lead from the Inside Out: Self-Coaching in the Storm

Anika, though outwardly composed, admitted in our first session:

"I feel like I am constantly reacting. I have not had time to think clearly in weeks."

We drew inspiration from Marcus Aurelius: *Before leading others, lead your own mind.*

She began a daily ritual—10 minutes of voice journaling on what she felt, feared, and needed clarity on. Within two weeks, her energy shifted. She stopped second-guessing herself in meetings and started asking sharper, more purposeful questions.

Soon, her self-coaching inspired others to reflect before reacting. The culture of panic began to slow.

2. Integrity Over Image: Building Trust Through Truth

In sprint reviews, the leadership had a habit of sugarcoating issues. The team had stopped believing in status reports. Anika changed that.

In one meeting, she openly admitted:

"We have overpromised and underdelivered. That is on me. Here is how I intend to course-correct."

The room fell silent—then, slowly, heads began to nod. That moment of raw honesty cracked open new trust. Her direct reports followed suit, and stand-ups turned from blame sessions to shared problem-solving.

As Marcus had done—Anika modelled *humble truth over heroic image.*

3. Responsibility Is Power: No More Finger-Pointing

When a critical deployment failed during a holiday sale, tension erupted. Fingers pointed between QA, Data, and DevOps.

But Anika gathered the full team and reframed it:

"We all own this. Let us fix the system, not fix the blame."

They ran a *blameless post-mortem*, restructured test responsibilities, and introduced paired code reviews. Morale improved. So did system resilience.

Responsibility shifted from defensive to **empowered**.

4. Wisdom Requires Many Voices: Listening to Lead

Previously, strategy decisions were top-down. The engineering team felt unheard, and designers felt blocked.

Anika changed the cadence—launching *cross-functional discovery circles* where every voice mattered. The junior UX researcher's insights led to a UX redesign that increased task completion by 21%.

And when the data PM challenged a key roadmap assumption, Anika invited debate—and changed the quarterly focus.

Like Marcus, she learned: **Humility is strategy. Listening is power.**

5. Obstacles Are the Way: Adversity Became Their Superpower

Midway through transformation, the team lost two senior devs unexpectedly. Spirits dipped. But instead of collapsing, they anchored back to their **"Why."**

In one of our coaching huddles, the engineering manager said:

"Let us treat this as a forge. We will redistribute load, upskill juniors, and document better."

That hardship-built resilience. Within six weeks, junior engineers stepped up, tech debt was reduced, and onboarding improved.

They stopped fearing problems. They started **growing through them**.

The Result?

- Cross-team trust soared

- Delivery cadence stabilized

- Employee engagement scores jumped by 34%

- And more importantly—**they rediscovered joy in the mission**

In our final retro, Anika said:

"I used to think leading was about being right. Now I know—it is about being real."

Final Reflection

Marcus Aurelius did not lead Rome through peace—but through chaos.

This product team did not transform through perfect plans—but through **self-awareness, honesty, shared ownership, open dialogue, and resilience**.

Transformation is not just what we build.

It is *who* we become in the process.

Story-13:

How Confucius's Philosophy Aligns with Modern Leadership and Personal Growth

> **"To put the world in order, we must first put the nation in order; to put the nation in order, we must first put the family in order; to put the family in order, we must first cultivate our personal life; we must first set our hearts right."**
>
> — *Confucius*

Confucius, one of the most influential figures in ancient philosophy, demonstrated principles that align closely with the **IMPACT Framework** for coaching, helping individuals develop into better leaders, thinkers, and overall, more self-aware, impactful human beings.

His wisdom has influenced both personal development and leadership coaching for millennia.

Let us break down how Confucius's philosophy and leadership approach correlate with each element of the **IMPACT Framework:**

1. I - Inspire Awareness & Identity (Self-Reflection, Behavioral Change, Neuroscience)

Confucius's teachings were heavily focused on **self-awareness** and **personal growth.** He said, *"The superior man understands what is right; the inferior man understands what will sell."*

This reflects a deep commitment to **self-reflection**—encouraging individuals to look inward and assess their actions, values, and identity. In his coaching, Confucius would ask his students to examine who they were and how they could improve, which directly connects with the concept of discovering one's strengths, values, and identity in the IMPACT framework.

Example from Confucius: He would often say, *"When we see men of a contrary character, we should turn inwards and examine ourselves."* This reflects **self-reflection** and the idea of behavioral change through self-awareness—one of the key elements of the **I** in IMPACT.

2. M - Mindset & Mastery Shift (Overcoming Fear, Belief Transformation, Mandela's Optimism, NLP & CBT)

Confucius believed in the **power of personal transformation and overcoming adversity.** His famous quote, *"Our greatest glory is not in never falling, but in rising every time we fall,"* speaks to the **growth mindset.** His philosophy emphasized that failure was a learning experience and that **fear** and **limiting beliefs** could be overcome through wisdom, perseverance, and resilience.

Example from Confucius: In his coaching, Confucius encouraged his followers to transform their thinking, turning every obstacle into an opportunity. This connects directly with the **M** in the IMPACT Framework, which focuses on overcoming limiting beliefs and **cultivating mental resilience.**

3. P - Purpose-Driven Goals & Strategy (Positive Psychology, Coaching Models, Leadership Goal-Setting)

Confucius was a strong advocate for aligning one's actions with **higher purpose.** He stated, *"The will to win, the desire to succeed, the urge to reach your full potential... these are the keys that will unlock the door to personal excellence."* He encouraged individuals to set goals based on their **values,** purpose, and the greater good, helping them align actions to a **higher mission.**

Example from Confucius: His entire philosophical system was about creating a **roadmap for life**—where individuals could set personal goals for **self-cultivation**, which is a form of **purpose-driven leadership.** His coaching helped individuals not just pursue **success,** but the **right kind of success** aligned with moral principles and societal betterment.

4. A - Action, Accountability & Adaptability (High-Performance Teams, Startup Success, Leadership Execution)

Confucius's teachings were not just about contemplation but about taking **action.** He said, *"He who learns but does not think, is lost. He who thinks but does not learn is in great danger."* This emphasizes the importance of balancing reflection with practical **action.**

Confucius stressed **accountability**—both personally and socially. He believed in the idea of **resilience** and adaptability in the face of hardship. Leaders must **take action,** track their progress, and **stay adaptable** to overcome challenges.

Example from Confucius: His disciples would regularly practice what they learned, holding each other accountable and making real-world decisions to demonstrate their understanding. This emphasis on **practicality, action,** and **adaptability** is core to the **A** in IMPACT.

5. C - Connection & Collaborative Growth (Coaching Impact, Mentorship, Team Empowerment, Aristotle's Leadership)

Confucius viewed **mentorship** and **collaboration** as essential for personal and collective growth. His emphasis on **"ren"** (humaneness) encouraged individuals to support each other, fostering a **sense of community** and collective responsibility.

Confucius believed that a wise leader should cultivate a **collaborative environment,** where everyone can grow together and support one another's development. He often said, *"A man who has committed a mistake and doesn't correct it, is committing another mistake."* This highlights the role of **mentorship** and **peer coaching**—helping others not only develop individually but **empower them** in a collective setting.

Example from Confucius: Confucius did not just instruct; he mentored and developed the character of his disciples. He would always engage in dialogue, asking thought-provoking questions, and guiding individuals toward **shared learning**, which nurtured **collaborative growth.**

6. T - Transform & Thrive (Digital Transformation, Business Coaching, Innovation, Legacy)

Confucius's legacy was one of **transformation.** His teachings have influenced not just his time but continue to **shape leadership and ethical thinking today.** The idea of **legacy-building** resonates deeply with the **T** in IMPACT, as Confucius's teachings aimed at leaving a **lasting impact** on his disciples and future generations. His focus on continuous **self-cultivation** and **lifelong learning** supports the idea of sustaining success through transformation.

Example from Confucius: Confucius is considered one of the **founding figures** of the ethical and moral framework of Chinese culture, and his teachings have had a **lasting impact** for over 2,000 years. His teachings show that a leader's transformation does not end with personal achievement—it evolves into a **legacy** that benefits future generations.

Confucius, through his deep philosophy and coaching practices, set the stage for the **IMPACT Framework** long before it was formalized. He focused on **self-awareness, mindset shifts, purpose-driven actions, accountability,** and **collaboration**—all essential components of personal and leadership development. His ideas on **legacy-building** are still relevant today, as they encourage individuals and leaders to continuously evolve, leaving a profound and **lasting impact** on both their personal lives and society at large.

In essence, Confucius's ancient coaching methods have **stood the test of time,** proving that the principles behind the **IMPACT Framework** are deeply rooted in the earliest practices of leadership and coaching.

Implementing the principles from Confucius's teachings can be challenging because they require us to step out of our comfort zones, change old habits, and engage in deep self-reflection and personal growth.

These are not easy feats, especially when life is fast-paced, filled with distractions, and when we are often overwhelmed with daily responsibilities. However, there are simple daily actions we can take to improve our approach to these principles, making them more accessible and manageable.

Let us break it down:

1. Self-Reflection & Self-Awareness (I)

In the hustle of daily life, finding time for deep reflection can feel like an impossible task. With busy schedules and endless demands on our attention, the idea of pausing for self-awareness might seem like a luxury. But the truth is, developing self-awareness does not require long hours or deep introspection. It begins with small, honest moments of reflection.

At the end of each day, carve out just five minutes for yourself. It does not need to be a lengthy or profound session—just a quiet moment to ask yourself one simple question: *Did my actions today align with my values?* This brief pause gives you the opportunity to check in with yourself. It is not about being perfect or having all the answers right away; it is about creating a habit of self-reflection.

By taking these few minutes each day, you will begin to notice patterns in your behaviour—where you are staying true to your values and where you may have strayed. This daily practice of reflection can lead to a deeper understanding of yourself and gradually reveal areas where you can improve. Over time, it becomes a natural part of your routine, helping you to live more intentionally and aligned with your true self.

2. Mindset Shift (M)

The morning sun streamed through the window, casting golden streaks across the wooden floor. Rohan sat on the edge of his bed, staring at the wall. His chest felt heavy; his mind cluttered with worries. Today would be just like yesterday—another day of doubt, another battle lost before it even began.

His phone buzzed. A reminder. "Start with a thought that serves you, not one that drains you."

He sighed, rubbing his temples. It felt pointless. How could a simple sentence change anything? Still, he muttered the words under his breath. *I am resilient. I learn from every challenge.* The words felt weak, like trying to hold back an ocean with a paper boat.

But then, the day began.

Emails flooded in—some urgent, some frustrating. His code refused to work, his inbox swelled with questions, and the deadline loomed like a storm cloud. A familiar tightness gripped his chest. The old voice returned, whispering, *you cannot handle this. You are going to fail.*

But this time, something was different.

Rohan paused. He inhaled deeply, feeling the air cool his lungs. The words from the morning returned, not as a distant echo, but as a steady hand on his shoulder. *I learn from every challenge.*

He leaned forward, eyes sharpening. One task at a time. One step forward. He tackled the problem before him—not with fear, but with quiet determination.

That evening, as he closed his laptop, he felt something strange. The stress had not disappeared; the challenges had not vanished—but the weight was lighter. His mind was not drowning; it was steady. And when he reflected on the day, he saw it—not failure, not struggle, but a small victory.

A single moment of resilience.

Tomorrow, he would do it again. And again. Until, one day, the old voice would be nothing but a whisper lost in the wind.

3. Purpose-Driven Goals (P)

The clock ticked steadily, but Aisha barely noticed. Her inbox was overflowing, her calendar packed, her to-do lists a relentless tide that never seemed to recede. She moved from one task to the next, checking boxes, replying to emails, sitting through meetings that blurred together. Productivity? Maybe. But fulfilment? That was a different question.

One evening, as she shut her laptop, an unsettling thought lingered—*What did I actually do today that mattered to me?* She could not answer.

The next morning, before diving into work, she paused. Instead of rushing straight into emails, she grabbed a sticky note and wrote: "Today, I will make time to mentor someone who needs guidance." It was small, simple, but different.

Hours passed. Deadlines loomed. She almost forgot about the note—until a junior colleague hesitated by her desk, struggling with a problem. The instinct was to brush it off, to say, *I will help later.* But the words from the morning stared back at her.

She exhaled, closed her inbox, and turned to listen.

The conversation was brief but meaningful. The colleague left with newfound clarity, and Aisha felt something she had not in a long time— purpose.

That night, she glanced at the note again. Unlike before, when the day felt like a blur, she now had an answer to the question: *What did I do today that truly mattered?*

One small habit. One intentional act. Tomorrow, she would do it again.

And maybe, just maybe, the real to-do list is not the one on our screens—but the one that shapes who we become.

4. Action & Accountability (A)

Rahul stared at his screen, the blinking cursor taunting him. A report was due, emails needed responses, and a dozen other tasks loomed over him like an approaching storm. He sighed, scrolling mindlessly through his phone instead. *I will start in five minutes... maybe after one more video.*

Minutes turned into an hour. The weight of undone work pressed heavier. *Why is it so hard to start?*

Then, a thought struck him. *What if I just focus on three things?*

He grabbed a sticky note and wrote them down:

1. Draft the first section of the report.

2. Reply to three important emails.

3. Schedule a team check-in.

No pressure to finish everything. Just these three.

With the first task in focus, he set a timer for 25 minutes and started typing. The words came slowly at first, but soon, momentum took over. The first section was done. A small victory. Encouraged, he moved to the next task.

By the end of the day, his note had three checkmarks. He felt lighter, more in control. Instead of drowning in an ocean of unfinished work, he had taken small, deliberate steps forward.

That night, he sent a quick message to his friend: "Held myself accountable today. Three tasks. All done."

The reply came instantly: "Nice! What is the plan for tomorrow?"

Rahul smiled. It turns out, progress is not about waiting for motivation—it is about starting, one small win at a time.

5. Collaboration & Growth (C)

Aisha hurried through the office hallway, her mind cluttered with deadlines, meetings, and the ever-growing to-do list waiting on her desk. She barely noticed Aman, her junior colleague, sitting alone near the coffee machine, his shoulders slumped, staring at his laptop.

She almost walked past him—but something made her stop.

"Hey, Aman. You good?"

Aman looked up, startled. He hesitated, then exhaled. *"Honestly? Struggling with this project. Feels like I'm going in circles."*

Aisha did not have extra time. But she had been there before—overwhelmed, unsure, feeling like she had to figure it all out alone.

"Let me see. Maybe I can help." She pulled up a chair. In ten minutes, they broke the problem into smaller pieces. Aman's shoulders relaxed as clarity replaced confusion.

"I didn't think anyone would notice," he admitted.

Aisha smiled. *"We're a team. We figure things out together."*

That evening, she reflected on that moment. It had not taken much—just a pause, a question, and a willingness to listen. Yet, it made a difference.

Success is not just about personal achievements. Sometimes, the greatest impact comes from lifting others up. Who will you check in on today?

6. Legacy & Transformation (T)

Ravi sat at his desk, staring at the blinking cursor on his screen. *Legacy?* The word felt too big—meant for people with statues, bestsellers, or grand achievements. Right now, he was just trying to make it through another exhausting workday.

Then his eyes drifted to the worn-out notebook beside him—the one he had promised himself he would fill with new ideas, learnings, and reflections. Dust had started to settle on its cover.

"Maybe tomorrow," he had told himself yesterday. And the day before that.

But today, he did something different. He flipped it open and wrote just one line: *"I will improve 1% every day."*

That evening, he watched a short video on leadership. The next day, he stayed an extra five minutes to mentor a junior colleague. By the end of the week, he had outlined a new approach to streamline his team's workflow.

None of these felt revolutionary on their own. But over time, they stacked up—small ripples creating waves.

Legacies are not built overnight. They grow in the moments we choose to take action, no matter how small.

What is the one step you will take today?

Making It Stick

The key to executing these principles is **consistency.** Rather than trying to overhaul everything at once, choose one action to focus on daily. As you consistently build these habits, they will become second nature, and you will start to see the bigger transformations over time.

The daily actions do not have to be perfect or monumental—what matters is that you are making progress, however small. In the grand scheme of things, these small, intentional actions will lead to the growth, change, and legacy you are striving for.

> **"The expectations of life depend upon diligence; the mechanic that would perfect his work must first sharpen his tools."**
>
> — *Confucius*

Key takeaways:

1. Self-Awareness is the Starting Point of Leadership (Inspire – "I")

Confucius emphasized deep self-reflection as the foundation for personal excellence. His teachings prompt us to look inward, examine our values and behaviours, and realign our identity with what is right rather than what is easy. Even 5 minutes a day asking, "Did I act according to my values?" begins the transformation.

"When we see men of a contrary character, we should turn inwards and examine ourselves." – Confucius

2. Mindset Shifts Create Resilience and Mastery (Mindset – "M")

Resilience is not born—it is practiced. Confucius taught that failing is not the problem; not rising after is. Cultivating daily mental resilience, like Rohan's moment of clarity, allows us to slowly replace fear and self-doubt with strength and growth.

"Our greatest glory is not in never falling, but in rising every time we fall." – Confucius

3. Purpose Fuels Meaningful Action (Purpose – "P")

Leadership without purpose becomes noise. Confucius encouraged alignment between one's goals and one's values. A small daily commitment to act with purpose—like mentoring someone—can bring deep fulfilment, as Aisha's story shows.

"The will to win... the urge to reach your full potential... unlock the door to personal excellence." – Confucius

4. Small Actions Build Accountability and Progress (Action – "A")

Knowing is not enough; doing matters. Confucius's wisdom is rooted in the balance of thought and action. Like Rahul's approach—breaking big tasks into small wins—progress is built one decision at a time, held together by daily discipline.

"He who learns but does not think, is lost. He who thinks but does not learn is in great danger." – Confucius

5. Legacy is Built Through Everyday Impact (Transform – "T")

True transformation is not always loud or immediate. It is in the notebook we dust off, the junior we mentor, the idea we finally share. Confucius's legacy was not just in what he said, but how he inspired generations to act, reflect, and grow.

> **"A man who has committed a mistake and doesn't correct it, is committing another mistake."**
>
> **– Confucius**

Story-14:

The Hidden Code of Success: How Napoleon Hill's Philosophy Mirrors the IMPACT Framework

> **"You are the master of your destiny. You can influence, direct, and control your own environment. You can make your life what you want it to be."**
>
> — *Napoleon Hill*

A young journalist sat nervously across from the richest man in the world. His notepad trembled in his hands as he prepared to ask a question that could change his life. Andrew Carnegie, the steel magnate, leaned forward with a knowing smile.

"Are you willing to dedicate the next twenty years of your life to uncovering the secrets of success?"

The room fell silent. The journalist, Napoleon Hill, swallowed hard. He had no wealth, no connections—only a burning curiosity. Yet, something in Carnegie's eyes told him that if he said yes, he would unlock something that even money could not buy.

Hill did not just agree. He **surrendered to a mission** that would take him across the world, interviewing over 500 of the greatest minds in business, science, and politics. What he discovered became the foundation of *Think and Grow Rich*—but it was far more than just a book. It was a **roadmap** for those daring enough to chase greatness.

And within that roadmap lies something astonishing—Hill's principles mirror the very DNA of what modern leadership frameworks, like **IMPACT**, teach us today.

1. Integrity & Authenticity – The Moment of Truth

Hill had a core belief: **"Success begins with a definite purpose."** But defining that purpose required brutal honesty.

One of his most striking interviews was with Henry Ford. In the early 1900s, Ford's dream of an affordable automobile seemed laughable.

Competitors mocked him. His own engineers quit, calling his vision impossible.

One evening, after yet another failure, Ford stood in his dimly lit garage, staring at his latest broken model. Any sane man would have given up. Instead, he wiped the grease from his hands and whispered, **"I will see this through."**

That night, **Ford made a choice**—to remain true to his vision, no matter the cost. It was the **IMPACT principle of Integrity & Authenticity** in action. A leader must stand firm, even when the world calls them a fool.

Lesson: True success starts when you refuse to betray your purpose.

2. Mastery & Continuous Growth – The Relentless Student

Every successful person Hill studied had one thing in common: **they never stopped learning.**

Take Thomas Edison. After thousands of failed attempts to invent the light bulb, reporters ridiculed him. One famously asked, **"How does it feel to fail 10,000 times?"**

Edison simply smiled. **"I did not fail. I found 10,000 ways that will not work."**

Hill recognized this as the hallmark of a **growth mindset.** It is not failure that stops people—it is their inability to learn from it. The greatest minds are not the smartest; they are the most **relentless.**

Lesson: Mastery is the art of seeing failure as fuel for growth.

3. Purpose & Impact-Driven Leadership – The Fire That Never Dies

Hill's research uncovered something chilling. The difference between those who made millions and those who died in obscurity had nothing to do with intelligence.

It had to do with **desire.**

He called it a **"burning obsession"**—the kind of purpose that consumes a person, pulling them through failures, rejections, and doubt.

When Nelson Mandela was thrown into prison, many expected him to fade into history. But while the world forgot him, he **held onto his vision of a free South Africa** like a man gripping the edge of a cliff.

For 27 years, he endured. And when the gates of Robben Island finally opened, he did not emerge as a bitter man—he stepped forward as a leader who would change the course of history.

Lesson: The strongest leaders do not chase success; they chase **meaning.**

4. Accountability & Ownership – The Unbreakable Will

There is a moment in every person's life when they must decide: **Will I take responsibility for my future, or will I blame circumstances?**

Hill believed this was the moment that separated winners from the rest. He called it **"definiteness of decision."**

Elon Musk embodies this principle today. When SpaceX's first three rocket launches exploded, he had a choice—walk away or **bet everything on one last attempt.** He **took ownership** of the outcome and pushed forward.

The fourth launch succeeded. The rest is history.

Lesson: Leaders do not wait for change; they **own** their fate.

5. Collaboration & Connection – The Power of a Mastermind

Hill discovered that no one succeeds alone. Every legendary figure he studied had a **"Mastermind Group"**—a network of **mentors, challengers, and visionaries** who fuelled their success.

Steve Jobs had Steve Wozniak. Bill Gates had Paul Allen. Even Edison had a group of thinkers and financiers backing him.

Success is not a solo journey—it is **a symphony of minds.**

Lesson: Your greatest asset is not your intelligence. It is **who you surround yourself with.**

6. Transformation & Adaptability – The Art of Reinvention

Perhaps the greatest lesson Hill left behind was this: **change is inevitable, but transformation is a choice.**

Look at Winston Churchill. When World War II erupted, many thought Britain had lost before the fight began. But Churchill understood something his enemies did not—**a leader must adapt faster than the crisis.**

He changed battle strategies overnight. He shifted public morale through electrifying speeches. He adapted, evolved, and ultimately led his nation to victory.

Lesson: Those who refuse to change will be left behind.

The Hidden Truth: Hill's Legacy Lives on in the IMPACT Framework

Napoleon Hill did not just write a book. He uncovered a **universal code for success.**

Every entrepreneur, leader, and innovator who followed in his footsteps—Ford, Edison, Mandela, Jobs, Musk—proved that his principles were not theories. They were **laws of achievement.**

And today, these same laws are embedded in the **IMPACT Framework**:

- **Integrity & Authenticity → Know your purpose and stand by it.**

- **Mastery & Continuous Growth → Never stop learning.**

- **Purpose & Impact-Driven Leadership → Find a mission greater than yourself.**

- **Accountability & Ownership → Take full responsibility for your life.**

- **Collaboration & Connection → Build a network of strong minds.**

- **Transformation & Adaptability → Embrace change before it forces itself upon you.**

Napoleon Hill's legacy is clear: **Success is not reserved for the lucky or the gifted. It belongs to those willing to follow the principles of achievement—those willing to act.**

Coaching Lessons & Actions from Napoleon Hill's Story

Napoleon Hill's journey from an unknown journalist to the architect of *Think and Grow Rich* is not just a story—it is a **blueprint for transformative coaching**. His research uncovered **six core principles of success**, principles that every coach must **embody, teach, and inspire** in their clients.

But here is the real challenge: **How do coaches turn these principles into action?**

Below are **six powerful coaching lessons** extracted from Hill's story—each paired with **specific actions** for coaches to implement immediately.

1. Integrity & Authenticity → Coaching the "Moment of Truth"

Henry Ford stood alone in his dimly lit garage, surrounded by broken parts and shattered expectations. Another prototype had failed. His engineers had walked away, convinced his vision was impossible. The world mocked his dream of an affordable automobile, calling it foolish, unrealistic. But in that silent moment, as the weight of doubt pressed down on him, Ford did not waver. He whispered to himself, *"I will see this through."*

Every great leader, every ambitious dreamer, faces this moment—the point where everything seems to be falling apart, where giving up feels easier than pressing forward. This is where true transformation happens. A coach's role is not just to provide strategies or advice; it is to be the voice that reminds clients why they started. It is to help them stay grounded in their deeper purpose when the noise of fear and failure threatens to drown it out.

To build this resilience, clients must define their *non-negotiables*—the values they refuse to compromise, no matter how hard things get. When everything feels uncertain, these core beliefs become their compass. One way to solidify this is by crafting a personal *Integrity Statement*—a written commitment to themselves, reinforcing the reasons they won't quit.

Because when the world questions their vision, when even those closest to them express doubt, one question will determine their fate: *What belief will keep you standing?*

2. Mastery & Continuous Growth → Coaching a Relentless Mindset

Thomas Edison spent years chasing a dream that seemed impossible. Each experiment ended the same way—failure. Time and time again, the light bulb refused to shine. Most would have given up, convinced they were not meant to succeed. But not Edison. When asked about his countless failures, he did not dwell on disappointment. He simply said, *"I found 10,000 ways that won't work."* To him, every misstep was a step forward, every mistake a lesson, every setback a necessary part of the journey.

This is the mindset that separates those who quit from those who break through. Too often, people see failure as a verdict—a sign to stop. Coaches must help their clients rewrite this belief. Failure is not an ending; it is a classroom. It is how people refine their skills, sharpen their strategies, and move closer to success.

One way to make this shift is by keeping a *Failure Log*—a space to track mistakes, but more importantly, to record what they taught. Instead of hiding from failure, clients should analyze it with curiosity. What worked? What did not? What adjustments can be made? This habit turns failure into fuel.

Growth is not about giant leaps. It is about tiny, consistent steps—1% improvement every day. Over time, that small daily progress compounds into mastery. The real question is: *If failure did not exist, what would you attempt?* Because in truth, failure *does not* exist—it is just learning in disguise.

3. Purpose & Impact-Driven Leadership → Coaching a Mission That Outlives the Client

For 27 years, Nelson Mandela sat behind prison bars, cut off from the world he had sworn to change. Each day was a test of endurance, a battle against hopelessness. Yet when he finally walked free, there was no anger in his heart. No thirst for revenge. Instead, he spoke of unity, of forgiveness, of a vision far greater than himself—a free and equal South Africa. His suffering had not broken him; it had strengthened his resolve.

This is the power of a true mission. Goals can motivate, but missions *pull* people through their darkest moments. When the road gets tough, a pay check or a promotion will not be enough to keep someone going. But a cause? A purpose beyond themselves? That is unshakable. Coaches must help their clients find that deeper reason—the thing that will keep them moving forward, no matter what stands in their way.

A powerful way to uncover this? Ask, *"If you could only be remembered for one thing, what would it be?"* Strip away the noise, the titles, the fleeting successes—what truly matters? Who benefits from their success beyond themselves? When people realize that others—family, community, the next generation—are counting on them, their fight becomes stronger.

Obstacles are not barriers to a mission. They are part of the mission. Mandela did not survive prison *despite* his vision—he survived *because* of it. His purpose turned suffering into fuel. So, ask yourself: *What would you fight for, even if you knew you might not win?* Because that's where true strength is found.

4. Accountability & Ownership → Coaching a No-Excuses Mindset

Elon Musk stood at the edge of total failure. Three rocket launches. Three explosions. Millions of dollars burned in seconds. Investors doubted him. Critics mocked him. Most people would have walked away. But Musk did not flinch. He gathered every last dollar he had, poured it into one final attempt, and launched. This time, it worked. SpaceX was saved—not by luck, but by an unshakable refusal to surrender.

This is the difference between those who succeed and those who do not. Winners do not wait for circumstances to improve. They do not blame the economy, the market, or bad timing. They take control. They *create* change. Coaches must instil this mindset in their clients—eliminating blame, replacing excuses with ownership, and shifting focus from problems to solutions.

Think about it—how often do people say, *"I can't because..."*? What if, instead, they asked, *"How can I...?"* The moment someone stops looking for reasons they *cannot* and starts searching for ways they *can*, everything shifts. A powerful exercise? Write down every excuse holding you back. Then, one by one, turn them into action steps.

Ownership is not just a mindset; it is a contract with yourself. When clients sign an *Extreme Ownership Contract*, they are making a written commitment—no more blame, no more waiting, no more wishing. Their success is in their hands.

So, ask yourself: *If no one else was responsible for your success—only you—what would you do differently?* Because the truth is, that is already the case.

5. Collaboration & Connection → Coaching the Power of the Mastermind

Napoleon Hill spent decades studying the world's most successful leaders, searching for the secret behind their extraordinary achievements. He found one undeniable pattern—none of them walked the path alone. Henry Ford had Thomas Edison. Steve Jobs had Bill Gates as both a rival and an inspiration. Every great mind had a circle of trusted advisors, challengers, and mentors—a *Mastermind Group*—that pushed them beyond their limits.

Yet so many people still believe success is a solo journey. They grind in isolation, convinced that sheer effort will be enough. But breakthroughs do not happen in a vacuum. The right relationships do not just open doors; they shatter ceilings. Coaches must help their clients see that who they surround themselves with will define their potential.

Take a moment and reflect: Who are the five people shaping your mindset every day? Are they fuelling your growth, or holding you back? If you want to rise, your environment must rise with you. Building a *Personal Mastermind*—a tight-knit circle of mentors, peers, and challengers—is not a luxury; it is a necessity. One conversation, one connection, one mentor could shift your entire trajectory.

The truth is, success is not just about what you know—it is about *who* you know and *how* they make you think. So, ask yourself: *Who in your life makes you think bigger? And how can you spend more time with them?* Because the right people will not just support your dreams—they will demand you make them a reality.

6. Transformation & Adaptability → Coaching Reinvention & Resilience

The war was very serious, and Britain was close to falling apart. Many cities were damaged, and people were losing hope. Fear was everywhere. But in the middle of this chaos, one man stayed strong—Winston Churchill.

He did not stick to old ways or wish things were different. Instead, he changed quickly, made new plans, and gave people hope. He believed they could still win. He understood that refusing to change could be just as bad as giving up. Instead of being afraid of the unknown, he accepted it and stayed ahead of the enemy. Because he adapted, Britain survived.

Change happens all the time, but many people try to avoid it until they cannot anymore. The world keeps moving forward, whether we are ready or not. That is why good leaders—like coaches—must help others prepare for change. They do not just react to it; they expect it and plan for it.

Imagine if you woke up tomorrow and your job or industry was gone— no warning at all. Would you panic, or would you already have a backup plan? Real adaptability means you are not surprised by change. The most successful people do not just get through change—they lead it. They keep learning and growing, even when things are uncertain.

Feeling uncomfortable does not mean you should stop. It usually means that change is coming. If you keep going, today's problems will become tomorrow's strengths. You grow by stepping out of your comfort zone, not by staying safe.

So, ask yourself: What change are you afraid of that could actually help you grow? The future is not going to wait—so why should you?

Final Coaching Challenge: Will You Apply These Lessons?

Napoleon Hill did not just discover success principles—he revealed a **repeatable system** that applies to **coaches, leaders, and high achievers today.**

Summary of Coaching Actions:

- **Integrity & Authenticity:** Help clients define their **non-negotiable values**.

- **Mastery & Growth:** Teach clients to **view failure as data, not defeat**.

- **Purpose & Impact:** Guide clients to discover a **mission bigger than themselves**.

- **Accountability & Ownership:** Eliminate **excuses** and install an **ownership mindset**.

- **Collaboration & Connection:** Help clients **build a Mastermind network**.

- **Transformation & Adaptability:** Train clients to **evolve before change forces them to**.

Final Question for Coaches: *Are you coaching people to think, or coaching them to act?*

Now, take one of these strategies and use it in your next coaching session. Because knowing is not enough—doing is what creates transformation.

"Whatever the mind can conceive and believe, it can achieve."

— Napoleon Hill

Key Takeaways:

1. Purpose Fuels Endurance

"The strongest leaders don't chase success; they chase meaning."

Hill's journey, Mandela's resilience, and Ford's defiance all prove one thing: without a deep, burning purpose, even the most brilliant minds will falter. Purpose is the internal engine that powers perseverance in the face of adversity.

Coaching Cue: Help clients define their mission. Ask: "What would you fight for, even if you knew you might not win?"

2. Failure Is Feedback, not a Finale

"Mastery is the art of seeing failure as fuel for growth."

Edison's 10,000 failed attempts were not setbacks—they were steps. Hill observed that successful people do not fear failure—they study it. They adapt, improve, and try again with greater wisdom.

Coaching Cue: Encourage a Failure Log. Frame mistakes as data. Ask: "What did you learn that makes your next attempt smarter?"

3. Own Your Outcome

"Leaders don't wait for change; they own their fate."

Elon Musk did not blame circumstances—he bet on himself when everything was crumbling. Hill saw this as the turning point in every leader's journey: the moment they stop waiting and start owning.

Coaching Cue: Create an Extreme Ownership Contract. Ask: "If no one else is coming to save you, what will you do differently?"

4. Growth Is a Group Sport

"Your greatest asset is not your intelligence. It is who you surround yourself with."

From Ford and Edison to Jobs and Wozniak, Hill found that greatness is never a solo act. Collaboration multiplies possibility. Success lives in connection.

Coaching Cue: Facilitate building a Mastermind Group. Ask: "Who challenges you to be better?"

5. Integrity is the Unshakable Foundation

"True success starts when you refuse to betray your purpose."

Ford's lonely moment in his garage was the ultimate test of belief. When everyone else walked away, he chose to stay rooted in his vision. Hill's research calls this unwavering self-alignment "Definiteness of Purpose."

Coaching Cue: Craft a client's Integrity Statement. Ask: "What value will you refuse to compromise, no matter what?"

Case study:

Coaching Rohan: From Overwhelmed to Empowered

Rohan, a bright student, arrived at my door burdened by the crushing weight of the engineering entrance exam. Despite his dedicated efforts, he was trapped in a cycle of low mock test scores, a gnawing feeling of being stuck eroding his confidence and planting seeds of doubt about his future.

Our coaching journey began with a deep dive into his core motivations, the very essence of what truly mattered to him.

Purpose Fuels Endurance

I posed a fundamental question: *"What would you fight for, even if victory seemed elusive?"* A visible uncertainty flickered across Rohan's face before he articulated, *"I want to become an engineer who can forge sustainable solutions for rural India, to alleviate the struggles my father faced with electricity."*

This was the spark. Rohan's motivation transcended the exam; it was rooted in a larger, deeply personal mission. Together, we sculpted his Mission Statement, a guiding star to revisit when the path grew arduous: *"To become an engineer who builds sustainable solutions for rural empowerment."* This became his anchor, a powerful reminder that pulled him back on course during the toughest storms of self-doubt.

Failure Is Feedback, not a Finale

Next, we confronted the recurring setbacks of his mock tests, the source of immense frustration. I challenged his perception with a simple yet potent question: *"What did you learn from that experience that will make your next attempt smarter?"*

Rohan began to see failure not as a dead end, but as invaluable data. Each mistake held a lesson waiting to be unearthed. We implemented a Failure Log, a space to dissect each setback: identifying the misstep, extracting the insight, and strategizing a different approach for the next attempt. For instance, he recognized that his problem-solving weaknesses demanded more targeted practice, and he consciously avoided repeating past errors. His mindset underwent a crucial shift: from the paralysis of defeat to the proactive engagement of learning.

Own Your Outcome

Rohan's next hurdle was embracing complete ownership of his success. He had a tendency to attribute his struggles to external factors – the study materials, distractions, even the test format. To dismantle this limiting mindset, I challenged him: *"If no external force is coming to rescue you, what will you do differently?"*

This question resonated deeply. Rohan realized he was passively waiting for ideal conditions. We then crafted an Extreme Ownership Contract, a personal declaration: *"I, Rohan, take full responsibility for my progress. No excuses. No distractions. I will act with unwavering focus and drive."* This pivotal moment marked a profound change. He ceased waiting for external circumstances to align and instead took decisive action to create the environment for his own success, recognizing that the power to transform his reality resided within him.

Growth Is a Group Sport

While diligently working, Rohan also understood that this journey did not necessitate solitude. I prompted him: *"Who challenges you to become a better version of yourself?"*

After thoughtful consideration, he recognized that his peers were navigating similar challenges, and a collective effort could propel them all forward. We explored the power of collaboration, and Rohan took the initiative to form a Mastermind Group with two like-minded classmates, each committed to mutual accountability. Their weekly meetings became a vital space for sharing progress, dissecting obstacles, and offering invaluable support, transforming potential competition into a powerful alliance.

Transformation & Adaptability

Throughout his preparation, an unexpected change in the exam format threatened to derail his progress. But this became an opportunity to embody a crucial coaching principle: *"Don't wait for change to disrupt you—lead the change within you."*

Instead of succumbing to panic or resistance, Rohan embraced adaptability. He proactively integrated new study materials, online mock tests, and digital tools to align with the updated structure. Rather than reacting to change, he anticipated it, staying ahead of the curve and cultivating the agility to navigate unforeseen challenges.

Integrity & Authenticity

Finally, we delved into Rohan's core values. I asked: *"What principle will you refuse to compromise, regardless of the pressure?"* His response, delivered with conviction, was: *"I will remain true to my principles. No shortcuts. No cheating."* This solidified into his Integrity Statement, a personal pledge to act with unwavering honesty and authenticity, irrespective of external pressures or temptations. He committed to navigating the challenging journey with his values as his unwavering guide.

The Results

The student who sat for his entrance exam was a far cry from the overwhelmed individual who first sought guidance. Rohan had undergone a profound transformation, evolving from someone paralyzed by the fear of failure into a driven, resilient individual fuelled by purpose and ownership.

His strong performance in the exam was a testament to this inner shift, a direct result of his unwavering commitment to his purpose, his ability to extract wisdom from setbacks, his proactive ownership of his outcomes, and his agile adaptability to change. Furthermore, the robust support network he cultivated through his Mastermind

Group and his steadfast adherence to his integrity provided an unshakeable foundation.

Rohan's journey stands as a powerful real-world embodiment of the IMPACT Coaching Framework, demonstrating how purpose, accountability, growth, collaboration, and integrity can indeed turn aspirations into tangible realities.

Reflection

Rohan's story resonates as a potent reminder of the transformative power of coaching, guided by the principles of the IMPACT framework. As you navigate your own challenges, I invite you to consider:

What one action can you take this week to embody these coaching qualities in your life?

Chapter summary:

Here are five action-oriented coaching questions and corresponding actions based on the insights shared:

1. Purpose Fuels Endurance

- **Coaching Question**: *What would you fight for, even if you knew you might not win?*

- **Action**: **Define Your Mission**: Create a clear statement of purpose that reflects your core beliefs and passions. Revisit it regularly to ensure your actions are aligned with this mission. When facing challenges, reconnect with your purpose as your driving force.

2. Failure Is Feedback, not a Finale

- **Coaching Question**: *What did you learn that makes your next attempt smarter?*

- **Action**: **Maintain a Failure Log**: Track your setbacks and treat each one as an opportunity to learn. For every failure, write down key insights and actions you can take to improve moving forward. Use this log to build resilience and a growth mindset.

3. Own Your Outcome

- **Coaching Question**: *If no one else is coming to save you, what will you do differently?*

- **Action**: **Create an Extreme Ownership Contract**: Write a contract with yourself where you take full responsibility for your success and failures. This accountability tool ensures that you stop waiting for circumstances to change and start actively driving your outcomes.

4. Growth Is a Group Sport

- **Coaching Question**: *Who challenges you to be better?*

- **Action**: **Build a Mastermind Group**: Surround yourself with individuals who push you to grow, challenge your thinking, and hold you accountable. Commit to regular meetings where you can share progress, discuss obstacles, and provide mutual support for personal and professional growth.

5. Integrity is the Unshakable Foundation

- **Coaching Question**: *What value will you refuse to compromise, no matter what?*

- **Action**: **Craft Your Integrity Statement**: Write a personal statement outlining the core values that define who you are. Make a pledge to yourself that no matter the external pressures, you will always act in alignment with these values. Refer back to it whenever faced with tough decisions.

These coaching questions and actions provide a structured path to transform intentions into meaningful, lasting change. By reflecting deeply and taking consistent action, you can harness the power of purpose, resilience, accountability, collaboration, and integrity to shape your leadership journey.

Concluding Reflection:

What one action can you take this week to embody the Coaching qualities discussed in the chapter?

These questions can help facilitate deeper reflection and dialogue, encouraging individuals to connect their personal experiences with the principles outlined in the text

Chapter 3

Coaching in Action — Historical & Legendary Leaders

Leadership is not just a theory we read about or a concept we study in classrooms; it is a dynamic force that thrives in the real world through action. It is forged in moments of adversity, shaped by challenges, and tested through the resilience of those who lead. In this chapter, we will journey through time, exploring the lives of legendary leaders who did not just understand leadership—they embodied it. These figures have transformed not only their own lives but also the world around them through the principles of coaching, resilience, and visionary thinking. Their stories offer profound insights into how the IMPACT Coaching Framework can be applied to create extraordinary results, not only for individuals but for entire nations and organizations.

As we delve into these historical and modern figures, we will see how their leadership journeys were marked by more than just tactical brilliance—they were powered by deep, purposeful coaching that focused on the growth and transformation of both themselves and those they led. From the strategic genius of Chandragupta Maurya and Chanakya to the unyielding leadership of Shackleton in the frozen wilderness, each of these leaders demonstrated how principles of coaching and personal development can shape destiny.

Through their experiences, we will uncover how the IMPACT Coaching Framework—through its focus on mindset, purpose-driven goals, adaptability, and fostering unity—can be an effective tool in shaping the leaders of tomorrow. Each story we share in this chapter serves as a powerful reminder that leadership is not static or born in a vacuum; it is cultivated, coached, and brought to life in action.

The narratives of these legendary figures, ranging from military leaders to nation builders, are not just historical accounts. They are practical examples of leadership in motion, showcasing how coaching can drive both personal and collective transformation. By studying these figures, we will gain insight into how to implement coaching techniques that foster resilience, adaptability, and sustainable success in any context. Through their actions, we will explore how coaching can help leaders conquer fear, build purpose, and create lasting legacies.

In this chapter, we will look at leaders like:

- Chandragupta Maurya and Chanakya, whose story is not just one of royal conquest but also of the wisdom of mentorship, vision, and purpose-driven leadership.

- Napoleon Bonaparte, whose leadership mindset transformed him from an ambitious officer to an emperor, shaping the future of nations with his bold strategies.

- Zhuge Liang, whose strategic brilliance, and leadership wisdom turned adversity into victory, creating a lasting legacy through his thoughtful leadership.

- Ernest Shackleton, whose unshakable will to survive and unwavering focus on his crew's safety guided them through the harshest conditions imaginable.

- Lee Kuan Yew, whose approach to nation-building was grounded in coaching, mentorship, and a relentless focus on transformation for the collective good.

- The Sierra Leone peacekeeping mission, which shows how collective leadership, collaboration, and coaching can rebuild nations from the brink of collapse.

In each of these stories, we will uncover how the powerful principles of coaching were applied to achieve not just short-term successes but transformative, long-lasting impact. As you read through these accounts, reflect on the lessons they offer for today's leadership challenges and imagine how the IMPACT Coaching Framework can be the key to unlocking extraordinary potential in your own leadership journey.

Key Topics:

- **The Fire That Forged a King: The Story of Chandragupta Maurya & Chanakya**

- **Napoleon Bonaparte: The Leader Who Transformed Himself and the World**

- **Zhuge Liang: The Mastermind of Leadership and Strategy**

- **Shackleton's Unbreakable Will: A Leadership Odyssey in the Frozen Wasteland**

- **Lee Kuan Yew: A Master Coach in Nation-Building and Leadership Development**
- **The Sierra Leone Peacekeeping Story: A Journey from Chaos to Stability**
- **From Chaos to Courage: How Coaching Can Rebuild a War-Torn Nation**

Story-15:

The Fire That Forged a King: The Story of Chandragupta Maurya & Chanakya

> **"A lion born in a cage never knows its own strength."**

The words echoed in **Chandragupta's mind** as he watched the Nanda king's golden chariots roll past. He was just a boy, barefoot and hungry, yet something inside him burned—a fire of defiance. He was not meant to beg for scraps. He was meant to rule. But who would believe that a lowborn child could change the fate of an empire?

The world saw him as nothing. But one man saw everything.

- **Identity: Discovering True Strengths (I)**

It was **Chanakya**, the exiled scholar, who found Chandragupta in the dusty streets of Takshashila. He studied the boy's sharp eyes, his unyielding stance. "You have the heart of a ruler," he said. "But a sword without a mind is just a piece of metal."

That night, under the moonlight, **Chanakya tested him**—could he endure pain? Deception? Loss? Chandragupta refused to break. His strength was not just in his muscles but in his **unyielding spirit**.

A king had been found. But a king without wisdom is just a tyrant.

- **Mindset: Developing a Success-Oriented Mindset (M)**

Chanakya was a harsh teacher. He made Chandragupta go **days without food**, fight against **skilled warriors twice his size**, and endure **humiliation without reaction**. "A ruler cannot be ruled by emotions," he said. "Anger is a weapon—use it wisely, or it will destroy you."

One day, a soldier **spat on Chandragupta**, mocking his dream of ruling Magadha. The boy clenched his fists but did not strike. Instead, he smiled. The soldier laughed. That same night, **that soldier's entire battalion switched sides**—Chandragupta had learned the art of patience.

- **Purpose: Setting Meaningful Goals (P)**

"Why do you want the throne?" Chanakya asked.

"Revenge," Chandragupta said.

"Then you will be no different from the tyrants before you," the scholar warned. "Rule must not be for anger, but for justice. The people suffer, and you must be their hope."

That night, **Chandragupta walked through the villages**, seeing the starving farmers, the broken streets. He saw his **own childhood in their eyes**. His purpose changed. It was not about vengeance. **It was about a future where no child would go to sleep hungry.**

- **Adaptability: Staying Committed to Change (A)**

The war for Magadha was not a straight path. Their first rebellion **failed miserably. Their men were captured, their food supplies burnt.**

But Chanakya smiled. "A battle lost is just a lesson learned."

They retreated into the forests, changed their tactics—**instead of attacking forts, they cut off supplies; instead of fighting armies, they turned villagers against their king.** Like water, they adapted, flowing around obstacles.

The Nanda king, once untouchable, now stood surrounded.

- **Connections: Building Strong Networks (C)**

Alone, Chandragupta was just a warrior. But with Chanakya, he was a **strategist**. With the villagers, he was a **leader**. With foreign allies, he became **unstoppable**.

He learned to **listen to wise counsel, to trust his generals, to unite enemies under a single cause.** Where others-built walls, **he built alliances.**

- **Transformation: Creating Lasting Success (T)**

And then, **on the fateful day**, the gates of Pataliputra swung open. Chandragupta, once a street boy, now rode in as a conqueror. The Nanda king knelt before him, the golden crown trembling in his hands.

But Chandragupta did not take revenge. **He let the old king live—proof that justice, not hatred, had won.**

His rule became the **foundation of an empire that lasted centuries.** His name became **legendary.** And at his side, **Chanakya smiled—not because the boy had become a king, but because he had become a ruler with purpose.**

History does not remember those who seek power. It remembers those who **use it for a greater cause**.

And so, the fire that once burned in the heart of a hungry boy **became the flame that lit an empire.**

> **"The strength of a ruler is not in his sword, but in his vision and wisdom."**
>
> **- Chanakya**

Key Coaching Messages for Coaches to Take Action:

1. **Unleash Potential, Not Just Skills** – A great coach does not just teach strategies; they reveal the leader hidden within. Like Chanakya saw the fire in Chandragupta, coaches must identify and nurture the untapped strengths of those they guide.

2. **Mindset Overcomes Circumstances** – True transformation begins in the mind. Help individuals shift from victimhood to leadership by cultivating emotional intelligence, resilience, and the ability to harness emotions like anger and fear into constructive power.

3. **Purpose Drives Sustainable Success** – Without a meaningful goal, talent is wasted. Coaches must instil a sense of higher purpose in their mentees—beyond personal gain—so they lead not just with ambition, but with vision and responsibility.

4. **Adaptability is the Key to Long-Term Impact** – Plans fail, battles are lost, but those who adapt thrive. Teach flexibility in thought, strategy, and execution so leaders can pivot when needed and turn setbacks into stepping stones.

5. **Leadership is Built Through Relationships** – No great leader rises alone. Coaches must emphasize the power of collaboration, mentorship, and alliances. Strength lies in the ability to unite, delegate, and empower others toward a common cause.

"Greatness isn't born—it's awakened. Just as Chanakya saw a king in a street boy, true coaching reveals the leader hidden within, ignites a resilient mindset, and aligns ambition with purpose to shape a legacy beyond self."

The main key takeaways from the story of **Chandragupta's journey** through **IMPACT coaching** could be:

- ***Unleash Inner Potential***: *Like Chanakya did for Chandragupta, coaches must look beyond what is visible and recognize the untapped potential within individuals. It is not just about teaching skills, but identifying and nurturing the inherent leadership qualities that can shape an extraordinary future.*

- ***Mindset is the Catalyst for Transformation***: *The transformation from a street boy to a king is a result of mindset. Success in coaching comes from helping individuals shift their perception and embrace resilience, emotional intelligence, and strategic patience. A powerful mindset is the foundation for overcoming obstacles and achieving greatness.*

- ***Purpose-Driven Leadership***: *Success is not defined by personal ambition or power, but by the meaningful purpose behind it. Coaches should guide individuals to discover their deeper purpose, whether in leadership or personal growth, so they can lead with vision, justice, and responsibility—not just for themselves, but for the greater good.*

Story-16:

Napoleon Bonaparte: The Leader Who Transformed Himself and the World

> **"Courage isn't having the strength to go on; it is going on when you don't have strength."**
>
> **– Napoleon Bonaparte**

The cold wind howled through the streets of Ajaccio, Corsica. A young boy, smaller than his peers, stood at the edge of the harbour, staring at the ships sailing toward distant lands. His clothes were simple, his accent marked him as an outsider, and his name carried little weight in the grand courts of Europe. Yet, in his heart, **Napoleon Bonaparte already saw himself as a leader.**

He had no title, no fortune, no noble lineage to secure his future. **But he had something far greater—a relentless belief in himself.** He knew that the world only remembered those who shaped it, and he was determined to carve his name into history.

Years later, the world would tremble at his name. **How did he do it?** How did an unknown Corsican rise to become one of history's most powerful rulers?

The answer lay in his ability to **reinvent himself**, to master his mind, and to apply timeless principles of leadership and transformation—principles that anyone can use to rise from ordinary to extraordinary.

Inspire Awareness & Identity – Know Yourself First

"A leader is a dealer in hope."

Napoleon was not born a general. He was not born a ruler. He was a boy who was mocked for his foreign accent, treated as an outsider in the elite military schools of France. **But he knew one thing—he was different.**

He studied history, strategy, and leadership. He watched how great rulers of the past had conquered not just lands, but the hearts of people.

He understood that before anyone else believed in him, he had to believe in himself.

The Turning Point:

At his coronation in 1804, Napoleon did something unheard of. Traditionally, the Pope placed the crown on the head of a new emperor, symbolizing divine authority. But as the Pope raised the crown, Napoleon took it from his hands and placed it on his own head. **The message was clear—he was not chosen by fate; he chose himself.**

Mindset & Mastery Shift – Overcoming Fear and Doubt

"Courage isn't having the strength to go on; it is going on when you don't have strength."

As a young officer, Napoleon was given command of a ragged army in Italy. **They were outnumbered, poorly supplied, and had little hope.** The generals before him had failed. The enemy had no fear of them.

Napoleon knew that battles were not just won with weapons; **they were won in the mind first.** He walked among his soldiers, speaking to them not as a superior, but as a man who understood their struggles. He told them of their potential, of the victories waiting for them.

They marched into battle not as a broken army, but as warriors with fire in their eyes. **They won battle after battle—not because they had more soldiers, but because they had more belief.**

The Lesson:

Every great leader, every successful person, faces doubt. The difference is that **they act despite their fear.**

Purpose-Driven Goals – A Vision Bigger Than Power

"Impossible is a word to be found only in the dictionary of fools."

Napoleon was not just a conqueror—**he was a builder.** While kings before him ruled with tradition, he ruled with vision. He saw a France where laws were fair, where talent mattered more than birth, where society moved with order and purpose.

To make this vision real, he created **the Napoleonic Code**, a system of laws that brought justice, equality, and order. **Today, that system still influences legal structures worldwide.**

The Lesson:

Success is not just about winning battles—it is about building something that outlives you. **What are you building? What will your legacy be?**

Action, Accountability & Adaptability – Thinking on His Feet

"Take time to deliberate, but when the time for action has arrived, stop thinking and go in."

Napoleon's genius was not just in planning—it was in action. **He made decisions faster than his enemies.** While others hesitated, he moved.

In 1806, he faced the powerful Prussian army at the Battle of Jena-Auerstedt. The Prussians believed they had the advantage. Napoleon studied their formations, saw their weakness, and struck with speed and precision. **The battle was over in hours.**

The Lesson:

Overthinking kills more dreams than failure ever will. **Action, not perfection, leads to success.**

Connection & Leadership – Earning Loyalty

"The strong man is the one who is able to intercept at will the communication between the senses and the mind."

Napoleon did not command from a throne. **He walked among his soldiers, shared their hardships, and fought beside them.**

His troops did not just respect him—they loved him. They followed him even when the odds were against them, even when exile and defeat loomed. **This was not blind loyalty—it was earned trust.**

The Lesson:

True leadership is not about power—it is about **inspiring others to believe in something greater than themselves.**

Transformation & Legacy – Leaving a Mark on the World

"Death is nothing, but to live defeated and inglorious is to die daily."

Even in exile, Napoleon's ideas reshaped the world. His legal reforms, his military strategies, and his leadership principles continued to influence nations.

The world remembers those who create, who build, who transform.

The Lesson:

You do not have to lead an army to create an impact. **Your life, your work, and your actions can leave a lasting legacy.**

How You Can Apply Napoleon's Principles in Your Own Life

Your journey to growth begins with self-awareness.

Take a moment to reflect—what are you naturally good at, and what is holding you back? Understanding yourself is the first step to unlocking your potential.

Fear is a constant companion, but it does not have to control you. Doubts will always whisper in the background, yet every step forward is a choice. You can either let fear stop you or use it as fuel to move ahead.

Clarity is power. What do you truly want? Picture it vividly and put it into words. A dream remains a dream until you define it—then it becomes a goal.

The perfect moment does not exist. The longer you wait, the more opportunities pass by. Take action now, with whatever resources you have. Growth comes from starting, not waiting.

Success is not just about personal achievement; it is about the impact you have on others. Real leaders lift people up, inspire change, and create opportunities for those around them.

And in the end, what will remain? Your legacy is shaped by the actions you take today. The way you lead, the way you inspire, and the way you contribute will determine how you are remembered. Every choice you make now leaves a mark on the future.

Napoleon was not born great. **He became great.**

And so can you.

Your journey starts with one step. **What will yours be today?**

Here are key coaching messages from this text:

1. ***Great Leaders Shape Their Own Identity***

   *True leadership begins with **self-awareness and belief** in oneself. Napoleon did not wait for external validation—he **chose himself** as a leader. Before others can follow you, you must first believe in your own potential. **Ask yourself:** What identity am I crafting? Am I waiting for permission, or am I stepping into leadership?*

2. ***Fear is Inevitable—Action is a Choice***

   *Courage is not the absence of fear but the decision to act despite it. Napoleon **transformed his army's mindset** by instilling belief, proving that mental strength often wins over external circumstances. **Ask yourself:** What fears are holding me back? How can I take one step forward today despite my doubts?*

3. ***Purpose-Driven Leadership Leaves a Legacy***

   *True success is not just about personal achievement—it is about **creating something that outlives you**. Napoleon's Napoleonic Code still influences laws today. **Ask yourself:** Am I just working for short-term wins, or am I building something meaningful?*

4. ***Decisiveness and Speed Drive Success***

   *Overthinking can kill progress. Napoleon's strength lay in **quick, strategic execution** rather than hesitation. Leaders must know when to **analyse and when to act**. **Ask yourself:** Am I stuck in analysis paralysis, or am I making bold moves toward my goals?*

5. ***Leadership is Earned Through Trust and Connection***

   *Napoleon's soldiers followed him not just because of his title, but because he **stood with them, understood their struggles, and led by example**. Leadership is not about control—it is* *about **inspiring people to believe in something greater**. **Ask yourself**: Am I leading with authority, or am I leading with connection and trust?*

*Each of these coaching messages is a call to **action**—to believe in yourself, act despite fear, create lasting impact, move with speed, and lead with trust. Napoleon was not born great—he **became** great. The same path is available to anyone willing to step into their potential.*

> **"Great ambition is the passion of a great character. Those endowed with it may perform very good or very bad acts. All depends on the principles which direct them."**
>
> **– Napoleon Bonaparte**

Story-17:

Zhuge Liang: The Mastermind of Leadership and Strategy

> ***"Great coaches, like Zhuge Liang, don't rush to lead—they wait for the moment when wisdom is truly valued over force."***

Zhuge Liang, also known as **Kongming,** was one of the most legendary strategists, statesmen, and scholars in Chinese history.

He lived during the tumultuous Three Kingdoms period, a time of intense warfare and shifting allegiances, yet he rose above the chaos with a mind as sharp as a blade and wisdom that transcended generations.

He was not just a military genius but also a master of diplomacy, governance, and leadership, shaping the course of history with his intellect and foresight.

The Rise of a Strategic Mastermind

Born in 181 AD in present-day Shandong, Zhuge Liang was orphaned at a young age and spent his early years in seclusion, studying philosophy, military strategy, and Confucian principles. Unlike many who sought fame and power, he remained humble and patient, believing that true leadership was not seized but earned. He compared himself to the mythical Sleeping Dragon, waiting for the right moment to awaken.

That moment came when Liu Bei, a warlord with ambitions to restore the Han Dynasty, sought his counsel. Unlike others who would have rushed to serve, Zhuge Liang tested Liu Bei's patience. He famously made him visit three times before agreeing to join his cause. This was not arrogance—it was a lesson in persistence, a challenge to prove that Liu Bei truly valued wisdom over brute force.

The Art of Leadership and Strategy

Once he stepped into Liu Bei's service, Zhuge Liang became the architect of his success. He was not merely an advisor; he was a teacher who shaped Liu Bei into a true leader. He crafted grand strategies that turned a struggling warlord into a powerful ruler. One of his most remarkable achievements was the "Longzhong Plan," a vision that guided Liu Bei in securing territories and forging key alliances to establish the Shu Han kingdom.

His battlefield strategies were legendary. He understood that victory did not always come from superior numbers but from superior thinking. One of his most famous moments was the "Empty Fort Strategy," where he bluffed an advancing army into retreating by leaving a city's gates wide open and sitting calmly on the walls, playing his guqin. The enemy, suspecting a trap, fled without a fight. This was not mere luck—it was psychological warfare at its finest.

A Master of Adaptability and Governance

Beyond military strategy, Zhuge Liang was a master administrator. When Liu Bei died, leaving behind a young heir, Zhuge Liang did not abandon the kingdom. Instead, he became its regent, guiding the next generation and ensuring stability. He reformed governance, built strong infrastructure, and upheld justice, earning the trust of his people. His ability to balance authority with compassion made him a revered leader.

But what truly set him apart was his resilience. He faced overwhelming odds, betrayals, and setbacks, yet he never wavered. When one plan failed, he adapted. When challenges arose, he found solutions. He led five northern campaigns to unify China, pushing forward despite exhaustion and dwindling resources. Even in his final days, as illness took hold, he continued to strategize, unwilling to let his vision fade.

Legacy of a Timeless Coach and Mentor

Zhuge Liang was not just a war strategist; he was a coach in the truest sense. He mentored leaders, instilled confidence in his soldiers, and inspired loyalty through wisdom rather than fear. His writings on leadership, strategy, and governance became timeless lessons, studied by emperors, scholars, and modern-day leaders alike.

His legacy remains alive not just in history books but in the very philosophy of leadership and strategic thinking. He taught that true power lies not in force, but in knowledge, foresight, and the ability to inspire others. Even centuries after his passing, his name symbolizes intelligence, perseverance, and the art of turning adversity into opportunity.

Zhuge Liang was not just a man of his time—he was a legend whose wisdom continues to shape the minds of leaders across generations.

Aligning Zhuge Liang's Coaching Philosophy with the IMPACT Coaching Framework

Zhuge Liang's coaching philosophy closely aligns with the **IMPACT** framework, which emphasizes **strategic awareness, mindset shifts, purpose-driven goals, adaptability, collaboration, and long-term transformation.** His approach to leadership, decision-making, and mentorship reflects the **same core principles** found in modern coaching. Here's how Zhuge Liang's methods align with IMPACT:

Inspire Awareness & Identity → Zhuge Liang Developed Leaders by Awakening Their Strategic Identity

Zhuge Liang's approach to leadership development centered on self-awareness and purpose, emphasizing that true success begins with a clear sense of identity. Before guiding others in action, he first helped them see their own potential and purpose. His coaching of Liu Bei exemplified this philosophy—rather than treating him as just another warrior, Zhuge Liang encouraged him to envision himself as a future ruler, a leader destined to restore the Han Dynasty. This shift in identity was crucial, as it transformed Liu Bei from a wandering fighter into a leader with a mission greater than himself.

Beyond inspiring Liu Bei, Zhuge Liang extended his wisdom to all those under his guidance, instilling in them the belief that they were fighting not just for survival but for a higher cause. His ability to recognize hidden talents allowed him to groom future leaders, selecting individuals who possessed both skill and conviction. He understood that leadership is not just about ability but about the mindset and vision behind it.

One of the most defining moments of this coaching philosophy was his initial reluctance to serve Liu Bei. Zhuge Liang tested Liu Bei's dedication, ensuring that he was truly committed to his purpose before accepting him as his leader. This mirrors the core principle of coaching—before taking action, one must first clarify their identity, values, and long-term goals. Just as Zhuge Liang refused to invest his efforts in a leader who lacked self-awareness, effective coaching today starts with deep introspection, ensuring that actions are aligned with a strong, purposeful vision.

Mindset & Mastery Shift → Zhuge Liang Transformed Fear into Resilient Leadership

Zhuge Liang's philosophy emphasized the power of mindset in leadership, demonstrating that fear could be transformed into confidence through wisdom, patience, and strategic thinking. He believed that true victory was not just a matter of physical strength but of mental resilience and tactical foresight. His coaching approach trained leaders to remain calm under pressure, turning uncertainty into an opportunity for decisive action. By reframing fear as a tool for strategy rather than an obstacle, he ensured that his allies made sound decisions even in the most dire situations.

One of the most famous examples of his mastery over perception and confidence was the "Empty Fort Strategy." Facing an overwhelming enemy force, Zhuge Liang made a bold move—he left his city gates open, played music calmly, and sat atop the walls in plain sight. His calculated display of confidence created the illusion that a hidden ambush awaited, leading the enemy to retreat without a single arrow being fired. This moment encapsulated his belief that a leader's mindset could shape reality; fear, when replaced with strategic thinking, becomes a tool for victory rather than defeat.

By applying this approach in coaching, modern leaders can learn to reframe their own fears, approach challenges with confidence, and use perception as a strategic advantage. Whether in business or personal growth, those who adopt Zhuge Liang's mindset shift from reactive decision-making to proactive leadership, ensuring that obstacles become stepping stones toward success.

Purpose-Driven Goals & Strategy → Zhuge Liang Created Step-by-Step Blueprints for Success

A core principle of the IMPACT framework is the alignment of vision with actionable goals, a concept Zhuge Liang mastered in his approach to leadership and strategy. Unlike leaders who acted impulsively, driven by short-term gains, Zhuge Liang emphasized the importance of long-term vision. His dream of restoring the Han Dynasty was not merely an abstract ideal—it was backed by a meticulously crafted roadmap, ensuring that every decision contributed to a greater purpose.

His strategy was holistic, considering battles, alliances, and negotiations as interconnected steps toward a larger objective. Rather than chasing immediate victories, Zhuge Liang guided Liu Bei to first establish a solid foundation. He knew that lasting success required securing key territories, resources, and political alliances before engaging in large-scale conflict. His ability to balance ambition with patience allowed him to turn seemingly impossible situations into strategic victories.

One of the greatest examples of this philosophy was his counsel to Liu Bei before the Battle of Red Cliffs. When Liu Bei, eager to expand his influence, wanted to launch an aggressive attack against his enemies, Zhuge Liang urged restraint. Instead of rushing into battle, he advised forming alliances—most notably with Sun Quan. This strategic patience ultimately led to one of the most decisive victories in Chinese history. The success at Red Cliffs was not a result of reckless ambition but of careful planning, diplomatic foresight, and a commitment to a long-term vision.

Zhuge Liang's approach mirrors modern leadership and coaching principles, where sustainable success comes from aligning one's grand vision with practical, well-structured goals. It serves as a reminder that true impact is not about immediate wins but about laying the groundwork for meaningful and lasting transformation.

Action, Accountability & Adaptability → Zhuge Liang Ensured Execution & Adjusted to Change

Execution, accountability, and adaptability were central to both Zhuge Liang's coaching philosophy and the IMPACT framework. His brilliance lay not just in devising grand strategies but in ensuring their disciplined execution. Unlike leaders who relied solely on rigid plans, Zhuge Liang instilled a culture of responsibility, learning, and continuous refinement.

He maintained strict accountability within his ranks, demanding precision and discipline from his army and leadership. Every officer understood their role, and failure was not met with blame but with constructive learning. His belief in adaptability was evident in his approach to warfare—he never adhered blindly to a single strategy but continuously adjusted his tactics based on new intelligence, shifting circumstances, and unexpected challenges.

A defining characteristic of Zhuge Liang's leadership was his ability to pivot when plans did not unfold as expected. Despite meticulous preparation, some of his military campaigns encountered unforeseen setbacks. Rather than retreating into defeat, he treated these setbacks as opportunities for recalibration. He shifted resources, altered battle formations, and devised new tactics—all while maintaining the morale and trust of his soldiers. His resilience ensured that obstacles did not derail his vision but instead strengthened his strategic agility.

His approach offers a valuable lesson for modern leadership and coaching. Success is not about rigidly following an initial plan—it is about execution with accountability and the ability to adapt when reality presents new challenges. Leaders who embrace this mindset foster teams that are not only disciplined but also agile, capable of overcoming adversity and driving sustained impact.

Connection & Collaborative Growth → Zhuge Liang Built Trust & Mentored Future Leaders

Just as the IMPACT framework emphasizes collaborative leadership, Zhuge Liang believed that true greatness lay in empowering others rather than ruling through fear. His leadership style was rooted in mentorship, trust, and the belief that collective strength always surpasses individual brilliance.

He personally mentored emerging leaders, including Liu Shan, guiding them through complex decisions, and preparing them for future responsibilities. Unlike leaders who hoarded power, Zhuge Liang created an environment where his officers felt valued and trusted. His ability to cultivate loyalty and teamwork ensured that his strategies were executed with precision and dedication. His officers followed him not out of obligation, but because they believed in his vision and leadership.

Zhuge Liang's commitment to building a strong, unified team was evident in his approach to governance and military strategy. He recognized that a well-coordinated team, where each individual understood their role and strengths, could achieve far more than even the most brilliant leader acting alone. His ability to align different talents towards a shared goal was one of his greatest strengths.

Even in his final moments, Zhuge Liang remained dedicated to his people. On his deathbed, he did not cling to power but instead ensured that responsibilities were delegated effectively. He left behind not only strategies for his successors but also a culture of wisdom, discipline, and teamwork. His legacy was not just in his victories but in the lasting impact of his teachings, proving that true leadership is about preparing the next generation to carry the vision forward.

Transform & thrive → Zhuge Liang's Leadership Philosophy Became a Timeless Coaching Model

IMPACT's final stage focuses on lasting transformation, ensuring that the lessons learned lead to sustained success. Zhuge Liang's influence extended far beyond his own lifetime—his principles of leadership, strategy, and mentorship continue to inspire leaders, military strategists, and scholars even today.

He was not merely a brilliant tactician; he was a transformational leader who shaped the destiny of his people. Under his guidance, Liu Bei evolved from a wandering warrior into an emperor, embodying the idea that true leadership is cultivated, not inherited. Zhuge Liang's coaching did not just focus on winning battles—it was about building enduring systems of governance, strategy, and leadership that would outlive him.

His impact was not confined to his era. The strategies he developed, the governance structures he implemented, and the psychological insights he applied to leadership have stood the test of time. His teachings continue to be referenced in modern business strategy, military training, and leadership development. His military texts and philosophies are still studied today, proving that great leadership transcends time.

Zhuge Liang's story is a testament to the power of coaching, mentorship, and vision-driven leadership. His legacy reminds us that true success is not measured by personal achievements alone but by the systems, knowledge, and inspiration we leave behind for future generations.

Zhuge Liang as an IMPACT Coach

Zhuge Liang's coaching methods perfectly align with the **IMPACT coaching framework.** His ability to **inspire awareness, shift mindsets, create strategic roadmaps, execute with adaptability, foster collaboration, and ensure long-term transformation** made him one of history's greatest coaches.

Just as IMPACT helps individuals unlock their full potential, Zhuge Liang's philosophy turned warriors into leaders, fear into confidence, and ambition into lasting success.

Unlocking Zhuge Liang's Strategic Wisdom Through the IMPACT Coaching Framework

Inspire Awareness & Identity

Zhuge Liang understood that leadership starts with self-awareness. He did not seek power for its own sake but waited until the right leader—Liu

Bei—recognized his potential. He was clear about his role, his strengths, and his purpose.

Lesson for You: Reflect on who you are as a leader. Are you seeking leadership for power, or do you truly want to create impact? Recognize your strengths, define your values, and embrace your role with clarity and confidence.

Mindset & Mastery Shift

Zhuge Liang's greatest weapon was not an army—it was his ability to outthink his enemies. He turned challenges into opportunities, whether through the Empty Fort Strategy or his meticulous battle plans. He saw every setback as a chance to learn and improve.

Lesson for You: Shift from a reactive mindset to a strategic one. Instead of fearing challenges, see them as opportunities to apply wisdom and creativity. Train yourself to think beyond obstacles and develop mastery in decision-making.

Purpose-Driven Goals & Strategy

Zhuge Liang's Longzhong Plan was not a short-term tactic—it was a long-term vision for restoring the Han dynasty. His strategies were clear, precise, and aligned with his greater mission.

Lesson for You: Define your vision with purpose. What is your ultimate goal? Break it down into clear, actionable steps. Whether in business, leadership, or personal growth, having a well-thought-out plan will set you apart.

Action, Accountability & Adaptability

Zhuge Liang was not just a thinker; he was a doer. He executed his plans with discipline and resilience. When one strategy failed, he adapted. When resources were low, he found creative solutions. He held himself accountable to his mission, ensuring his actions always aligned with his principles.

Lesson for You: Take decisive action. Don't just plan—execute. Hold yourself accountable to your goals. Adapt to changing situations while staying true to your purpose. Resilience and flexibility are the keys to sustained success.

Connection & Collaborative Growth

He did not fight alone. He built alliances, mentored warriors, and inspired loyalty. Even in times of war, he focused on creating strong relationships *based on trust and shared purpose. His ability to unite people was as powerful as his strategic mind.*

Lesson for You: *Build meaningful connections. Leadership is not a solo journey. Empower others, create trust, and foster collaboration. Great success comes from working together toward a common goal.*

Transform & Thrive

Zhuge Liang's leadership was not just about winning battles—it was about shaping the future. His influence lasted far beyond his lifetime, inspiring countless leaders who followed. His ability to combine wisdom, resilience, and strategic action made him a timeless figure in leadership and coaching.

Lesson for You: *True transformation comes when you apply these principles consistently. Leadership is about leaving a lasting impact. Focus on continuous growth, refine your strategies, and commit to a purpose greater than yourself.*

*By applying the **IMPACT Coaching Framework**, Zhuge Liang's wisdom becomes more than just history—it becomes a practical guide for leadership, strategy, and personal growth. Whether in business, personal development, or team leadership, these principles can help you think smarter, act decisively, and create a lasting impact in your field.*

> **"True leadership is not about seizing power, but shaping destiny with patience, purpose, and profound strategy."**
>
> **- Anonymous**

Story-18:

Shackleton's Unbreakable Will: A Leadership Odyssey in the Frozen Wasteland

> **"The greatest leader is not necessarily the one who does the greatest things. He is the one that gets the people to do the greatest things."**
>
> **— Ronald Reagan**

In the biting cold of Antarctica, where the wind howled like a beast and the ice stretched endlessly in all directions, Sir Ernest Shackleton faced the ultimate test of leadership. It was 1914, and he had set out on an ambitious journey—the Imperial Trans-Antarctic Expedition, aiming to be the first to cross the frozen continent. But nature had other plans.

The **Endurance,** his ship, became trapped in the pack ice, a prisoner to the unrelenting polar grip. Shackleton and his 28 men could only watch as the ice slowly crushed the ship, their lifeline to civilization sinking beneath the frigid waters. With no radio, no way to send for help, and temperatures plunging to deadly lows, hope could have easily faded into despair. But Shackleton refused to surrender to fear.

Rather than allowing panic to take hold, he transformed the crisis into a mission—not of exploration, but of survival. He **became the anchor** his men needed, keeping their minds sharp and their spirits alive. He enforced daily routines, encouraged laughter, and never allowed despair to settle in. He understood that in a fight against nature, **the mind was just as critical as the body.**

Months passed. The ice floes carried them farther from their intended path, forcing them to camp on a shifting frozen ocean. When survival seemed impossible, Shackleton made the boldest decision of his life. He would take a small lifeboat and sail **800 miles across the world's most violent seas** to South Georgia, where he could find help. The journey was madness—16 days of unrelenting storms, waves taller than buildings, and freezing spray that turned their clothes into ice.

Starving, exhausted, and frostbitten, they finally reached land— but they had landed on the wrong side of the island. No time for rest. Shackleton and two men set off on foot, hiking **36 hours without stopping,** crossing glaciers and mountains, until they stumbled into a whaling station. Shackleton, covered in ice and nearly unrecognizable, had done the impossible. He had reached help.

But his mission was not over. His men were still stranded, waiting for him to return. Over the next few months, Shackleton led a rescue effort and, after two years in Antarctic isolation, brought back **every single one of his crew alive.** Not one man had perished under his command.

Shackleton's leadership was more than strategy—it was sheer mental fortitude. He never allowed doubt to control him, **adapting at every**

turn, making decisions not just with logic but with an intuitive understanding of human resilience. He knew that survival wasn't just about physical endurance, but about **keeping the spirit unbroken.**

His story remains one of the greatest testaments to **courage, adaptability, and the power of the human will.** In the face of impossible odds, he proved that a leader's mindset is the force that can turn defeat into triumph.

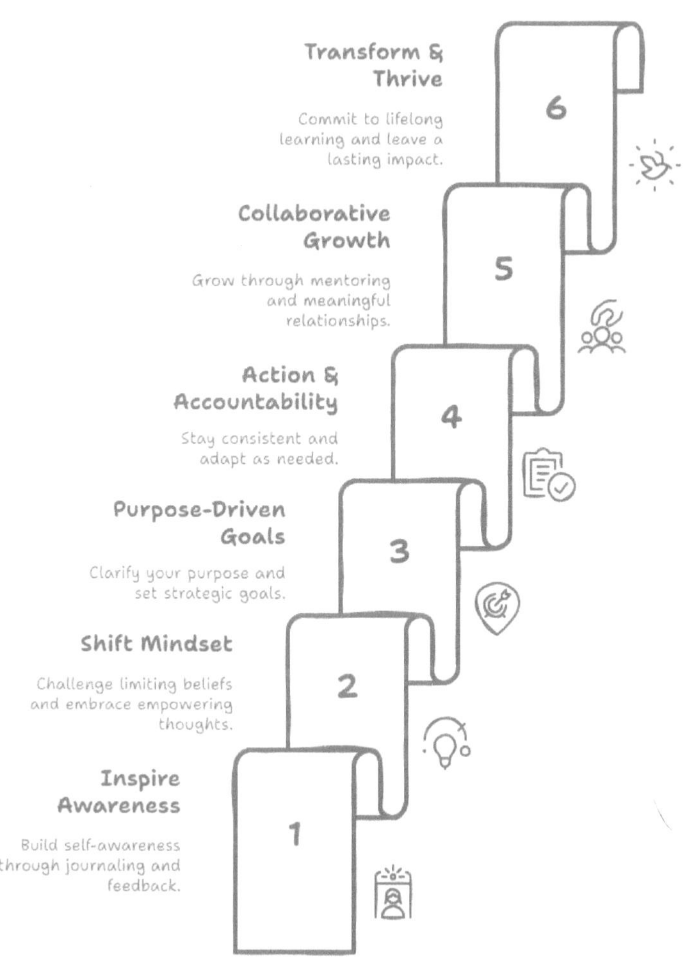

Applying the IMPACT Framework to Shackleton's Leadership Story

Sir Ernest Shackleton's survival against impossible odds during the Endurance Expedition is a powerful example of leadership, mental agility, and resilience. By mapping his actions to the **IMPACT Coaching Framework,** we can uncover **hidden coaching elements** that helped him and his crew survive.

1. I - Inspire Awareness & Identity

The biting Antarctic wind cut through the air as Shackleton surveyed his men—exhausted, hungry, and stranded on an endless sheet of ice. Just months ago, he had been an explorer chasing history, eager to cross Antarctica. Now, history no longer mattered. Survival did.

The weight of leadership pressed heavy on his shoulders. This wasn't about reaching the South Pole anymore—it was about bringing every man home. He took a breath, steadying himself. Who was he now? Not just a captain, not just a visionary, but a protector. His crew didn't need grand ambitions; they needed hope, structure, and unwavering confidence.

Doubt tried to creep in, whispering that the odds were against them. He silenced it. Fear had no place here. Every word, every action, every decision he made had to reinforce one thing: *we will survive.* He listened closely to his crew, watching their body language, adjusting his leadership with each passing day. If their spirits faltered, so would their will to fight. He could not allow that.

A leader is not just the sum of their ambitions but the strength they bring to others in their darkest moments. Shackleton redefined himself, not by his original mission, but by the lives he refused to lose.

When everything falls apart, who are you?

2. M - Mindset & Mastery Shift

The ice groaned, then roared like a living beast. Shackleton stood motionless for a moment, watching his ship—the *Endurance*—splinter and sink beneath the frozen wasteland. Everything was gone. No vessel, no supplies, no escape route. Just an endless stretch of ice and the howling Antarctic wind. Fear could have taken hold, but Shackleton refused to let it.

He turned to his men, their eyes wide with uncertainty. "Ship and stores have gone," he said, his voice steady. "Now we go home." There was no room for panic, no space for despair. His belief became their belief. If he had shown fear, it would have spread like frostbite. Instead, he rewrote the story: this was not the end—this was a new beginning.

Like Mandela, locked away in a prison cell for 27 years yet never surrendering to hopelessness, Shackleton carried an unwavering optimism. He saw beyond the present hardship and focused on what *could* be done. Every night, he told stories, cracked jokes, and lifted spirits, ensuring his men remained mentally strong. He trained them to shift fear into action, to see problems as obstacles to be conquered rather than threats to survival.

Fear is a choice, and so is action. When faced with adversity, which will you choose?

3. P - Purpose-Driven Goals & Strategy

The moment the *Endurance* was swallowed by the ice, Shackleton's mission shattered. The dream of crossing Antarctica was gone. But where most would see failure, he saw a new purpose—survival. Every decision, every step forward, was no longer about exploration; it was about bringing every single man home alive.

He wasted no time mourning what was lost. Instead, he redrew the map in his mind. The goal had changed, but his leadership remained unshaken. First, he moved the team to stable ice. Then, as conditions worsened, he led them on a gruelling journey in lifeboats, battling the merciless sea until they reached the barren safety of Elephant Island. But survival there was impossible—rescue was 800 miles away, across some of the most treacherous waters on Earth. And so, with only a handful of men, Shackleton set off again, sailing in an open boat through hurricane-force winds, navigating by instinct and the stars, until they reached South Georgia.

Every step of the journey was a calculated move. He did not rely on hope—he relied on strategy, planning, and the unbreakable trust of his crew. Success was no longer about glory; it was about *life itself.*

Shackleton understood a fundamental truth: when faced with uncertainty, clear goals and decisive actions make the difference between survival and collapse. What does success look like for you? And more importantly—do you have a plan to get there?

4. A - Action, Accountability & Adaptability

The ice cracked like gunfire beneath them. Shackleton's ship, *Endurance*, groaned as the frozen sea tightened its grip, splintering the wooden hull. The dream of reaching Antarctica was gone. Now, survival was the only goal.

Without hesitation, Shackleton moved. There was no time for mourning lost plans. He gathered his men, his voice firm, unwavering. "We adapt, or we die." The mission had changed, and so had he.

Gone was the explorer who had meticulously mapped out each stage of the journey. In his place stood a leader who understood that rigidity meant failure. He discarded old plans like useless maps, crafting new strategies as the situation evolved. One moment, he was a navigator; the next, a hunter, a cook, a caretaker. Whatever was needed, he became.

But adaptability was not enough. Leadership demanded more. Shackleton bore the weight of every life on his shoulders. He did not send men into the cold—he walked with them. He did not demand endurance—he embodied it. When food ran low, he gave up his portion. When spirits wavered, he told stories by firelight, weaving hope into the frozen night.

Each decision was deliberate. *What must I do right now?* He set survival protocols, rationed supplies, and maintained strict discipline. *How do I ensure I follow through?* He held himself to the highest standard, never wavering, never allowing despair to take root.

He did not just react to change—he anticipated it, adjusted, and thrived within the chaos. And because he refused to break, neither did his men.

True leadership is not about the plan that gets you there. It is about the choices you make when everything falls apart.

5. C - Connection & Collaborative Growth

The wind howled through the ice, a relentless reminder of the brutal conditions Shackleton and his men faced. Each day was a battle—not just against the cold, but against despair. Starvation gnawed at their stomachs. The endless white stretched in every direction, a frozen prison with no clear escape.

Shackleton knew that survival was not just about rations or endurance—it was about morale. A broken spirit was more dangerous than the bitter Antarctic cold. He moved among his men, listening, observing, reading the exhaustion in their eyes and the tension in their voices.

Some suffered in silence, their fear masked by forced smiles. Others grew restless, their patience fraying with each passing day. Shackleton took action. He did not just command—he connected. He assigned the most anxious, the most cynical men to his own tent, keeping them close where he could personally lift their spirits. At night, he shared stories of home, of adventures yet to come, painting a future beyond the ice. He made sure no man felt forgotten; no mind was left to fester in the grip of fear.

Leadership was not about standing above—it was about standing *with*. He delegated tasks with care, ensuring that everyone played a vital role. He turned hardship into shared responsibility, making each man feel necessary, valued. In the darkest moments, he reminded them: *We survive together, or not at all.*

He was more than their captain. He was their mentor, their counsellor, their unwavering pillar of strength. And because he believed in them, they believed in themselves.

True leadership is not just about guiding a team—it is about *lifting them up* when the weight of the world threatens to bring them down.

6. T - Transform & Thrive

The ice eventually released its grip, but Shackleton's legacy remained frozen in time—etched into the fabric of leadership itself. His survival was not just a triumph over nature, but a testament to the power of resilience, adaptability, and unwavering purpose.

Long after he and his men returned home, his story travelled farther than any of his expeditions. Military officers studied his strategies. CEOs examined his crisis management. Leadership coaches dissected his every move. How did one man hold together a team facing certain death? How did he turn fear into courage, exhaustion into endurance?

The answer was simple—he never led for himself. Shackleton's leadership was not about personal glory; it was about the survival, strength, and growth of those he led. Every action, every decision, was made with the long game in mind. His legacy was not in the miles he travelled, but in the lives he shaped.

Even now, boardrooms and battlefields echo his lessons. His name is invoked in times of crisis, a reminder that leadership is not about commanding—it is about *lifting others up* when the weight of the world threatens to crush them.

The real test of leadership is not what you accomplish in your own lifetime, but how your lessons endure long after you are gone. Shackleton did not just survive—he ensured his story would guide generations to come. What will your legacy be?

How the IMPACT Framework Unlocked Shackleton's Survival Success

The frozen wasteland stretched endlessly before them. Shackleton stood at the center of his men; their breath visible in the bitter cold. The mission had collapsed—their ship, *Endurance*, crushed and swallowed by the unforgiving ice. But defeat was not an option. This was not the end of their story.

With every passing day, he redefined his purpose. He was no longer just an explorer; he was their lifeline, their source of strength. Fear threatened to take hold, but he refused to let it fester. Instead, he transformed it—turning anxiety into action, despair into determination.

Each decision became a matter of life or death. Shackleton did not just issue orders; he built a roadmap—moving camp to solid ice, navigating lifeboats across treacherous waters, and charting a desperate 800-mile journey to South Georgia. The goal was clear: *survival at any cost.*

He knew that strategy alone was not enough—his men needed hope. He walked among them, listening, mentoring, ensuring their spirits remained unbroken. He assigned the most fearful to his own tent, guiding them through the dark nights. Morale was as vital as food and shelter.

Shackleton did not just survive—he left a legacy. His leadership transformed crisis into triumph, proving that resilience, adaptability, and a coaching mindset could overcome even the harshest conditions.

In moments of crisis, will you endure—or will you lead?

> **"Success is not final, failure is not fatal: It is the courage to continue that counts."**
>
> **— Winston Churchill**

Here are the key messages:

Sir Ernest Shackleton's survival story during the *Endurance* expedition is a masterclass in transformational leadership under extreme adversity. By aligning his actions with the **IMPACT Coaching Framework**, the narrative reveals how Shackleton's **identity**, **mindset**, **purpose**, **action**, **connection**, and **transformation** not only saved lives but forged an enduring leadership legacy.

Summary of Core Messages by IMPACT Elements:

1. **I – Inspire Awareness & Identity**

   Shackleton redefined himself not as an explorer chasing glory, but as a guardian of his crew's lives. In crisis, true leadership begins with self-awareness and inspiring hope.

2. **M – Mindset & Mastery Shift**

   Faced with total loss, he chose unwavering optimism over fear— teaching his team to mentally reframe adversity as a challenge they could overcome together.

3. **P – Purpose-Driven Goals & Strategy**

   He shifted focus from exploration to survival, setting clear, actionable goals with strategic execution to keep his crew moving forward against impossible odds.

4. **A – Action, Accountability & Adaptability**

   Shackleton modelled courage and flexibility, adapting quickly to every setback while holding himself accountable to the highest standards of leadership.

5. **C – Connection & Collaborative Growth**

   He strengthened team morale by forging deep emotional bonds, addressing individual needs, and ensuring everyone felt seen, heard, and valued.

6. **T – Transform & Thrive**

   Shackleton's enduring legacy lies not just in survival, but in how he transformed adversity into a story of growth, resilience, and leadership that inspires generations.

Core Takeaways:

Great leaders are not defined by goals achieved, but by how they lead when everything falls apart. Shackleton did not just survive—he uplifted, transformed, and left a legacy that continues to coach leaders long after his time.

Story-19:

Lee Kuan Yew: A Master Coach in Nation-Building and Leadership Development

> *"Before you are a leader, success is all about growing yourself. When you become a leader, success is all about growing others."*
>
> **— Jack Welch**

Lee Kuan Yew was more than the founding Prime Minister of Singapore—he was a master coach who shaped leaders, policies, and an entire nation's mindset. His leadership extended beyond governance; he was deeply invested in mentoring those around him, instilling discipline, and building a resilient, high-performance society. His coaching principles transformed Singapore from a struggling island nation into a global economic powerhouse and continue to influence leaders worldwide.

Coaching Through Vision and Strategic Thinking

Lee understood that leadership is not just about managing the present but about crafting a vision for the future. He taught his protégés the importance of long-term planning, pragmatism, and adaptability. He firmly believed that a leader must define the future and prepare people to embrace change, rather than reacting to it passively.

Young politicians and civil servants under his guidance learned that every decision must be grounded in reality, with a focus on sustained progress rather than short-term political gains. He personally mentored Goh Chok Tong, who would later become Singapore's second Prime Minister, coaching him on making decisive choices under pressure and handling economic challenges with a pragmatic mindset. Through his leadership, Singapore's future leaders learned that vision alone is not enough—it must be supported by meticulous execution.

Coaching Leadership Discipline and Accountability

Lee Kuan Yew's coaching was as rigorous as it was transformative. He set high expectations for ministers, civil servants, and business leaders, insisting on excellence, integrity, and discipline. His governance was built on a meritocratic system where only the most capable individuals could rise to leadership roles.

Transparency and accountability were non-negotiable under his mentorship. He demanded that government officials be data-driven and results-oriented, ensuring that their policies benefited the nation rather than personal interests. His strict but fair approach to leadership development shaped figures like Tharman Shanmugaratnam, who later became a key economic strategist and, ultimately, Singapore's President. Through his mentorship, Tharman learned the art of balancing economic foresight with social equity, a principle that remains central to Singapore's governance.

Coaching Resilience and Crisis Management

Resilience was at the heart of Lee's coaching philosophy. He believed that strong leaders must be able to navigate uncertainty, stay calm in crises, and make decisions based on data rather than fear. Whether facing racial tensions, economic downturns, or geopolitical challenges, he trained his government officials to think critically and act decisively.

One of the defining moments of his crisis coaching came during the 1997 Asian Financial Crisis. While many countries panicked, Lee guided Singapore's policymakers to take calculated measures, stabilizing the economy without resorting to reactionary decisions. His lesson was clear: true leadership is not about following opinion polls but about shaping public confidence and guiding people through difficult times.

Personal Mentorship and Knowledge Transfer

Lee Kuan Yew was deeply invested in nurturing future leaders. He believed that leadership is not inherited but cultivated through constant learning, exposure, and experience. He often held one-on-one sessions with ministers, challenging them to think critically, question assumptions, and refine their leadership abilities.

His coaching style emphasized continuous self-improvement. He encouraged leaders to read widely, travel extensively, and learn from successful models around the world. "Read, observe, and learn from the best," he would advise. His mentorship of Goh Chok Tong was a perfect example of this philosophy—starting with small responsibilities and gradually expanding them until his protégé was ready to lead.

Coaching a Nation: Building a Strong National Identity

Beyond mentoring political leaders, Lee Kuan Yew coached an entire nation, shaping the mindset of Singaporeans to be disciplined, hardworking, and forward-thinking. He instilled the values of meritocracy, teaching that success should be based on effort and ability rather than privilege. He emphasized self-reliance, reminding

Singaporeans that "no one owes us a living," reinforcing the idea that progress is achieved through personal and collective effort.

His coaching extended to fostering social cohesion, actively promoting racial and religious harmony in a diverse society. He used speeches, policies, and educational initiatives to reinforce the importance of mutual respect and unity. Under his leadership, Singaporeans internalized a culture of excellence, leading to the city-state's reputation for efficiency, innovation, and global competitiveness.

A Lasting Legacy in Leadership Coaching

Lee Kuan Yew's influence as a coach extends far beyond Singapore. His leadership principles continue to inspire politicians, business executives, and thought leaders worldwide. His ability to mentor with both tough love and strategic foresight set the gold standard for leadership development.

His legacy endures not only in the policies he implemented but, in the leaders, he nurtured, the institutions he built, and the culture of excellence he instilled. Today, Singapore stands as a testament to his coaching philosophy—an example of what disciplined, visionary leadership can achieve.

Lee Kuan Yew was not just a leader; he was a masterful coach who understood that the true measure of leadership is not personal success but the ability to develop others into great leaders. His philosophy serves as a timeless guide for anyone seeking to create lasting impact, whether in governance, business, or personal development.

Lee Kuan Yew's Leadership Coaching Through the IMPACT Framework

Lee Kuan Yew's transformation of Singapore was not just about economic growth and governance—it was an extraordinary case study in leadership coaching. His approach aligns seamlessly with the **IMPACT** coaching framework, which emphasizes self-awareness, mindset shifts, purpose-driven strategy, action, collaboration, and long-term transformation.

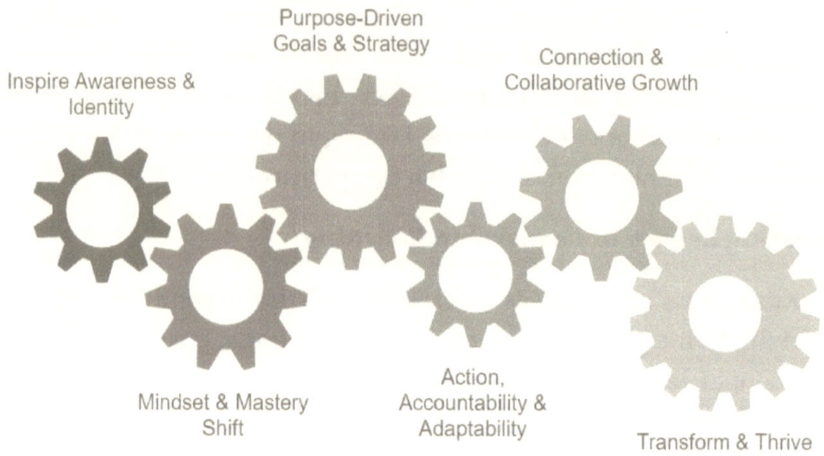

Here's how his coaching philosophy fits within the **IMPACT** framework:

1. I - Inspire Awareness & Identity

Lee Kuan Yew believed that leadership was not just about managing the present—it was about defining the future and preparing people to adapt to it. His deep understanding of identity, both at an individual and national level, allowed him to shape Singapore into a nation of resilience, pragmatism, and self-awareness. He instilled in his leaders and citizens a clear understanding of their strengths, responsibilities, and the mindset required to build a successful and adaptive society.

One of Lee's most impactful coaching strategies was encouraging young politicians and civil servants to reflect on their role in shaping Singapore's future. He emphasized meritocracy, teaching leaders to assess their capabilities objectively and develop the skills necessary to lead effectively. Beyond individual leadership, he carefully cultivated Singapore's national identity—one rooted in discipline, pragmatism, and resilience—through his speeches and policies, ensuring that these values became ingrained in the country's DNA.

His commitment to leadership development was evident in his mentorship of Goh Chok Tong. Recognizing the young leader's potential, Lee provided continuous feedback, helping Goh refine his political identity and strategic thinking. Through this guidance, Goh gained clarity on his leadership strengths and areas for growth, allowing him to step confidently into the role of Singapore's second Prime Minister.

Lee's legacy proves that leadership is not just about governing the present—it is about shaping the future by developing leaders who can carry a nation forward with vision and purpose.

2. M - Mindset & Mastery Shift

Lee Kuan Yew understood that true leadership is not about following popular opinion but about shaping it. As he famously stated, *"You do not lead by following opinion polls. You lead by shaping opinions."* His leadership was rooted in the power of mindset transformation—he instilled a culture of self-reliance among Singaporeans, shifting their perspective from dependency to one of resilience and opportunity.

Within his government, Lee trained his ministers to navigate uncertainty and external pressures by prioritizing data-driven decision-making over emotions or political expediency. He reinforced the belief that failure was not a setback but a stepping stone for improvement, ensuring that mistakes became lessons rather than excuses. His governance model was defined by pragmatism over ideology, coaching leaders to remain flexible, solutions-focused, and willing to adapt to changing realities rather than clinging to rigid doctrines.

This leadership philosophy was particularly evident during Singapore's early years of independence. Faced with economic vulnerability and political instability, Lee coached his ministers to adopt a mindset of economic survival, pushing them to think beyond immediate hardships and focus on long-term growth strategies. By instilling this forward-thinking mentality, he not only secured Singapore's prosperity but also cultivated a leadership culture that continues to drive the nation's success today.

3. P - Purpose-Driven Goals & Strategy

Lee Kuan Yew was deeply aware of the dangers of complacency, once warning, *"What I fear is complacency. When things always become better, people tend to want more for less work."* His leadership was rooted in a philosophy of relentless accountability, adaptability, and integrity, ensuring that both leaders and citizens took full ownership of their roles in nation-building.

In his governance model, accountability was non-negotiable. He held ministers to exceptionally high standards, swiftly removing those who failed to deliver results. His leadership style emphasized adaptability, constantly fine-tuning Singapore's policies to maintain a competitive edge in an ever-changing global landscape. Beyond performance, integrity was a cornerstone of his administration—he waged a relentless battle against corruption, ensuring that Singapore's governance remained efficient, transparent, and trusted by its people.

The impact of this leadership philosophy was particularly evident during the 1997 Asian Financial Crisis. While many nations struggled with instability, Lee's coaching ensured that Singapore's government remained composed, following data-driven fiscal policies to navigate the crisis with precision. His insistence on accountability and adaptability not only stabilized the economy but reinforced Singapore's reputation as a resilient and well-governed nation. His legacy serves as a powerful reminder that true leadership demands both discipline and the willingness to evolve.

4. A - Action, Accountability & Adaptability

Lee Kuan Yew was deeply aware of the dangers of complacency, once warning, *"What I fear is complacency. When things always become better, people tend to want more for less work."* His leadership was rooted in a philosophy of relentless accountability, adaptability, and integrity, ensuring that both leaders and citizens took full ownership of their roles in nation-building.

In his governance model, accountability was non-negotiable. He held ministers to exceptionally high standards, swiftly removing those who failed to deliver results. His leadership style emphasized adaptability, constantly fine-tuning Singapore's policies to maintain a competitive edge in an ever-changing global landscape. Beyond performance, integrity was a cornerstone of his administration—he waged a relentless battle against corruption, ensuring that Singapore's governance remained efficient, transparent, and trusted by its people.

The impact of this leadership philosophy was particularly evident during the 1997 Asian Financial Crisis. While many nations struggled with instability, Lee's coaching ensured that Singapore's government remained composed, following data-driven fiscal policies to navigate the crisis with precision. His insistence on accountability and adaptability not only stabilized the economy but reinforced Singapore's reputation as a resilient and well-governed nation. His legacy serves as a powerful reminder that true leadership demands both discipline and the willingness to evolve.

5. C - Connection & Collaborative Growth

Lee Kuan Yew understood that true leadership is never a solitary pursuit. As he famously stated, *"If you want to reach your goals and dreams, you cannot do it alone. You must stand on the shoulders of others."* His success was built on a foundation of mentorship, collaboration, and shared responsibility—principles that continue to drive Singapore's leadership excellence today.

Rather than relying on individual brilliance, Lee cultivated a high-performance leadership ecosystem that ensured long-term national success. He personally mentored multiple generations of leaders, engaging directly with rising politicians to pass down knowledge and insights. His governance model prioritized teamwork and inter-ministerial collaboration, ensuring that government agencies operated with efficiency and unity. More importantly, he embedded a culture of mentorship, where experienced leaders were expected to coach and develop the next wave of political and administrative talent.

The strength of this structured approach is evident in Singapore's smooth leadership transitions. From Lee Kuan Yew to Goh Chok Tong, and later to Lee Hsien Loong, the transfer of power was seamless, preserving stability and continuity. His legacy demonstrates that leadership coaching, when embedded into a nation's governance structure, can create lasting impact for generations to come.

6. T - Transform & Thrive

Lee Kuan Yew's leadership journey was a masterclass in nation-building, a testament to the power of vision, strategy, and unwavering commitment. Reflecting on his life's work, he once said, *"I have spent my life, so much of it, building up this country. There is nothing more that I need to do. At the end of the day, what have I got? A successful Singapore."* These words encapsulate his ultimate coaching success—the transformation he orchestrated not just within his government, but across an entire nation.

Lee's leadership principles continue to shape Singapore's economic, political, and social fabric long after his passing. His governance model was built to endure, ensuring that the foundations he laid would outlast him and drive the country's continued success. His influence extended beyond Singapore, inspiring policymakers worldwide to study and adapt his development strategies. Through decades of mentorship, he instilled resilience, innovation, and excellence—qualities that define Singapore to this day.

The impact of his leadership philosophy is evident. Singapore remains one of the world's most stable and prosperous nations, a direct reflection of the values and governance structures he embedded. His legacy stands as a powerful example of leadership coaching in action, proving that visionary leadership can shape not just a government, but an entire nation's destiny.

Final Takeaways: Lee Kuan Yew's Mastery of the IMPACT Framework

Lee Kuan Yew's leadership journey was an unparalleled demonstration of the **IMPACT** coaching framework in action. His ability to inspire self-awareness, shift mindsets, set purpose-driven goals, drive accountability, foster collaboration, and create lasting transformation makes him one of history's greatest leadership coaches.

For leaders, entrepreneurs, and policymakers seeking to create a lasting impact, his approach serves as an enduring blueprint for success.

Enhancing Coaching Outcomes: Lessons from Lee Kuan Yew's Leadership Coaching

Lee Kuan Yew's legacy as a leadership coach offers valuable insights for anyone looking to refine their coaching skills. By applying his methods, we can create a more impactful coaching experience for our clients. Below are key learning points from his story and how we, as coaches, can integrate them into our practice.

1. Inspire Awareness & Identity: Help Clients See Their True Potential

Lee Kuan Yew, the founding father of modern Singapore, understood that the foundation of great leadership is self-awareness. He did not just lead with vision—he shaped future leaders by helping them understand who they were at their core. One of his key mentees, Goh Chok Tong, benefited greatly from Lee's ability to guide others in recognizing their unique strengths and refining their leadership identity. Lee believed that before someone could lead a nation, they had to first lead themselves.

In coaching, this principle becomes powerful. Helping clients reflect deeply on their values, beliefs, and strengths is essential. Through self-reflection and honest inquiry, leaders can discover the core of what makes them effective. By asking thoughtful questions like "Who are you as a leader?" and "What strengths do you bring to the table?" coaches can open up transformational dialogue. Tools like journaling, strengths assessments, value clarification exercises, and 360-degree feedback allow clients to gain both internal and external insights into their leadership style. This process not only builds confidence, but also forms a strong, authentic foundation for leadership growth.

2. Shift Mindsets & Overcome Barriers

Lee Kuan Yew was a master of transforming mindsets. He guided an entire nation—and its future leaders—away from fear, complacency, and defeatism toward resilience, realism, and pragmatism. His leadership was not just about policies; it was about changing how people thought, especially in times of crisis. By fostering adaptability, he ensured that Singapore's leaders could not only withstand turbulent times but thrive in them.

In a coaching context, this approach is deeply relevant. Many clients carry limiting beliefs that quietly sabotage their potential. As a coach, helping individuals identify these inner roadblocks is the first step. Then comes the shift—using tools from neuro-linguistic programming (NLP) and cognitive-behavioural techniques (CBT), coaches can guide clients to reframe their narratives and replace negative thought patterns with empowering ones. Fostering a growth mindset—where setbacks are seen as stepping stones—turns fear into fuel. Practical tools like NLP exercises, reframing strategies, and CBT worksheets become powerful aids in this mindset transformation.

3. Set Purpose-Driven Goals & Strategy

Lee Kuan Yew led with clarity and purpose. He was never swayed by short-term wins or popular opinion. Instead, he focused on building a strong foundation for Singapore's future. Every decision was rooted in long-term strategy, and he instilled the same discipline in his ministers. He taught them to resist the temptation of immediate gratification and to always align their actions with a larger national vision.

This strategic mindset is a powerful lesson for coaching. Leaders often struggle with scattered priorities or reactive decision-making. As a coach, helping clients reconnect with their long-term vision brings focus and intentionality. Tools like SMART goals and OKRs (Objectives and Key Results) allow clients to set precise, meaningful targets. Asking thought-provoking questions like, "How does this serve your bigger vision?" pushes them to think beyond the now. Through vision-mapping and structured goal-setting, clients can build a clear execution plan with measurable progress points—turning ambition into strategy.

4. Drive Action, Accountability & Adaptability

Lee Kuan Yew was not just a visionary—he was a master executor. Once a decision was made, he ensured it was carried out with discipline and precision. He held his ministers to the highest standards, expecting them to take full ownership of their actions. But he also understood that no plan survives unchanged. So, he built a culture that embraced adaptability and resilience, making space for continuous learning in the face of evolving realities.

This approach is deeply relevant in coaching. Many leaders struggle with follow-through or become overwhelmed when plans shift. As a coach, establishing accountability systems—like regular check-ins or action plans—keeps clients committed. Encouraging adaptability helps them pivot when challenges arise without losing sight of their goals. Resilience strategies support clients through uncertainty, helping them stay grounded and solution-focused. With the right tools, such as habit trackers and adaptability models, coaches can transform good intentions into consistent, high-impact action.

5. Build Connection & Foster Growth Through Mentorship

Lee Kuan Yew understood that leadership is not a solo pursuit—it is a legacy passed forward. He believed deeply in mentorship and collaboration, ensuring that each generation of leaders was prepared to lead with wisdom, not just power. His guidance of successors like Goh Chok Tong reflected this commitment to knowledge transfer, shared purpose, and unity.

For coaches, this legacy reminds us of the power of connection. Leaders grow stronger when they seek out mentors, cultivate meaningful relationships, and invest in others. Coaching clients to build supportive networks, influence with integrity, and collaborate with their teams can dramatically expand their leadership impact. Active listening and empathy—skills that Lee himself practiced—are essential tools for both coaches and the leaders they guide. Techniques like peer coaching, mentorship circles, and collaborative exercises help instil a culture of trust, openness, and growth that lasts far beyond one person's tenure.

6. Create Lasting Transformation & Legacy

Lee Kuan Yew did not just lead for the present—he led with the future in mind. His vision for Singapore was not about quick wins or temporary fixes; it was about building a foundation that would stand strong long after he stepped away. His legacy is visible in Singapore's resilience, global presence, and continued prosperity. That is the mark of truly sustainable transformation.

In coaching, this principle reminds us to help clients think beyond their immediate goals. It is about guiding them to define a leadership legacy—something that reflects their deepest values and long-term aspirations. Encouraging continuous learning, adaptability, and regular self-reflection allows leaders to evolve, stay relevant, and make an enduring impact. Tools like leadership legacy planning, personal transformation journeys, and learning roadmaps help clients stay grounded in their purpose while growing toward their future.

Becoming a Master Coach

By integrating Lee Kuan Yew's leadership coaching principles with structured frameworks like **IMPACT**, we can **enhance our coaching outcomes** and create meaningful, lasting transformations for our clients.

> *"Leadership is the capacity to translate vision into reality."*
>
> — **Warren Bennis**

Key Coaching Practices to Apply:

- Help clients build **self-awareness and identity clarity**
- Shift **mindsets from fear to confidence**
- Align goals with **long-term purpose and vision**
- Foster **accountability and adaptability**
- Encourage **mentorship and collaborative leadership**
- Focus on **sustainable transformation, not just short-term wins**

Chapter Summary:

Core Messages Aligned with the IMPACT Framework

1. Inspire Identity & Self-Awareness

- **Message:** True leadership begins with understanding who you are. It is rooted in knowing your values, strengths, and purpose. Great leaders are self-aware and able to align their actions with their authentic selves.

- **Action:** Leverage journaling, reflection, and feedback tools such as 360-degree assessments to help leaders uncover and refine their leadership identity. These practices foster deeper self-awareness and personal growth.

2. Mindset Shift Fuels Resilience

- **Message:** Fear is a natural part of leadership, but it is how you respond that defines your success. Shifting your mindset from fear to focus opens doors to new possibilities and builds emotional resilience.

- **Action:** Use Cognitive Behavioural Therapy (CBT), Neuro-Linguistic Programming (NLP) techniques, reframing exercises, and storytelling to enhance emotional intelligence and mental strength. These tools help leaders build the mindset necessary to thrive under pressure.

3. Purpose-Driven Goals Create Meaningful Impact

- **Message:** Leadership is not just about short-term wins—it is about leading with a purpose that aligns with a greater vision. Purpose-driven leadership brings lasting transformation that transcends immediate results.

- **Action:** Set SMART goals and leverage Objectives and Key Results (OKRs) to align your actions with a higher purpose. Coaching around long-term vision ensures that leaders' efforts are purposeful, meaningful, and impactful.

4. **Accountability & Adaptability Lead to Real Results**

   o **Message:** Success in leadership requires both discipline and the ability to adapt in dynamic situations. Leaders must be accountable to their goals while maintaining the agility to pivot when necessary.

   o **Action:** Implement accountability systems such as regular check-ins, KPIs, and scorecards. Encourage experimentation, role rotation, and retrospectives to cultivate adaptability and continuous improvement in leadership practices.

5. **Connection & Collaboration Build Strong Cultures**

   o **Message:** Trust, mentorship, and shared responsibility are the pillars of strong leadership cultures. Leaders who foster deep connections with their teams create environments of collaboration, which lead to sustainable growth.

   o **Action:** Facilitate peer coaching, establish mentorship programs, and encourage shared storytelling to build relational bonds. By nurturing these connections, leaders can create cultures that thrive on mutual respect and collaboration.

6. **Transformative Leadership Leaves a Legacy**

   o **Message:** Great leaders think beyond their own success. They build systems, cultivate cultures, and establish values that endure long after their tenure. The legacy of a transformative leader extends far beyond their lifetime.

   o **Action:** Guide clients in defining their leadership legacy, mapping the ripple effects of their decisions, and documenting the transformative journeys they embark on. This encourages leaders to focus on creating lasting change that influences future generations.

7. **Collaboration & Partnerships Solve Complex Challenges**

   o **Message:** The world's most complex challenges—such as global peacebuilding or environmental sustainability—

require systemic change, which can only be achieved through collaboration with diverse stakeholders.

- o **Action:** Train leaders in co-creation, active listening, and cross-cultural collaboration. By developing these skills, leaders can engage with others to address large-scale challenges through partnerships and collective effort.

Bonus: Cross-Cultural Lessons for Timeless Leadership

The stories of legendary figures such as Zhuge Liang, Shackleton, Napoleon, Lee Kuan Yew, and Chandragupta offer powerful insights that transcend cultures and eras:

- **Coaching as Strategic Visioning:** Coaches are not just motivators—they are strategic visionaries. Just as Chanakya and Zhuge Liang shaped the futures of nations, coaches guide leaders to shape the future of organizations and communities.

- **Legacy through Mindset, Purpose, and Execution:** The leadership legacies of Napoleon, Shackleton, and Lee Kuan Yew underscore the importance of mindset, purpose, and execution. Napoleon's speed, Shackleton's grit, and Lee Kuan Yew's long-term vision demonstrate that leadership is defined by the ability to persist, adapt, and execute with a purpose.

Concluding Reflection:

Like the great leaders throughout history, your impact will be defined by your mindset, purpose, and execution. Embrace coaching qualities, build collaborative cultures, and strive for a legacy that endures.

What one action can you take this week to embody the Coaching qualities discussed in the chapter?

Chapter 4

The Modern Coaching Revolution

Where Strategy Meets Soul, and Transformation Begins

What do a steel magnate from the 19th century, a Pixar genius, a football coach, and a global entertainment empire have in common?

They all cracked the code of transformation—not with more power, but through purposeful coaching.

In today's high-speed world, coaching is not a luxury. It is the fuel that powers reinvention. Whether in boardrooms, locker rooms, or war zones, coaching has become the compass for those navigating change, challenge, and crisis.

In this chapter, we travel through time and industries—from the roaring furnaces of Carnegie's steel empire to the digital phoenix rising from Disney's ashes. We will step inside the minds of creators, visionaries, and courageous leaders who redefined success—not just for themselves, but for generations to come.

At the heart of their breakthroughs? The IMPACT Coaching Framework—a timeless blueprint rooted in identity, mindset, purpose, action, connection, and transformation.

These stories are not just case studies. They are lessons in human potential. They show us how coaching creates a ripple effect—from inner growth to global innovation. From Pixar's radical honesty rooms to Facebook's fractured friendships, high school hardwood of Coach Carter's gym—coaching turns breakdowns into breakthroughs.

This chapter is not about theory—it is about revolution. You will discover how coaching lights the fire of identity in a disoriented team, re-aligns a mission gone off course, and breathes purpose into performance. So, whether you are a leader, coach, or simply someone standing at a crossroads—this chapter will hand you a mirror, a torch, and a map.

Welcome to the revolution. Let us make coaching your competitive edge.

Key Topics:

- **Impact in Steel: The Leadership Secrets of Andrew Carnegie**

- **Ed Catmull's Leadership Transformation and Coaching: The Architect of Creative Excellence**

- **Disney's Digital Comeback: A Story of Transformation**

- **Ferguson's IMPACT on Leadership & Coaching**

- **IMPACT in Motion: Leadership Lessons from The Social Network**

- **Beyond the Game: The Coach Who Changed Lives**

- **How Businesses Overcame Challenges with Structured Planning and the IMPACT Framework**

Story-20:

Impact in Steel: The Leadership Secrets of Andrew Carnegie

> **"What we do for ourselves dies with us. What we do for others and the world remains and is immortal."**
>
> — *Albert Pine*

The air in Pittsburgh hung thick with the scent of molten metal, the clang of hammers on steel ringing through the streets. Smoke curled from towering chimneys, painting the sky in shades of gray. Amidst this symphony of industry, a boy with calloused hands and dirt-streaked clothes stood still, his sharp eyes drinking in the relentless energy of the mills. He was an immigrant, a nobody in a city of giants, but deep within him burned a fire that would one day reshape an industry. That boy was Andrew Carnegie.

He did not inherit wealth or prestige. He earned them—through shrewd decisions, an unbreakable will, and a belief in something greater than himself. His journey from a penniless factory worker to the mastermind behind Carnegie Steel Company was not just about business; it was about mindset, strategy, execution, and legacy—the very essence of the IMPACT framework.

Inspire Awareness & Identity (Self-Reflection & Understanding Strengths)

The telegraph office smelled of ink and hot metal, wires buzzing with messages that shaped the nation's fate. Young Carnegie sat, his fingers dancing over the keys, absorbing every word, every opportunity hidden between the lines. He was not just relaying messages; he was learning, observing, connecting dots others missed.

Self-awareness propelled him forward. He saw beyond his station, recognizing that his sharp mind and ambition could take him further than the factory floor. He refused to lament his lack of formal education, instead devouring knowledge, treating every encounter as a lesson. One evening, as the telegraph machine clicked urgently, Carnegie swiftly decoded a message before his superior even glanced at it. The impressed Thomas Scott, a railroad tycoon, saw potential in him. That moment set him on a path from an ordinary worker to a strategic thinker in the business world.

Mindset & Mastery Shift (Overcoming Limiting Beliefs & Strategic Thinking)

The wooden bridge trembled under the weight of a heavy locomotive. Carnegie stood at the riverbank, watching as the structure groaned, failing its test. Most men saw a disaster. Carnegie saw an opportunity.

With a growth mindset, he immersed himself in learning about iron and steel, understanding how innovation could rewrite the rules of construction. He placed bold bets, investing in iron bridges when skeptics clung to outdated wooden structures. He was not reckless—he was calculated, studying the future when others stayed bound by the past. When war broke out, Carnegie doubled down on steel production, believing infrastructure would drive the next economic era. His gamble paid off, setting the stage for his empire.

Purpose-Driven Goals & Strategy (Aligning Actions with a Bigger Vision)

The blueprint lay across his desk, smudged with the fingerprints of engineers and dreamers alike. The Brooklyn Bridge—a marvel of human ambition—would stand because of Carnegie steel.

Carnegie was not just making money; he was reshaping cities, industries, and the future. With clear goals, he introduced cost-saving methods, making steel an accessible foundation for expansion. Profits mattered, but legacy mattered more. The completion of the Brooklyn Bridge in the 1880s was not just an architectural triumph; it was a symbol of Carnegie's foresight in betting on steel as the backbone of modern civilization.

Action, Accountability & Adaptability (Execution, Resilience & Agility)

The steel mill was a beast, its furnaces roaring, consuming iron, spitting out beams that would shape America. But efficiency was the key, and Carnegie knew it. He walked the factory floor, eyes scanning every movement, identifying waste, refining processes.

He demanded better, faster, cheaper production without sacrificing quality. Holding himself and his managers to ruthless standards, he ensured rapid execution. As technology advanced, he did not resist— he led the charge, always staying ahead of competitors. When the steel industry faced market instability, Carnegie did not panic. He expanded, acquired competitors, and tightened efficiency, securing his dominance.

Connection & Collaborative Growth (Building High-Performance Teams & Leadership Impact)

The room buzzed with the sound of sharp minds at work—engineers, chemists, business strategists. Carnegie sat among them, not as a distant owner, but as a leader who listened, challenged, and empowered.

He understood that success was amplified through collaboration. He recruited top talent, investing in continuous learning. Even in an era of brutal industry, his workers saw him as someone who understood both ambition and humanity. By fostering partnerships and empowering teams, he ensured his company was not just surviving—it was innovating.

Transform & Thrive (Sustaining Success & Leaving a Legacy)

The ink on the deal had dried. Carnegie Steel was now part of J.P. Morgan's empire. But instead of retreating into luxury, Carnegie looked beyond himself. What would his wealth mean if it died with him?

He believed fortune should serve humanity, not just individuals. Transforming from industrialist to philanthropist, he became the world's most famous patron of libraries, universities, and peace initiatives. Selling Carnegie Steel for $480 million was not an end—it was a beginning. His name would no longer be tied to industry, but to knowledge, progress, and a better world.

Lessons from Carnegie's Self-Coaching & Leadership Transformation

Modern leaders can draw immense wisdom from Carnegie's story. His journey illustrates the power of self-awareness, strategic execution, and lasting impact:

- **Develop self-awareness → Identify your unique strengths.**
- **Shift your mindset → Turn failures into learning experiences.**
- **Define your purpose → Align your goals with a bigger vision.**

- **Execute with precision** → **Make decisions and adapt quickly.**
- **Build strong teams** → **Success is amplified through collaboration.**
- **Create lasting impact** → **Wealth and success mean nothing without a legacy.**

Andrew Carnegie's story was not just about steel—it was about transformation, resilience, and shaping the future. His success, like that of any great leader, was not just about what he achieved; it was about how he IMPACTed the world.

Top Key Messages for Coaches from Andrew Carnegie's Leadership Journey

- **Self-Awareness is the Catalyst for Growth**

  Carnegie's rise from a poor immigrant to an industrial titan began with **self-reflection and recognizing his strengths**. He treated every experience as a learning opportunity and sought **mentors** who helped him refine his vision. Coaches should encourage leaders to assess their skills, embrace continuous learning, and build on their unique strengths.

- **Mindset Shift Unlocks Opportunities**

  While others saw obstacles, Carnegie saw opportunities. His decision to invest in steel when others clung to wood exemplifies a growth mindset and strategic risk-taking. Coaches must help leaders challenge limiting beliefs, embrace innovation, and develop strategic thinking skills to navigate change.

- **Purpose-Driven Goals Drive Long-Term Success**

  Carnegie was not just chasing wealth—he was **reshaping industries and cities**. His steel empire laid the foundation for America's infrastructure. Coaches should guide leaders to define their bigger purpose, align goals with impact, and focus on long-term value creation rather than short-term gains.

- **Execution, Adaptability & Accountability Define Leaders**

  Carnegie's relentless focus on **efficiency, quality, and continuous improvement** made his company the most powerful in the steel industry. He adapted to market shifts, improved processes, and held his teams to high standards. Coaches should emphasize the importance of taking decisive action, being adaptable, and holding themselves accountable for results.

- **Collaboration & Legacy Elevate Leadership**

  Carnegie built a high-performance team, **empowered others**, and ultimately transitioned from business to philanthropy. His wealth was not just for personal gain—it was reinvested into libraries, education, and social progress. Coaches should instil the value of collaboration, leadership impact, and building a legacy that goes beyond personal success.

> **"Success is not about standing alone at the top—it's about lifting others along the way."**
>
> *– Andrew Carnegie*

Story-21:

Ed Catmull's Leadership Transformation and Coaching: The Architect of Creative Excellence

> **"Getting the right people and the right chemistry is more important than getting the right idea."**
>
> *—On why leadership should focus on culture and talent rather than just strategies.*

Ed Catmull, the co-founder of Pixar Animation Studios and former president of both Pixar and Walt Disney Animation Studios, is widely recognized as one of the most transformative leaders in the creative industry. His leadership journey is not just about managing teams—it is about fostering an environment where creativity thrives, innovation flourishes, and people feel empowered to do their best work.

From an aspiring computer scientist with dreams of making the first computer-animated film to a visionary leader who shaped the culture of two of the world's most successful animation studios, Catmull's leadership transformation is a testament to his commitment to continuous learning, adaptability, and the belief that great leaders create great teams—not the other way around.

From Technologist to Inspirational Leader

Catmull's transformation as a leader did not come from traditional management techniques but from his deep understanding of the creative process and the human dynamics that drive it. He started as a computer scientist with a passion for animation, but as he rose to leadership, he realized that fostering creativity was not just about technology—it was about people.

At Pixar, he built a culture where risks were encouraged, mistakes were embraced as learning opportunities, and open collaboration was the norm. Unlike many leaders who fear uncertainty, Catmull saw it as an essential part of innovation. He believed that true creativity requires a safe space where people feel comfortable sharing ideas, challenging assumptions, and admitting when they are wrong.

Key Leadership Transformations & Coaching Philosophy

1. Creating a Culture of Candor

One of Catmull's most profound leadership transformations was his shift toward fostering radical honesty within teams. He understood that in creative industries, people often hesitate to share honest feedback for fear of offending others. However, he knew that without open communication, ideas could not evolve, and innovation would stagnate.

To address this, he established the **Braintrust,** a feedback mechanism at Pixar where directors, writers, and animators could openly critique a film in progress without hierarchy or egos getting in the way. The

Braintrust's success lay in its **no-authority dynamic**—everyone was encouraged to challenge ideas, but no one was forced to implement changes. This approach created a psychologically safe environment where constructive criticism was embraced rather than feared.

◈ **Leadership Lesson:** Great leaders create an environment where truth is valued more than hierarchy. Encouraging honest feedback leads to better decision-making and stronger innovation.

2. Embracing Failure as a Learning Tool

Early in his leadership journey, Catmull recognized that perfectionism stifles creativity. He shifted his mindset from preventing mistakes to learning from them, making failure an essential part of Pixar's culture.

He famously stated, *"All our movies suck at first." Instead of expecting instant success, he encouraged teams to refine ideas through iteration. By embracing failure, Pixar transformed rough concepts into masterpieces like Toy Story, Finding Nemo, and Inside Out.*

Coaching Insight: A leader's job is not to prevent failure but to create a culture where failures are stepping stones to success. Instead of punishing mistakes, use them as learning opportunities.

3. Leading with Humility and Continuous Learning

Despite his success, Catmull never claimed to have all the answers. He openly admitted that leadership is a continuous learning process. He sought feedback from employees at all levels, challenged his own biases, and remained adaptable to change.

One of his biggest transformations as a leader came when Pixar merged with Disney Animation. Instead of imposing Pixar's culture on Disney, he took time to understand the existing dynamics at Disney Animation and helped rebuild the studio from within. By empowering Disney's creatives and applying Pixar's collaborative methods, he helped turn around the struggling studio, leading to a resurgence of films like *Frozen, Zootopia, and Moana.*

Leadership Takeaways: Great leaders do not dictate change— they enable it by listening, learning, and adapting. True transformation comes from empowering others rather than enforcing control.

4. Balancing Structure and Creativity

One of the biggest challenges in creative leadership is balancing artistic freedom with organizational discipline. Catmull mastered this balance by giving teams autonomy while ensuring they had the right support and structure.

At Pixar, he ensured that teams had creative control but also implemented guiding principles that kept projects on track. He trusted his teams to make creative decisions but provided leadership support when needed. This approach allowed Pixar to maintain both its artistic integrity and its commercial success.

Coaching Principle: Leaders should empower teams with autonomy while providing clear structures that prevent chaos. Creativity flourishes in an environment with both freedom and accountability.

Ed Catmull's Coaching Philosophy for Leaders

Catmull's leadership style has become a model for modern coaching in innovation-driven organizations. His approach focuses on:

✓ **Building Trust & Safety – Creating environments where people feel safe to express ideas and challenge norms.**

✓ **Encouraging Constructive Criticism – Fostering open dialogue without ego or hierarchy.**

✓ **Accepting Uncertainty – Embracing change and iteration rather than fearing failure.**

✓ **Empowering Others – Trusting people to make decisions rather than micromanaging.**

✓ **Staying Humble – Leading with curiosity and always being open to learning.**

The Legacy of Catmull's Leadership Transformation

Ed Catmull's transformation from a scientist to a visionary leader is a masterclass in leadership evolution. His ability to foster creativity, embrace failure, and empower teams has not only shaped Pixar's legendary success but also influenced leadership strategies across industries. His coaching insights remind us that leadership is not about control—it is about cultivating an environment where people can thrive.

If more leaders adopted Catmull's philosophy, workplaces would become more innovative, resilient, and fulfilling. His journey serves as an inspiration for anyone looking to lead with authenticity, creativity, and wisdom.

As Catmull himself put it: *"If you give a good idea to a mediocre team, they will screw it up. But if you give a mediocre idea to a great team, they will either fix it or come up with something better."*

Leadership is not about having the best ideas—it is about building the best teams.

Ed Catmull's Leadership Transformation Through the IMPACT Framework

Ed Catmull, co-founder of Pixar and former president of Walt Disney Animation Studios, is a perfect example of **how the IMPACT framework** can shape a visionary leader. His journey—from an aspiring computer scientist to the leader behind some of the most successful animated films—reflects the principles of self-awareness, mindset shifts, purpose-driven strategy, action, collaboration, and long-term transformation.

"If you give a good idea to a mediocre team, they will screw it up. But if you give a mediocre idea to a great team, they will either fix it or come up with something better." — On the power of teams.

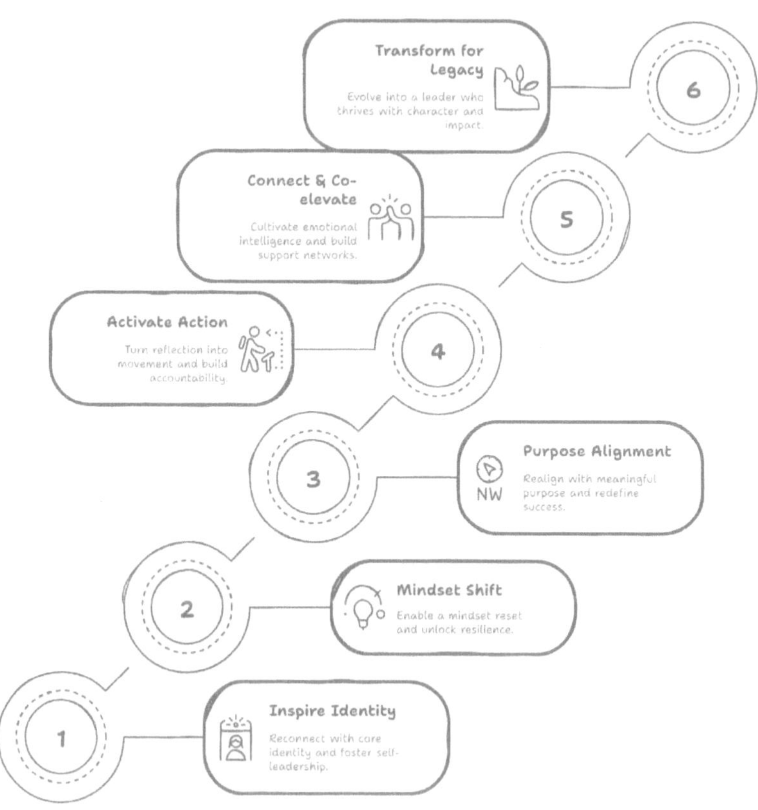

1. I - Inspire Awareness & Identity: Discovering the True Role of a Leader

What if the key to success was not just innovation, but the ability to lead others toward it?

Early in his career, Ed Catmull was a brilliant computer scientist with a bold dream—to create the first computer-animated feature film. He saw himself as a technologist, someone who would push the boundaries of what computers could do. But as Pixar took shape, he faced a deeper challenge. Cutting-edge technology alone would not make Pixar great. The real challenge was not in the code—it was in the people.

Catmull found himself asking hard questions. What kind of company did he want to build? How could he create a culture where both artists and technologists thrived? What kind of leader did he need to become for Pixar to succeed?

His transformation came when he realized that leadership was not about having all the answers—it was about fostering an environment where the best ideas could emerge. He built a culture where creativity flourished, where risk-taking was safe, and where failure was not punished but seen as a step toward mastery. His true legacy was not just technological breakthroughs—it was the people he empowered to create something extraordinary.

The question is, are you only focusing on innovation, or are you also building the culture that makes it possible?

How to Apply:

- Take time for self-reflection—what is your true leadership identity?

- Seek feedback from your team to understand how they perceive your leadership.

2. M - Mindset & Mastery Shift: Embracing Failure & Uncertainty

What if the fear of failure was the very thing holding back your greatest success?

In Pixar's early days, uncertainty loomed like a storm cloud. Before *Toy Story*, the company struggled financially, and many doubted whether computer animation could ever produce a successful feature film. The pressure was immense. The fear of failure could have paralyzed them. But Ed Catmull saw things differently.

Instead of resisting failure, he embraced it as an essential part of creativity. "Early on, all of our movie's suck. Our job is to go from suck to not-suck," he famously said. He knew that no great idea was born perfect—it had to be shaped, refined, and even broken before it could truly shine.

To make this mindset a reality, Catmull built a culture that welcomed honest feedback and fearless experimentation. Pixar's *Braintrust* became a space where directors could receive constructive criticism without ego or punishment. Teams were encouraged to take risks, to push creative boundaries, to fail safely. Psychological safety was not just a buzzword—it was the foundation of Pixar's success, ensuring that even the most junior employees felt empowered to contribute.

The result? A company that did not just survive uncertainty but thrived in it. The question is, are you creating a space where creativity can grow, or are you letting fear keep it small?

How to Apply:

- Shift from a perfectionist mindset to a **growth mindset.**

- Create an environment where feedback is honest but constructive.

3. P - Purpose-Driven Goals & Strategy: Defining Pixar's Creative Mission

What if success was not the finish line, but the biggest threat to innovation?

After *Toy Story* became a groundbreaking success, Pixar could have played it safe. They could have followed a formula, replicated what worked, and settled into a cycle of predictable hits. But Ed Catmull saw the hidden danger—complacency. Creativity thrives on risk, not routine. If Pixar stopped pushing boundaries, their magic would fade.

To keep innovation alive, Catmull anchored Pixar in a clear purpose: *"To tell great stories with heart, humor, and innovation."* This was not just a mission statement—it was a guiding principle for every creative and business decision.

To execute this vision, Pixar institutionalized innovation. They invested heavily in R&D, developing cutting-edge animation tools that pushed the limits of what was possible. No film was rushed to market—every story was refined, iterated, and reworked until it met Pixar's impossibly high standards. Profit was never prioritized over storytelling excellence.

The result? A studio that never stopped evolving, delivering masterpiece after masterpiece. The question is, are you letting success make you comfortable, or are you using it as a launchpad for your next big breakthrough?

How to Apply:

- Align your goals with a larger purpose—what drives you and your team?

- Ensure that every strategy connects back to that bigger vision.

4. A - Action, Accountability & Adaptability: Building a Sustainable Creative Process

How do you balance creativity with discipline without killing innovation?

At Pixar, the challenge was not just about having great ideas—it was about turning those ideas into exceptional films, again and again. Too much structure could stifle creativity. Too much freedom could lead to chaos. Ed Catmull knew that the magic of Pixar was not just in its talent, but in how that talent was nurtured and guided.

Instead of rigid control, Pixar developed creative workflows that balanced structure with flexibility. Teams were given accountability—they owned their work, but also had the freedom to refine and improve. Filmmakers were not locked into their first ideas; they could iterate, change course, and rework stories until they found something truly great.

This balance paid off. Pixar produced one masterpiece after another—*Finding Nemo, The Incredibles, Ratatouille, Up, WALL-E*—each film pushing the boundaries of storytelling and animation. High standards were maintained, not through micromanagement, but through trust, feedback, and a relentless pursuit of excellence.

The lesson? Creativity thrives in the right environment—not too loose, not too tight. The question is, have you built a system that fuels innovation, or one that stifles it?

How to Apply:

- Focus on **consistent execution rather than waiting for perfection.**

- Build accountability systems—regular check-ins, progress tracking.

5. C - Connection & Collaborative Growth: Nurturing Pixar's Creative Community

What if the greatest threat to success was not competition—but the walls within your own company?

At Pixar, the challenge was not just making great films. It was making sure the artists, engineers, and business teams worked together seamlessly. Without collaboration, creativity would stall, innovation would suffer, and the company's magic would fade. Ed Catmull saw the danger of silos and knew that if Pixar wanted to thrive, its people could not work in isolation.

So, he made a radical shift—he tore down the walls, both literally and figuratively. Leaders did not hide behind closed doors; they sat in open workspaces, accessible to anyone. Cross-disciplinary teams were not just encouraged—they were essential. Artists and engineers tackled problems together, blending creativity with technology. And to make collaboration a lifelong habit, Catmull created *Pixar University*, where employees could take courses outside their expertise, learning from one another and strengthening the bonds across teams.

The result? A company where everyone felt like a valued contributor, not just a worker. A culture where the best ideas came not from one department, but from the fusion of many. The question is, are you fostering collaboration in your own organization, or are invisible walls holding your team back?

How to Apply:

- Build a culture of mentorship and teamwork—collaborate rather than compete.

- Create spaces for open dialogue where ideas can be shared freely.

6. T - Transform & Thrive: Leaving a Lasting Legacy

What if true leadership was not about making decisions, but about building a culture where creativity thrives?

Under Ed Catmull's leadership, Pixar transformed from a struggling startup into the gold standard for innovation and storytelling. His impact was not just in the films Pixar created—it was in the way he led, the culture he built, and the lessons he left behind.

His leadership proved that creativity flourishes in an environment of trust and collaboration. That failure is not a roadblock—it is a stepping stone to innovation. That great leaders do not just give orders; they create spaces where people feel safe to take risks, challenge ideas, and push boundaries.

Even after his retirement, Catmull's influence remains deeply embedded in Pixar and Disney Animation Studios. His book, *Creativity, Inc.*, has become a guidebook for leaders who want to unlock innovation in their own organizations.

The question is, how are you shaping the culture around you? Are you simply managing, or are you leading in a way that will leave a lasting impact?

Final Thought: How You Can Apply This to Your Own Leadership Journey

What if the key to extraordinary leadership is not just what you do—but how you think?

Great leadership starts with self-awareness—defining who you are and what you stand for. The most successful leaders do not fear failure; they see it as fuel for growth. They align their goals with a bigger mission, ensuring that every decision moves them closer to lasting impact. They take consistent action, building habits and accountability systems that turn ideas into results. But true transformation does not happen alone—it thrives in collaborative spaces where creativity and teamwork flourish.

The real question is not just how to lead—it is what kind of legacy you want to leave behind. Are you building something that will outlast you?

By following the IMPACT framework, just like Ed Catmull, you can create a culture of innovation, collaboration, and long-term success

> **"Fear of failure leads to a mindset of self-protection, which in turn leads to rigidity, inflexibility, and ultimately failure."**
>
> *—On why leaders must create a safe space for creative risks.*

Key Themes & Takeaways:

1. From Technologist to Transformational Leader

- Ed Catmull began as a computer scientist but became a visionary creative leader.

- His transformation was driven not by management techniques, but by understanding human dynamics and nurturing creative environments.

2. Creating a Culture of Candor

- **The Braintrust** at Pixar promoted radical honesty without ego or hierarchy.

- Truth was valued over authority, fostering innovation through open and fearless feedback.

- **Lesson:** Honest conversations without fear create stronger teams and better outcomes.

3. Embracing Failure as Fuel for Innovation

- Catmull made failure part of the creative process: "All our movies suck at first."

- Iteration, not perfection, was the goal.

- **Insight:** Great leaders normalize failure as a stepping stone to brilliance.

4. Leading with Humility & Continuous Learning

- Despite his stature, Catmull sought feedback from everyone.

- His humility was most evident in the Disney merger, where he listened first and led through collaboration.

- **Takeaway:** Transformation starts with humility and a willingness to learn.

5. Balancing Creative Freedom with Structure

- Catmull ensured teams had autonomy within a supportive framework.

- Creativity needs boundaries that prevent chaos but do not stifle imagination.

- **Coaching Principle:** Freedom + Accountability = Sustainable Creativity

Story-22:

Disney's Digital Comeback: A Story of Transformation

> **"Times and conditions change so rapidly that we must keep our aim constantly focused on the future."**
>
> — *Walt Disney*

Disney's 2024 streaming success was a testament to the power of strategic transformation. After years of financial losses in the competitive streaming market, the company redefined its approach, prioritizing profitability over rapid expansion. This shift was not an overnight success but the result of carefully planned and executed changes across multiple business areas.

A key factor in Disney's turnaround was cost-cutting, which included operational streamlining, workforce reductions, and budget reallocations. The company also optimized its content strategy, focusing on high-impact franchises like Marvel, Star Wars, and Pixar while reducing underperforming productions. Rather than chasing unsustainable subscriber growth, Disney prioritized engagement, retention, and revenue generation.

Strategic partnerships played a crucial role in this transformation. By integrating Hulu into Disney+ and expanding ESPN+ offerings, Disney created a seamless, value-driven experience for its subscribers. Pricing adjustments and bundled services increased average revenue per user, while advanced data analytics helped refine content recommendations and audience targeting.

At its core, Disney's success was driven by a leadership mindset shift—one that embraced adaptability, long-term vision, and disciplined execution. This transformation not only stabilized its streaming division but also reinforced Disney's position as a leader in the entertainment industry, setting the stage for sustainable growth in the digital age.

In 2024, Disney achieved what once seemed impossible—its streaming division finally turned a profit after years of losses.

This was not just luck; it was the result of a carefully crafted transformation, a journey shaped by the principles of the **IMPACT Coaching Framework.**

The Awakening: A Moment of Realization

For years, Disney had dominated traditional entertainment, but as streaming giants surged ahead, the company found itself at a crossroads. The old ways were no longer enough. Executives gathered in a high-stakes strategy session, reflecting on a critical question: *Who are we in this new digital era?*

This self-reflection marked the first step—**Inspire Awareness & Identity.** Disney acknowledged its legacy in storytelling but also recognized the urgent need to evolve. The company's strengths—iconic franchises, unmatched brand loyalty—had to be repurposed for the streaming age.

A Shift in Mindset: Breaking Free from Tradition

Letting go of traditional distribution was not easy. For decades, Disney had thrived on box office releases and cable TV deals. But as Netflix and other competitors redefined entertainment, Disney had to shift its thinking—**Mindset & Mastery Shift.**

The company made a bold move: investing heavily in digital infrastructure, revamping Disney+, and pivoting to a subscriber-first strategy. Innovation became the new norm, and agility was embraced at every level. The leadership knew that clinging to the past meant losing the future.

Purpose-Driven Strategy: Aiming for Profitable Growth

Disney's mission had always been to deliver **magical entertainment experiences**—but now, profitability was key. Instead of flooding the platform with content, the focus sharpened—**Purpose-Driven Goals & Strategy.**

Executives outlined a clear roadmap: maximize beloved franchises like Marvel and Star Wars, optimize content schedules, and create exclusive must-watch experiences. Every move was intentional, ensuring engagement and retention while steering towards financial sustainability.

Taking Bold Action: Adapting in Real Time

No transformation is smooth, and Disney faced its fair share of hurdles—rising production costs, market skepticism, and fluctuating subscriber growth. Yet, instead of resisting change, they embraced it with **Action, Accountability & Adaptability.**

Subscription models were revised, operational costs were trimmed, and content strategies were fine-tuned based on real-time user feedback. The leadership held itself accountable, openly communicating progress with stakeholders and quickly adapting to market shifts.

Collaboration Over Competition: Unifying the Ecosystem

Disney understood that siloed platforms were holding it back. To create a seamless experience, they took a radical step—integrating Hulu with Disney+ and introducing ESPN+ into the mix. This was **Connection & Collaborative Growth** in action.

By merging these platforms, Disney offered customers a richer, all-in-one entertainment experience while streamlining internal operations. Departments that once worked separately were now collaborating towards a common goal—delivering top-tier entertainment while driving revenue.

The Triumph: A New Era of Success

Months of relentless execution paid off. **Transform & Thrive** was no longer just an idea—it was reality. For the first time, Disney's streaming division turned profitable.

This was not just a financial victory; it was a statement to the industry. Disney had redefined itself, proving that even legacy giants could innovate, adapt, and thrive in the digital era.

Their journey serves as a powerful lesson—**with the right mindset, strategy, and execution, transformation is always possible.**

Business Coaching Lessons from Disney's Transformation

Disney's remarkable turnaround provides a powerful case study for business coaches. It highlights key coaching principles that can drive organizational change, inspire leaders, and enable sustainable success. Here is what business coaches can learn—and how they can apply these lessons to any organization.

1. Self-Awareness & Identity: Helping Organizations Discover Their Core Strengths

A company at its peak—successful, admired, and deeply rooted in its core strengths—can sometimes become trapped by its own success. What once made it great may turn into the very thing that prevents it from evolving. The key question is: will it recognize the need for change before it is too late?

This was the challenge Disney faced. For decades, it was the dominant force in traditional entertainment—movies, television, and theme parks defined its empire. But as the world shifted toward streaming, Disney found itself at a crossroads. Would it cling to the past or embrace the future? The turning point came when the company engaged in deep self-assessment, leading to the bold decision to launch Disney+. This move redefined its business model, ensuring it remained a powerhouse in the digital era.

The lesson is clear: transformation begins with self-discovery. Before an organization can innovate or break new ground, it must first take an honest look at itself—its strengths, blind spots, and untapped potential. Companies that shape the future are those that proactively redefine themselves rather than waiting for the world to force them to adapt.

As a coach, you can help businesses navigate this process by guiding them through structured self-reflection. Encourage them to clarify their vision, values, and market positioning. Use strategic tools such as SWOT analysis and competitive mapping to reveal hidden strengths and opportunities that may not be immediately obvious. Most importantly, ask the game-changing question: *Who are we today, and who do we want to become?*

The organizations that embrace this mindset will be the ones that lead the future—not just react to it.

2. Mindset Shift: Encouraging Adaptability and Growth

For decades, Disney defined entertainment with its blockbuster films, cable networks, and iconic theme parks. But the rise of streaming demanded a choice: cling to tradition or boldly embrace the future.

Disney+'s launch was a mindset shift, not just a strategy. They did not fear disruption; they seized the chance to reimagine their strengths for a digital era. By breaking old Molds and embracing digital innovation, Disney did not just survive—it thrived.

The key takeaway: change is opportunity, not a threat. Transformation happens when leaders see challenges as pathways to innovation.

As a coach, help leaders reframe challenges as opportunities. Guide them to see disruption as a call for evolution. Encourage a growth mindset where experimentation is routine, building resilience and adaptability. Use role-playing to shift teams from fear to bold, forward action.

The future belongs to creators, not resisters.

3. Purpose-Driven Strategy: Aligning Goals with Organizational Mission

Disney is not just about movies, theme parks, or merchandise—it is about magic. It is the kind of magic that makes a child's eyes light up at

Cinderella's Castle, that turns animated characters into lifelong friends, and that keeps families returning for generations. But behind the magic is something deeper: a strategy fuelled by an unwavering commitment to exceptional experiences and financial sustainability.

When Disney expanded into streaming with Disney+, it was not merely following a trend. It was a deliberate move that aligned with its core purpose—delivering unforgettable storytelling experiences while securing long-term business success. This was not just about competing in the streaming wars; it was about evolving while staying true to the very essence of Disney. The result? A seamless fusion of creativity and strategy that continues to captivate audiences worldwide.

The key lesson here is that a strong vision drives sustainable success. Businesses thrive when every decision—big or small—is rooted in a clear and compelling purpose.

As a coach, you can guide businesses to achieve this level of clarity by facilitating vision-setting workshops, helping them articulate their purpose and ensuring that every strategy reflects their core values. Encourage leaders to define clear, actionable objectives that go beyond short-term wins, fostering long-term growth and impact. Inspire purpose-driven leadership where decisions are made with integrity, sustainability, and a deep commitment to lasting success.

Because when a company stays true to its purpose, success is not just possible—it is inevitable.

4. Action & Accountability: Turning Plans into Results

A vision alone is inert; it requires the spark of action to become reality. Disney did not just envision digital streaming—they acted boldly. They restructured, adapted subscription models, optimized content, and strategically acquired, moving beyond legacy to compete. This was not passive; it was deliberate execution.

Strategy without execution is just a wish. Disney's success hinged on ownership, adaptability, and relentless follow-through. The Disney+ vision demanded full leadership commitment, adjusting tactics with market shifts while maintaining storytelling quality.

The core lesson: bold action turns vision into reality. Agile companies that act and refine their approach lead the way.

As a coach, help businesses move from vision to action by implementing accountability frameworks that drive ownership. Use SMART goals to break down big changes into measurable steps. Encourage regular reviews to enable agile adjustments for maximum impact.

Success is not about perfect plans—it is about acting, learning fast, and moving forward.

5. Collaboration & Integration: Breaking Silos for Greater Impact

Disney's transformation was not just about launching Disney+— it was about seeing the bigger picture. The company realized that its true strength was not in isolated platforms but in their synergy. By integrating Hulu, ESPN+, and Disney+ into a unified streaming ecosystem, Disney enhanced the user experience, streamlined operations, and leveraged its vast content library more effectively. This was not just a technological shift; it was a strategic alignment that maximized efficiency and amplified Disney's market power.

The same principle applies to organizations. When teams and departments operate in silos, innovation slows, communication breaks down, and opportunities are lost. But when they collaborate, transformation becomes possible. True growth happens when teams align, moving beyond isolated success toward a shared vision.

As a coach, you can help businesses break down silos by fostering cross-functional teamwork. Encouraging collaboration between departments ensures that resources are used efficiently and that everyone is working toward a common goal rather than competing for influence. Team coaching can be a powerful tool, aligning leadership and employees to drive strategic execution. Running design thinking workshops can also inspire teams to approach challenges creatively, leveraging collective intelligence to spark breakthrough innovation.

Because the future is not built by lone geniuses—it is built by teams that think, adapt, and grow together.

6. Resilience & Adaptability: Coaching Through Uncertainty

Disruption forces a critical choice: resist and risk obsolescence, or adapt, evolve, and thrive. Disney's journey exemplifies relentless agility, proactively anticipating industry shifts and consistently leading. Their enduring success, from box office dominance to streaming navigation, stems from continuous reinvention, not luck.

Agility is no longer a choice—it is essential for survival and leadership. The ability to pivot amidst market shifts, consumer behaviour changes, and technological advancements distinguishes thriving businesses.

As a coach, you build resilience by developing composed leaders through stress management training. Fostering continuous learning cultivates a culture that embraces agility. Scenario planning enables proactive strategies against potential disruptions.

The future belongs to those who master change, not fear it.

7. Transformation & Thriving: Long-Term Success Through Leadership Development

Transformation is not just about making financial decisions or strategic pivots—it is a mindset shift. Disney's evolution was never about chasing short-term wins but about reshaping its future, embracing innovation, and sustaining long-term growth. It recognized that success is not a final destination but an ongoing journey, requiring constant adaptation and reinvention.

True transformation is not a one-time event—it is a continuous commitment to progress. Companies that remain at the forefront do not settle for past achievements; they stay ahead by cultivating resilience, curiosity, and a willingness to evolve.

As a coach, you can empower leaders for long-term success by focusing on executive coaching that builds forward-thinking, adaptable leadership. Planning for the future through well-defined succession strategies ensures that transformation efforts extend beyond current leadership, keeping the momentum alive. Embedding a culture of innovation within organizations guarantees that progress does not stall after the first breakthrough but becomes an integral part of the company's DNA.

Real success is not just about reaching the top—it is about staying there, constantly redefining what is possible.

> **"The only way you survive is you continuously transform into something else. It is this idea of continuous transformation that makes you an innovation company."**
>
> — *Ginni Rometty, Former CEO of IBM*

Final Takeaways: Business Coaching is the Catalyst for Change

Disney's transformation did not happen by accident—it was a result of intentional leadership, strategic execution, and adaptability. Business coaches play a crucial role in guiding organizations through similar transformations by:

The Blueprint for Thriving in a Changing World

The boardroom is silent, except for the faint hum of a projector. Charts flash across the screen—numbers climbing, dipping, shifting unpredictably. The air is thick with the scent of fresh coffee, but no one takes a sip. Eyes scan reports, brows furrowed. The question hangs in the air: What is next?

Some leaders freeze in moments like this, gripped by uncertainty. Others see opportunities where others see roadblocks. What makes the difference?

- Recognizing the Tides of Change

  The world does not stand still. Can you hear the distant rumble of disruption before it reaches your doorstep? The rustle of shifting market trends? The whispers of customer expectations evolving? Companies that listen closely see challenges coming before they arrive.

- Shifting Mindsets—From Fear to Innovation

  The weight of past successes can be heavy. It is easy to cling to what worked before. But the scent of fresh ideas—the excitement of a bold experiment—breathes life into companies willing to evolve. The question is not *should* we change, but *how fast can we adapt?*

- Aligning Goals with Purpose

  A company without a clear mission feels like wandering through a dense fog—each step uncertain, every direction unclear. But when goals align with purpose, the path is illuminated—like city lights guiding the way on a dark night.

- Turning Ideas into Action

  Brainstorming is exciting, but execution is where success is built. It is the sound of keyboards clicking as strategies come to life, the sight of whiteboards filled with action plans, the energy in the room when teams take ownership and move forward.

- Collaboration—Breaking Down Walls

  Imagine a workplace where departments work in silos, doors closed, emails left unanswered. Now picture an open space buzzing with discussion, ideas flowing like fresh air through an open window. Which environment fosters innovation?

- Building Resilience to Face the Unknown

  The storm will come. Will you hear the sharp crack of panic in the air, or the steady resolve of a team prepared to pivot? Companies that survive do not just react—they anticipate, adapt, and stay steady in the face of uncertainty.

Preparing Leaders Who Carry the Torch Forward

Leadership is not about a single moment—it is a legacy. The question is not just who leads today, but who is being prepared to lead tomorrow? The future belongs to those who plant the seeds today.

The Future is Being Built Now

The scent of opportunity is in the air. The hum of innovation is rising. Are you ready to step forward?

Want to transform your organization like Disney? Business coaching can help you master change, lead with purpose, and drive sustained success.

Key takeaways:

1. Transformation Begins with Self-Awareness and a Shift in Identity

Disney's turnaround started with a bold *inward look*—recognizing that past success could not guarantee future relevance. This moment of reflection, identifying core strengths and acknowledging market changes, was the first step toward purposeful reinvention.

Coaching Insight: Help leaders ask the hard questions—*Who are we today? Who do we need to become?*

2. Mindset Shifts Unlock New Possibilities

Letting go of legacy models and embracing a digital-first, innovation-driven strategy marked a massive mindset shift for Disney. It was not just about launching Disney+—it was about unlearning old assumptions and mastering agility.

Coaching Insight: Guide clients through mindset transitions, from fear of disruption to embracing it as an opportunity for growth.

3. Purpose-Driven Strategy Ensures Focused, Sustainable Growth

Disney realigned its strategic goals with its enduring mission—creating magical, meaningful experiences. Profitability was no longer pursued through quantity, but through quality, focus, and franchise-driven storytelling.

Coaching Insight: Encourage organizations to tether every strategy to their *core purpose*, ensuring alignment, clarity, and long-term value.

4. Action, Accountability & Adaptability Drive Real Results

Disney did not just plan—it *executed*. From restructuring teams and cutting costs to leveraging real-time analytics and pivoting quickly, action was consistent and responsive.

Coaching Insight: Support clients in translating strategy into measurable action plans. Accountability and agility are the engines of real transformation.

5. Collaboration Breaks Silos and Builds Scalable Innovation

Disney unified Hulu, ESPN+, and Disney+ into an integrated ecosystem, boosting efficiency, synergy, and user value. This collaborative approach also extended internally, as departments aligned toward a shared vision.

Coaching Insight: Coaches should help clients foster cross-functional collaboration to replace fragmented efforts with unified momentum.

Story-23:

Ferguson's IMPACT on Leadership & Coaching

> **"In Ferguson's world, leadership wasn't given; it was earned. He made every player, coach, and staff member step up and embrace their role in the team's journey."**

Sir Alex Ferguson is one of the greatest football managers in history. His leadership at **Manchester United** was not just about tactics and talent—it was about **transforming players into winners**.

His coaching philosophy aligns closely with the **IMPACT Coaching Framework**, as he instilled **identity, discipline, adaptability, teamwork, and an unshakable winning mentality** in his players.

Let us break down how **Ferguson's coaching philosophy maps into the IMPACT model**:

1. Inspire Awareness & Identity – Building the Manchester United DNA

At Manchester United, giving up was never an option. Sir Alex Ferguson did not just build a football team—he created a winning identity. Whether it was academy graduates or superstar signings, he made sure every player understood what it truly meant to wear the Manchester

United shirt. He inspired them to believe they were part of something far greater than themselves.

Ferguson instilled a never-say-die attitude in legends like Ryan Giggs, Roy Keane, and Paul Scholes, ensuring they carried the torch of resilience. He constantly reinforced United's legacy—its history of attacking football, dramatic comebacks, and absolute dominance. Beyond tactics and fitness, he built a leadership culture where senior players mentored the younger ones, passing down the club's values and expectations.

This aligns perfectly with coaching strategies that help individuals build strong identities and resilient mindsets. Just as Ferguson shaped a team that thrived under pressure, great coaches empower individuals to see challenges not as obstacles, but as opportunities to rise.

2. Mindset & Mastery Shift – Turning Talent into Champions

Winning was not just a goal for Sir Alex Ferguson—it was an expectation. He did not settle for talent alone; he demanded that his players develop the mindset of relentless competitors. For him, skill was just the foundation—mental resilience, discipline, and hunger were what separated the good from the great.

Cristiano Ronaldo arrived at Manchester United as a flashy, skilful youngster, but under Ferguson's guidance, he transformed into a disciplined, goal-driven machine. Ferguson made him focus on efficiency, end product, and consistency rather than just entertaining the crowd. Similarly, he toughened up Wayne Rooney, channelling his natural aggression into controlled, productive energy on the pitch.

Complacency had no place in Ferguson's teams. Even after major victories, his message was clear: "Enjoy it tonight, but tomorrow we go again." He instilled a mentality where success was not a destination—it was a constant pursuit.

This aligns perfectly with coaching strategies that push individuals beyond their comfort zones. True mastery is not just about what you achieve—it is about how you sustain and elevate that success over time.

3. Purpose-Driven Goals & Strategy – Long-Term Vision & Game Plans

Sir Alex Ferguson understood that sustained success requires constant evolution. He was not just reacting to immediate challenges—he was always thinking ahead, planning for the future, and building a legacy. His ability to balance short-term performance with long-term vision made Manchester United dominant for over two decades.

He rebuilt squads every few years, recognizing that even the greatest teams must evolve to stay competitive. Instead of settling for one victory, he always had his eye on the next title, the next generation of leaders, and the next tactical innovation. By mentoring and grooming captains like Roy Keane, Gary Neville, and Nemanja Vidić, he ensured that his teams had strong leadership embedded in their DNA.

Ferguson's philosophy aligns perfectly with purpose-driven coaching. Just as great coaches help clients set meaningful, long-term goals, he ensured that United's success was not just a fleeting moment but a sustained legacy. Success is not just about winning today—it is about building systems, mindsets, and habits that ensure you keep winning for years to come.

4. Action, Accountability & Adaptability – The Hairdryer Treatment & Tactical Shifts

Sir Alex Ferguson's leadership was built on discipline, accountability, and adaptability. His famous "Hairdryer Treatment"—a fiery and direct method of confronting players—was not about intimidation but about demanding the highest standards. He understood that managing elite professionals required a balance of control, motivation, and adaptability.

If a player underperformed, Ferguson addressed it immediately, making it clear that mediocrity was unacceptable. He was not afraid to change tactics mid-season, shifting formations and strategies based on his opponents. More importantly, he instilled a mentality of resilience, teaching his players to thrive under pressure. One of the greatest examples of this was Manchester United's legendary 1999 Champions League final comeback, where they scored twice in injury time to secure victory.

Just as great coaches push their clients to take action, be accountable, and continuously evolve, Ferguson ensured his team never became complacent. His approach highlights a crucial lesson: sustained success requires a relentless commitment to improvement, adaptability, and a refusal to settle for anything less than excellence.

5. Connection & Collaborative Growth – Creating a Family Culture

Sir Alex Ferguson was more than just a coach—he was a mentor, leader, and father figure to his players. His philosophy went beyond tactics and training; he believed that understanding and supporting people on a personal level was just as important as developing their skills on the pitch.

He took the time to know his players personally, offering guidance through their struggles and celebrating their successes. He built strong bonds with his staff, ensuring that the coaching, medical, and scouting teams worked together seamlessly. More importantly, he created a culture of mentorship, where senior players were expected to guide and inspire the younger ones, fostering a cycle of leadership that sustained Manchester United's success for decades.

Ferguson's leadership aligns perfectly with the IMPACT framework—he emphasized mentorship, connection, and collaboration as key drivers of long-term transformation. Just as great coaches empower their clients by building trust, relationships, and a strong support system, Ferguson ensured that his team operated as a family, united by a shared vision of success.

6. Transform & Thrive – Leaving a Legacy of Excellence

At Manchester United, second place was never an option. Ferguson's relentless pursuit of excellence shaped a club that dominated English football for over two decades. His players did not just succeed under him—they carried his lessons forward into their own careers, embodying the mindset he instilled.

Many of his former players, like Ole Gunnar Solskjær and Ryan Giggs, transitioned into coaching, applying his leadership principles to their own teams. His philosophy of discipline, teamwork, and adaptability influenced generations of footballers, ensuring that his impact extended far beyond his own tenure. Even after retirement, Ferguson's legacy continues to shape leadership in sports and business, proving that true coaching success is not just about short-term victories—it is about creating leaders who thrive long after the coaching journey ends.

"Ferguson's coaching went beyond the X's and O's. It was about creating a mindset where leadership, commitment, and relentless pursuit of success were non-negotiables."

Sir Alex Ferguson & IMPACT Coaching: The Perfect Alignment

IMPACT Coaching Principle:

How IMPACT enables?

- **Inspire Awareness & Identity:** Built the **Manchester United DNA**—never give up, never settle.

- **Mindset & Mastery Shift:** Developed **mental toughness**—turned talent into champions.

- **Purpose-Driven Goals:** Created **long-term winning strategies** beyond just one season.

- **Action, Accountability & Adaptability:** Demanded **high standards, constant adaptation, and responsibility**.

- **Connection & Collaborative Growth:** Fostered **team unity, mentorship, and deep personal connections**.

- **Transform & Thrive:** Left a **legacy of excellence** that still inspires leaders today.

Final Thoughts: Ferguson's IMPACT on Leadership & Coaching

Sir Alex Ferguson was not just a football coach—he was a **master strategist, motivator, and leader** who transformed individuals and teams. His principles align seamlessly with **IMPACT coaching**, proving that the best coaches do not just **teach skills—they inspire transformation, resilience, and leadership**.

Whether in **sports, business, or life**, the **Ferguson mindset** teaches us that:

- **Discipline, focus, and belief turn ordinary people into legends.**

- **Adapting to change ensures long-term success.**

- **The best leaders create more leaders, not just followers.**

"A great coach doesn't just shape players on the field; they build leaders for life. Ferguson's leadership philosophy shaped minds, not just teams."

Here are **5 key coaching questions and actionable steps** inspired by how Sir Alex Ferguson's leadership maps to the **IMPACT Coaching Framework**—ideal for use in leadership development, coaching sessions, or self-reflection prompts:

1. Inspire Awareness & Identity

Key Question:

What core identity do you want your team or organization to be known for?

Action:

Define and communicate a clear vision and set of values. Create rituals, symbols, or stories (like Ferguson did with the "United way") that reinforce this identity in daily work.

2. Mindset & Mastery Shift

Key Question:

Are you cultivating a culture where growth, grit, and consistency are valued more than raw talent?

Action:

Introduce mindset coaching sessions. Celebrate effort and resilience over short-term success. Set goals that challenge comfort zones and reward consistency.

3. Purpose-Driven Goals & Strategy

Key Question:

Are your short-term actions aligned with your long-term purpose and legacy?

Action:

Create a "legacy map"—a strategic plan that blends quick wins with future development. Mentor successors to sustain vision, just as Ferguson groomed future leaders.

4. Action, Accountability & Adaptability

Key Question:

Do you hold yourself and others accountable to high standards while staying flexible in your approach?

Action:

Run regular check-ins with clear KPIs and feedback loops. Embrace feedback—even if it is tough ("Hairdryer moments" when needed). Be ready to pivot strategies without compromising on values.

5. Connection & Collaborative Growth

Key Question:

How are you investing in personal relationships to foster loyalty, trust, and collaboration?

Action:

Schedule one-on-one time regularly with team members—not just for performance talks, but to understand their lives, motivations, and challenges. Build cross-functional mentorship structures.

Story-24:

IMPACT in Motion: Leadership Lessons from The Social Network

> **Until you make the unconscious conscious, it will direct your life and you will call it fate."**
>
> — *Carl Jung*

In *The Social Network*, we follow Mark Zuckerberg, a Harvard student with a brilliant mind and a passion for coding. The film opens with a conversation between Mark and his girlfriend, Erica Albright, who breaks up with him over his obsession with school and lack of emotional understanding. This pivotal moment sets Mark on a path of ambition and personal vengeance, driving him to create a platform that will change the world.

Mark, with his friend Eduardo Saverin, starts developing a social networking site called "Facemash" in his dorm room. The project quickly evolves, and soon, they begin working on "The Facebook," a platform designed for college students to connect and share their lives. Mark eventually brings in Sean Parker, the co-founder of Napster, who helps the project gain attention and secure funding. However, the movie takes a turn as it focuses on the conflicts and betrayals that emerge between the key figures involved.

Key Conflicts and Challenges:

- **Betrayal and Friendship:** The relationship between Mark and Eduardo, who initially started Facebook together, begins to break down. Eduardo, who provided initial funding for the project, becomes increasingly sidelined as Mark becomes more focused on the business side of Facebook, influenced by Sean Parker. The tension builds when Eduardo finds out that Mark and Sean have made business decisions without his knowledge or approval.

- **Legal Battles:** The film portrays the legal drama that follows, with Eduardo suing Mark for diluting his ownership stake in Facebook. At the same time, the Winklevoss twins, who claim that Mark stole their idea for the social network, file a separate lawsuit, accusing Mark of intellectual property theft. The movie depicts the growing animosity between Mark and these individuals, as their lawsuits progress.

- **The Moral Struggle:** As the story unfolds, Mark's ambition drives him further away from his values and relationships. He becomes consumed by the idea of success and is willing to sacrifice his friendships and moral compass to grow Facebook into the global giant it becomes. The emotional cost of his actions is portrayed through his strained relationships and the isolation he experiences.

IMPACT Framework

I - Inspire Awareness & Identity: Self-reflection, behavioral change, neuroscience, Aristotle's coaching

M - Mindset & Mastery Shift: Overcoming fear, belief transformation, Mandela's optimism, NLP & CBT

P - Purpose-Driven Goals & Strategy: Positive psychology, coaching models, leadership goal-setting

A - Action, Accountability & Adaptability: High-performance teams, startup success, leadership execution

C - Connection & Collaborative Growth: Coaching impact, mentorship, team empowerment, Aristotle's leadership

T - Transform & Thrive: Digital transformation, business coaching, innovation, legacy

Introducing the "IMPACT" Coaching Framework

IMPACT stands for:

1. I - Inspire Awareness & Identity

- Focus: Self-reflection, strengths discovery, and purpose
- Draws from: The Power of Self-Reflection, Breaking the Chains of the Shoulds, Aristotle's legacy

- Key coaching questions:
  - Who am I as a leader/person?
  - What are my values, beliefs, and strengths?
  - What inner barriers hold me back?
- Coaching Tools: Strength's assessments, 360-degree feedback, self-reflection journals

2. M - Mindset & Mastery Shift

- Focus: Rewriting beliefs, breaking fears, and developing a growth mindset
- Draws from: The Power of Beliefs, Breaking the Chains of Fear, CBT for Coaching
- Key coaching questions:
  - What limiting beliefs are stopping my growth?
  - How can I shift fear into action?
  - What new perspectives will empower me?
- Coaching Tools: NLP techniques, cognitive-behavioral coaching, visualization exercises

3. P - Purpose-Driven Goals & Strategy

- Focus: Clarity, goal-setting, and building a roadmap for success
- Draws from: CLEAR Model, Coaching for Leadership, Scaling Success
- Key coaching questions:
  - What does success look like for me/team?
  - How can I align my actions with my purpose?
  - What strategies will help me reach my goal?
- Coaching Tools: SMART goals, OKRs, action planning frameworks

4. A - Action, Accountability & Adaptability

- Focus: Taking action, developing resilience, and tracking progress

- Draws from: Coaching Without Ego, Building High-Performance Teams, Agile Mindset

- Key coaching questions:

    o What action steps must I take?

    o How will I stay accountable to my commitments?

    o How can I embrace adaptability in my journey?

- Coaching Tools: Habit trackers, peer accountability groups, resilience-building exercises

5. C - Connection & Collaborative Growth

- Focus: Building strong teams, mentorship, and leadership impact

- Draws from: The Ripple Effect, Empowering Leadership, The Garden of Growth

- Key coaching questions:

    o How can I empower others through coaching?

    o What role does mentorship play in success?

    o How can collaboration drive better outcomes?

- Coaching Tools: Team coaching, leadership mentoring, active listening techniques

6. T - Transform & Thrive

- Focus: Sustained success, legacy building, and continuous learning

- Draws from: The Catalyst, The Digital Revolution, The Future of Coaching

- Key coaching questions:
  - How will I sustain my transformation?
  - What is my long-term vision?
  - How can I create impact beyond myself?
- Coaching Tools: Growth mindset strategies, reflection exercises, leadership legacy planning

Why "IMPACT" is a Powerful Coaching Framework:

The **IMPACT framework** is a structured coaching methodology designed to facilitate measurable growth, empower transformational leadership, and ensure long-term success. It provides both coaches and clients with a roadmap to navigate personal and professional development, ensuring that every step is intentional and aligned with meaningful progress.

For coaches, the framework offers a clear and structured approach to guiding their clients effectively. By integrating principles of self-awareness, mindset mastery, goal-setting, leadership development, collaboration, and long-term impact, IMPACT transforms the coaching process into a deeply insightful and results-driven journey. Coaches who adopt this framework can elevate their practice, enhance client outcomes, and establish themselves as thought leaders in their field.

For clients—whether individuals, teams, or organizations—IMPACT serves as a comprehensive guide to personal and professional growth. It helps leaders refine their self-awareness, overcome limiting beliefs, and align their goals with a larger purpose. By fostering collaboration, adaptability, and resilience, the framework ensures that success is not just an individual pursuit but a shared journey that creates a lasting legacy. Unlike traditional coaching models that focus solely on motivation or tactical execution, IMPACT integrates mindset work with strategic leadership practices, creating a holistic transformation that is both meaningful and sustainable.

One of the most compelling aspects of the IMPACT framework is its marketability. The name itself is powerful, memorable, and universally resonant, making it an attractive tool for professionals in the personal development, leadership coaching, and corporate transformation sectors. Its structured yet adaptable approach ensures that it can be applied across various coaching niches, from leadership development to executive coaching, life coaching, and team coaching.

Leadership coaches can leverage this framework to help their clients develop vision, emotional intelligence, and strategic thinking. Business and executive coaches can use it to refine leadership effectiveness, enhance decision-making, and drive organizational success. Life and transformation coaches can apply it to help individuals cultivate resilience, shift their mindset, and unlock their full potential. Team and organizational coaches can utilize the framework to foster collaboration, strengthen workplace culture, and build high-performing teams.

Whether used in one-on-one coaching, team coaching, or large-scale organizational transformation, the IMPACT framework is grounded in psychological principles, neuroscience, and leadership research. By combining scientific insights with practical coaching techniques, it ensures that success is not just about achieving short-term milestones but about fostering long-term, meaningful change.

The *IMPACT* framework offers a robust structure to tackle team challenges like those seen in *The Social Network*, where the main issue revolves around conflict, betrayal, and shifting team dynamics. By applying each of its principles, coaches can guide leaders and teams through the emotional and strategic hurdles they face, ultimately helping them reach their highest potential. Here is how this framework can be applied to address the situation:

1. Inspire Awareness & Identity (I)

In the case of Mark Zuckerberg and Eduardo Saverin, a coaching framework would begin with deep self-reflection, helping them explore their identities as leaders and partners. Their conflict was not just about business—it was a clash of values, leadership styles, and emotional responses to the rapid evolution of Facebook. Mark's relentless drive for success and control contrasted with Eduardo's emotional attachment and expectation of loyalty, leading to misalignment in their decision-making.

A coach would guide them through introspective exercises, prompting questions such as: *Who are you as a leader in this relationship? How do your personal values shape your decisions? What strengths and weaknesses do you each bring to the table?* These reflections would allow both to recognize the underlying motivations driving their choices and the impact of their leadership styles on their partnership.

To facilitate this process, tools such as *strengths assessments, 360-degree feedback, and journaling* would provide valuable insights. Strength's assessments could highlight complementary skills that, when leveraged correctly, could have strengthened their collaboration. 360-degree feedback from peers and mentors would reveal blind spots and help each of them see how their leadership styles affected the team. Journaling would encourage self-awareness, allowing them to track emotional triggers and recurring patterns in their decision-making.

By first understanding themselves and their leadership approaches, Mark and Eduardo could have built a stronger, values-aligned partnership—one that balanced ambition with trust and personal drive with shared purpose.

2. Mindset & Mastery Shift (M)

The challenges between Mark and Eduardo go beyond business disagreements; they are rooted in deep-seated fears and limiting beliefs that shaped their actions and responses. Mark feared losing control and being overshadowed, while Eduardo believed that his financial contributions warranted equal decision-making power. These internal struggles created an emotional divide that ultimately led to conflict and betrayal.

To rebuild trust and collaboration, they needed a *Mindset & Mastery Shift*—a transformation in how they perceived their fears and beliefs. Instead of seeing each other as threats, they needed to recognize the value in their differences and reframe their perspectives to support mutual growth.

Key coaching questions would include: *What limiting beliefs are holding you back from finding a mutual solution? How can you shift your fear into action and focus on growth together?* These questions encourage self-awareness and introspection, helping them break free from narratives that fuel division.

To facilitate this shift, *Cognitive-Behavioral Techniques (CBT)* could be used to reframe negative thought patterns. By identifying cognitive distortions—such as Mark's fear-driven need for control or Eduardo's resentment over perceived exclusion—they could develop new, empowering beliefs. This process would help them understand each other's fears, communicate with greater empathy, and rebuild their partnership on a foundation of trust and respect.

By addressing their mindset first, Mark and Eduardo could have moved beyond conflict and toward a shared vision, strengthening both their leadership and Facebook's long-term success.

3. Purpose-Driven Goals & Strategy (P)

Mark and Eduardo's partnership suffered because their individual ambitions and definitions of success began to diverge. Mark was focused on rapid innovation and expansion, while Eduardo prioritized stability and traditional business growth. Without a shared vision, their relationship became strained, leading to miscommunication, frustration, and ultimately, betrayal.

To rebuild trust and collaboration, they needed to *realign their goals* around a *purpose-driven strategy*. This required open dialogue about what success truly meant for both of them—not just individually, but for Facebook as a whole. By understanding each other's aspirations and concerns, they could have worked toward a collective vision rather than pulling in opposite directions.

Key coaching questions would include: *What does success look like for both of you in this venture? How can you align your goals and actions for the greater good of Facebook?* These questions encourage them to move beyond personal grievances and focus on shared objectives.

To ensure alignment, they could implement structured goal-setting frameworks such as *SMART goals* and *OKRs (Objectives and Key Results)*. These tools would help define clear, measurable targets, ensuring that their individual contributions complement Facebook's broader vision. A *strategic action plan* would then serve as a roadmap, breaking down their roles, responsibilities, and collaborative efforts into actionable steps.

By fostering alignment through clarity and structure, Mark and Eduardo could have strengthened their partnership, ensuring Facebook's growth was driven by a unified vision rather than conflicting priorities.

4. Action, Accountability & Adaptability (A)

The breakdown of Mark and Eduardo's partnership stems from two key issues: a lack of accountability and the failure to adapt to Facebook's rapid evolution. As the company grew, their leadership styles and expectations diverged, with Mark becoming more focused on product and expansion, while Eduardo remained anchored in traditional business models. This misalignment created tension, ultimately leading to conflict and distrust.

To rebuild their partnership, both needed to take *concrete, accountable actions* rather than letting unresolved issues fester. Mark had to acknowledge and address Eduardo's concerns, ensuring transparency in decision-making and reaffirming their partnership. Eduardo, on the other hand, needed to adapt his approach to leadership, recognizing the shifting demands of a fast-growing tech startup and finding ways to contribute effectively in that environment.

A coaching process centered on accountability would involve key reflective questions: *What actions can each of you take to restore trust and accountability in this partnership? How can you remain flexible in responding to the growing demands of Facebook?* These questions push them to move beyond blame and take responsibility for proactive change.

To ensure follow-through, practical tools like *accountability systems*—including *habit trackers* and *action plans*—could be implemented. These tools provide measurable ways to track commitments, monitor progress, and reinforce trust through consistent action. By embracing accountability and adaptability, Mark and Eduardo could have strengthened their collaboration, ensuring their partnership evolved alongside Facebook's exponential growth.

5. Connection & Collaborative Growth (C)

One of the central issues in the story is a breakdown in collaboration, leading to misalignment and conflict. Mark isolates himself with Sean Parker, making key decisions without Eduardo, while Eduardo feels sidelined and undervalued. This lack of communication and mutual support strains their partnership, ultimately causing resentment and division.

The *Connection & Collaborative Growth* step in the coaching process would address these challenges by fostering a culture of open dialogue, trust, and shared purpose. True collaboration is not just about working together—it is about ensuring that both individuals feel empowered, respected, and valued within the team. For Mark and Eduardo, rebuilding their partnership means finding ways to align their strengths and leverage their unique perspectives for the greater success of Facebook and their personal growth as leaders.

Key coaching questions to reflect on include: *How can both of you empower each other? How can your collaboration enhance not only the success of Facebook but also personal growth?* These inquiries encourage them to shift from competition to cooperation, recognizing that their combined efforts can create a more powerful and sustainable impact.

To facilitate this transformation, practical tools such as *active listening techniques* and *mentorship models* can be introduced. Active listening ensures that both parties feel heard and understood, reducing misunderstandings and fostering mutual respect. Mentorship models help establish structured ways to support one another's leadership development, creating an environment where constructive feedback and shared learning become the norm.

By embracing these strategies, Mark and Eduardo can move beyond past conflicts and build a partnership rooted in trust, communication, and a shared commitment to long-term success.

6. Transform & Thrive (T)

The ultimate goal for both Mark and Eduardo is to transform their working relationship into a thriving, collaborative partnership that not only strengthens their personal and professional growth but also creates a lasting impact. By learning from past experiences, they have the opportunity to rebuild trust, refine their leadership approaches, and establish a shared vision that extends beyond Facebook. True leadership is not just about building companies—it is about fostering relationships, adapting to change, and ensuring long-term success through continuous growth and learning.

To achieve this transformation, they must engage in deep reflection and forward-thinking strategies. Key questions to consider include: *How can you both ensure that the mistakes of the past do not define your future? What long-term vision can you create for yourselves individually and as partners?* These inquiries encourage self-awareness and help align their personal aspirations with their professional goals.

Practical tools can further support their journey. Reflection exercises allow them to analyse past conflicts objectively and extract valuable lessons. Leadership legacy planning ensures that their actions contribute to a greater mission, fostering a culture of growth, mentorship, and ethical leadership. A commitment to developing a growth mindset will enable them to embrace change, learn from setbacks, and continuously evolve as leaders.

By integrating these principles, Mark and Eduardo can redefine their partnership—not just as business collaborators but as visionary leaders shaping the future with wisdom, integrity, and a renewed sense of purpose.

Applying the *IMPACT* framework to the situation between Mark and Eduardo would involve guiding both individuals through self-reflection, shifting mindsets, and developing collaborative strategies. With actionable steps and a focus on their long-term vision and growth, they could both not only heal their rift but thrive as leaders in a complex and competitive environment.

"The quality of your life is the quality of your relationships."

— *Tony Robbins*

Key takeaways:

1. Inspire Awareness & Identity (I)

- **Key Message**: Self-awareness is the foundation for resolving conflict and building stronger partnerships. Leaders must reflect on their identities, values, and leadership styles to identify misalignments and gain clarity on what drives their decisions.

- **Application**: For Mark and Eduardo, understanding their personal motivations (Mark's ambition vs. Eduardo's loyalty) would have highlighted the emotional divides and allowed them to rebuild trust based on mutual values and complementary strengths.

2. Mindset & Mastery Shift (M)

- **Key Message**: The foundation of conflict resolution lies in shifting limiting beliefs and fears into growth-oriented perspectives. Leaders must challenge their fears and limiting assumptions to move from adversarial positions to mutual understanding.

- **Application**: Mark and Eduardo needed to confront their fears—Mark's fear of losing control and Eduardo's belief in equal power—and shift their mindsets to embrace each other's differences as opportunities for growth, not threats.

3. Purpose-Driven Goals & Strategy (P)

- **Key Message**: Alignment of goals and strategic vision is crucial for long-term success. Leaders must clearly define shared objectives and create a strategy that unites their individual aspirations for the collective good.

- **Application**: The lack of a shared purpose between Mark and Eduardo created tension. A coaching intervention would focus on re-aligning their goals around a unified vision for Facebook, fostering a collective purpose to guide decision-making.

4. Action, Accountability & Adaptability (A)

- **Key Message**: Accountability and adaptability are essential for sustainable progress. Leaders must take ownership of their actions, adapt to changing circumstances, and commit to solutions that prioritize the health of the team and the business.

- **Application**: For their partnership to recover, Mark and Eduardo needed to take concrete actions to rebuild trust, be accountable for past missteps, and adapt to Facebook's evolving needs, ensuring that both could contribute to its growth in complementary ways.

5. Connection & Collaborative Growth (C)

- **Key Message**: Effective collaboration goes beyond teamwork—it involves empowering each other, embracing diverse strengths, and creating a culture of trust and open communication.

- **Application**: Rebuilding their connection required Mark and Eduardo to actively listen to each other, value their unique perspectives, and engage in collaborative decision-making, ensuring that both felt respected and included in the leadership of Facebook.

6. Transform & Thrive (T)

- **Key Message**: Transformation is the result of continuous self-improvement, reflection, and growth. Leaders must not only address past conflicts but also develop a shared vision for the future that reflects both personal and professional aspirations.

- **Application**: Mark and Eduardo's transformation could only be achieved through ongoing reflection, setting a new course for their partnership that integrates past lessons and fosters long-term personal and professional growth, ensuring both thrive individually and as co-leaders.

Story-25:

Beyond the Game: The Coach Who Changed Lives

> **"A coach is someone who can give correction without causing resentment."**
>
> — *John Wooden*

In Coach Carter (2005), the coaching approach is centered around discipline, academic excellence, and personal growth, with a heavy emphasis on accountability. Coach Carter (played by Samuel L. Jackson) is hired to coach the Richmond High School basketball team, which is struggling both on and off the court. His coaching approach is unique because he challenges his players to excel not just in basketball, but also in their academic pursuits, teaching them valuable life lessons that extend beyond sports.

The storyline follows Carter's decision to bench the entire team after discovering that their grades are below the standards he has set. His goal is to teach his players that academic success and character are just as important as athletic success. As the players struggle with this new approach, they initially resist Carter's strict rules, but over time, they realize that his discipline and commitment to their futures are acts of care and leadership.

The themes explored in the movie include:

1. **Discipline** – Coach Carter sets strict standards for his players, emphasizing the importance of commitment, hard work, and responsibility both on the court and in life.

2. **Academic Excellence** – Carter's rule that players must maintain a certain GPA to play basketball challenges the idea that sports should come before education.

3. **Teamwork** – Through basketball, Carter teaches his players the value of collaboration, sacrifice, and support for each other.

4. **Leadership and Accountability** – Carter holds his players accountable for their actions and decisions, teaching them the value of leadership and integrity.

5. **Personal Growth** – Throughout the movie, the players learn valuable life skills, such as self-respect, confidence, and perseverance, that help them achieve success off the court.

The ultimate message of the movie is that success is not defined by talent alone but by hard work, education, and strong character. Coach Carter's tough love ultimately helps his players grow into more responsible and capable individuals, illustrating the profound impact a dedicated coach can have on a team's lives.

In *Coach Carter* (2005), the coaching approach aligns closely with the **IMPACT Framework,** which emphasizes self-awareness, mindset shifts, purpose-driven goals, action and accountability, collaboration, and transformation. Let us trace how Coach Carter's approach to coaching mirrors this framework:

1. Inspire Awareness & Identity (I)

The gymnasium echoed with the sound of bouncing basketballs and the rhythmic squeak of sneakers against polished wood. The Richmond High players had always seen the court as their escape—a place where they could forget the struggles of their daily lives. But Coach Carter had a different vision.

He stood before them, clipboard in hand, eyes sharp with determination. "This is bigger than basketball," he said, his voice cutting through the room. The players exchanged confused glances. Basketball was all they had. What else was there?

Then, the contract appeared. A simple piece of paper, but one that carried weight far beyond the game. Good grades. Respect. Responsibility. If they wanted to wear the jersey, they had to live up to these standards—not just as athletes, but as students, as young men preparing for something greater.

At first, there was resistance—grumbles, defiance, rolled eyes. But Carter did not back down. He pushed them to look in the mirror, to see past their circumstances, to realize they were capable of more.

When he locked the gym, cancelling games despite their winning streak, frustration boiled over. But slowly, reality set in. Their coach was not punishing them—he was elevating them. He was teaching them that success was not just about scoring points; it was about character, discipline, and the belief that they were more than their environment dictated.

By the end of the season, they were not just players. They were scholars. Leaders. Young men who had confronted their fears and rewritten their own stories.

Coach Carter did not just change their game—he changed their lives.

2. Mindset & Mastery Shift (M)

The tension in the gym was thick, hanging in the air like an unspoken challenge. The Richmond High players slouched in their chairs, eyes downcast, waiting for Coach Carter to finish his lecture. He paced in front of them, arms crossed, his gaze piercing through their excuses.

"You're not just basketball players," he said, his voice firm but steady. "You are young men with the potential to be great. But if you don't believe that, then none of these matters."

Silence. A few players shifted uncomfortably. They had spent years being told otherwise—by teachers, by the world around them, by their own doubts whispering that they were not good enough.

Carter was not just asking them to play better; he was asking them to see themselves differently.

He raised the bar, not just on the court but in the classroom. He set strict academic expectations, refusing to let their dreams be defined by a game. Some resisted at first, their fear of failure masquerading as defiance. But Carter saw through it. He knew what fear looked like— the hesitation before taking a shot, the avoidance of hard questions, the quiet surrender to low expectations.

So, he pushed harder. When they stumbled, he made them stand back up. When they doubted themselves, he reminded them of their progress. He held them accountable, not just for their talent but for their future.

And then, something changed. They started to believe. In the classroom, in their work, in their ability to rise above the statistics that had written their futures for them.

By the end of the season, they were not just a winning team. They were young men who had learned that success was not just about what happened on the court—but what they chose to believe about themselves long after the final buzzer sounded.

3. Purpose-Driven Goals & Strategy (P)

The gym echoed with the sound of sneakers squeaking on polished wood. The Richmond High players ran drill after drill, exhaustion weighing heavy on their shoulders. But Coach Carter was not just watching their footwork or their shooting form—he was watching their discipline, their mindset.

"Stop," he called out, tossing a clipboard onto the bench. "How many of you want to play college ball?"

Hands shot up. Some players raised theirs hesitantly, as if afraid to believe it was possible.

Carter nodded, pacing in front of them. "And how many of you are putting in the work off the court to make that happen?"

Silence. A few players looked at each other. They knew the answer.

Coach Carter walked over to a pile of papers and held them up. "These are your contracts," he said. "Not basketball contracts—life contracts. You will maintain a 2.3 GPA. You will sit in the front of your classes. You will show up to study hall." His voice hardened. "You will not be another statistic."

Some players grumbled. "Coach, we're here to play ball."

Carter's gaze sharpened. "And what happens when the ball stops bouncing?" He let the question hang in the air, watching as realization dawned on their faces. "You think winning a game is success? No. Success is being in control of your future. Success is making sure you have choices."

At first, resistance came in the form of rolled eyes and muttered complaints. But over time, something shifted. The team started showing up to class. They began taking pride in their academics as much as their game. They studied together, held each other accountable.

By the season's end, their victories were not just on the scoreboard. Scholarships were earned. Futures were changed.

Coach Carter had not just coached a team—he had redefined their definition of success. It was no longer just about the game. It was about the life that came after it.

4. Action, Accountability & Adaptability (A)

The gym doors swung open, and the Richmond High basketball team walked in, expecting another day of practice. But instead of whistles and drills, they found their coach standing in the centre of the court, arms crossed, a clipboard clutched in his hand. The scoreboard remained dark. No basketballs were in sight.

"Take a seat," Coach Carter said, his voice calm but firm. The players hesitated, confused.

"You think you've earned the right to be here?" he asked, scanning the room. "You think talent alone keeps you on this team?"

The players glanced at each other. Some shifted in their seats.

Carter held up a stack of papers. "These are your grade reports." He dropped them onto the bench with a thud. "Too many of you failed to meet the contract you signed. That means one thing—practice is over."

Murmurs rippled through the team.

"You can't do that, Coach!" one player protested. "We've got a big game coming up!"

Carter's eyes did not waver. "And you had an even bigger responsibility— to your future." He stepped closer. "Basketball is temporary. Your education is not."

The gym fell silent.

For days, the court remained locked. No practices. No games. The players grumbled, angry, frustrated. But as the weight of Carter's decision settled in, something changed. They started hitting the books. Study groups formed. The team held each other accountable, making sure no one fell behind.

When they finally earned their way back onto the court, it was not just about playing—it was about proving to themselves that they could rise above setbacks.

Coach Carter had not just benched his team. He had forced them to take responsibility, to see that discipline was not just about basketball—it was about life.

5. Connection & Collaborative Growth (C)

The gym echoed with the rhythmic squeak of sneakers against polished wood. Sweat dripped, breaths came heavy, but the real challenge was not the drills—it was the lesson Coach Carter was about to teach.

"Suicide drills. Go." His voice was sharp, cutting through the exhaustion in the air. The players groaned but sprinted without hesitation.

Then it happened. Jason, one of the team's most promising players, collapsed to his knees, gasping for air. His teammates slowed, hesitating, waiting for Carter's next move.

Carter crossed his arms. "Get up," he said, his voice even.

"I... I cannot, Coach," Jason admitted, his chest heaving.

Silence.

Then, a voice from the back. "I'll run for him." It was Cruz, the player who had once resisted Carter's rules the most.

A pause.

Another voice. "Me too."

One by one, the teammates stepped forward, splitting Jason's remaining sprints among them. No one was left behind.

Carter watched, a flicker of pride crossing his face. "That," he said finally, "is what a team looks like."

From that moment on, the players did not just play for themselves—they played for each other. They studied together, pushed each other, grew stronger as individuals and as a unit.

It was not about basketball anymore. It was about trust, respect, and knowing that when one-man stumbles, another will be there to lift him up.

6. Transform & Thrive (T)

The final game had ended. The scoreboard no longer mattered.

The locker room, once filled with the rowdy energy of a team hungry for victory, now held a different kind of silence—a heavy, reflective one. The players sat, jerseys damp with sweat, eyes locked on Coach Carter as he stood before them.

"You think this is about basketball?" Carter's voice was calm but firm. He looked at each of them, his gaze lingering as if memorizing their faces. "It never was."

Some of them shifted uncomfortably. Others just listened.

"This was about your future. About the kind of men, you choose to be." He glanced at the walls lined with academic contracts—the ones they had signed at the start of the season. "Look at what you have done. Look at how far you have come."

Jason, who once dismissed school as a waste of time, had pulled his grades up high enough to apply for college. Cruz, who had nearly thrown his life away in the streets, now carried himself with a quiet confidence, a man who knew his worth. The whole team, once a group of individuals playing for themselves, had become something greater—a brotherhood, bonded not just by the game, but by the belief that they were capable of more.

Carter stepped back; his voice softer now. "I am proud of you. But this is just the beginning."

The players exchanged glances, the weight of his words settling in. Because they understood now—this was not about the season. It was not about the wins or losses.

It was about the legacy they carried forward. The lessons of discipline, resilience, and self-respect. The understanding that success was not measured by a final score, but by the choices they would make every day.

As they stood up, one by one, something had shifted. They were not just players anymore. They were leaders, ready to take on whatever came next.

Coach Carter had given them more than basketball.

He had given them the belief that they could build their own futures.

By using the **IMPACT Framework,** *Coach Carter* illustrates a coaching journey that goes far beyond the basketball court.

Through his disciplined approach, Carter empowers his players to believe in themselves, set meaningful goals, take consistent action, support each other, and ultimately thrive as individuals. The movie demonstrates how effective coaching can transform lives, creating a legacy that extends well beyond the team's athletic achievements.

From a coaching perspective, *Coach Carter* offers valuable lessons on how coaches can be better at their craft by following a structured approach like the **IMPACT Framework.**

Let us break down the key coaching takeaways from the movie and how a coach can apply them to be more effective:

1. Inspire Awareness & Identity (I)

A great coach goes beyond just teaching skills or strategies—they help players understand who they are beyond the game. This means guiding them to reflect on their personal values, motivations, and aspirations. True growth comes not just from improving technical abilities but from developing a strong sense of identity and purpose. When players understand their strengths, challenges, and deeper goals, they become more committed, both on and off the court.

In *Coach Carter*, Carter challenges his players to see themselves as more than just basketball players. He pushes them to reflect on their academic performance, their future, and how they represent themselves. His coaching is not just about winning games—it is about shaping responsible, self-aware individuals who take ownership of their actions and choices. By forcing them to confront difficult truths about their effort, discipline, and mindset, he helps them redefine who they are and who they can become.

To instil this level of self-reflection, coaches need to engage in meaningful conversations with their players. Asking questions like, "What do you want to achieve beyond basketball?" or "What kind of person do you want to be?" helps athletes think beyond immediate goals and consider their long-term growth. Encouraging journaling, team discussions, or even personal storytelling can provide players with the space to explore their motivations and challenges.

Using practical tools like strengths assessments and self-reflection exercises allows players to gain deeper clarity about their values and identity. Regular feedback sessions help reinforce progress, ensuring that players not only develop their skills but also build the self-awareness needed to succeed in life. A coach who fosters this kind of reflection creates not just better athletes, but better individuals.

2. Mindset & Mastery Shift (M)

A great coach understands that the biggest obstacle to success is often not external challenges, but the self-imposed limitations players place on themselves. Fear, self-doubt, and negative beliefs can hold them back from reaching their full potential. A coach's role is to help players break free from these mental barriers, teaching them to see failure as a learning experience rather than a reason to give up. By shifting their mindset, players can step beyond their comfort zones and achieve more than they ever thought possible.

In *Coach Carter*, the players start with the belief that they are "just athletes" and that success outside of basketball is out of reach. Coach Carter refuses to let them be defined by these limitations. He pushes them to expect more from themselves, both academically and personally, helping them see that their future is not determined by where they come from, but by the choices they make. Through discipline, encouragement, and high expectations, he transforms their mindset, making them believe in their own potential.

To help players overcome limiting beliefs, coaches must actively foster a growth mindset. This means framing challenges as opportunities rather than threats and reinforcing the idea that failure is simply part of the learning process. Positive reinforcement plays a key role—reminding players that they are capable, strong, and resilient. Simple affirmations like, "You've got this," or "I believe in you" can have a profound impact on an athlete's confidence.

Practical tools such as Neuro-Linguistic Programming (NLP) techniques and cognitive-behavioural strategies can help players reframe their thinking. Visualization exercises, where athletes mentally picture themselves succeeding in difficult situations, can also be powerful in building self-confidence. By guiding players to rewire their thought patterns and embrace a mindset of growth, a coach not only improves their game but also prepares them for success in life.

3. Purpose-Driven Goals & Strategy (P)

A great coach does more than teach skills; they help players see the bigger purpose behind their hard work. Setting meaningful goals is crucial in guiding athletes toward success, both on and off the field. A coach must ensure that players understand how their daily efforts contribute to both short-term victories, like winning games, and long-term achievements, such as academic success and personal growth. When players connect their actions with a larger purpose, they become more motivated and committed to their journey.

In *Coach Carter*, the coach sets high standards, not just for basketball performance but for academic excellence as well. He instils in his players the belief that their success on the court is directly linked to their personal and educational goals. By refusing to let them settle for mediocrity, he teaches them that discipline and dedication will shape their futures. His leadership helps the players recognize that their talent is not enough; they must also focus on their education and long-term ambitions.

To improve as a coach, it is important to guide players in setting goals that go beyond the sport. Encouraging them to think about their future and aligning their personal aspirations with the team's objectives creates a sense of purpose. Regular check-ins can help ensure that both individual and team goals remain on track. Using structured goal-setting methods, such as SMART goals and OKRs, allows players to measure their progress, both in academics and athletics. A strong coach does not just push for victories in games—they push for victories in life.

4. Action, Accountability & Adaptability (A)

A strong coach instils both accountability and adaptability in their players. Athletes must take responsibility for their actions, decisions, and commitments, understanding that success comes from discipline and follow-through. At the same time, setbacks are inevitable, and a good coach teaches resilience—helping players adapt, learn from mistakes, and keep moving forward. A team that embraces both accountability and adaptability become stronger, more disciplined, and better prepared for challenges on and off the field.

In *Coach Carter*, accountability is a central theme. When the players fail to meet their academic standards, he benches the entire team, making it clear that actions have consequences. His approach teaches them that discipline and commitment go beyond basketball; they must also excel in their education. However, he does not abandon them in their struggle—he supports their efforts to improve, showing that failure is not the end, but an opportunity to adapt and grow. This balance of strict accountability and compassionate guidance transforms his players into responsible young men.

To become a more effective coach, it is crucial to establish clear expectations from the start and create a structured system of accountability. This could include peer check-ins, where teammates support and challenge each other to meet their goals, or designated accountability partners who provide encouragement and constructive feedback. Coaches can also use practical tools like habit trackers to monitor progress and resilience-building exercises such as scenario planning to help players navigate setbacks. By fostering both accountability and adaptability, a coach not only builds a winning team but also prepares players for success in life beyond the game.

5. Connection & Collaborative Growth (C)

A great coach understands that success is not just about skill and strategy but also about trust and relationships. By forming personal connections with each player, a coach can inspire and motivate them to reach their full potential. When players feel valued and supported, they are more likely to stay committed and push themselves to improve. Beyond individual growth, a coach must also nurture teamwork, helping players realize that their success is tied to the team's success. When a team works together, supporting and relying on one another, they become stronger as a unit.

In the movie *Coach Carter*, the coach goes beyond teaching basketball skills. He becomes a mentor, guiding his players not only in the game but in life. He emphasizes that teamwork is not just about winning matches but about standing by each other through challenges. His leadership transforms his players, instilling discipline, responsibility, and a sense of purpose that extends beyond the court.

To improve as a coach, it is essential to build meaningful relationships with each player. Offering mentorship and guidance helps individuals grow both as athletes and as people. Creating a team-oriented culture, where players encourage and support one another, strengthens the entire group. Using techniques like team coaching, leadership mentoring, and active listening allows a coach to understand each player's needs and foster an environment of trust and growth. True coaching is not just about developing skills—it is about shaping character and preparing individuals for success in all aspects of life.

6. Transform & Thrive (T)

A great coach does not just focus on winning games—they shape individuals who are prepared for life beyond the sport. True coaching is about creating a lasting impact, equipping players with the mindset, skills, and habits they need to succeed long after their athletic careers are over. This means teaching resilience, leadership, discipline, and the ability to navigate challenges, both on and off the court.

In *Coach Carter*, the true measure of success is not just the team's performance on the basketball court—it is the transformation of the players as individuals. Carter instils discipline, accountability, and a vision for their future, pushing them to excel academically and see themselves as more than just athletes. His coaching is not about short-term victories but about preparing young men to become responsible, successful individuals in life.

To create this kind of long-term transformation, a coach must help players see beyond their immediate circumstances. Encouraging them to develop leadership skills, time management abilities, and emotional intelligence fosters growth that extends into their personal and professional lives. It is not just about how well they perform in the game but about how well they handle adversity, make decisions, and shape their future.

Using leadership development programs, mentorship opportunities, and strategies for continuous learning can help players build a solid foundation for the future. Implementing legacy planning—where players reflect on the kind of impact they want to leave behind—can further reinforce the importance of long-term growth. A coach's greatest achievement is not just a winning season—it is the success of the individuals they have guided long after the game has ended.

Coach Carter exemplifies the principles of the **IMPACT Framework** in his coaching approach, demonstrating how a coach can be more effective by helping players reflect on their identities, transform their mindsets, set purposeful goals, be accountable, collaborate as a team, and ultimately thrive. Coaches who adopt this comprehensive, transformational approach will likely create environments where players not only excel in sports but grow as individuals capable of leading successful, fulfilling lives.

> **"Success is peace of mind which is a direct result of self-satisfaction in knowing you made the effort to become the best of which you are capable."**
>
> — *John Wooden*

Here is a breakdown of the key coaching takeaways from _Coach Carter_, using the IMPACT Framework to enhance a coach's effectiveness:

1. Inspire Awareness & Identity (I)

A great coach goes beyond teaching skills—they guide players to discover their deeper sense of self. By fostering self-awareness and reflection, players understand their values, motivations, and aspirations, which enhances both their performance and their life off the court. Coaches can inspire this growth by engaging in reflective conversations, encouraging journaling, and using tools like strengths assessments to help players develop a strong sense of identity. This process empowers players to take ownership of their actions and choices.

2. Mindset & Mastery Shift (M)

Coaches must help players overcome self-imposed limitations like fear and self-doubt. By shifting their mindset, players can see failure as a stepping stone, not a setback. In _Coach Carter_, the players learn to expect more from themselves both academically and personally, broadening their vision of what they can achieve. Coaches can encourage a growth mindset by framing challenges as opportunities, using positive reinforcement, and applying cognitive strategies like visualization and NLP to help players break through mental barriers.

3. Purpose-Driven Goals & Strategy (P)

Successful coaches help players understand the bigger purpose behind their efforts. By aligning daily actions with long-term goals— whether related to sports, education, or personal growth—players become more motivated and committed. _Coach Carter_ emphasizes that basketball performance is connected to academic success and life goals. Coaches should guide players in setting purposeful goals and use structured methods like SMART goals or OKRs to track both athletic and personal growth, reinforcing the importance of discipline and dedication.

4. Action, Accountability & Adaptability (A)

A great coach instils a sense of accountability and resilience in their players. Setbacks are inevitable, but a coach's role is to teach players how to adapt and keep moving forward. In *Coach Carter*, accountability is a central theme, as players face consequences for failing to meet academic standards. To foster this, coaches can create a system of accountability through peer check-ins, habit trackers, and resilience-building exercises. This empowers players to be disciplined and adaptable, preparing them for both the game and life.

5. Connection & Collaborative Growth (C)

Coaching is not just about skill development; it is about building strong, trusting relationships. A great coach forms personal connections with players, inspiring them to reach their full potential. *Coach Carter* demonstrates this by becoming a mentor who guides players not only in basketball but also in life. Coaches can foster a team-oriented culture, where players support each other and collaborate to improve. Techniques like team coaching and leadership mentoring can strengthen both individual and team growth, leading to greater overall success.

6. Transform & Thrive (T)

A coach's impact extends beyond the game; it is about shaping individuals for success in life. *Coach Carter* focuses on the long-term transformation of his players, teaching them discipline, leadership, and resilience. To create lasting change, coaches should encourage leadership development, emotional intelligence, and legacy planning, preparing players for challenges beyond their athletic careers. By nurturing personal growth and helping players visualize their future success, a coach can create lasting impact far beyond the game.

Coach Carter exemplifies the IMPACT Framework by guiding players through self-discovery, mindset shifts, purpose-driven actions, accountability, teamwork, and long-term transformation. Coaches who adopt this holistic, transformational approach create an environment where players excel in both sports and life, becoming well-rounded individuals capable of thriving in any challenge they face.

Story-26:

How Businesses Overcame Challenges with Structured Planning and the IMPACT Framework

> **"Strategy without tactics is the slowest route to victory. Tactics without strategy is the noise before defeat."**
>
> — *Sun Tzu*

Successful businesses do not just stumble upon success—they follow structured frameworks, embrace challenges, and execute their strategies with discipline.

Below are **detailed, real-life stories** of companies that faced significant obstacles, overcame them using structured planning, and transformed into industry leaders.

I - Inspire Awareness & Identity: How Starbucks Rediscovered Its Soul

Losing Identity in the Pursuit of Growth

In the early 2000s, Starbucks was expanding at an incredible pace, opening thousands of stores worldwide. However, in this race for growth, the company lost something essential—its original identity. Baristas, once passionate about crafting high-quality coffee, were now trained to serve drinks faster, prioritizing speed over craftsmanship. The cozy and inviting ambiance that once defined Starbucks stores gradually faded, replaced by an impersonal, efficiency-driven atmosphere. Customers began to notice that Starbucks no longer felt like the unique coffeehouse they had once loved. Instead, it was becoming just another generic coffee chain. Without realizing it, Starbucks had lost touch with what made it special in the first place. As a result, sales declined, customer dissatisfaction grew, and the company's stock price plummeted.

How Starbucks Found Its Identity Again

In 2008, Howard Schultz, the company's former CEO, returned to lead its revival. His approach was rooted in self-awareness and a return to

Starbucks' core values, aligning with the first pillar of the **IMPACT Framework**—identity and purpose. One of his first major decisions was to shut down 7,100 stores for a full day to retrain baristas, reminding them of the artistry behind making espresso. This symbolic move was more than just a training session; it was a statement that Starbucks was reclaiming its commitment to quality. Schultz also refocused the company on its original mission: *"To inspire and nurture the human spirit – one person, one cup, and one neighbourhood at a time."* This shift in strategy led to the closure of hundreds of underperforming stores, prioritizing experience, and quality over unchecked expansion.

The Key Lesson

When a business loses its identity, it also loses its customers. Starbucks' turnaround proves that success is not just about growth—it is about staying true to purpose. By taking a step back, reflecting on what made them great, and realigning their strategy with their core values, Starbucks was able to reconnect with both its mission and its customers.

M - Mindset & Mastery Shift: Netflix's Bold Leap into the Unknown

Facing Extinction in a Changing Industry

In the early 2000s, Netflix was still a DVD rental company, battling against Blockbuster, the dominant force in the industry. However, the landscape was shifting. Digital streaming technology was emerging, and consumer habits were changing. Fewer people were renting physical DVDs, opting instead for the convenience of on-demand content. Many industry experts doubted that streaming would succeed, arguing that internet speeds were too slow to support it. Blockbuster executives dismissed Netflix's vision, convinced that customers would always prefer renting physical DVDs over watching movies online.

Like many businesses facing disruption, Netflix found itself at a crossroads: cling to the familiar and risk becoming obsolete, or embrace change and transform into something entirely new. The fear of change often holds companies back, just as it does for individuals. But instead of resisting the inevitable, Netflix chose to reinvent itself.

How Netflix Reinvented Itself

Under the leadership of CEO Reed Hastings, Netflix underwent a complete transformation, guided by a key principle of the **IMPACT Framework**—embracing change as an opportunity rather than a threat. Hastings made the bold decision to pivot away from DVDs and invest heavily in online streaming. Recognizing the potential of personalized content, he introduced a data-driven algorithm that recommended shows and movies tailored to each user's preferences, making the experience more engaging and addictive. But Netflix did not stop there. Instead of just distributing content, it became a creator, investing in original programming. The launch of groundbreaking shows like *House of Cards* and *Stranger Things* gave Netflix a unique competitive edge that no other platform could replicate.

Meanwhile, Blockbuster refused to evolve, clinging to its outdated business model. As Netflix soared, Blockbuster collapsed, eventually filing for bankruptcy. Today, Netflix is a $200 billion powerhouse, dominating the entertainment industry and reshaping how the world consumes content.

The Key Lesson

Businesses, like individuals, must adopt a **growth mindset** and take calculated risks. Fear and rigid thinking are the enemies of innovation. Netflix's success is proof that those who embrace change, adapt quickly, and dare to challenge conventional wisdom are the ones who survive—and thrive.

P - Purpose-Driven Goals & Strategy: Tesla's Master Plan for Revolutionizing the Auto Industry

Competing Against Giants with No Resources

When Tesla first emerged, the idea of electric cars was dismissed as impractical, unrealistic, and even laughable. The automobile industry was firmly controlled by massive corporations like Ford, General Motors, and Toyota—companies with decades of experience and billions of dollars in resources. On top of that, the infrastructure to support electric vehicles barely existed. Charging stations were rare, and most people believed that EVs were slow, unreliable, and incapable of competing with traditional gasoline-powered cars.

Under these overwhelming odds, most startups would have folded. But Elon Musk had a plan—not to fight the giants directly, but to take a structured, step-by-step approach, much like the **Purpose-Driven Goals** principle in the **IMPACT Framework**.

How Tesla Transformed the Industry

Rather than attempting to mass-produce affordable electric cars immediately, Tesla started at the top of the market and worked its way down. The first step was to create an expensive, high-performance electric sports car—the **Tesla Roadster**. This was not designed for mass appeal but rather to prove that EVs could be fast, exciting, and cutting-edge. With the Roadster's success, Tesla gained credibility and funding to move to the next phase.

With growing resources, Tesla expanded its lineup by developing the **Model S** luxury sedan and the **Model X** SUV, making electric vehicles more accessible to high-end consumers. These cars demonstrated that EVs could be stylish, long-range, and technologically advanced. The success of these models provided the financial foundation for Tesla's biggest leap—the launch of the **Model 3**, an affordable mass-market EV designed for everyday consumers. This final step brought electric vehicles to millions, disrupting an industry that had remained unchanged for over a century.

The Key Lesson

Without a **clear strategic roadmap**, companies can drift aimlessly, failing to make meaningful progress. Tesla's success was not based on luck—it was a result of **deliberate, phased execution** that built momentum over time. By following a structured plan and proving its value at each stage, Tesla did not just survive in a hostile industry—it became the most valuable car company in the world.

A - Action, Accountability & Adaptability: Amazon's Relentless Execution

Scaling While Maintaining Customer Obsession

Amazon began as a small online bookstore, but Jeff Bezos had a vision far beyond selling books—he aimed to build the most customer-centric company in the world. As the company expanded, its operations became increasingly complex. Managing logistics, supply chains, and fulfilment centres on a global scale required constant innovation. Traditional retail giants like Walmart dismissed Amazon's ability to compete, believing that e-commerce could never match the efficiency of brick-and-mortar stores. Meanwhile, rapid growth meant Amazon could not rely on a rigid business model; constant adaptation was essential for survival.

How Amazon Achieved Unmatched Growth

Amazon's success was not just about having a great idea—it was about **relentless execution, accountability, and adaptability**. Jeff Bezos instilled an obsessive focus on customer feedback, ensuring that every decision aligned with customer needs. Whether it was through faster deliveries, personalized recommendations, or better pricing, Amazon always put the customer first.

At the same time, the company pursued **extreme efficiency in execution**. Amazon pioneered automation, robotics, and AI-driven logistics to streamline operations at a massive scale, making it nearly impossible for competitors to keep up. Instead of staying confined to e-commerce, Amazon continually **reinvented itself** by expanding into cloud computing (AWS), subscription services (Prime), and AI-driven products like Alexa. This willingness to pivot and embrace new opportunities kept Amazon ahead of the competition.

The Key Lesson

A **brilliant plan is useless without action and adaptability**. Amazon did not become a global powerhouse by sticking to a single idea—it **executed relentlessly** while continuously evolving. Its ability to balance **customer obsession, operational excellence, and innovation** ensured its dominance in multiple industries.

C - Connection & Collaborative Growth: Microsoft's Cultural Transformation

Transforming a Toxic, Siloed Work Culture

Under former CEO Steve Ballmer, Microsoft was plagued by a **highly competitive and fragmented work environment**. Employees were pitted against each other, prioritizing personal success over teamwork. Internal divisions made collaboration difficult, stifling innovation. Leadership was also resistant to **external partnerships**, refusing to work with Linux, Apple, and other tech companies. As a result, **morale declined**, and while Microsoft struggled with stagnation, competitors like Google and Apple surged ahead, leaving the tech giant at risk of falling behind.

How Satya Nadella Transformed Microsoft

When Satya Nadella took over as CEO, he recognized that Microsoft's biggest problem was not its technology—it was its culture. He **dismantled the toxic, cutthroat environment** and promoted a team-oriented mindset, where employees worked together rather than against each other. He also embraced **collaboration beyond Microsoft**, forming strategic partnerships with open-source communities, cloud computing competitors, and even longtime rivals like Linux.

Beyond just partnerships, Nadella introduced a cultural shift cantered on **continuous learning and growth**. Microsoft evolved from a rigid "know-it-all" culture to a **"learn-it-all" culture**, where curiosity and adaptability were encouraged at every level. This change in mindset unlocked new innovations, reignited employee engagement, and helped Microsoft regain its position as a tech leader.

The Key Lesson

Long-term success is built on **collaboration and connection, not competition and isolation**. By shifting its focus from internal rivalries to **teamwork, partnerships, and a growth mindset**, Microsoft regained its dominance, eventually becoming a **$2 trillion company** and one of the most influential technology firms in the world.

T - Transform & Thrive: Apple's Reinvention

Apple's Near Bankruptcy and Ultimate Transformation

In the 1990s, Apple was on the verge of collapse, struggling with declining sales, lack of focus, and poor leadership. The company had too many products, no clear direction, and was rapidly losing market share to competitors like Microsoft. Many analysts predicted Apple's downfall, and bankruptcy seemed inevitable.

How Steve Jobs Revived Apple

When Steve Jobs returned to Apple in 1997, he radically simplified the company's product lineup, cutting unnecessary projects and focusing on innovation. He introduced a design-first approach, ensuring that Apple's products were not only technologically advanced but also intuitive and beautiful. This design-thinking philosophy led to the creation of iconic products like the iMac, iPod, iPhone, and MacBook, setting Apple apart from its competitors.

Beyond products, Jobs also built a seamless ecosystem, where Apple devices worked together flawlessly. This approach created long-term customer loyalty, turning Apple into more than just a technology company—it became a lifestyle brand.

The Key Lesson

Transformation is not a one-time event—it is an ongoing process. Apple's success was not just about one great product; it was about continuous innovation, reinvention, and a relentless focus on simplicity, design, and customer experience. Today, Apple is the most valuable company in the world, proving that true transformation comes from adapting, evolving, and staying ahead of the curve.

Final Takeaways: The Power of the IMPACT Framework

These companies **succeeded because they followed structured planning** rather than relying on luck.

Great businesses thrive on **clarity, strategic execution, leadership, and adaptability**—the same principles that drive personal growth. By applying these **IMPACT-based coaching questions** within a business setting, organizations can unlock potential, align teams, and drive sustainable success.

Let us explore how each category of questions can **transform businesses**, using **real-world examples** of companies that overcame challenges by leveraging these insights.

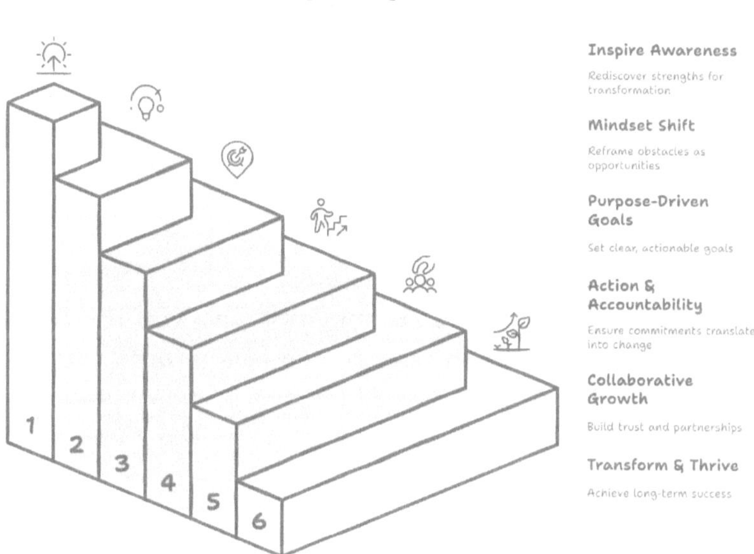

I - Inspire Awareness & Identity: Aligning Business Vision & Values

In today's competitive business world, companies often find themselves adrift without a clear sense of purpose and identity. Without these guiding principles, businesses can lose their way, struggling to differentiate themselves and risking customer trust. A strong identity, rooted in core values and a well-defined vision, is not just a tool for marketing—it is the foundation for growth and sustainability.

Airbnb's story is a prime example of how a company can turn uncertainty into market leadership by clarifying its purpose. When

Airbnb first launched, it faced an uphill battle. The concept of renting homes to strangers was not only unfamiliar, but it also raised concerns about safety and reliability. Hosts were hesitant, and guests were unsure about trusting the platform. In this challenging environment, Airbnb's leadership team understood that they had to look inward before they could move forward.

They began by asking themselves tough questions about their mission, values, and how they were perceived by their customers. Questions like:

- *What is our company's core mission, and how does it set us apart?*

- *Are we consistently living by our values in every customer interaction?*

- *How do customers perceive us, and what can we improve to build stronger trust?*

Through this deep reflection, Airbnb discovered that its true value was not just in providing a marketplace for rentals—it was in creating a sense of trust, belonging, and community. This was the vision that could set them apart. With this renewed sense of purpose, Airbnb began making crucial changes, such as introducing verified host profiles, secure payment systems, and guest reviews. These features not only built trust but also reassured both hosts and guests, making Airbnb more than just a platform—it transformed into a global leader in hospitality.

The key lesson from Airbnb's journey is clear: businesses that lack clarity in their purpose will struggle to build lasting relationships with customers. In contrast, a company that defines its mission, lives by its core values, and listens to its customers is positioned for growth. Airbnb's transformation shows that when a company aligns its actions with a clear sense of purpose, it does not just build a brand—it builds a movement that resonates with people and drives long-term success.

M - Mindset & Mastery Shift: Breaking Through Business Growth Barriers

Many companies hold themselves back not because of a lack of resources or talent, but because of limiting beliefs. These are the silent saboteurs—the "what ifs," the doubts, and the outdated assumptions that create fear of change. Organizations that cling to the status quo often find themselves stuck, while those willing to challenge those internal narratives open doors to innovation and growth. Netflix is a powerful example of what happens when a company chooses courage over comfort.

When Netflix started, it was a DVD rental business trying to carve out a space in a market dominated by Blockbuster. The idea of mailing DVDs seemed revolutionary at the time, but soon, digital streaming technology began to emerge. This presented Netflix with a dilemma: stick to the model that was working or bet on a future that had not fully arrived yet.

Inside Netflix, questions began to swirl. Was the world really ready for streaming? Would customers adapt? Would slow internet speeds kill the experience? These were real concerns, and many companies in their place might have hesitated. But Netflix did not let fear become a roadblock. Instead, the company leaned into a growth mindset—a belief that the future could be shaped, not feared.

Rather than asking what might go wrong, Netflix began asking what old beliefs were holding them back. They challenged their assumptions, considered the risks, and reimagined the entire landscape of home entertainment. By treating disruption as a doorway rather than a danger, they moved boldly into streaming.

And they did not stop there. Netflix did not just adapt—they led. They used data to personalize viewing experiences, invested in original shows and films, and redefined what it meant to consume entertainment. In doing so, they did not just survive the streaming revolution—they created it.

The real lesson? Success does not come from playing it safe. It comes from having the mindset to question everything, the vision to imagine something better, and the courage to act on it—even when the outcome is not guaranteed. Netflix's story is a reminder that the biggest breakthroughs happen when you stop asking, "What if it fails?" and start asking, "What if it works?"

P - Purpose-Driven Goals & Strategy: Setting Clear Business Objectives

A powerful vision can inspire, but it takes clear goals and consistent action to make that vision real. Many organizations talk about changing the world—but few take the structured steps needed to truly do it. Tesla is one of the rare companies that turned a bold mission into a global movement, not by rushing, but by planning each move with precision.

Tesla's vision is simple but ambitious: accelerate the world's shift to sustainable energy. This was not something that could be achieved overnight, and Elon Musk knew it. Instead of trying to change the auto industry all at once, he created a roadmap—a strategic blueprint that would build momentum over time.

The journey started with the Tesla Roadster, a high-performance electric sports car designed to shatter the myth that EVs were boring or impractical. Once Tesla proved that electric vehicles could be exciting, they reinvested the profits into creating more premium models like the Model S and Model X. These were not just cars—they were statements of innovation, luxury, and what the future could look like. The final stage? The Model 3—an affordable, mass-market electric car aimed at making clean transportation accessible to everyone.

What made this strategy work was not just vision—it was the discipline to break it down into realistic goals. Along the way, Tesla asked critical questions: What does long-term success really look like? What are the measurable steps that will get us there? And when obstacles arise—as they always do—how do we adapt without losing sight of the mission?

The real lesson here is this: bold visions alone are not enough. Strategic goal-setting is what bridges the gap between dreaming and doing. Tesla did not just disrupt an industry by thinking big—they did it by thinking smart, staying focused, and turning their mission into a series of clear, actionable steps. And that is how they became one of the most valuable and transformative companies in the world.

A - Action, Accountability & Adaptability: Driving Execution and Innovation

Having a brilliant strategy is important—but without consistent action, even the most inspiring vision will fade away. Many companies dream big, yet few succeed in turning those dreams into reality. Amazon is a powerful example of what happens when bold vision meets relentless execution.

Amazon started as a simple online bookstore, but Jeff Bezos had something far more ambitious in mind. He wanted to create the most customer-centric company in the world. That kind of transformation did not happen overnight—and it certainly was not easy. As Amazon began to grow, it faced enormous challenges: managing complex logistics, scaling operations, and going head-to-head with retail giants like Walmart. But instead of sticking rigidly to a single playbook, Amazon kept evolving.

The secret? A deep, ongoing commitment to execution. The company constantly analysed customer behaviour, experimented with new ideas, and made fast, data-driven decisions. It was not afraid to change course or test bold new models—whether launching Amazon Web Services (AWS), introducing Prime subscriptions, or stepping into physical retail with Amazon Go and Whole Foods. At the heart of it all was a simple idea: move fast, stay accountable, and put the customer first—always.

Amazon's success came from asking tough but powerful questions: What actions do we need to take today to make progress? How can we ensure every team is accountable for outcomes? And what will we do if our first plan does not work?

The biggest lesson from Amazon's story is this: strategy sets the direction, but it is execution that takes you to the finish line. By staying adaptable, acting quickly, and staying focused on customers, Amazon did not just grow—it redefined what execution-driven innovation really looks like.

C - Connection & Collaborative Growth: Strengthening Teamwork and Leadership

What really makes a team successful? Google wanted to find out. So, through a deep study called *Project Aristotle*, they explored why some teams thrive while others do not. They discovered something powerful and surprising: the secret to high-performing teams was not just talent or intelligence—it was **psychological safety**. In other words, it was about how safe people felt to speak up, share ideas, ask questions, or even admit mistakes without fear.

Even at a place filled with brilliant minds, Google saw that innovation slowed down when people did not feel comfortable expressing themselves. Without trust, teams became quiet, careful, and disconnected. Creative energy faded. But when people felt safe, supported, and heard, something incredible happened—they collaborated more freely, took bold steps, and solved complex problems together.

To build this kind of culture, Google focused on a few key things. Leaders were trained not just to manage, but to truly listen. They created open environments where everyone could share thoughts without judgment. Mistakes were not seen as failures but as valuable lessons. Teams were encouraged to take risks and learn. Managers became mentors—people who uplifted and supported their team members rather than just assigning tasks.

The big lesson from Google's journey is this: it is not enough to gather smart people in a room. What truly matters is the environment you create around them. When you lead with trust, nurture open communication, and turn mistakes into stepping stones, you create a space where people can do their best work. That is how real innovation happens—and that's how Google keeps pushing the boundaries of what is possible.

T - Transform & Thrive: Ensuring Long-Term Business Growth and Legacy

There was a time when Microsoft, once the undisputed tech giant, began to feel like it was falling behind. As the tech world moved rapidly toward cloud computing and artificial intelligence, Microsoft struggled to keep up. Under Steve Ballmer's leadership, the company stayed focused on its traditional PC software business, even as competitors like Google and Amazon raced ahead with bold new innovations. The world was changing, and Microsoft risked becoming irrelevant.

Then came a turning point. When Satya Nadella took over as CEO, he brought with him a fresh perspective and a deep sense of urgency. He did not just want to fix Microsoft—he wanted to reinvent it. He asked hard but necessary questions: How can Microsoft stay relevant in a rapidly evolving industry? What new innovations should we embrace now to shape the future? And what kind of impact do we want to leave behind?

Under Nadella's leadership, Microsoft transformed. The company adopted a "cloud-first" mindset, pouring energy and investment into Azure, its cloud computing platform, to compete with Amazon's AWS. It embraced artificial intelligence, supported open-source projects, and made strategic acquisitions like LinkedIn and GitHub to extend its influence in the digital world. Most importantly, Microsoft moved away from a narrow focus on software and began positioning itself as a leader in cloud services, enterprise AI, and digital transformation.

The real lesson in Microsoft's story is not just about technology—it is about mindset. Success today is not about clinging to what worked yesterday. It is about having the courage to adapt, the vision to innovate, and the patience to build for the long run. By choosing transformation over tradition, Microsoft not only regained its edge but became a powerful example of how reinvention is the true key to lasting success.

Final Thoughts: Why Coaching Questions Matter in Business

The **right coaching questions** drive **clarity, innovation, and execution** in business just as they do in personal growth. Companies that ask these questions **consistently evolve, adapt, and lead.**

Coaches can learn several key insights from this story, particularly around leadership, transformation, and strategic execution. Here are the top coaching takeaways:

1. Self-Awareness & Identity Are Foundational

- Lesson: Just like Starbucks, businesses (and leaders) lose their way when they drift from their core identity.

- Coaching Takeaway: Help teams reflect on their purpose, values, and unique strengths. Regularly ask: *"Are we staying true to what makes us special?"*

2. Mindset Shift Drives Innovation

- Lesson: Netflix thrived because it embraced a growth mindset instead of resisting change.

- Coaching Takeaway: Encourage clients to reframe challenges as opportunities. Ask: *"What assumptions are limiting us? What risks are we avoiding out of fear?"*

3. Purpose-Driven Strategy Fuels Sustainable Growth

- Lesson: Tesla did not just innovate—it followed a structured, phased plan to disrupt the industry.

- Coaching Takeaway: Guide teams to set long-term goals with actionable steps. Ask: *"What is our roadmap to success? How do today's actions align with our long-term vision?"*

4. Action, Accountability & Adaptability Are Non-Negotiable

- Lesson: Amazon scaled because it prioritized execution, customer feedback, and constant adaptation.

- Coaching Takeaway: Push leaders to act decisively and track progress. Ask: *"How do we ensure accountability? What is our plan if things do not go as expected?"*

5. Collaboration & Connection Strengthen Culture

- Lesson: Microsoft's transformation under Nadella was driven by teamwork, open learning, and partnerships.

- Coaching Takeaway: Foster psychological safety and collaboration. Ask: *"Are we enabling open communication? How can we better support and challenge each other?"*

6. Continuous Transformation is Key to Long-Term Success

- Lesson: Apple and Microsoft succeeded because they embraced ongoing reinvention.

- Coaching Takeaway: Encourage leaders to plan for the future. Ask: *"How will we stay relevant five years from now? What skills and innovations do we need to invest in today?"*

Final Takeaways for Coaches

A structured coaching approach—focused on awareness, mindset shifts, purpose, action, collaboration, and transformation—can help businesses thrive, just like these global leaders. Coaching is not just about advice; it is about asking the right questions to unlock potential and drive meaningful change.

> **"In the middle of difficulty lies opportunity."**
>
> — *Albert Einstein*

Key Takeaways

1. Clarity Over Chaos: Purpose Is the Starting Line

"Businesses do not drift into greatness—they design it with purpose. Like Airbnb, clarity of mission builds trust, direction, and long-term loyalty."

2. Growth Demands Grit: Mindset Makes or Breaks Momentum

"Innovation is not born from certainty—it is born from questioning limits. Netflix won by challenging fear with forward-thinking courage."

3. Dreams Need a Map: Strategy Converts Vision into Victory

"Tesla did not disrupt by accident—they planned it, step by step. Purpose-driven strategy turns bold ideas into unstoppable execution."

4. Speed + Accountability = Execution Excellence

"Amazon's secret? Relentless action, radical customer focus, and fearless adaptability. Execution is not an act—it is a habit."

5. Transformation Thrives on Trust and Teamwork

"Real growth is not solo—it is shared. Like Microsoft and Google, when you build psychological safety and collaborative culture, you spark innovation that lasts."

Chapter Summary

Top Coaching Questions & Actions to Unlock Transformation

I – Inspire Awareness & Identity

Coaching Questions:

- Who are you at your core as a leader?

- What do you want your team or organization to be known for?

- Which past experiences shaped your identity and current leadership style?

Action Steps:

- Write a personal leadership manifesto.

- Create and share a team purpose statement.

- Reflect on moments of transformation in a leadership journal.

M – Mindset & Mastery Shift

Coaching Questions:

- What limiting belief is holding you or your team back?

- Where do you need to shift from fear to curiosity or courage?

- Are you rewarding progress, not just perfection?

Action Steps:

- Conduct a "belief audit" to reframe negative narratives.

- Run monthly mindset growth sessions with your team.

- Celebrate a "failure that led to insight" each quarter.

P – Purpose-Driven Goals & Strategy

Coaching Questions:

- Are your daily actions aligned with your long-term purpose?
- What legacy do you want to leave behind?
- What goals reflect meaning, not just metrics?

Action Steps:

- Create a "Legacy Map" with short-term wins and long-term purpose milestones.
- Lead a session where your team craft's individual purpose statements.
- Design strategic OKRs that tie to mission, not just performance.

A – Action, Accountability & Adaptability

Coaching Questions:

- What bold action are you avoiding right now?
- How are you creating structures for accountability and adaptability?
- When was the last time you pivoted in response to new insights?

Action Steps:

- Set up weekly reflection huddles with KPIs + "pivot moments."
- Use the "accountability triangle" (responsibility – feedback – growth).
- Create a "Red Flag Ritual" to catch misalignment early and adapt fast.

C – Connection & Collaborative Growth

Coaching Questions:

- Who on your team needs more support, trust, or recognition?

- Are you building bridges across silos—or walls?

- How are you nurturing leadership in others?

Action Steps:

- Implement monthly 1:1 "human check-ins," not just performance reviews.

- Start a mentorship or buddy program across departments.

- Share team wins in visible ways that highlight collaboration.

T – Transform & Thrive

Coaching Questions:

- What is your next bold evolution as a leader?

- What inner transformation needs to happen before outer success follows?

- How are you ensuring your impact lasts beyond your current role?

Action Steps:

- Design a personal development roadmap: mindsets, skills, and relationships to evolve.

- Conduct a "transformation timeline" with past, present, and desired future growth.

- Start a legacy project—something that benefits others beyond your tenure.

End-of-Chapter Reflection Prompt:

"Of all the lessons from Carnegie, Catmull, Coach Carter, and others—what's the one insight I will act on in the next 7 days to become the coach or leader I aspire to be?"

Concluding Reflection:

What one action can you take this week to embody the Coaching qualities discussed in the chapter?

These questions can help facilitate deeper reflection and dialogue, encouraging individuals to connect their personal experiences with the principles outlined in the text

Chapter 5

Coaching the Future — Legacy, Children & Global Challenges

"The dreams of the future are born in the hearts of the young—and shaped by the hands of those who choose to lead with purpose today."

In a world grappling with disruption and division, one truth remains: **the future will be shaped by the leaders we empower now.** These leaders will not just be adults in boardrooms or politicians on podiums—they will be **children in classrooms**, young minds sparking under starlit skies, and courageous voices rising in communities across the globe.

This chapter is a call to **coach not for today's success, but for tomorrow's legacy**.

Drawing inspiration from the stories of bold changemakers like Dr. A.P.J. Abdul Kalam and Jacinda Ardern, we explore how leadership is not about domination, but **transformation**—and how the **IMPACT Coaching Framework** can awaken this potential in anyone, anywhere.

We journey into the hearts of three interwoven truths:

- That **leadership begins with self-awareness**—a child learning to believe in their voice.

- That **fear is not the end, but the beginning of courage**—a young leader daring to act in uncertainty.

- And that **true legacy is built not through titles, but through people**—through every mind we ignite and every life we lift.

From humble beginnings in Rameswaram to launching satellites from Thumba, from classrooms to global conferences, the leaders of tomorrow are waiting. They need not permission—but **coaching, connection, and purpose**.

Because legacy is not what we leave behind—it is who we leave empowered.

And the question this chapter asks is simple, yet profound:

Will we be the generation that coaches the future—or the one that fails it?

Key Topics:

- **From Potential to Power: Transforming Children into Leaders with the IMPACT Coaching Framework**

- **Igniting Minds, Inspiring Generations: The Story of Dr. APJ Abdul Kalam**

- **How the IMPACT Coaching Framework Empowers Leaders to Solve Global Challenges**

- **IMPACT in the Depths: A Story of Resilience, Leadership, and Transformation**

- **IMPACT Coaching in Action: The Mighty Ducks (1992)—A Journey of Transformation and Excellence**

- **Elon Musk and the Growth of SpaceX: A Real-Life Example of Lateral Thinking in the IMPACT Framework**

- **IMPACT in Action: A Woman's Journey from Self-Help to Social Impact**

- **From Breakdown to Breakthrough: How Coaching Saved Ford's Future**

Story-27:

From Potential to Power: Transforming Children into Leaders with the IMPACT Coaching Framework

> **"True leadership stems from individuality that is honestly and sometimes imperfectly expressed... Leaders should strive for authenticity over perfection."**
>
> – Sheryl Sandberg

Imagine a young girl growing up in a small rural town in New Zealand—her name is **Jacinda Ardern**. Raised in a modest household with a deep sense of community, young Jacinda was not the loudest in the room, nor did she demand attention. She was observant, thoughtful, and deeply moved by the struggles of those around her.

In school, she noticed inequality early on—some classmates came to school without lunches, while others faced bullying in silence. Jacinda did not yet know what "leadership" meant in a political sense. But she knew what fairness felt like. And she could not ignore the discomfort in her heart when others were treated unfairly.

This quiet fire inside her marked the beginning of a journey—the very kind of transformation the **IMPACT Coaching Framework** is designed to support. Not through authority or titles, but through deep, values-driven action.

1. Inspire Awareness — Awakening the Inner Mirror

Leadership begins not with strategy but with self-awareness. Even as a child, Jacinda spent time questioning how things could be better—not just for herself, but for her peers. When others overlooked a classmate in need, she paid attention. When rules felt unjust, she asked why.

That curiosity, paired with a strong internal compass, laid the foundation of her identity—not just as a student, but as someone who believed in *people first*. The IMPACT Framework starts here—by helping children like Jacinda discover who they are, what they feel, and why it matters.

2. Mindset Shift — Turning Fear into Fuel

It is easy to believe that great leaders are fearless. But the truth is, like young Jacinda, many of them started out with doubt. She once described feeling "like an outsider" in her early years—not always fitting into traditional molds of popularity or power. Yet, she never let that discomfort silence her voice.

Instead, she leaned into it. She joined the student council not because she loved speaking, but because she cared about change. Her courage did not roar—it whispered. She spoke up when it was hard. She stood up for others when no one else did. Through practice and perseverance, she rewired fear into fuel, embodying the essence of the **Mindset Shift** principle.

3. Purpose-Driven Vision — Discovering the Why

Jacinda's early exposure to social issues shaped her purpose early on. As a teenager, she joined a youth political organization—not for power, but to be of service. Her leadership was not driven by ambition, but by a relentless question: *"How can I help?"*

This sense of purpose did not arrive all at once—it was built through reflection, listening, and staying connected to the people she wanted to uplift. In the **Purpose-Driven Vision** phase of the IMPACT framework, we help children like Jacinda explore what lights them up and who they want to become—not in terms of careers, but in terms of character.

4. Action and Accountability — From Dreams to Deeds

Jacinda never sat idle with her ideas. Even as a youth, she volunteered, organized, and acted. Whether it was standing up for others at school or voicing her thoughts at local council meetings as a young adult, she took initiative—not perfectly, not always confidently, but consistently.

This reflects the **Action & Accountability** principle. Ideas only become impact when they are lived. Children learn this when we create space for them to act—when we treat their ideas as real, and their dreams as valid.

5. Collaborative Growth — Building Together, Not Alone

One of Jacinda's greatest strengths as a leader is her ability to unite people. That began early, when she led not with domination but with empathy. She listened more than she spoke. She created coalitions, not competition.

As Prime Minister, she would later demonstrate this during moments of national crisis—showing the world that leadership can be both powerful and gentle, commanding, and compassionate. But those seeds were planted in childhood—in the way she connected with others, valued their voices, and shared her spotlight.

This is what **Collaborative Growth** teaches children: that leadership is not about being above others, but walking beside them.

6. Transform & Thrive — A Lifestyle of Leadership

Jacinda did not just grow into a leader—she grew into someone who *lives* her values. Her leadership was a reflection of years of practice in integrity, compassion, and authenticity. Her story shows us that real transformation is not a single event—it's a way of being.

Children who are taught this from a young age carry it into adulthood—not to become prime ministers necessarily, but to become the kind of leaders who lift others up in every room they enter.

The IMPACT Coaching Framework is not a theoretical model—it is a lived path, one that leaders like Jacinda Ardern have walked in their own way.

By nurturing awareness, rewiring fear, anchoring in purpose, taking action, collaborating deeply, and committing to growth, we give children the tools to lead—not someday, but today.

When we invest in their inner world, we do not just create future professionals—we cultivate compassionate, courageous changemakers. And the world needs more of them now than ever.

Key Takeaways:

- **Self-Awareness as the Foundation of Leadership**

   Leadership begins with self-awareness. Just like Jacinda Ardern, who observed the inequalities around her and questioned the status quo, the IMPACT Coaching Framework encourages children to reflect on their values and identity. Understanding who they are and what they care about is essential for becoming a values-driven leader.

- **Turning Fear into Fuel**

Great leaders do not necessarily lack fear; they transform it into motivation. Jacinda Ardern's early struggles with fitting in did not stop her from taking action. The Mindset Shift principle in the IMPACT framework teaches children to reframe fear as an opportunity for growth, encouraging them to act despite their discomfort.

- **Leadership is About Collaboration, Not Domination**

True leadership is about lifting others up, not standing above them. Jacinda's leadership style, rooted in empathy and collaboration, demonstrates that leadership is about building relationships and uniting people for a common cause. The IMPACT Coaching Framework emphasizes that leadership involves working with others, valuing their voices, and fostering collective growth.

> **"Leadership is not about being in charge. It's about taking care of those in your charge."**
>
> – Simon Sinek

Story-28:

Igniting Minds, Inspiring Generations: The Story of Dr. APJ Abdul Kalam

> **A nation's future is written not in policies, but in the dreams of its young minds**
>
> **— and Dr. Kalam gave those dreams wings**

The small town of **Rameswaram** smelled of salt and fresh fish. Wooden boats rocked gently against the shore as fishermen unloaded their catch.

In the midst of the morning hustle, a young boy ran barefoot across the sandy streets, a bundle of newspapers clutched tightly in his hands. His name was **Abdul Kalam**, and though the world saw him as just another boy from a poor family, he knew, deep inside, that he was meant for something greater.

No one could have imagined then that this boy—born to a simple boat owner—would one day **lead India's missile program, inspire millions, and become the President of the nation.** But he did. Not because of luck, not because of privilege, but because he understood something powerful:

Greatness is built. One decision, one action, one dream a t a time.

Here's how **IMPACT framework** can transform

Inspire Awareness & Identity: The Spark of a Dream

Late at night, under the flickering glow of a **kerosene lamp,** Kalam sat cross-legged on the floor, his fingers running over the pages of a borrowed science book. His family was poor; they could not afford luxuries like electricity or expensive textbooks. But what they lacked in money, they made up for in values—**hard work, discipline, and a love for knowledge.**

His father was a quiet, thoughtful man who spent hours in prayer and meditation. His mother, a kind-hearted woman, cooked meals for anyone in need. Kalam absorbed everything from them—his father's wisdom, his mother's generosity—but above all, he learned the power of **self-awareness.**

One evening, his **science teacher, Siva Subramania Iyer,** called him aside after class. The man's sharp eyes shone with something close to excitement.

"Kalam," he said, placing a hand on the boy's shoulder, "you have a gift. You must learn, grow, and one day, you will help India fly."

Those words **lit a fire inside him.** That night, as he lay on his thin mattress, staring at the ceiling, he made a promise to himself:

One day, I will build something that touches the sky.

Mindset & Mastery Shift: The Power of Failing Forward

Years later, the sky over Chennai buzzed with the roar of aircraft. **Kalam, now a young engineering student at Madras Institute of Technology (MIT), stood watching in awe.** The dream that had once flickered under a kerosene lamp was now burning bright. He was studying aeronautics, learning the mechanics of flight.

But his journey was not easy.

One day, a professor handed him a complex project—designing an aircraft model. The deadline was impossible. The challenge was immense. And Kalam, for the first time, felt fear creep into his heart.

"You have three days," the professor said, his voice firm. "If you fail, you will lose your scholarship."

That night, Kalam barely slept. He **sketched, erased, rebuilt, and tested.** He pushed himself beyond exhaustion, refusing to give up. On the final day, he stood before his professor, his hands trembling as he presented his design.

The professor looked at it for a long moment. Then, he nodded.

"This," he said, "is excellent."

Kalam had done it.

That day, he realized something important: **Fear is just an obstacle. The only way past it is to keep moving forward.**

Purpose-Driven Goals & Strategy: Building India's Space Dream

A few years later, Kalam found himself standing inside **a small, abandoned church in Thumba, Kerala.** The wooden benches had been pushed aside, the walls lined with blueprints and scientific equipment. This was no longer a place of worship—it was now the **heart of India's first space research center.**

The government had little funding. The world doubted India's ability to build rockets. But Kalam and his team refused to accept defeat. **They had a goal: To launch India's first satellite into space.**

Day and night, they worked. **They carried rocket parts on bicycles.** They tested engines on beaches. They faced failures, explosions, setbacks—but they never lost sight of their purpose.

And then, in **1980,** the world watched as **India successfully launched its first satellite, Rohini, into orbit.** The ground shook as the rocket soared into the sky, carrying with it the dreams of a billion people.

Kalam looked up; his eyes filled with pride.

India had touched the stars.

Action, Accountability & Adaptability: The Rise of the Missile Man

Kalam's hunger to learn never faded. From rockets, he moved on to missiles, leading the development of **Agni, Prithvi, and BrahMos— India's most powerful defense weapons.**

The weight of responsibility was enormous. **If these projects failed, the entire country's defense program would be at risk.** But Kalam knew one thing:

Leaders do not blame others. They take responsibility.

When the **first missile test failed,** journalists surrounded him, demanding answers. But instead of shifting the blame, he stood before the cameras and said,

"I take full responsibility. We will learn. We will succeed."

And they did. **Within a few years, India became a nuclear-capable nation, a force to be reckoned with.**

Kalam had turned failure into fuel.

Connection & Collaborative Growth: A Leader Who Listened

Despite his success, Kalam remained humble. He never saw himself as a boss, but as a **mentor, a guide, a teacher.**

He would walk through laboratories, talking to young scientists, **listening to their ideas.** He believed that the best leaders were not the ones who gave orders, but the ones who **inspired others to think.**

One evening, a young scientist nervously approached him.

"Sir," he said, "I have an idea, but I'm not sure if it will work."

Kalam smiled. "The only way to know," he said, "is to try."

That scientist would go on to invent new missile guidance technology, changing India's defense capabilities forever.

Transform & Thrive: A Legacy That Lives On

Years later, when Kalam was elected as the **President of India,** he did not move into the grand Presidential palace like his predecessors. Instead, he **chose to live simply, in a small room filled with books.**

Even as the leader of the nation, he remained the same humble scientist, the same curious student, the same dreamer who had once stared at the sky.

He spent his final years traveling from city to city, speaking to **students, urging them to dream big, work hard, and never stop learning.**

On **July 27, 2015,** while delivering a lecture at IIM Shillong, he collapsed on stage. His last words before he fell?

"Keep learning, keep dreaming, keep working."

Even in his final moments, **Dr. Kalam was inspiring the world.**

The IMPACT of APJ Abdul Kalam

The young boy sat by the seashore, watching birds soar effortlessly across the sky. His heart swelled with curiosity—how did they fly? That question lit a fire in his mind, a love for learning that would never fade.

When he faced failure, he did not break. Instead, he gathered the pieces, studied his mistakes, and turned them into stepping stones toward success. He refused to let setbacks define him.

With a heart full of purpose, he set his sights on the stars. He built India's space and missile programs, transforming dreams into reality with unwavering determination.

When challenges arose, he never blamed his team. He stood tall, taking responsibility for failures and leading with integrity, proving that true leadership means owning both success and struggle.

But his greatest achievement was not missiles or satellites—it was the young minds he mentored. He shared knowledge freely, inspiring countless students to chase their own dreams.

And when he left this world, he did not leave empty-handed. He left behind a legacy of knowledge, courage, and hope—a reminder that dreams, when nurtured, have the power to lift an entire nation.

Dr. Kalam's story is proof that greatness is not given—it is built.

What dream will YOU chase?

How the IMPACT Coaching Framework Drives Structured Coaching for Transformation

Transformation does not happen by chance. It requires a **structured approach,** clear **guidance,** and a **repeatable process** that helps individuals and teams move from where they are to where they need to be. The **IMPACT coaching framework** provides this structure, ensuring that coaching is **not random, but intentional, strategic, and results-driven.**

How IMPACT Helps in Coaching for Transformation

Each element of the **IMPACT** framework ensures that coaching is not just motivational but **actionable, measurable, and sustainable.**

1. **Inspire Awareness & Identity → Creating Self-Discovery and Clarity**

Without awareness, transformation is impossible.

Many people struggle because they do not understand:

- **Where they currently stand** (strengths, weaknesses, limiting beliefs)

- **Who they want to become** (vision, purpose, identity)

- **What is holding them back** (fear, doubt, past failures)

How IMPACT helps:

A coach using the IMPACT framework does not simply give advice—they unlock doors within the mind.

With each carefully crafted question, they guide individuals to pause, reflect, and dig deeper into their own thoughts. A simple "Why do you believe that?" can unravel years of limiting beliefs. A thoughtful "What would happen if you tried a different approach?" can open a world of possibilities.

They become a mirror, helping individuals see the hidden patterns of thinking that have held them back for years. Fear, doubt, and hesitation begin to lose their grip as awareness grows.

Slowly, a shift happens. The person who once said, "I can't" begins to ask, "What if I could?" Instead of seeing failure as an end, they start to see it as a lesson. Their mindset transforms—not just for today, but for a lifetime.

This is the power of structured coaching. This is the power of IMPACT.

Example: A professional struggling with career growth **feels stuck.** Through structured coaching, they realize that **fear of failure** has been stopping them from taking leadership roles. Once they recognize this, they start actively **shifting their mindset** and taking bold steps.

Without IMPACT? The coaching would lack depth, and the individual would focus on surface-level solutions without understanding the **root cause** of their struggles.

2. Mindset & Mastery Shift → Rewiring Limiting Beliefs for Breakthroughs

Success is 80% mindset, 20% strategy.

People often fail to transform because they:

- Stay stuck in **fixed mindsets** ("I'm not good enough," "I cannot change")

- Fear **failure** and avoid taking action

- Lack **resilience** when facing obstacles

How IMPACT helps:

A coach using the IMPACT framework does not just offer encouragement—they challenge perspectives, breaking down the invisible walls that hold people back.

When someone says, *"I'm not good enough,"* the coach leans in and asks, *"Says who?"* When they whisper, *"I always fail,"* the coach counters, *"Or have you been learning all along?"*

With structured tools, they help individuals reframe failure—not as proof of incompetence, but as stepping stones to mastery. The sting of past mistakes fades, replaced by curiosity: *"What did this teach me?"*

Excuses dissolve. Blame shifts into responsibility. Suddenly, the person who once felt powerless now stands tall, realizing that the pen to rewrite their story has been in their hands all along.

This is more than coaching—it is transformation.

Example: A startup founder is **afraid of rejection** and hesitates to pitch to investors. Through the **IMPACT framework,** they learn that rejection is **part of growth.** By reprogramming their thinking, they **build confidence** and finally secure funding.

Without IMPACT? The founder might stay stuck in self-doubt, delaying action, and missing out on opportunities. A lack of structured coaching would mean they **never shift their mindset,** leading to **zero transformation.**

3. Purpose-Driven Goals & Strategy → Aligning Actions with a Bigger Vision

Transformation is not just about action—it is about the right action.

Many people fail to change because they:

- Set **vague** or **uninspiring** goals

- Focus on **short-term tasks** instead of long-term purpose

- Lack a **clear strategy** to turn goals into results

How IMPACT helps:

A coach using the IMPACT framework does not just ask, *"What do you want?"* They dig deeper—*"Why does it matter to you?"* Because a goal without purpose is like a ship without a compass—drifting, uncertain, easily lost.

With clarity comes direction. The coach helps break down big dreams into actionable steps, turning overwhelming ambitions into achievable milestones. Progress is no longer a vague hope but a structured journey, with each step reinforcing confidence.

When exhaustion sets in, when doubts creep in, the coach brings them back to their **WHY**—that burning reason they started in the first place. With that fire reignited, they do not just push forward—they thrive.

Example: A manager wants to become a **C-level executive,** but their daily tasks keep them distracted. Through **IMPACT coaching,** they map out a clear **5-year plan, delegate tasks,** and start focusing on **high-impact leadership activities.**

Without IMPACT? The manager would keep working hard but without direction. Years later, they might **still be stuck in the same role** because they never strategically aligned their actions.

4. Action, Accountability & Adaptability → Moving from Thinking to Execution

Knowledge without action is useless.

Many people **know** what to do, but they do not:

- Take **consistent** action
- Hold themselves **accountable**
- Adapt when things do not go as planned

How IMPACT helps:

A dream without a deadline is just a wish. A coach using the IMPACT framework turns vague aspirations into concrete plans—step by step, deadline by deadline. There is no room for *"I'll do it someday."* The roadmap is clear, and the journey begins now.

But action alone is not enough. Life throws obstacles, doubts creep in, and old habits fight to return. This is where accountability becomes the game-changer. The coach checks in, not to judge, but to remind— *"You committed to this. How is it going?"* That gentle pressure keeps momentum alive.

And when setbacks hit—as they always do—the coach does not let failure become a dead end. Instead, they ask, *"What can you learn from this?"* They reframe struggles as stepping stones, ensuring the individual rises stronger, more determined, and ready to push forward.

Example: An aspiring author wants to write a book but **keeps postponing.** Through IMPACT, they commit to a **writing schedule,** have **weekly check-ins,** and adapt their strategy based on progress. In 6 months, the book is finished.

Without IMPACT? The book stays a dream. The author keeps "thinking" about writing but never **executes.**

5. Connection & Collaborative Growth → Expanding Success Through Others

Great transformations do not happen alone.

Many people **struggle in isolation** because they:

- Try to do everything **themselves**

- Lack **mentorship** and **support systems**

- Do not know how to **build strong networks**

How IMPACT helps:

Success is rarely a solo journey. A coach using the IMPACT framework helps individuals recognize the power of the right environment—the people who challenge, inspire, and uplift them.

Instead of struggling alone, they learn to seek mentorship, to stand on the shoulders of those who have already walked the path. *"Who has already achieved what you are striving for? What can you learn from them?"* A simple question, but one that shifts the mindset from isolation to growth.

And it does not stop there. The framework fosters a culture of collaboration. Success is no longer just personal—it is multiplied. When individuals connect, share ideas, and support each other, progress accelerates. *One person's breakthrough sparks another's, and together, they achieve what seemed impossible alone.*

Example: A corporate leader wants to expand their influence. Through coaching, they start building a personal brand, networking with top executives, and attracting career-changing opportunities.

Without IMPACT? The leader would keep working hard but **in isolation,** missing out on the power of collaboration.

6. Transform & Thrive → Making Success Sustainable

Short-term wins are easy. Sustained success is the real challenge.

Many people **achieve success** but then:

- **Lose momentum** and stop growing

- Forget to **give back and inspire others**

- Do not create **systems to sustain long-term success**

How IMPACT helps:

True transformation is not just about achieving a goal—it is about sustaining success long after the initial breakthrough. A coach using the IMPACT framework helps individuals build habits that do not fade with time but become a natural part of who they are.

By shifting focus from short-term wins to long-term impact, individuals begin to see their growth as more than just personal success. They start thinking beyond themselves. *"How can your journey inspire others? How can your success create opportunities for those who come after you?"*

With this mindset, transformation is no longer temporary. It becomes a way of life. The lessons learned, the habits formed, and the impact made continue to ripple outward—creating a legacy that lasts.

Example: A successful entrepreneur, after scaling their company, **mentors' young founders,** ensuring their knowledge **impacts future generations.**

Without IMPACT? Success might fade. Without structured coaching, they **burn out,** lose focus, or fail to sustain their impact.

What Happens If We Do Not Use a Framework Like IMPACT?

Without IMPACT coaching, transformation becomes:

Without a structured framework like IMPACT, both personal and professional growth can feel slow, frustrating, and directionless. Without clear guidance, individuals often struggle to figure out where to start or what steps to take, relying on trial and error that wastes valuable time. Progress becomes random rather than intentional, leading to inconsistent growth where breakthroughs happen more by chance than by strategy. This lack of structure can be frustrating, as people find themselves repeating the same mistakes and feeling stuck rather than evolving.

Even when success is achieved, it tends to be short-lived without accountability and long-term habits to sustain it. Motivation fades, and people often slip back into old patterns. The absence of mentorship and collaboration makes the journey even harder, as individuals miss out on valuable insights, feedback, and encouragement that could accelerate their progress. A structured coaching framework like IMPACT provides a clear roadmap, ensuring that transformation is not just temporary but a lifelong journey of deliberate, effective, and sustainable growth.

Example of a failed transformation: A company tries to implement a **leadership transformation** but without a structured framework:

- Employees attend one-off training sessions but **never apply what they learn.**

- No one follows up, so **momentum is lost.**

- There is no accountability, so **nothing really changes.**

The result? Waste of time, money, and effort—without real transformation.

Why IMPACT Coaching is Essential for True Transformation

The IMPACT framework transforms coaching into a structured and effective journey of growth and success, eliminating guesswork and uncertainty. It provides a clear roadmap, ensuring individuals follow a guided approach rather than relying on trial and error. By driving mindset shifts, it helps people overcome limiting beliefs, learn from failures, and build confidence for lasting change. Every action aligns with a greater purpose, making goals more meaningful and sustainable rather than short-lived achievements.

The framework also maintains momentum through accountability, with regular check-ins and support to prevent stagnation and procrastination. Beyond personal growth, it fosters collaboration and leadership, encouraging mentorship and teamwork that benefit entire communities. Most importantly, it creates lasting success by instilling habits and strategies that ensure transformation is not just a temporary phase but a lifelong journey. With the IMPACT framework, success is intentional, structured, and enduring, leading to continuous development and meaningful progress.

True transformation is not just about knowing what to do—it is about having the right framework to do it.

"He didn't just launch rockets; he launched a generation to believe, to dream, and to dare beyond the impossible."

Key Takeaways:

1. **Dreams Are Born in the Ordinary — and Built Through Purpose**

From barefoot newspaper boy in Rameswaram to the President of India, Kalam's journey shows that greatness is not given—it is **earned through vision, values, and relentless effort**. The IMPACT framework begins by **Inspiring awareness and identity**, just like young Kalam's first spark under the kerosene lamp.

2. Failures Are not Final — They are Fuel for Mastery

Kalam's MIT project deadline, which nearly cost him his scholarship, became the moment he broke through fear. With the **Mindset & Mastery Shift**, failure became his teacher, not his end. Structured coaching helps people **reframe failure as progress**, not proof of inadequacy.

3. Purpose Powers Progress — Even Without Resources

At ISRO's humble Thumba center, Kalam and his team launched dreams into orbit with **purpose-driven strategy** and passion—not privilege. Coaches help clients align big dreams with **clear goals and strategies**, making the impossible, possible.

4. Leadership is Action, Not Position

When missile tests failed, Kalam did not point fingers. He stood tall, took responsibility, and adapted. Through **accountability and adaptability**, he modeled that real leaders own both success and struggle. Coaching through IMPACT ensures execution meets intention.

5. Legacy Lives Through People, Not Titles

Kalam mentored, listened, and believed in the next generation. His true impact was not just technological—it was **human transformation**. The final step—**Transform & Thrive**—reminds us that leadership is about lifting others, leaving a trail of hope, courage, and vision.

Story-29:

How the IMPACT Coaching Framework Empowers Leaders to Solve Global Challenges

> **"We cannot solve our problems with the same thinking we used when we created them."**
>
> — *Albert Einstein*

As the world steps into 2025, the air is thick with uncertainty. Leaders across industries wake each morning to a rapidly shifting reality. Political conflicts shake global stability, economic downturns cast long shadows over businesses and livelihoods, and artificial intelligence rewrites the rules of entire industries overnight. Climate change accelerates at an alarming pace, food and water shortages tighten their grip on vulnerable populations, and the chasm between the privileged and the struggling grows deeper.

The burden on leaders has never been heavier. They are no longer just decision-makers; they are the architects of tomorrow, the ones expected to bring clarity amidst chaos, solutions where none seem to exist. But how does one lead when the very ground beneath their feet is constantly shifting?

In the heart of this uncertainty, a guiding force emerges—the **IMPACT Coaching Framework.** It is more than just a leadership model; it is a blueprint for transformation. It does not merely teach leaders how to manage crises—it forges them into individuals who **anticipate, adapt, and create meaningful change.** This is not about survival. This is about rewriting the future.

I - Inspire Awareness & Identity

A young diplomat stands at the negotiation table, the weight of two nations' futures on her shoulders. The room is tense, distrust thick in the air. She could react to the hostility, let emotion dictate her response, or she could pause, take a breath, and **lead with awareness and integrity.**

Leadership begins with understanding oneself. Without self-awareness, decisions are clouded by biases, fears, and personal insecurities. But with it, a leader gains clarity, the ability to **see beyond immediate reactions and into the heart of the issue.**

Through deep introspection, behavioral assessments, and guided coaching, IMPACT leaders uncover their **core values and leadership identity.** They ask themselves:

- Who am I when the world is watching?

- What do I stand for when no one else does?

- How do my actions shape the future of my organization, my community, and beyond?

With this clarity, a leader does not just **solve problems**—they **unite people across divisions,** fostering trust, diplomacy, and ethical leadership that transcends borders.

M - Mindset & Mastery Shift

A seasoned CEO stares at a screen filled with unsettling reports—automation has made thousands of jobs obsolete overnight. His team looks to him for answers, fear lurking behind their questions. Will he resist change, clinging to old ways? Or will he see **disruption as an opportunity?**

The world is changing at a pace humanity has never seen before. Artificial intelligence, digital transformation, and automation are not on the horizon—they are **already here.** But fear is not a strategy.

IMPACT coaching reshapes mindsets, teaching leaders to **break free from outdated beliefs** and embrace a future of possibilities. Through neuroscience-backed techniques and cognitive-behavioral coaching, leaders learn to:

- Recognize and dismantle self-imposed limitations.

- Shift from fear-driven leadership to innovation-driven action.

- Develop the mental resilience to **navigate the unknown** with confidence.

True mastery comes from reframing challenges as opportunities. The leaders who **adapt and evolve** are the ones who **shape the industries of tomorrow.**

P - Purpose-Driven Goals & Strategy

A scientist stands before a panel of investors, her research on renewable energy a beacon of hope. The world desperately needs sustainable solutions, but will the decision-makers **prioritize long-term impact over short-term profit?**

The greatest crises of our time—climate change, pandemics, resource scarcity—demand **leaders who act with purpose.** Without a clear vision, strategies crumble. Without measurable goals, progress is an illusion.

IMPACT coaching equips leaders to:

- Align business and policy goals with sustainability efforts.

- Design clear, actionable roadmaps that turn aspirations into reality.

- Implement frameworks like OKRs and SMART goals to **measure true impact.**

Purpose-driven leadership is no longer an option. It is the only way forward.

A - Action, Accountability & Adaptability

A prime minister watches as protestors flood the streets. His policies have been questioned, his leadership doubted. He has two choices: dismiss the voices of the people, or **listen, adapt, and lead with accountability.**

Ideas and strategies mean nothing without execution. The best leaders are those who **turn vision into reality** through disciplined action.

IMPACT coaching instills a mindset of execution and adaptability, ensuring leaders:

- Develop high-performance habits and peer accountability structures.

- Build resilience strategies to handle setbacks with grace.

- Master agile leadership principles to **pivot when external conditions demand it.**

Leaders who embrace accountability and adaptability do not **merely react** to crises—they **shape the future with unwavering resolve.**

C - Connection & Collaborative Growth

A young activist steps onto a stage, a sea of diverse faces watching. They come from different nations, different struggles, yet they all seek the same thing—**a leader who listens, who unites.**

In an era of division, leaders must be **connectors, not separators.** True leadership is about bringing people together, fostering inclusivity, and ensuring every voice is heard.

IMPACT coaching fosters:

- A culture of inclusive leadership where diverse perspectives drive progress.

- Global collaborations that bridge political, racial, and economic divides.

- Mentorship networks that **empower future leaders** to continue the cycle of transformation.

A leader who chooses connection over competition builds not just an organization—but a movement.

T - Transform & Thrive

A visionary founder walks through the halls of his company, knowing he may never see its full impact in his lifetime. Yet, he is at peace, **because he has built something that will outlive him.**

The world's greatest leaders do not just **react to crises**—they **anticipate and shape the future.** True transformation comes from a commitment to continuous learning, adaptability, and legacy-building.

IMPACT coaching equips leaders to:

- Develop foresight and strategic agility to remain resilient in an unpredictable world.

- Build a legacy of innovation, ensuring lasting societal impact.

- Commit to lifelong growth, ensuring they never become obsolete.

A leader who embraces transformation does not just survive. They thrive, inspire, and redefine the world.

The Future Demands IMPACT-Driven Leaders

The world does not need more leaders who simply **manage crises.** It needs **visionaries who anticipate them,** innovators who solve them, and mentors who **empower the next generation.**

Through the IMPACT Coaching Framework, leaders gain the clarity, resilience, and adaptability to **navigate the world's toughest challenges with confidence and purpose.**

> **"Leadership is not about a title or a designation. It is about impact, influence, and inspiration."**
>
> — *Robin S. Sharma*

Key Takeaways:

1. The World is at a Crossroads – and So is Leadership

2025 presents unprecedented global turbulence—geopolitical tensions, AI disruption, climate urgency, and deepening inequality. Leaders can no longer rely on old paradigms. **Leadership today is not about control—it is about conscious transformation.**

2. The IMPACT Coaching Framework is a Blueprint for Thriving Amid Chaos

More than a model, **IMPACT is a lifeline**. It shifts leaders from reactive to proactive, helping them:

- Reclaim their **identity** in confusion (Inspire)

- Shift **mindsets** to fuel innovation (Mindset)

- Lead with **purpose** that serves both people and planet (Purpose)

- Build the discipline for **action and agility** (Action)

- Cultivate **connection** across divides (Connection)

- And **transform** to create lasting impact (Transform)

3. Self-Awareness is the First Step to Global Impact

Leadership starts from within. The courage to pause, reflect, and lead with integrity builds trust and fuels ethical decisions. Leaders must ask:

"Who am I when the world is watching? What legacy am I building?"

4. Mindset is a Leader's Most Strategic Asset

In a world shaped by disruption, fear cannot guide action. Leaders must unlearn limitations and **embrace agility, curiosity, and mastery** to stay relevant.

5. Purpose is Not Optional—It is the New Currency of Leadership

The leaders who thrive in 2025 will **align their missions with global good**—whether it is climate solutions, social equity, or public health. Purpose fuels not just performance, but deep impact.

6. Accountability & Action Separate Visionaries from Dreamers

Without action, vision is fantasy. The framework teaches **habits of high performance, feedback-driven growth, and agile adaptation—** vital for executing in volatile conditions.

7. Connection is the Antidote to Division

In times of polarization, leaders must become **unifiers**—embracing diversity, nurturing global partnerships, and mentoring the next generation to carry forward the torch.

8. Legacy is Built Through Continuous Transformation

The greatest leaders do not just navigate uncertainty—they **shape the future**, leave a mark, and **prepare others to go further**. True leadership is about legacy, not just tenure.

9. The Call to Action: The Future Demands IMPACT

The message is clear:

"The world doesn't need more managers of crisis—it needs coaches of courage, creators of change, and cultivators of collective resilience."

Through the **IMPACT Coaching Framework**, any leader can rise—not just to survive the storm, but to **lead the dawn of a new era**.

Story-30:

IMPACT in the Depths: A Story of Resilience, Leadership, and Transformation

> **"It is not the strongest of the species that survive, nor the most intelligent, but the one most responsive to change."**
>
> **– Charles Darwin**

In August 2010, the world held its breath as news spread about a catastrophic collapse in the San José mine in northern Chile. Thirty-three miners, who had gone deep into the earth to extract copper, found themselves trapped nearly 700 meters underground. The mine, once a site of labor and industry, had become a dark tomb, an inescapable prison of rock and dust. With limited food, no light, and the crushing weight of time bearing down on them, the miners could do nothing but wait.

Above ground, the news spread like wildfire. The world was watching. The families of the miners gathered outside the mine, clutching onto hope in a place where hope seemed to have died. Meanwhile, engineers and rescue teams from all corners of the globe rushed in to find a way to bring the miners back to the surface.

But this was not just an engineering challenge. It was a test of human will. It was a story of **leadership**, **resilience**, and **human spirit**—one that would unfold through the application of a powerful coaching framework.

Inspire Awareness & Identity

Deep below the surface, the miners faced the unimaginable. Days stretched into weeks, and the weight of despair threatened to consume them. But amidst the fear and uncertainty, one man stepped up. Luis Urzúa, the shift boss, became the guiding force. He did not impose authority through commands; instead, he **inspired awareness**.

He gathered the miners and asked them to step into leadership roles themselves. Each man took on a duty: distributing food, checking on each other's health, keeping the group's morale intact, recording their stories. **They began to define their own identity**, not as victims of circumstance, but as leaders of their own fate.

Above ground, the engineers and rescue leaders were undergoing a transformation of their own. They faced a daunting reality: **they were not just engineers anymore—they were lifelines**. The work they were doing was more than just technical; it was about **purpose**. They, too, needed to reframe their roles. They needed to see themselves as **hope-bringers**, not just problem-solvers.

Mindset & Mastery Shift

Inside the mine, the passage of time was a test of endurance. Panic, fear, and hopelessness could have consumed the men. But instead, they turned inward and began to develop a **growth mindset**. Every day was a battle not just to stay alive, but to stay mentally strong.

Luis Urzúa became their coach. He led the men in rituals of **positive thinking**, reminding them that survival was not just about physical strength—it was about keeping their minds sharp. He encouraged them to write in journals, to stay connected to their loved ones through messages, to envision a future beyond the mine.

Above ground, the engineers faced their own battles. The first drilling plan failed. Then the second. But with each failure came a lesson, and instead of being paralyzed by setbacks, the team adopted the mindset that **failure was not an end, but a learning opportunity**. Andrés Sougarret, the head engineer, looked at his team and said, "Each failure is a blueprint. Let us learn and adapt." And so, they did. **Failure became fuel for innovation**.

Purpose-Driven Goals & Strategy

The mission of rescuing the miners was no longer just about getting them out; it was about **getting them out alive, safely, and with dignity**. That purpose became the driving force behind every decision, every action taken.

The rescue leaders were not just setting technical milestones—they were setting **human-centered goals**. They measured success not in feet of drill, but in hope:

- **Days to establish contact with the miners**.

- **Days to send them food and supplies**.

- **Days to begin boring the rescue shaft**.

On the ground, the miners themselves had personal goals to keep their spirits alive. Some made plans for the future—dreams of starting businesses, of reuniting with their families. Others kept writing letters to their loved ones, preserving their connection to the world above.

Action, Accountability & Adaptability

As days turned to weeks, the miners on the ground developed a powerful rhythm. They held **daily meetings**, rotated leadership roles, and ensured that every man stayed accountable to the collective well-being of the group. When one person faltered, others lifted them up. They knew their survival depended not just on their individual actions, but on **working together as a team**.

Above ground, the engineers worked tirelessly, constantly refining their approach. The first drill plan failed. Then the second. But there was no room for hesitation. They adapted. They shifted focus to the third plan. And as time passed, they learned that **parallel action was the key**. Three drilling plans were run simultaneously, each one inching them closer to their goal.

Every action had its own accountability. Every success, no matter how small, was celebrated. **Adaptability became their greatest tool**. When Plan B succeeded in breaking through to the miners, the world rejoiced. But the engineers knew there was still much work to do. They immediately pivoted to ensure the miners' safe extraction.

Connection & Collaborative Growth

This was not just a mission for engineers and miners—it was a **global effort**. NASA provided expertise. Drill manufacturers in the U.S. and Canada collaborated. Chilean doctors consulted with psychologists and leadership coaches.

Underground, despite the oppressive darkness, the miners found ways to **stay connected** to each other, to their families, and to the world above. Every day, they communicated with their loved ones, sending messages of hope. The families of the trapped miners formed a **community of resilience** outside the mine. They camped together, sharing their experiences, their grief, and their unwavering belief that they would be reunited with their loved ones.

Above ground, engineers, psychologists, and coaches worked together, pooling their knowledge and resources. Their collective effort was not just about **drilling**; it was about **human connection**, the shared belief that no one should face such a crisis alone.

Transform & Thrive

Sixty-nine days after the collapse, the miners were pulled from the depths of the earth, one by one. As the last man emerged from the mine, the world erupted into cheers. But for those who had witnessed the journey from start to finish, the real miracle was not just the physical rescue—it was the **transformation** that had taken place.

The miners had gone from being victims of an unimaginable tragedy to becoming **symbols of resilience**. Many of them went on to become motivational speakers, sharing their stories of survival and leadership. They inspired millions, showing the world that, even in the darkest of times, the human spirit could endure.

Above ground, engineers, psychologists, and coaches reflected on the lessons learned from the crisis. **Resilience was not just a trait of the miners—it was a global collaboration**, and it had changed everyone involved.

The Chilean mine rescue was not just a success in terms of engineering—it was a testament to the power of **leadership**, **coaching**, and the **IMPACT framework**. It showed that when human spirit meets structured coaching, even the earth's depths cannot trap our potential.

"Leadership is not about being in charge. It's about taking care of those in your charge." – Simon Sinek

Key Coaching Lessons:

- **Inspire Ownership and Empower Others**: As seen in the miners' experience, true leadership is not about commanding or controlling—it is about **inspiring others** to take charge of their own journey. Encourage your clients to step into leadership roles, both for themselves and others, and help them develop a sense of **agency** in their lives.

- **Cultivate a Growth Mindset**: The miners, despite being trapped underground, showed incredible mental strength by adopting a mindset that **embraced challenges** as opportunities for growth. As a coach, guide your clients to focus on **resilience** and the power of perseverance, especially when faced with setbacks.

- **Set Purpose-Driven Goals**: Just as the engineers set purposeful, human-centered goals, coaches must help their clients define goals that go beyond achievement and focus on **impact**. Every decision should be made with a sense of purpose, whether personal or professional.

- **Promote Accountability and Adaptability**: The miners and engineers both embraced accountability for their roles in the rescue process, continuously **adapting** to new information and challenges. As a coach, create environments where clients hold themselves accountable, and help them stay adaptable, pivoting when necessary to achieve their goals.

- **Foster Connection and Collaboration**: Leadership thrives in **collaboration**. Whether in a corporate setting or personal development, encourage your clients to **build strong support systems**, seek out diverse perspectives, and collaborate toward collective growth. **Shared experiences and mutual support** make transformation not only possible but sustainable.

- **Transform Through Adversity**: The true measure of leadership lies not in comfort but in **how we rise through adversity**. Encourage your clients to see difficult situations as opportunities for **personal growth and transformation**. What challenges can be reframed as moments of potential growth?

- **Celebrate Every Step of Progress**: Whether small or large, each success should be celebrated. Recognizing progress reinforces the **positive momentum** that drives sustained growth. This mindset shifts from a focus on the end result to a focus on the **journey** and its transformative power.

By applying these principles, coaches can create a **space of growth, accountability, and resilience** that enables their clients to unlock their full potential, even in the face of daunting challenges.

Story-31:

IMPACT Coaching in Action: The Mighty Ducks (1992)– A Journey of Transformation and Excellence

"The Mighty Ducks" (1992) is not merely a sports film about hockey. It is a heartwarming tale of transformation, where a group of misfits—unmotivated, disillusioned kids—are turned into champions. But this is not just about learning to skate or scoring goals; it is about discovering untapped potential, developing resilience, and building relationships that transcend the rink. Through Coach Gordon Bombay's guiding hand, these young players experience a profound change, learning lessons that will shape them far beyond the game. This is where the **IMPACT Coaching Framework** comes into play, guiding Coach Bombay's approach and helping him elevate his team in ways that are both powerful and transformative.

Inspire Awareness & Identity (I)

At the beginning of the movie, the team is a collection of individuals who have little faith in themselves or each other. But Coach Bombay sees beyond their external circumstances. He does not just want them to play well; he wants them to realize their worth, both on and off the ice.

How does he do this? He creates a new identity for them—**The Mighty Ducks**. He changes their jerseys, their mindset, and their sense of purpose. He does not just want them to play as a team; he wants them to **believe** that they *are* a team—worthy, capable, and powerful. The Mighty Ducks are born, and with them, a new identity: they are no longer a bunch of misfits—they are a force to be reckoned with.

Mindset & Mastery Shift (M)

In the beginning, doubt clouds the minds of his players. Many of them feel they are destined to fail. Coach Bombay sees this and sets out to change that. He teaches them that true strength lies in **mindset**, and that every setback is an opportunity to grow.

How does he do this? Through hard-fought practice sessions, Coach Bombay shows them that victory is not given; it is earned. He encourages the players to embrace **persistence**, to view mistakes as stepping stones, not failures. As they confront and overcome their fears, they begin to shift from victims of circumstance to architects of their own success.

Purpose-Driven Goals & Strategy (P)

Coach Bombay shifts the focus from individual glory to collective success. This is not just about scoring points—it is about working together as one cohesive unit. He teaches them that the key to success is **purpose**—playing not for themselves, but for each other. Their goal is not just to win games; it is to honour their commitment to the team and the values they represent.

How does he do this? By creating strategies cantered around teamwork, Coach Bombay emphasizes collaboration over personal achievement. He teaches them that every pass, every block, and every shot is not just about individual success but about working together toward a **common purpose**. This unity becomes their strength, and it is through this lens that they begin to see victory not as an individual feat but as a shared triumph.

Action, Accountability & Adaptability (A)

Accountability is not just a rule—it is a lifestyle. Coach Bombay holds his players accountable, not just for their actions on the ice but also for their behaviours off it. And when things go wrong, he teaches them the power of **adaptability**—the ability to adjust, learn, and grow through adversity.

How does he do this? When a player fails to meet expectations, Coach Bombay does not just scold them—he pushes them to take responsibility for their actions. Whether it is a missed shot, a poor attitude, or a lack of discipline, the lesson is clear: take ownership, **adapt**, and try again. With each failure comes the chance to **learn** and **evolve**, and Coach Bombay makes sure they never forget that growth happens through action, accountability, and resilience.

Connection & Collaborative Growth (C)

The real strength of a team lies in the relationships that bind its members together. Coach Bombay understands that true **connection** goes beyond the rink—it is about trust, respect, and mutual support. This is where the Mighty Ducks begin to truly shine. As they come together as a team, they learn to trust each other, communicate openly, and support one another through thick and thin.

How does he do this? He fosters an environment where every player's role matters. From the most skilled to the least experienced, each player feels valued and essential. Coach Bombay instils in them the power of **collaborative growth**—where every victory and every defeat is shared, and no one is left behind. Through this unity, they learn that their individual success is tied to the success of the team, and that together, they are greater than the sum of their parts.

Transform & Thrive (T)

Coach Bombay's ultimate goal is not just to teach his players how to play hockey—it is to transform them into better, more resilient individuals. By the end of the movie, the team has grown from a group of misfits into a cohesive unit that has not only improved as athletes but as people. The lessons they have learned are now ingrained in who they are, and they are ready to take on life with renewed confidence and purpose.

How does he do this? Through his unwavering belief in their potential, Coach Bombay has helped his players transform their lives. The final game is not just about winning; it is about proving to themselves that they can rise above adversity and achieve greatness, not just in hockey, but in life. They have learned that success is about **teamwork**, **resilience**, and **self-belief**—values they will carry with them long after the final buzzer.

The transformation of the Mighty Ducks is the perfect example of how the **IMPACT Coaching Framework** can be used to unlock the true potential of individuals and teams. Coach Bombay does not just coach hockey—he coaches life. Through his belief in his players, his commitment to their growth, and his focus on teamwork, accountability, and transformation, he helps them become better people. In the end, their victory is not just about the final score—it is about the lifelong lessons they have learned about perseverance, connection, and personal growth.

The Mighty Ducks teaches us that true coaching is not just about teaching the game—it is about teaching life. The journey from **misfits to champions** is a testament to the power of **IMPACT Coaching** and its ability to inspire, empower, and transform.

Key Learnings and Messages about Coaching for Readers:

1. **Coaching is About Transformation, Not Just Skill Development**

   The Mighty Ducks highlights that coaching is not solely about teaching technical skills. It is about **transforming** individuals, helping them grow as people, and building their confidence. A good coach does not just improve performance; they unlock untapped potential and inspire lasting personal change.

2. **Mindset is Key to Overcoming Challenges**

   One of the most powerful messages from the film is how **mindset** can shift from self-doubt to self-belief. **Coaching** helps individuals confront negative thoughts, embrace challenges, and see failure as a stepping stone to success. This shift from a fixed mindset to a growth mindset is crucial for anyone looking to excel in life and work.

3. **Purpose-Driven Goals Foster Teamwork and Success**

   A successful coach fosters a sense of **purpose** that unites individuals toward a shared vision. Coach Bombay emphasizes that success is not just about individual achievements but about the collective success of the group. By encouraging teamwork and aligning individual goals with the team's mission, a coach creates a **cohesive** and motivated group focused on mutual success.

4. **Accountability Drives Growth**

   Accountability is a central pillar of coaching. Holding individuals responsible for their actions, while also empowering them to learn and adapt, is essential. **Coaching** helps people take ownership of their actions and decisions, encouraging them to take responsibility for their growth and development.

5. **Connection and Trust Are the Foundation of Team Success**

Strong **teamwork** does not just happen; it is built on trust, open communication, and a sense of shared responsibility. A good coach fosters these connections, creating an environment where each person feels valued and supported. When individuals trust each other, the collective energy of the group becomes unstoppable.

6. **Coaching Is About Life Lessons, Not Just Winning**

The true measure of a coach's success is not how many games are won but how many lives are changed. **Coaching** empowers people with the resilience to face challenges beyond the field, preparing them for life's ups and downs. The transformation the Mighty Ducks undergo teaches that **coaching** is about preparing people for life's bigger battles.

7. **Adaptability is Essential for Overcoming Obstacles**

Flexibility and adaptability are essential for personal and team growth. A coach's role is to help individuals adapt to new challenges, adjust their strategies, and remain resilient in the face of setbacks. Learning to pivot and adjust to changing circumstances is one of the most valuable life skills a coach can teach.

8. **True Leadership Is About Empowerment**

Coaching is also about empowering others. **Coach Bombay** does not just lead; he empowers his players to become leaders themselves. A great coach helps others realize their potential, teaching them how to lead themselves and inspire those around them.

Story-32:

Elon Musk and the Growth of SpaceX: A Real-Life Example of Lateral Thinking in the IMPACT Framework

Elon Musk's journey with SpaceX is a remarkable example of how **lateral thinking** and the **IMPACT Coaching Framework** can help overcome challenges and drive extraordinary success. Musk, with his unconventional approach and relentless drive, transformed SpaceX from a struggling startup into a leading force in the aerospace industry. His story is filled with lessons on how to push through challenges, think differently, and achieve the seemingly impossible.

Inspire Awareness & Identity: Finding His True Identity

When Musk started SpaceX, he did not have the typical background many expected. Without a formal degree in aerospace engineering, he was often doubted by experts in the industry. Early on, he dealt with feelings of **imposter syndrome**, questioning whether he truly belonged in such a high-stakes industry.

Instead of allowing this lack of formal experience to hold him back, Musk used it to his advantage. He practiced **first-principles thinking**, which allowed him to break down problems to their most basic elements and find innovative solutions. This mindset, rooted in **lateral thinking**, gave him a unique perspective that helped him rethink the traditional ways of aerospace engineering. Rather than following the crowd, he embraced his identity as a visionary who was willing to take risks and challenge the status quo.

Mindset & Mastery Shift: Overcoming Fear of Failure

SpaceX's early years were full of setbacks. The company's first three rockets failed to launch successfully, and SpaceX was on the brink of financial collapse. The weight of these failures brought tremendous pressure, and many believed that Musk was facing a losing battle.

Instead of succumbing to the **fear of failure**, Musk saw each failure as a lesson. Rather than retreating or playing it safe, he chose to embrace a **growth mindset**, one that viewed challenges as opportunities for learning and improvement. His ability to persist, despite repeated failures, showcased his commitment to **long-term success**. Musk's approach was a perfect application of **lateral thinking**—he used his setbacks not as proof of failure, but as stepping stones toward a bigger goal.

Purpose-Driven Goals & Strategy: Setting Clear and Actionable Goals

Musk's ultimate vision for SpaceX was to colonize Mars, an ambition that seemed wildly unrealistic to many. The enormity of the goal often left people questioning how such a dream could ever be realized. Early on, it appeared that SpaceX lacked a clear, actionable strategy to reach that end.

However, Musk broke down this massive objective into smaller, manageable goals. Instead of focusing solely on Mars, he set his sights on building reusable rockets and reducing the cost of space travel. Each small success, like the first successful rocket landing, built momentum and kept the team focused. Musk's ability to take **purpose-driven goals** and break them down into clear, **actionable steps** is a perfect example of using **lateral thinking** to overcome seemingly insurmountable challenges.

Action, Accountability & Adaptability: Staying Committed

Despite the immense challenges and financial pressure, maintaining consistent progress was a constant struggle. There were moments when **procrastination** and **lack of accountability** threatened to derail the project.

To address this, Musk created a strong culture of **accountability** within SpaceX. He ensured that his team had clear responsibilities, deadlines, and expectations. Musk also encouraged adaptability—when plans did not go as expected, he quickly helped the team pivot and find new solutions. Instead of sticking rigidly to a single path, he fostered a culture of **flexibility**, which allowed SpaceX to remain agile in the face of setbacks.

Connection & Collaborative Growth: Building a Strong Team

SpaceX's success did not come from Musk's vision alone. Early on, the company faced challenges in finding the right talent. In an industry dominated by established giants, it was difficult to build a team with the right expertise and innovation.

Musk did not just rely on traditional aerospace experts; instead, he sought out people from diverse fields who could bring **creative problem-solving** skills to the table. He valued **team collaboration** and encouraged his employees to think beyond the conventional. By offering them **ownership** in the company, including stock options,

Musk created a sense of **shared responsibility** for the company's success. This collaborative environment played a key role in SpaceX's ability to push boundaries and stay ahead of the competition.

Transform & Thrive: Long-Term Growth and Sustainability

Despite overcoming early failures, SpaceX continued to face the risk of **burnout** and the challenge of maintaining **sustainability**. The long hours and intense pressure could have easily led to exhaustion, but Musk understood that for the company to thrive, they needed to focus on long-term success.

Musk helped SpaceX maintain its momentum by encouraging the team to **work smarter**, not harder. Instead of pushing employees beyond their limits, he focused on building **sustainable systems** that improved efficiency. He also stressed the importance of **adaptability** and continuous learning, ensuring that the company could evolve with industry changes and technological advancements.

Conclusion:

Elon Musk's story with SpaceX is a testament to the power of **lateral thinking** and the **IMPACT Coaching Framework**. Through resilience, creativity, and a commitment to long-term goals, Musk transformed SpaceX into a revolutionary force in the aerospace industry. His approach proves that by embracing challenges, breaking down large goals into actionable steps, fostering accountability, and adapting to change, you can achieve extraordinary success.

Musk's story shows us that with the right mindset and strategic thinking, even the most ambitious goals can be achieved. If you are facing challenges in your own journey, remember that the key is not to shy away from them, but to think differently, stay committed, and never stop learning.

Key Learnings from Elon Musk's SpaceX Journey: Applying the IMPACT Framework

- **Embrace a Growth Mindset**: Musk's resilience in the face of failure teaches us that setbacks are stepping stones to success.

Instead of fearing failure, view it as an opportunity to learn and grow. By maintaining a **growth mindset**, you can turn challenges into valuable lessons and continuously improve.

- **Break Big Goals into Actionable Steps**: Musk's vision of colonizing Mars was enormous, but by breaking it down into smaller, achievable milestones (like reusable rockets), he made progress manageable. **Purpose-driven goals** are crucial, but so is breaking them down into **clear, actionable steps** to stay focused and avoid feeling overwhelmed.

- **Leverage Lateral Thinking to Innovate**: Rather than following traditional paths, Musk used **lateral thinking** to find creative solutions to complex problems. Whether it was rethinking rocket design or overcoming engineering challenges, thinking outside the box allowed SpaceX to innovate and disrupt the industry.

- **Build Accountability and a Strong Team**: Musk ensured that everyone at SpaceX had clear roles, responsibilities, and goals. This sense of **accountability** within the team fostered collaboration and encouraged everyone to take ownership of their work. Building a **strong team** with diverse expertise and empowering them to contribute ideas was key to their success.

- **Adapt and Stay Flexible**: Musk's ability to adapt to setbacks—whether technical or financial—was crucial to SpaceX's ability to thrive. By maintaining **flexibility** and quickly pivoting, when necessary, he ensured the company could overcome obstacles and continue to move forward.

- **Focus on Long-Term Sustainability**: Musk's success was not just about hitting short-term milestones but ensuring **long-term sustainability**. Building a business that thrives over time requires **balance**—not just working hard, but working smart and continuously evolving with the industry.

- **Invest in Continuous Learning**: Musk is known for being a voracious learner, always seeking new knowledge and applying it to solve problems. By prioritizing **continuous learning**, he was able to lead SpaceX through innovation after innovation.

Story-33:

IMPACT in Action: A Woman's Journey from Self-Help to Social Impact

> **"Success is the sum of small efforts, repeated day in and day out."**
>
> **— Robert Collier**

Lata Sahu: From Housewife to Changemaker

Lata Sahu's story began in the **quiet fields of Chhattisgarh**, born into modest circumstances where opportunities were scarce but her **inner spark was strong**. As a young girl, she **loved going to school**, her eyes lighting up at the sight of books and the blackboard. But that light dimmed when she was **married off at just 19**.

Her dreams took a backseat as she transitioned into life as a housewife in a farmer's home, carrying the burdens of **financial hardship, household responsibilities, and raising children**. The situation worsened when her **husband quit his job**, leaving the family dependent on **small-scale farming on a tiny plot of land**. The **rain-fed fields yielded little**, and money was always tight.

"There were days when I wondered if I would ever have a voice beyond the four walls of my home," she later said.

But change was on the horizon.

A New Beginning Through SHG

Everything shifted when **DAY-NRLM (BIHAN)** entered her village and began forming **Self-Help Groups (SHGs)**. Though hesitant at first, Lata joined and eventually became the **secretary** of her SHG. It was a small role on paper, but a monumental shift for her confidence.

She took a **loan of ₹5,000**—a leap of faith—and opened a small shop selling everyday items. It was not easy. She had to **learn how to manage money**, deal with suppliers, and **convince villagers— especially men—to trust her business**. But she persevered.

As the shop began earning modest profits, she reinvested and took another loan—this time ₹30,000. The shop grew. With ₹50,000, she bought a refrigerator and diversified her stock. For the first time, her family was not just surviving—they were beginning to **thrive**.

Becoming a Farming Changemaker

It was not enough for Lata to succeed alone. She wanted others to grow with her. When she got the opportunity to be trained in **sustainable and organic farming**, she **applied those techniques in her own field**—testing everything before recommending it to others.

From **organic composting** to **bio-pesticides**, she **experimented, failed, adjusted, and learned**. Then she began **training other farmers**, walking miles to reach remote villages. Many were sceptical.

"They asked, 'You are just a woman. What can you teach us about farming?'" she recalled.

But she won them over—not with authority, but with **experience, sincerity, and evidence**. Yields improved. Costs dropped. And soon, **word of her success spread**.

From Fields to Forums

Lata did not stop there. She became a **Community Resource Person (CRP)**, then a **Master Trainer**, and eventually began **speaking at public forums, agricultural seminars, and national programs**.

Her journey came full circle when she started **mentoring other SHG women**, helping them build shops, try kitchen gardening, or adopt sustainable farming. Over time, she directly influenced **more than 650 farmers**, changing not just harvests—but **mindsets and livelihoods**.

Despite her rising profile, Lata remains deeply grounded. She continues **learning, experimenting**, and investing her energy into building **a better future for her village**.

What Makes Her Journey So Powerful?

- **Early marriage did not define her future.**
- **Poverty did not silence her dreams.**

- **Being a woman in a male-dominated farming world did not stop her voice from rising.**

- She faced **doubt, social pressure, logistical hardship**, and still kept moving.

- She proved that with **community support, coaching, and inner resilience**, anyone can become a **catalyst for change**.

How Lata Sahu Showed Mental Agility?

- **Adaptability in Crisis:** When her husband lost his job and they faced financial distress, Lata did not panic or give up. She quickly adapted and found alternatives—like starting a shop using SHG loans—showing *flexibility under pressure*.

- **Open to Learning New Skills:** Despite limited formal education, she embraced **25+ trainings**, absorbed technical knowledge on organic farming, pest control, seed treatment, and even advanced farming models like **SRI and Trellis**. This shows her *mental openness and learning agility*.

- **Experimenting and Applying Knowledge:** She did not just learn concepts—she **tested them in her own fields**, validated the results (e.g., increased paddy yield from 16 to 24 quintals), and adjusted her methods. This is classic **agile mindset—learn, experiment, adapt**.

- **Resilience to Self-Doubt:** She felt nervous attending her first state-level training in Raipur, but still showed up. That courage to act despite fear is a key trait of mental agility.

- **Role Transition with Ease:** She smoothly transitioned from being a homemaker → SHG secretary → shop owner → CRP → AKM → Master Trainer, each requiring a **shift in mindset and identity**, showing *cognitive flexibility*.

- **Problem-Solving Orientation:** Instead of taking a high-interest loan, she explored viable, sustainable alternatives through community resources—this reflects *strategic thinking under uncertainty*.

- **Social Intelligence in Coaching Others:** She tailored her coaching to guide 650+ farmers, using simple, relatable demonstrations. That requires *empathy, communication agility,* and the ability to *connect diverse knowledge to real needs.*

Mental agility, at its core, is the ability to think flexibly, learn rapidly, unlearn old habits, and act effectively under change—and Lata exemplified all of it.

Coaching Aspects We Can Learn from Lata Sahu's Story

1. Empowerment Through Small Wins

- She began with a small loan of ₹5,000 and turned it into a sustainable business.

- *Lesson for Coaches:* Help coachees identify small, achievable goals that build momentum and self-belief.

2. Coaching Begins with Listening and Trust

- DAY-NRLM professionals did not impose a solution—they engaged the community and co-created a SHG.

- *Lesson:* Trust-building and co-creating goals with your client is more effective than giving top-down advice.

3. Growth Mindset and Continuous Learning

- Lata attended 25+ trainings, despite early nervousness.

- *Lesson:* A coach should encourage curiosity and a learning mindset—growth comes from openness to new knowledge.

4. Field-Driven Learning and Experimentation

- She tested new methods on her own farm before guiding others.

- *Lesson:* Encourage coachees to test ideas in real-world settings and learn from outcomes—not just theory.

5. From Coachee to Coach

- She evolved from a learner to a CRP, AKM, and Master Trainer.

- *Lesson:* Great coaching enables people to coach others—multiplying impact.

6. Systemic Coaching Awareness

- She did not just solve her own problems—she mobilized 650 farmers.

- *Lesson:* Think beyond the individual. Help clients see the system they influence—team, family, community.

7. Overcoming Limiting Beliefs

- From being a nervous trainee to confidently addressing ministers.

- *Lesson:* As a coach, support clients to reframe self-doubt and see their potential through new lenses.

8. Agility and Resilience

- She adapted to setbacks (husband's job loss) and pivoted strategies without losing hope.

- *Lesson:* Reinforce the value of resilience and help clients build agility in uncertain times.

9. Coaching with Simplicity and Connection

- Lata did not use jargon—she connected with farmers in relatable ways.

- *Lesson:* Coaching works best when it is human, grounded, and simple.

Final Reflection:

Lata's story reminds us that coaching is not about authority or perfection—it is about **unlocking potential, nurturing resilience, and guiding transformation** with empathy and real-world action.

Personal Growth and Self-Reflection

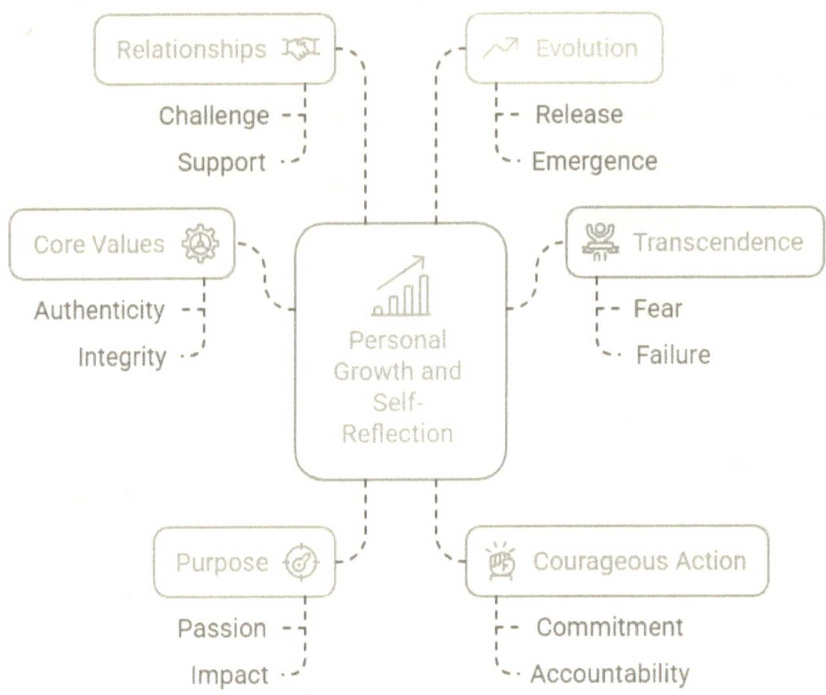

1. When no one is watching, who are you—and what core values define that version of you?

– Anchors Integrity & Authenticity

Clarifies inner identity and moral compass, independent of external validation.

2. What fear or failure have you transcended—and how has it shaped your strength today?

– Reflects Mastery & Growth

Transforms past struggles into lessons that forge confidence and capability.

3. If you knew you could not fail, what purpose would you devote your life to—and why?

– Uncovers Purpose & Impact

Reveals the client's deepest mission beyond limitation or self-doubt.

4. What courageous action will you commit to right now—and who will hold you accountable for it?

– Drives Accountability & Ownership

Creates momentum with clear intention and built-in follow-through.

5. Who are the five people who challenge, support, and elevate your growth—and how will you nurture those relationships?

– Builds Collaboration & Connection

Strengthens the network that multiplies success through shared vision and trust.

6. What part of your current self must evolve—or be released— for the next version of you to emerge?

– Catalyzes Transformation & Adaptability

Encourages intentional shedding of old patterns to embrace growth

Validating the IMPACT Coaching Framework Through Lata Sahu's Story

Lata Sahu's journey perfectly demonstrates how the **IMPACT Coaching Framework** enables real transformation. Each stage of **IMPACT**—from self-awareness to sustained growth—can be seen in her evolution from a struggling homemaker to an empowered community leader and trainer.

1. Inspire Awareness & Identity (I)

In the nascent stages of her journey, Lata navigated a landscape defined by financial limitations and the restrictive boundaries of societal norms, hindering her ability to envision a future where she could lead or innovate. The concept of entrepreneurship remained a distant star. The introduction to Self-Help Groups (SHGs) through the DAY-

NRLM intervention acted as a catalyst, igniting a vital spark of self-awareness within her. As she stepped into the roles of SHG secretary and bookkeeper, embracing the responsibilities of organization and community engagement, previously dormant strengths in leadership began to emerge. Lata's unfolding experience serves as a compelling validation, underscoring the profound truth that the inaugural and indispensable step towards any meaningful transformation is the clear recognition and confident embrace of one's intrinsic strengths, deeply held values, and unique purpose in the world.

2. Mindset & Mastery Shift (M)

Lata's initial steps into unfamiliar territories, such as attending state-level training, were marked by a common human experience: hesitation. Like many embarking on new ventures, she grappled with the insidious grip of fear of failure, the persistent whisper of self-doubt, and the unsettling weight of imposter syndrome. However, the principles of IMPACT coaching became her compass and her courage. Instead of succumbing to these internal barriers, she actively cultivated a path of consistent learning, diligently applying newly acquired knowledge, and embracing calculated risks, exemplified by her foray into organic farming. This deliberate engagement with growth fostered a profound internal shift. The fear of judgment that once held her back gradually transformed into a burgeoning confidence rooted in experimentation and the burgeoning recognition of her own leadership capabilities. Lata's journey powerfully validates the core tenet of IMPACT coaching: its ability to guide individuals in reframing their limiting beliefs and constructing a resilient and empowering growth mindset.

3. Purpose-Driven Goals & Strategy (P)

Lata faced the critical challenge of transitioning her family's financial stability beyond the limitations of small, individual loans, yet lacked a clear strategy for scaling her efforts. However, the principles of the IMPACT framework guided her towards a structured and visionary approach to growth. She strategically staged her financial expansion, beginning with a modest ₹5,000 loan, then progressively securing larger amounts of ₹30,000 for her shop and subsequently ₹50,000 to fuel further expansion. Crucially, when the opportunity for sustainable agriculture training arose, she did not view it in isolation. Instead, she consciously aligned this new skill set with a broader mission of creating a positive impact within her community. Lata's experience vividly validates a core strength of the IMPACT framework: its ability to empower individuals to connect their daily, often incremental efforts to a compelling long-term vision, thereby preventing the pitfalls of aimless hard work and fostering purposeful progress.

4. Action, Accountability & Adaptability (A)

The most formidable hurdle Lata faced lay in overcoming the inertia of inaction, the daunting prospect of taking that initial leap – whether it was unlocking the door to her new shop, committing to the unfamiliar practices of organic farming, or stepping into the role of a trainer for others. Adding to this challenge was the inevitable need to navigate the setbacks of failures and the anxieties of financial uncertainties. However, the principles of IMPACT coaching instilled in her a powerful bias towards consistent action. Before imparting knowledge to others, she diligently experimented with new techniques within her own field, building a foundation of practical experience. Furthermore, she cultivated a strong sense of accountability by meticulously tracking her results and regularly reporting her progress to both the Self-Help Group (SHG) and the Village Organization (VO). Crucially, when an approach proved ineffective, Lata demonstrated resilience, adapting her strategies rather than succumbing to the temptation to quit. Her journey powerfully validates a key strength of IMPACT coaching: it empowers individuals to maintain unwavering commitment to execution while fostering the essential flexibility to navigate and adjust to the ever-shifting landscape of circumstances.

5. Connection & Collaborative Growth (C)

In her initial efforts, Lata's primary focus was understandably on securing her family's survival. However, the principles of IMPACT coaching illuminated a more expansive truth: true and lasting impact is realized when knowledge is shared and collective growth is fostered.

Embracing this understanding, Lata transitioned from individual striving to community empowerment, diligently training over 650 farmers in the practices of sustainable agriculture, thereby ensuring a pathway to shared success within her community. Furthermore, she actively cultivated robust peer networks through the Self-Help Groups (SHGs), the Village Organization (VO), and her engagement with PRADAN, reinforcing the powerful principle that progress accelerates and becomes more resilient when individuals are supported by a strong and collaborative community. Lata's journey powerfully validates a core tenet of IMPACT coaching: that leadership transcends the boundaries of personal achievement and truly thrives when it is channeled into empowering others to rise alongside you.

6. Transform & Thrive (T)

While many individuals experience fleeting periods of improvement, the challenge often lies in cultivating enduring growth and long-term sustainability. However, Lata's journey, guided by the principles of IMPACT coaching, transcends these temporary gains. Her success was not a singular event; instead, it became a launchpad for ever-expanding influence. She ascended to the role of a Master Trainer, actively engaging with policymakers and extending her impact far beyond the confines of her own village. Demonstrating a continuous drive for growth and a commitment to legacy, Lata has now diversified her efforts into initiatives like mushroom cultivation, vermicomposting, and, crucially, mentoring aspiring entrepreneurs. Her ongoing trajectory powerfully validates a core tenet of IMPACT coaching: it is not merely about achieving short-term victories, but rather about embedding the principles of transformation so deeply that individuals sustain their growth and actively build legacies that extend far beyond their immediate achievements.

Final Conclusion: Does the IMPACT Framework Work?

Lata Sahu's real-life journey **validates** the **IMPACT Coaching Framework** because:

- **She started with self-awareness.**

- **She overcame limiting beliefs with learning.**

- **She aligned goals with purpose.**

- **She took action and stayed accountable.**

- **She empowered others, creating collective impact.**

- **She sustained her growth and continued evolving.**

Her story is living proof that **when people follow the IMPACT framework, they do not just improve their lives—they transform entire communities.**

> **"The greatest glory in living lies not in never falling, but in rising every time we fall."**
>
> **— Nelson Mandela**

Story-34:

From Breakdown to Breakthrough: How Coaching Saved Ford's Future

Journey to Long-Term Success

A true coaching transformation using the IMPACT Framework

In the early 2000s, Ford Motor Company—once the pride of American innovation—was a ship taking on water. It was bleeding billions. Product quality was slipping. Market share was shrinking. The company had mortgaged everything, including its iconic blue oval logo. Behind the scenes, Ford's leadership meetings were tense, quiet, and full of rehearsed optimism. Executives presented glowing reports that did not match the grim reality. The culture was steeped in fear, silos, and secrecy.

Into this turmoil stepped **Alan Mulally**, a Boeing executive with no automotive experience. But what he lacked in car industry knowledge, he made up for with a coach's mindset and a transformational leadership style grounded in **curiosity, compassion, and clarity**.

"I"—Inspire Awareness & Identity

Mulally's first act was not to overhaul Ford's production lines. It was to hold up a **mirror** to its leadership. He introduced the *Business Plan Review* (BPR), a weekly meeting where every leader was required to share the status of their key projects using a simple red-yellow-green system.

Week after week, every slide was green—even when everyone in the room knew things were failing.

Finally, **Mark Fields**, then-president of the Americas, nervously showed a red status for a launch delay. The room went silent. People held their breath. In the old Ford, this kind of honesty meant termination.

But Alan smiled and **clapped**.

"Mark," he said, "That's great visibility! What can we all do to help you?"

That moment was a **catalyst**. Leaders began to drop their masks. They admitted what was not working. They asked for help. Vulnerability was no longer weakness—it was a strength.

This was the coaching essence of **"Inspire Awareness & Identity."** Alan helped Ford's leaders **rediscover who they were** as people—not just professionals. He replaced fear with honesty. He created psychological safety in a room that had long lacked it.

"M"—Mindset & Mastery Shift

Ford's culture had long been rooted in self-preservation. Executives feared transparency. Departments competed for resources. Failure was hidden, not discussed.

Mulally flipped the script. "You can't manage a secret," he repeated often. He championed **learning over perfection**, progress over posturing. One by one, his team began to shift.

Instead of asking, *"Who's to blame?"* leaders began asking, *"What did we learn?"*

Mulally was not scolding failures—he was **coaching through them**. He offered **feedback without judgment**, creating room for new thinking to emerge. This mindset shift—moving from control and fear to growth and learning—sparked the second stage of IMPACT: **Mindset & Mastery Shift**.

Ford began to rewire itself from the inside out.

"P"—Purpose-Driven Goals & Strategy

With the team growing more open and self-aware, Alan knew it was time to reignite a deeper sense of purpose. He launched the rallying cry:

"One Ford. One Team. One Plan. One Goal."

It was more than a tagline—it was a **mission mantra**. This new vision unified everyone: from the C-suite in Dearborn to factory floors across the world.

The company aligned behind a bold strategy: simplify the product lineup, focus on fuel efficiency and quality, and build vehicles that customers truly wanted. Suddenly, every team knew where they were headed and why. People were not just assembling cars; they were **driving a turnaround**.

This was pure **"Purpose-Driven Coaching"**—bringing clarity to chaos, aligning hearts with roadmaps, and fuelling progress with intention.

"A"—Action, Accountability & Adaptability

Every Thursday morning at 7:00 a.m., the BPR became a **coaching circle**, not a punishment zone. Mulally's questions were not interrogations—they were invitations:

- "What's working?"

- "Where do you need help?"

- "What are we learning this week?"

Instead of hiding problems, executives surfaced them early. Resources were reallocated swiftly. Cross-functional support became the norm. There was no tolerance for blame—but infinite support for solutions.

Mulally turned Ford into an **agile learning organization**, where accountability was not top-down—it was team-driven. Every leader became a coach for their teams. Every meeting was a chance to learn, adapt, and act.

"C"—Connection & Collaborative Growth

Ford was once a fractured organization. Engineering and design rarely talked. Marketing and manufacturing worked in silos. Mulally made **collaboration a core value**.

He instilled a mantra: *"Everyone is included. Everyone is accountable."*

He modeled humility by praising others, seeking feedback, and celebrating cross-functional wins. Over time, trust replaced turf wars. Peer coaching became common. People stopped hoarding power and started sharing ideas.

This was coaching at the level of **culture**—a shift from individual egos to collective elevation. The **"C" in IMPACT** had come alive.

"T"—Transform & Thrive

By 2009, the global auto industry was in freefall. Chrysler and GM were bailed out. Ford was not.

Not because it did not need help—but because it had already **helped itself**. Through coaching, Ford had become leaner, wiser, and bolder.

The company launched bestsellers like the Ford Fusion and a reinvented F-150. Its stock rebounded. So did employee pride.

But the greatest transformation was not financial—it was **cultural**.

Alan Mulally left in 2014 with a powerful legacy: a company that **knew how to coach itself forward**, with honesty, resilience, clarity, and connection. Ford's DNA had changed. The coach had coached a **culture into existence**.

Reflection:

Ford's story is not just a business case study—it is a **coaching masterclass**. Alan Mulally did not manage a company. He *coached a movement*. And the IMPACT Framework—Inspire, Mindset, Purpose, Action, Connection, transform—was quietly at play in every meeting, every conversation, and every breakthrough.

- the coaching skills, coaching questions, and actionable outcomes from Alan Mulally's story through the lens of the IMPACT Coaching Framework, so readers (and coaches!) can use the same approaches when working with clients.

1. I—Inspire Awareness & Identity

- **Coaching Skills Displayed:**
  - Deep listening
  - Emotional safety building
  - Observation without judgment
  - Holding space for truth

- **Coaching Questions:**
  - What is really going on beneath the surface?
  - What are you not saying out loud yet?
  - Who are you as a leader when no one is watching?

- **Actions & Outcomes:**
  - Created psychological safety in meetings
  - Encouraged truth-telling and self-reflection
  - Sparked self-awareness of leadership blind spots
  - Leaders moved from denial to personal ownership

2. M—Mindset & Mastery Shift

- **Coaching Skills Displayed:**
  - Reframing limiting beliefs
  - Normalizing vulnerability
  - Encouraging a growth mindset
  - Modelling non-judgment

- **Coaching Questions:**
  - What are you afraid might happen if you are honest?
  - What could this mistake teach you?
  - What if asking for help was a strength, not a weakness?

- **Actions & Outcomes:**
  - Shifted from fear to curiosity
  - Normalized failure as learning
  - Encouraged interdependent leadership
  - Built courage and resilience within teams

3. P—Purpose-Driven Goals & Strategy

- **Coaching Skills Displayed:**
  - Vision elicitation
  - Strategic alignment
  - Storytelling for motivation
  - Communicating purpose with clarity

- **Coaching Questions:**
  - What future are we trying to create together?
  - How does your role serve this bigger vision?
  - What is the one goal that truly aligns us all?

- **Actions & Outcomes:**
  - Unified teams under "One Ford. One Team. One Goal."
  - Established shared goals and direction
  - Clarified departmental and personal contributions
  - Reconnected people with a larger "why"

4. A—Action, Accountability & Adaptability

- **Coaching Skills Displayed:**
  - Accountability coaching
  - Feedback facilitation
  - Real-time reflection
  - Encouraging action-based transparency

- **Coaching Questions:**
  - What is working? What is not?
  - What did you learn this week?
  - Where are you stuck, and what support do you need?

- **Actions & Outcomes:**
  - Held weekly Business Plan Reviews (BPRs)
  - Made failure discussable, not punishable
  - Fostered a coaching culture around execution
  - Encouraged learning loops and agile adaptation

5. C—Connection & Collaborative Growth

- **Coaching Skills Displayed:**
  - Relationship coaching
  - Team coaching and group facilitation
  - Trust building
  - Empathy in communication

Coaching Questions:
  - How well are you working with your peers?
  - Where is trust missing in your team?
  - Who needs your support right now?

- **Actions & Outcomes:**
  - Dismantled silos between teams
  - Fostered collaboration and mentorship
  - Turned competition into cooperation
  - Built a human-first, supportive work culture

6. T—Transform & Thrive

- **Coaching Skills Displayed:**
  - Long-term transformation thinking
  - Legacy and identity coaching
  - Cultural change facilitation
  - Sustained reflective practice

- **Coaching Questions:**
  - What kind of leader do you want to be remembered as?
  - What values do you want this organization to live by?
  - What will make your culture sustainable?

- **Actions & Outcomes:**
  - Transformed Ford's culture from fear to future-focused
  - Embedded coaching into operations and leadership practices
  - Enabled long-term performance and resilience
  - Left behind a lasting legacy of empowered leadership

Here are the key takeaways from Alan Mulally's coaching transformation at Ford through the IMPACT Framework:

1. **Inspire Awareness & Identity**: Mulally fostered psychological safety and encouraged honesty by introducing the Business Plan Review (BPR), where leaders admitted challenges openly, shifting from fear to vulnerability as a strength.

2. **Mindset & Mastery Shift**: Mulally created a culture of growth by reframing failure as a learning opportunity and promoting transparency. Leaders stopped hiding mistakes and instead focused on continuous learning.

3. **Purpose-Driven Goals & Strategy**: Mulally unified Ford under a common vision with the mantra "One Ford. One Team. One Goal," aligning all departments toward a shared purpose, igniting a collective sense of ownership and clarity.

Through these shifts, Ford evolved from a fearful, siloed company to one with a thriving, collaborative, and growth-driven culture, ultimately leading to its turnaround.

"True transformation doesn't come from commands — it comes from courageous conversations. Alan Mulally didn't just lead Ford; he coached it into a culture of honesty, agility, and shared purpose."

Chapter Summary: Nurturing Future Leaders

1. **Inspire:** *"Who are the emerging leaders around me, and how am I helping them dream boldly?"*

   o **Action:** Identify 1–2 individuals—whether they are children, students, or team members—that you interact with regularly. Take the time to ask them about their dreams and goals. Create a safe space for them to share what excites them. Encourage them to reflect on why these dreams matter to them and how they see them shaping their future.

2. **Mindset:** *"What fears or limiting beliefs might be holding them back, and how can I help them reframe those stories?"*

   o **Action:** Have a candid conversation about fear. Share your own experiences of overcoming self-doubt to create relatability. Help them write down one fear or limiting belief they hold and work together to transform it into a "power question" such as, *"What if this challenge is helping me grow stronger?"* This reframing technique allows them to approach challenges from a growth mindset.

3. **Purpose:** *"How can I help them connect their passions to a larger purpose?"*

   o **Action:** Guide them through a thought-provoking reflection: *"What problem in the world do you wish you could solve?"* Help them brainstorm tangible, small actions they can take now that contribute to solving this problem. This gives their passion a clear, purposeful direction.

4. **Action:** *"What habits or support systems can I help them build to act on their vision?"*

   o **Action:** Work together to set a 7-day micro-goal—a small but meaningful step toward their vision. This could be something like starting a journal, speaking up in class, or writing a blog post. Create an accountability loop where you check in regularly, celebrate their efforts, and reflect on their progress. This establishes a consistent rhythm of action and support.

5. **Connection:** *"Am I creating a space of belonging, listening, and mentorship?"*

   o **Action:** Dedicate time for a "connection chat" each week—just 15 minutes where the individual feels truly heard. Avoid offering advice; instead, create space for them to express themselves freely. Additionally, consider introducing them to a role model or peer community that aligns with their interests and goals. This helps foster a sense of belonging and further connection.

6. **Transform:** *"What legacy am I shaping through the way I show up for others today?"*

   o **Action:** Reflect deeply and journal your thoughts: *"What values do I want to pass on through my coaching or leadership?"* Consider the lasting impact you hope to have. Write a "Letter to the Future" for someone you mentor, sharing your hopes for who they will become and the positive change they will create. This exercise helps solidify your role as a transformative leader who nurtures lasting growth in others.

Concluding Reflection:

What one action can you take this week to embody the Coaching qualities discussed in the chapter?

These questions can help facilitate deeper reflection and dialogue, encouraging individuals to connect their personal experiences with the principles outlined in the text

Case studies

Case study - 1

From Overwhelm to Ownership: How IMPACT Coaching Transformed Priya's Leadership Journey

Priya, a mid-level product manager in a bustling Bangalore-based tech startup, had always been seen as smart, reliable, and driven. But beneath the surface, she was struggling. Every client presentation came with a wave of anxiety. She avoided difficult conversations with stakeholders, fearing conflict. Her calendar was overflowing, yet she often felt she was achieving little of real value. The pressure to deliver, lead, and climb the corporate ladder was mounting—and it was taking a toll on her confidence and health. She felt like she was merely surviving, not leading.

When Priya's manager offered her a spot in a leadership coaching program that used the **IMPACT Coaching Framework**, she was sceptical but hopeful. She knew something had to change. What followed was not just a skill upgrade—it was a transformation from the inside out.

The journey began with a deep dive into **Inspire Awareness & Identity**. Through thoughtful conversations, reflection exercises, and journaling prompts, Priya started uncovering the patterns that had shaped her behaviour. She realized that much of her leadership anxiety stemmed from a fear of not being "enough." She had spent years trying her self-worth to performance metrics and external validation. For the first time, she articulated her values—integrity, curiosity, and empathy—and recognized that her identity as a leader needed to grow from that authentic foundation.

With this newfound awareness, her coach guided her into the next stage: **Mindset & Mastery Shift**. Here, Priya began unpacking the limiting beliefs that had kept her stuck in self-doubt. She always assumed that conflict led to broken relationships, which kept her silent during critical discussions. But with coaching, she explored new perspectives. Through structured mindset exercises and roleplays, she learned to reframe her inner dialogue. "I'm not ready" turned into "I'm growing." She began seeing challenges not as threats, but as chances to practice courage and growth.

As her mindset shifted, Priya was ready to reconnect with direction and ambition in the **Purpose-Driven Goals & Strategy** phase. Together with her coach, she articulated a vision: to grow into a strategic product leader who could shape not just products, but people and culture. They broke this vision into actionable goals and milestones. Her six-month challenge was to lead a cross-functional product launch, aligning multiple teams around a clear, customer-focused roadmap. This clarity gave her energy; for the first time in months, she felt aligned and on track.

With goals set, the coaching moved into **Action, Accountability & Adaptability**. Priya developed rituals of weekly planning, reflection, and intentional prioritization. Rather than chasing every task, she began focusing on what mattered most. Mistakes still happened—but instead of spiralling into self-blame, she learned to pause, assess, and adapt. Her coach introduced her to strategies for resilience, helping her build momentum even through moments of uncertainty. What changed was not just her productivity—it was her relationship with action itself.

However, Priya knew that leadership was not just about her own progress. In the **Connection & Collaborative Growth** stage, she began focusing on how she showed up for others. She had always hesitated to offer feedback, fearing it would be taken the wrong way. But now, equipped with tools in active listening, emotional intelligence, and coaching conversations, she started initiating regular check-ins and retrospectives with her team. Instead of directing, she began co-creating solutions. One of her proudest moments was mentoring a junior PM, helping her navigate the same confidence issues Priya once faced.

The final stage of her transformation was **Transform & Thrive**. At this point, the change in her was not just visible to her coach—it was being noticed across the organization. She was not just managing deadlines; she was shaping strategy. She was invited to present at the quarterly leadership meeting, where she confidently outlined a product roadmap that blended market insight with team collaboration. That presentation led to a new role with broader influence. But what truly mattered to Priya was not the promotion—it was the sense of alignment. She finally felt that her career was a reflection of her values, strengths, and vision.

Through each stage of the IMPACT Coaching Framework—**Inspire, Mindset, Purpose, Action, Connection, transform**—Priya evolved from a reactive, overwhelmed contributor to an intentional, authentic leader. Her journey was not about fixing flaws; it was about uncovering her true power and leading from that place of clarity and courage.

Case study - 2

Healing the Healer: How Dr. Meera Rekindled Her Purpose Through IMPACT Coaching

Dr. Meera Sharma had spent over 15 years serving as the Head of Operations in a large multi-specialty hospital in Pune. To her team, she was known as dedicated, meticulous, and unshakably composed. But behind her calm demeanour was a soul quietly burning out. The COVID-19 pandemic had pushed the hospital—and her—to the edge. Staffing crises, supply shortages, 18-hour days, emotional strain from patient losses, and endless bureaucracy had left her physically drained and emotionally brittle.

She found herself constantly firefighting—handling urgent issues while strategic projects remained stalled. Her team had grown distant. Once collaborative and inspired, many had grown resentful, overworked, and disengaged. At home, her teenage son barely saw her. And when he did, she was distracted, often on the phone or replying to emails late into the night.

Meera knew something had to give. That is when her hospital's leadership partnered with a coaching initiative built around the **IMPACT Coaching Framework**. Sceptical but desperate, Meera joined.

Her journey began with the **Inspire Awareness & Identity** phase. Through early coaching conversations, she began to unpack the layers of roles she had been carrying for years—doctor, administrator, mother, leader, fire extinguisher—and in the process, lost sight of *Meera*, the human being. Her coach gently guided her to reflect on her core identity beyond her designations. For the first time in years, she asked herself, "Why did I enter medicine in the first place?" The answer was clear—*to heal, to connect, to make systems humane*. That forgotten inner compass began to glow again.

In the **Mindset & Mastery Shift** stage, Meera confronted beliefs that had been silently sabotaging her. "If I slow down, people will suffer." "I must be available 24/7." "Delegation means failure." These beliefs had become shackles. Through reflective exercises, she learned that sustainable leadership required not self-sacrifice, but self-awareness. She practiced letting go of control, trusting her team more, and honouring her boundaries. Her coach introduced her to mindfulness practices— brief rituals that allowed her to center herself before high-stakes decisions. Slowly, the chaos around her began to feel manageable.

With her mind clearer, she was ready for **Purpose-Driven Goals & Strategy**. Meera articulated a vision not just for hospital operations, but for a culture of compassionate care. She envisioned a leadership model where empathy, efficiency, and emotional wellness were equally valued. Her strategic goals emerged from this purpose: reducing nurse burnout, implementing cross-departmental empathy training, and improving patient satisfaction scores—all by creating space for team voices to shape solutions.

The **Action, Accountability & Adaptability** stage brought energy and momentum. Meera started having weekly "Wellness Rounds" not just for patients, but for her staff. She empowered nurse leaders to co-design workflow improvements, reducing redundant paperwork and increasing breaks. She blocked "sacred hours" on her calendar—non-negotiable time for family, rest, and strategic thinking. Her adaptability improved. When a crisis emerged, she did not react out of panic—she paused, assessed the situation, and responded with clarity.

In the **Connection & Collaborative Growth** phase, she reconnected deeply with her team. Where before she had been seen as distant or overloaded, she now became a more empathetic and vulnerable leader. She began to host storytelling circles with frontline workers—spaces to share wins, frustrations, and gratitude. Her own vulnerability, when she shared how overwhelmed she had felt, created a ripple effect of openness and healing. She mentored junior doctors, not just in medicine, but in resilience and boundaries.

By the time she reached the **Transform & Thrive** phase, Meera was no longer operating from burnout, but from balance. Her department's patient satisfaction scores had risen. Nurse retention improved. But more importantly, her son said something she had not heard in years: *"Mom, you smile more now."*

The hospital board took notice, inviting her to lead a broader initiative on compassionate leadership across departments. But for Meera, the biggest success was not the title or the numbers—it was the feeling of alignment. She was finally living in rhythm with her values, leading from wholeness, and modelling what healing leadership truly looks like.

Through each dimension of the **IMPACT Coaching Framework— Inspire, Mindset, Purpose, Action, Connection, transform**—Meera had not just rediscovered her strength. She had reawakened her calling.

Case study - 3:

From Dust to Destiny: How a Village Farmer in Kenya Found His Way Through Coaching

In a sunbaked village near **Kitui County**, eastern Kenya, lived **Kilonzo**, a 45-year-old smallholder farmer. His land, once lush with sorghum and maize, now cracked under the weight of droughts and failing rains. The seasonal rivers had dried, and every planting season became a gamble against climate.

Kilonzo had grown up believing the soil would always provide—his father had said so. But over the years, hope had withered like his crops. He had tried hybrid seeds, borrowed for fertilizer, and even leased a neighbour's land to increase yield, but the returns were poor. Debts began to mount, and with each passing harvest, his family ate less, worried more, and dreamed less.

One day, a community development organization arrived in the village with a rural resilience program that integrated the **IMPACT Coaching Framework**. At first, Kilonzo was sceptical. He had seen many NGOs come and go, handing out training manuals that gathered dust. But something about the word *"coaching"* felt different. It was not about giving—it was about growing.

In his first session, the coach gently led with **Inspire Awareness & Identity**. "Tell me," The coach asked, "when did you last feel proud of your work?" That question hit Kilonzo like a wave. He spoke about his younger days—how he once harvested enough to donate food during a flood in a neighbouring village. How his hands, rough from work, had once symbolized pride, not struggle. That memory rekindled something buried under years of hardship: a sense of *worth*.

As they moved into **Mindset & Mastery Shift**, Kilonzo confronted his internalized doubts— *"I am just a poor farmer. Nothing I do will change the weather."* The coach helped him reframe these limiting beliefs. He began to learn about climate-smart agriculture, mulching, and intercropping. Instead of focusing on what was out of his control—like the rains— he focused on what he could influence: his soil, his water usage, his planting techniques.

With a restored sense of identity, he progressed to **Purpose-Driven Goals & Strategy**. "Why do you want to farm?" the coach asked. "To feed my family—and to show my son that farming is not failure," Kilonzo said, his voice steady. That clarity drove his planning. He decided to shift one portion of his land to drought-tolerant crops like cowpeas and millet. He built zai pits to conserve water. And he began a small kitchen garden near his home, tended by his wife and daughter, that provided vegetables even in dry months.

In the **Action, Accountability & Adaptability** phase, he set simple, realistic goals. He recorded crop yields, tested soil moisture levels, and began composting. His coach checked in regularly—sometimes in person, sometimes by phone—to support, challenge, and cheer him on. When pests attacked his maize, instead of panicking, he sought advice from a neighbouring farmer and switched to neem-based organic sprays. Failure was no longer the end—just a lesson.

The true shift came during the **Connection & Collaborative Growth** stage. Kilonzo, once isolated and quiet, began organizing Saturday meetings with other farmers under a large baobab tree. They shared stories, tools, and seeds. He introduced ideas he had tried—zai pits, vertical sack gardening—and encouraged others to experiment too. One day, he invited the local chief to speak on land conservation. The village, once fragmented by survival mode, began to act like a community again.

By the time he reached **Transform & Thrive**, Kilonzo was no longer farming just to survive. He had set up a cooperative to sell surplus cowpeas to the nearby market. His son, once set on moving to Nairobi, now asked to learn more about sustainable farming. His wife started selling dried herbs and sun-dried tomatoes to a women's savings group. They weren't rich—but they were resilient, self-reliant, and thriving.

When asked what changed, Kilonzo smiled and said, *"I did not change the weather. I changed myself. And that changed everything."*

Through the **IMPACT Coaching Framework**, Kilonzo did not just improve his land. He rewrote his story—from drought and despair to dignity and direction. His footprints across the dry fields were no longer heavy with hopelessness—they were filled with purpose.

The Legacy of IMPACT – Coaching as a Catalyst for Transformation

The fire crackled in the dimly lit chamber, casting flickering shadows on the stone walls. A young boy, no more than twelve, sat cross-legged before his mentor. His clothes were tattered, his face smudged with the dust of the streets he once wandered alone. But his eyes—his eyes burned with an intensity that defied his past. Across from him, a man with piercing intellect and an unshakable resolve spoke in measured tones.

"You will not remain a child of misfortune," he said, his voice steady. "You will become a king."

It was an absurd claim. A child with no name, no family, no power. Yet, through sheer will, discipline, and the relentless coaching of his mentor, Chandragupta Maurya would one day rise from a street urchin to an emperor, ruling one of the greatest dynasties in history.

This was not a story of luck. It was a story of mentorship, strategy, and transformation—a story that has repeated itself across history in different forms, with different faces, in different lands. A Corsican soldier who reshaped Europe. A young monk who awakened a nation's soul. A steel magnate who transformed an industry. A weary explorer who refused to let his men perish in the ice. A digital empire brought back from the brink of collapse.

Each of them was forged in fire, guided by vision, and empowered through coaching.

But what about you?

What forces will shape your leadership? What mentor will challenge your assumptions, push you beyond your comfort, and refine you into something greater? More importantly—who will you coach, and whose destiny will you change?

The answers lie in the IMPACT Coaching Framework, a model rooted not just in theory but in the struggles, setbacks, and triumphs of history's greatest leaders.

A World Built on Coaching

If we strip away the grand monuments, the towering skyscrapers, the billion-dollar industries—what remains?

People. Relationships. Growth.

At its core, civilization has been built not just by visionaries but by coaches—those who see potential in others before they see it in themselves.

Picture a young Napoleon Bonaparte, ridiculed for his Corsican accent, dismissed as an outsider. Had he been left to the ridicule of his peers; he would have faded into obscurity. But instead, he found mentors in the art of strategy, guiding him from an unknown officer to a man who reshaped the world.

Or consider Andrew Carnegie, the son of a Scottish weaver, who arrived in America with nothing but hunger in his heart. Had he not been taken under the wing of Thomas Scott, who taught him the ropes of the railroad industry, he might have remained another struggling immigrant. Instead, he became a titan of steel, a master of leadership, and a mentor to others who would shape the future.

Even empires of business have teetered on the brink of collapse, only to be revived through coaching. Disney, once the pinnacle of animation, fell into creative stagnation, losing its magic. It took mentorship, reinvention, and coaching at the highest level to bring it back from decline, proving that even the greatest organizations must be coached through transformation.

And yet, for every success story, there is a tragedy where coaching was absent.

The fall of Nokia was not due to a lack of resources or intelligence—it was the absence of fearless leadership and open coaching cultures that sealed its fate. Employees saw the dangers ahead but lacked the voice or mentorship to change course. Fear stifled growth, and a once-dominant empire crumbled.

If there is one lesson from history, it is this: **coaching is not a luxury. It is the backbone of growth, survival, and success.**

And that applies to you, right now, more than you realize.

The Science of Transformation: Why IMPACT Works

It is easy to dismiss coaching as something abstract—something that "sounds good" but has little practical weight. But science tells a different story.

Imagine you are standing at the edge of a cliff, heart pounding, as the wind howls around you. Below lies a vast, uncharted territory—the future you have always wanted but never dared to reach. Your mind is screaming with doubts.

Now, imagine a voice behind you—calm, confident, unwavering.

"You can do this," it says. **"I have been here before. Follow my lead."**

Your breath steadies. The fear does not disappear, but it transforms into something else—focus, resolve, action.

This is the power of coaching. It rewires the brain, reframes fear, and ignites action. Studies in neuroscience confirm that mentorship and structured guidance accelerate learning, increase resilience, and create long-term behavioural change.

The IMPACT Coaching Framework is built on this foundation, combining:

- **Ancient wisdom** (Seneca's stoicism, Confucius's teachings, Rumi's introspection).

- **Modern leadership strategies** (Carnegie's mentorship model, Napoleon Hill's success philosophy).

- **Behavioural science and psychology** (Cognitive behavioural coaching, neuro-linguistic programming).

This is why it works—it aligns with how human beings grow, adapt, and achieve mastery.

The True Purpose of Leadership: Creating a Ripple Effect

Think back to the greatest leader you have ever known—not someone famous, but someone in your own life. A teacher. A manager. A parent. A mentor.

Why do they stand out?

Because they did not just tell you what to do. **They made you believe in what you could become.**

True leadership is not about accumulating power—it is about distributing it. It is about ensuring that your success is measured by how many others you empower.

We saw this in:

- **Swami Vivekananda**, whose words ignited an entire nation's spiritual awakening.

- **Lee Kuan Yew**, who coached an entire country into prosperity through discipline and vision.

- **Marcus Aurelius**, who coached himself through self-reflection, proving that the greatest mentors are sometimes within.

The real question is—**who will you empower?**

Because leadership is not measured by the empires you build, the money you accumulate, or the titles you wear.

It is measured by the people who rise because of you.

What Will Be Your IMPACT?

The pages of this book will close. The words will fade. But one thing remains—**what you choose to do next.**

Will you remain an observer, inspired but unchanged? Or will you step into the role of a leader, a coach, a force for transformation?

Because the world does not need more followers.

It needs more coaches.

- **Who will you mentor?**
- **Who will challenge you to grow?**
- **How will you apply the IMPACT Framework in your life, your team, your vision?**

The answers will define your legacy.

Because in the end, success is fleeting. Power fades. Titles disappear.

But the lives you touch, the people you uplift, the leaders you create—

That is your true impact.

And that is what will remain long after you are gone.

"Coaching isn't about telling someone what to do; it's about helping them discover the answers within themselves. IMPACT Coaching ignites that process."

"I've noticed something interesting as I've worked with individuals and organizations: people often don't seem to care about the IMPACT Coaching Framework, and life continues as usual. It makes me wonder, why is that?"

Here is what I have observed:

1. Comfort with the Status Quo

What I see: People seem content in their routines, even if they are unfulfilling. The idea of stepping out of that comfort zone—into something transformative like IMPACT—just does not appeal to them.

My Reflection: Change is uncomfortable. It is easier to stay in a place that feels familiar, even if it is draining. I have seen countless individuals who, when faced with the challenge of personal growth, choose to remain where they are. And it is not because they do not *want* success—it is because the discomfort of change feels too overwhelming.

2. Lack of Emotional Connection

What I see: Frameworks like IMPACT can sound abstract or theoretical to many. I have found that people only start truly caring when they **feel** the change—not when they just understand it intellectually.

My Reflection: When I have worked with others, I have noticed that unless the framework becomes deeply emotional and personal—unless people connect with it in a way that speaks to their heart—it remains just a tool, like any other. They need to see how it will transform them, not just in theory but in practice.

3. No Immediate Payoff

What I see: We live in a world that is obsessed with instant results. People want quick rewards, and IMPACT, with its depth and emphasis on long-term growth, does not offer those immediate wins.

My Reflection: It is frustrating to watch because I have seen individuals try IMPACT for a week, maybe two, and when they do not see immediate success, they abandon it. They miss the point that true transformation takes time, consistency, and patience. But the world is not built for patience anymore.

4. It is Just "Another Framework"

What I see: I have noticed that people, especially those who are already overwhelmed with so many tools and models, tend to dismiss IMPACT as just another "framework" on the shelf.

My Reflection: I have seen this happen all too often. The frameworks and buzzwords pile up, and without a deeper emotional connection, they all start blending together. People do not see how IMPACT differs from the rest because no one is showing them exactly how this framework leads to lasting change.

5. No One Is Modelling It

What I see: One of the most significant reasons people do not care about IMPACT, or any coaching framework for that matter, is that they do not see anyone around them truly living it.

My Reflection: As I reflect on the effectiveness of coaching, it is clear that the real game-changer is when someone—preferably a leader—embodies the principles. When leaders are not living the IMPACT framework, others do not take it seriously. I have seen firsthand how leadership can inspire massive change, but only if those in charge lead by example.

It is clear to me that people do not ignore IMPACT because it is not valuable. They ignore it because they have not yet experienced its power to change their lives—mainly because it is not being modelled for them, or they have not seen the results for themselves. Without emotional connection, without visible leadership, and without the patience to see it through, IMPACT just stays another theoretical model.

I believe the only way to truly make IMPACT meaningful is to live it. When we start embodying it, others will notice. That is when things will change.

To enhance the application of the **IMPACT Coaching Framework** in personal life, individuals need to develop key skills, tools, and actions that align with the framework's six pillars. These components allow individuals to create lasting, meaningful change, both in their personal growth and professional life. Here is a breakdown of the essential elements for effective application:

Key Skills for Personal Life Impact

1. **Self-Awareness** (I - Inspire Awareness & Identity)

   o Skill: Reflective Thinking and Self-Assessment

   o Action: Journaling, seeking 360-degree feedback, and identifying core values and limiting beliefs.

- o Tool: Self-assessment tools (e.g., StrengthsFinder, Johari Window)

2. **Growth Mindset** (M - Mindset & Mastery Shift)

- o Skill: Cognitive Reframing and Resilience Building

- o Action: Embrace challenges, reframe failures as learning experiences, and adopt a growth mindset through continuous learning.

- o Tool: Cognitive Behavioral Therapy (CBT), Neuro-Linguistic Programming (NLP), Reframing Techniques

3. **Purpose Alignment** (P - Purpose-Driven Goals & Strategy)

- o Skill: Goal Setting and Alignment with Core Values

- o Action: Setting meaningful, purpose-driven goals aligned with long-term visions and values.

- o Tool: SMART Goals, OKRs (Objectives and Key Results), Vision Board

4. **Consistent Execution** (A - Action, Accountability & Adaptability)

- o Skill: Habit Formation and Consistency

- o Action: Create habits that align with goals, track progress consistently, and be adaptable to changing circumstances.

- o Tool: Habit trackers (e.g., Habitica), resilience exercises, daily micro-commitments

5. **Collaboration & Networking** (C - Connection & Collaborative Growth)

- o Skill: Relationship Building and Mentorship

- o Action: Engage with mentors, coaches, and peers for continuous feedback, support, and growth.

- o Tool: Peer learning groups, mastermind groups, mentorship platforms

6. **Sustained Growth & Legacy** (T - Transform & Thrive)

   o Skill: Reflection, Legacy Planning, and Continuous Learning

   o Action: Regularly reflect on progress, adapt strategies, and plan for a lasting impact.

   o Tool: Leadership legacy planning tools, continuous education platforms

Key Tools for Effective Application

1. **Self-Assessment & Reflection Tools**

   o **Journals**: Keeping a daily journal helps to track thoughts, emotions, and actions, fostering greater self-awareness.

   o **360-Degree Feedback**: Gathering feedback from various sources can help identify blind spots.

   o **StrengthsFinder**: A tool to uncover inherent strengths, helping individuals align actions with their natural capabilities.

2. **Mindset Reframing Tools**

   o **Cognitive Behavioral Therapy (CBT)**: This helps in changing negative thought patterns and fostering a growth mindset.

   o **Neuro-Linguistic Programming (NLP)**: Techniques that reframe thought patterns and reduce fear of failure.

   o **Visualization Exercises**: Helps reframe challenges as opportunities for growth, enhancing resilience.

3. **Goal-Setting Frameworks**

   o **SMART Goals**: Provides clarity on what needs to be achieved and how it will be measured.

   o **OKRs**: A framework that enables individuals to align their personal goals with larger life objectives and track progress.

4. **Habit-Tracking and Accountability Tools**

   o **Habitica**: A digital habit tracker that makes habit formation fun and motivating by gamifying progress.

o **Resilience Exercises**: Regular practices to build mental and emotional resilience.

o **Accountability Groups**: Partnering with peers or a coach to track progress and keep each other motivated.

5. **Collaboration and Networking Tools**

o **Mastermind Groups**: These groups of individuals with shared goals provide mutual support, feedback, and shared accountability.

o **Mentorship Platforms**: Access to experienced mentors who guide personal and professional development.

6. **Transformation & Legacy Tools**

o **Leadership Legacy Planning**: Tools that help individuals align their actions with their legacy, ensuring long-term impact.

o **Continuous Education Platforms**: Learning resources (e.g., online courses, seminars) that foster lifelong learning and growth.

Key Actions to Maximize Impact

1. **Embrace Regular Reflection** (I - Inspire Awareness & Identity)

o Action: Dedicate time daily or weekly to self-reflection, identifying personal strengths, weaknesses, and growth opportunities.

2. **Adopt a Growth Mindset** (M - Mindset & Mastery Shift)

o Action: Practice resilience in the face of challenges, view failures as opportunities for learning, and push beyond comfort zones.

3. **Set Purposeful, Aligned Goals** (P - Purpose-Driven Goals & Strategy)

o Action: Define clear, purpose-driven goals aligned with personal values and long-term objectives. Break larger goals into smaller, actionable steps.

4. **Commit to Consistent Action** (A - Action, Accountability & Adaptability)

   o Action: Build daily habits, track progress, and hold oneself accountable. Stay adaptable and flexible to unforeseen challenges and opportunities.

5. **Foster Meaningful Connections** (C - Connection & Collaborative Growth)

   o Action: Invest in building relationships with mentors, peers, and other like-minded individuals. Seek collaboration for mutual growth and learning.

6. **Reflect and Plan for Legacy** (T - Transform & Thrive)

   o Action: Regularly review personal growth, reflect on long-term impact, and adapt strategies for continuous improvement and sustained legacy.

By mastering these **skills**, using the appropriate **tools**, and committing to consistent **actions**, individuals can effectively apply the IMPACT Framework to personal development. This comprehensive approach leads to significant, long-term growth and a powerful, lasting impact on one's life and career.

IMPACT Coaching Maturity Assessment Framework

Below is a structured Maturity Assessment Matrix you can use for evaluation, coaching sessions, or leadership development programs:

Stage	Maturity Level	Observable Indicators	Sample Validation Tools & Questions
I – Inspire Awareness & Identity	◈ **Beginner**: Low self-awareness, unclear values. ◈ **Intermediate**: Some reflection, knows strengths/ weaknesses. ◈ **Advanced**: Deep identity clarity, values-aligned actions.	- Speaks in vague terms about self - Blames external forces - Cannot articulate core values or strengths	☑ Self-reflection journal review ☑ 360° feedback summary ☑ Questions: • "Who are you at your best?" • "What values guide your daily decisions?"
M – Mindset & Mastery Shift	◈ **Beginner**: Dominated by fear, fixed mindset. ◈ **Intermediate**: Aware of limiting beliefs, starting to reframe. ◈ **Advanced**: Regularly practices growth mindset & reframing.	- Avoids risk or feedback - Uses language like "I can't" or "I'm not good at…" - Struggles with confidence under pressure	☑ Mindset quiz (Carol Dweck's model) ☑ NLP or CBT pattern identification ☑ Questions: • "What belief is limiting your next step?" • "When did you last reframe a fear into growth?"

Stage	Maturity Level	Observable Indicators	Sample Validation Tools & Questions
P – Purpose-Driven Goals & Strategy	◈ **Beginner**: Vague dreams, no plan. ◈ **Intermediate**: Some goal clarity but misaligned with values. ◈ **Advanced**: Crystal-clear goals tied to personal mission.	- Has no written goals or strategy - Acts reactively vs. intentionally - Cannot explain why a goal matter	☑ SMART/OKR audit ☑ Vision statement review ☑ Questions: • "Why is this goal meaningful to you?" • "What's your roadmap to get there?"
A – Action, Accountability & Adaptability	◈ **Beginner**: Procrastinates, avoids ownership. ◈ **Intermediate**: Takes some action but lacks consistency. ◈ **Advanced**: Demonstrates follow-through, resilient under change.	- Misses deadlines or resists change - Avoids accountability - Reluctant to experiment or adjust plans	☑ Weekly habit tracker ☑ Coaching accountability logs ☑ Questions: • "What actions have you completed this week?" • "How do you respond when plans change?"

Stage	Maturity Level	Observable Indicators	Sample Validation Tools & Questions
C – Connection & Collaborative Growth	◈ **Beginner**: Self-focused, poor listener. ◈ **Intermediate**: Values collaboration but not consistent. ◈ **Advanced**: Actively mentors, empowers, and influences others.	- Doesn't seek feedback or team input - Struggles with difficult conversations - Rarely acknowledges others' efforts	☑ Team feedback survey ☑ Listening & collaboration audit ☑ Questions: • "Whom have you empowered this month?" • "What does great collaboration mean to you?"
T – Transform & Thrive	◈ **Beginner**: Short-term thinker, fears uncertainty. ◈ **Intermediate**: Striving for impact, but not sustainable. ◈ **Advanced**: Operates with legacy mindset, system thinker, inspires others.	- Focused on survival not significance - Burnout risk is high - Cannot articulate long-term vision or broader impact	☑ Legacy worksheet ☑ Future vision coaching canvas ☑ Questions: • "What's the legacy you want to leave?" • "How are you building for long-term impact today?"

6-Month IMPACT Transformation Checklist Agenda

Each month is focused on a key pillar of the IMPACT Framework to drive sustainable transformation. Follow this path to align purpose, spark action, and scale growth.

Month 1 – I: Inspire Awareness & Identity

Theme: Reignite purpose. Realign people.

- Conduct a Purpose Alignment workshop with leadership
- Map out Vision, Mission, and Core Values using the Identity Canvas
- Share 3 internal stories of when your team made an authentic impact
- Launch a "Why We Exist" internal campaign
- Pulse survey: Ask teams to define what purpose means to them

Checkpoint: Have we clarified and communicated our True North?

Month 2 – M: Mindset & Mastery Shift

Theme: Build the emotional foundation for change.

- Run a "Mindset Reset" session to uncover limiting beliefs
- Introduce Growth Mindset principles in weekly standups
- Identify 3 outdated processes that need unlearning
- Host a Failure Story Friday: Normalize setbacks as learning
- Launch peer coaching or mentoring for mastery development

Checkpoint: Are we embracing challenges with curiosity instead of fear?

Month 3 – P: Purpose-Driven Goals & Strategy

Theme: Align strategy with soul.

- Co-create long-term goals aligned with organizational purpose
- Cascade 3-year vision into Q2 OKRs with leadership
- Build a Strategic Alignment Ladder: From values to deliverables
- Review which goals feel misaligned or mechanical
- Communicate the "why" behind every major goal to the teams

Checkpoint: Are we choosing goals that matter and energize?

Month 4 – A: Action, Accountability & Adaptability

Theme: Drive agile execution and clear ownership.

- Build Accountability Maps for top 5 priorities
- Prune 3 slow, bureaucratic processes
- Run a "Rapid Action Week" with quick wins and time-boxed goals
- Assign "Adaptability Leads" in each team to flag blockers
- Introduce a 15-minute weekly review: "What did we learn?"

Checkpoint: Are we moving fast, learning fast, and adjusting quickly?

Month 5 – C: Connection Across Teams

Theme: Bridge silos. Build culture.

- Launch "Voices of Innovation" forum with cross-functional groups
- Conduct a Culture Health Survey
- Create Inclusion Pods to brainstorm diversity challenges
- Highlight unsung heroes from different departments weekly
- Host monthly "Walk in My Role" empathy swaps

Checkpoint: Do people feel seen, heard, and connected across boundaries?

Month 6 – T: Transform & Scale

Theme: Cement habits. Celebrate transformation.

- Host a 6-month retrospective: wins, failures, lessons
- Share 3 transformation stories organization-wide
- Refresh the playbook based on real feedback
- Identify top 3 practices to scale company-wide
- Celebrate the teams that lived the IMPACT values boldly

Checkpoint: Are we evolving from activity to real transformation?

Final Action: Legacy Activation

- Design your "Next 6 Months" based on momentum and insights

- Mentor rising leaders to take ownership of the IMPACT journey

- Embed IMPACT rituals in hiring, onboarding, and recognition

- Create a Transformation Wall of Fame to spotlight team stories

As we draw the final page of this journey through the IMPACT Coaching Framework, it is important to recognize that true transformation goes far beyond the theoretical concepts and methodologies shared within these chapters.

While frameworks, strategies, and tools can provide the roadmap, the real magic happens when we, as leaders, begin to internalize these ideas and translate them into tangible actions. The power of the IMPACT framework lies not in its academic merit but in its ability to shape our day-to-day behaviors, decisions, and interactions.

When we embrace these principles—Inspire, Mindset, Purpose, Action, Connection, and Transformation—we begin to see leadership not as a title or a position to be attained but as a living, breathing practice that demands commitment, growth, and continuous self-reflection. It is about being present, setting the example, and embodying the values we wish to cultivate in others. The true essence of leadership is not measured in accolades or milestones but in the impact, we have on those around us and the legacy we leave behind.

The changes we seek in the world, in our teams, and in ourselves start with this simple truth: leadership is an ongoing journey, not a destination. It is about showing up, day after day, with purpose and a mindset focused on growth. As we lead with clarity, empathy, and resilience, we inspire others to do the same. This ripple effect—one rooted in authenticity and a relentless commitment to improvement—creates the possibility for profound, long-lasting change.

It is this very kind of leadership that sparks the potential in others, encourages a culture of trust and collaboration, and fosters an environment where everyone can thrive. In the end, leadership is not just about achieving success for ourselves; it is about creating an ecosystem where others can achieve theirs. By leaving behind a legacy built on empowerment, trust, and unwavering purpose, we can build a future that is not only different but better.

So, as you step forward from this moment, take with you the knowledge that the true power of leadership lies not in what we know but in how we choose to live and lead by example. It is in this commitment to be our best selves and to guide others to do the same that we transform not just individuals but entire communities. Leadership is the ultimate act of service—and in that service, we transform the world around us.

The **IMPACT Coaching Framework** stands apart from other coaching models by offering a **holistic, integrated approach** to leadership and personal transformation. While many frameworks focus on immediate actions or short-term results, **IMPACT** is designed to create lasting change by addressing the full spectrum of a leader's development. Here's how **IMPACT** delivers unique advantages over other popular models such as **GROW, OSKAR, CLEAR, STEPPA**, and **FUEL**:

Coaching Frameworks Comparison Table

Dimension	IMPACT	GROW	CLEAR	OSKAR
1. Starting Point	Self-awareness, identity, and purpose (Inspire)	Goal-setting	Contracting / setting agenda	Outcome-focused
2. Mindset & Inner Game	Strong focus: rewiring beliefs, emotional blockers	Limited	Lightly addressed	Minimal
3. Goal Alignment	Aligned with life purpose, values, and legacy	Performance-based goals	Client-defined goals	Practical solutions
4. Action Orientation	Action & adaptability systems built in (Act)	Strong action planning	Reflective action planning	Solution brainstorming
5. Accountability Support	Deep, with momentum tools and coaching loops	Light	Varies	Coach-led follow-ups
6. Collective Growth / Connection	Yes—emphasizes mentorship, collaboration, community	No	No	No
7. Legacy & Sustainability	YES—focuses on building legacy systems & transformation	Ends at goal achievement	Limited	Ends with review
8. Emotional Intelligence Integration	High—coaching the whole person	Low	Medium	Low
9. Flexibility / Customization	Modular tools for different niches & use cases	Basic model	Some flexibility	Structured, less flexible
10. Cultural / Philosophical Depth	Inspired by global leaders & timeless wisdom	Lacks depth	Western model	Solution-focused therapy influence

1. A Holistic, Transformative Approach

Unlike models that focus purely on goal-setting or short-term outcomes, **IMPACT** takes a **comprehensive approach** to transformation. It integrates six interconnected pillars—**Awareness, Mindset, Purpose, Action, Connection, and Transformation**—that drive long-term growth and success. This approach fosters **sustained change**, focusing not only on achieving immediate goals but also on **deep personal growth** and lasting leadership impact.

2. Deeper Self-Awareness

The first pillar of **IMPACT**, **Inspire Awareness & Identity**, goes beyond typical coaching frameworks by encouraging profound **self-reflection** and **identity exploration**. Unlike **GROW** or **CLEAR**, which primarily focus on actions and external goals, **IMPACT** begins with helping individuals understand **who they truly are**—their values, strengths, and how these influence their leadership style. This deep sense of self-awareness is crucial for cultivating authentic and effective leadership.

3. Mindset & Mastery for Lasting Change

The **Mindset & Mastery Shift** pillar of **IMPACT** addresses the root cause of barriers to success: **limiting beliefs** and **fear**. While frameworks like **GROW** and **OSKAR** focus on the **current reality** or **scaling solutions**, **IMPACT** takes a more transformative approach by helping individuals **reframe their mindset**. This shift is not just about solving problems—it is about changing how leaders **think** and **perceive challenges**, setting them up for **sustainable success** in the long run.

4. Purpose-Driven Goal Alignment

IMPACT goes beyond traditional goal-setting models like **FUEL** or **CLEAR**, which focus on understanding motivations and setting plans. Instead, the **Purpose-Driven Goals & Strategy** pillar centers on aligning actions with **core values** and a **personal sense of purpose**. This approach ensures that goals are not just achievable but also deeply meaningful, providing **long-term fulfilment**. **IMPACT** encourages leaders to think beyond short-term metrics and focus on creating a vision that resonates with both personal and professional aspirations.

5. Collaborative Leadership & Team Empowerment

Where many frameworks like **GROW** or **STEPPA** focus on individual progress, **IMPACT** emphasizes **collaborative leadership**. Its **Connection & Collaborative Growth** pillar encourages leaders to build teams, foster **mentorship**, and create an environment of mutual support. **IMPACT** recognizes that **leadership success is not just about individual achievement** but about creating a **culture of collaboration**, where teams thrive together. This focus on empowerment and mentorship is vital for sustainable, collective success.

6. Long-Term Growth & Legacy Building

The final pillar of **IMPACT**, **Transform & Thrive**, sets it apart by focusing not just on immediate success, but on **long-term growth** and **legacy**. While models like **OSKAR** and **FUEL** emphasize scaling and understanding, **IMPACT** incorporates **legacy building** as a key element. It challenges leaders to think about their **lasting impact**—how they will be remembered and how their influence will continue to shape their organizations, teams, and communities long after their tenure.

Key Differences Between IMPACT and Other Frameworks:

- **GROW**: A simple and effective model primarily focused on **goal-setting** and **action**. **IMPACT** delves much deeper into the **mindset, identity**, and **long-term transformation**, providing a fuller, more **sustainable approach** to leadership development.

- **OSKAR**: While **OSKAR** is strong in **scaling** and **solution-finding**, **IMPACT** places more emphasis on **belief transformation**, **personal values**, and creating **lasting impact**. It is about **transforming the person** as well as the problem.

- **CLEAR**: **CLEAR** is valuable for building trust and understanding at the start of coaching relationships, but **IMPACT** goes further by focusing on **long-term leadership transformation** and identity, helping individuals become **visionary leaders** with a legacy mindset.

- **STEPPA**: **STEPPA** integrates emotional awareness and self-regulation but is more narrowly focused on the individual's emotions. In contrast, **IMPACT** is **broader**—it covers **accountability**, **adaptability**, and **team empowerment** while fostering **long-term change**.

- **FUEL**: **FUEL** is great for **understanding motivations** and creating plans, but **IMPACT** ensures that these actions are not just reactive but aligned with a **deeper purpose** and **vision**, making it more holistic and impactful.

Why IMPACT is Truly Unique:

IMPACT is not confined to the transactional realm of tactical achievements; it is a journey into the very essence of leadership transformation, a holistic evolution encompassing the recalibration of mindset, the crystallization of identity, the deep grounding in core values, and the conscious shaping of leadership style. By artfully integrating the introspective power of self-awareness, the unwavering compass of purpose-driven goals, the amplifying force of collaboration, and the long-horizon perspective of legacy building, IMPACT provides a transformative architecture for leaders driven by a desire to forge change that endures and resonates with profound meaning. It is about nurturing leaders who not only navigate the present with exceptional skill but also sow the seeds of a powerful legacy that will blossom for generations to come.

If you seek a coaching framework that transcends the ephemeral nature of action plans, one that empowers you to sculpt your leadership journey into a testament of enduring impact, a legacy that speaks volumes long after your immediate presence, then IMPACT offers the true and sustainable path to realizing that profound vision.

Final comment:

The final page turns, but the journey of impact stretches endlessly before you. We stand now at the confluence of self-awareness, purposeful leadership, and the enduring ripple of legacy. This book has been a guide, illuminating a path that begins with the foundational power of coaching transformation and extends through the wisdom of ages, the triumphs of historical figures, the innovations of modern pioneers, and, most importantly, into the fertile ground of future potential.

Within these chapters, we have unearthed the transformative power of the IMPACT Coaching Framework, a tool not just for achieving goals, but for catalysing profound personal and collective evolution. We have explored the science that validates its consistent results, its remarkable adaptability to leadership, self-coaching, and the art of mentorship. This framework is not a static structure; it is a vibrant, living process, breathing with every conscious step you take, every empowering mindset shift you embrace, every purpose-driven decision you make.

Remember the initial spark in Chapter 1, acknowledging the unique headwinds facing young leaders and confronting the silent saboteurs that often impede their ascent? Overcoming these internal barriers is the very crucible in which unshakeable growth is forged in our ever-evolving world.

Reflect on the timeless wisdom shared in Chapter 2 by Vivekananda, Seneca, Rumi, and others, their philosophies resonating deeply with the core tenets of the IMPACT Coaching Framework. Their enduring teachings remind us that the wellspring of true leadership lies as much in the inner landscape as in the external world. Transformation, at its heart, is an inside job.

Witness again the extraordinary power of coaching manifested in the lives of Chandragupta Maurya, Napoleon, Shackleton, and Lee Kuan Yew in Chapter 3. Their greatness was not a birthright; it was sculpted by the trials they faced and illuminated by the guidance they received. Their journeys stand as powerful testaments to the fact that coaching and mentorship can ignite extraordinary transformations, even in the most challenging circumstances.

Revisit the modern coaching revolution unveiled in Chapter 4, where visionaries like Carnegie, Catmull, and Ferguson applied coaching principles to build empires, navigate the storms of crisis, and spark the flames of creative excellence. The IMPACT Coaching Framework transcends the boundaries of time, a timeless and indispensable compass in the intricate tapestry of the modern world.

And finally, remember our hopeful gaze towards the future in Chapter 5, focusing on the unbridled potential of the next generation. The IMPACT Coaching Framework is a seed of empowerment, nurturing young minds to overcome global challenges, embody their purpose, and rise above the limitations of fear. The truest legacy of leadership is not measured in titles or accolades, but in the lives, we uplift and the generations we inspire to reach for their own greatness.

Now, as you pause at the culmination of this shared journey, let these questions resonate within you: **How will you weave the principles of the IMPACT Coaching Framework into the very fabric of your life? How will you become the guiding light, coaching the next generation of leaders to soar to unprecedented heights?** The future is not a passive entity; it is being actively shaped by the way we choose to coach, to empower, and to lead with unwavering purpose.

Remember this profound truth: true leadership is not merely about changing the world; it is about the deeply human act of transforming the people within it. Whether you guide a team, mentor a young spirit, or coach yourself through the inevitable trials, your enduring legacy will be etched in the impact you have on the lives of others.

The time for reflection has nurtured the seed. **The time for action has arrived.** As you step forward, embrace the understanding that the journey of leadership and transformation is an unending cycle of growth, action, and profound self-awareness. Embrace its power.

This is not farewell, but a powerful invitation. Rise. Lead with intention. Coach with purpose. Transform with unwavering heart.

📓 Continue Your Journey

Want to go deeper with the tools, templates, and free resources mentioned in this chapter?

☞ Visit **chandanpatary.com** to access exclusive downloads, bonus workbooks, and updates on upcoming coaching programs.

By working through this book and applying the IMPACT framework, here's where you will arrive:

- **Inspire**: You will define your unique identity as a coach, aligned with your values and vision — no more imposter syndrome.

- **Mindset**: You will release limiting beliefs around money, visibility, and value — and gain rock-solid coaching confidence.

- **Purpose**: You will design a **signature offer** that solves real problems and attracts your ideal clients consistently.

- **Action**: You will set up marketing systems, lead magnets, content calendars, and sales funnels that feel authentic and aligned.

- **Connection**: You will build a referral engine through community, partnerships, and collaborations — clients will come looking for you.

- **Transform**: You will scale through group programs, digital products, and transformational experiences — turning your coaching into a legacy.

Notes

- The Coaching Habit: Say Less, Ask More & Change the Way You Lead Forever by Michael Bungay Stanier (1st Edition, 2016, Published by Box of Crayons Press)

- Becoming a Professional Life Coach: Lessons from the Institute for Life Coach Training by Patrick Williams and Diane S. Menendez (2nd Edition, 2015, Published by W. W. Norton & Company)

- Trillion Dollar Coach: The Leadership Playbook of Silicon Valley's Bill Campbell by Eric Schmidt, Jonathan Rosenberg, and Alan Eagle (1st Edition, 2019, Published by Harper Business)

- The Prosperous Coach: Increase Income and Impact for You and Your Clients by Steve Chandler and Rich Litvin (1st Edition, 2013, Published by CreateSpace Independent Publishing Platform)

- Co-Active Coaching: The Proven Framework for Transformative Conversations at Work and in Life by Henry Kimsey-House, Karen Kimsey-House, and Phillip Sandahl (4th Edition, 2018, Published by Nicholas Brealey Publishing)

- Flourish: A Visionary New Understanding of Happiness and Well-being by Martin E. P. Seligman (1st Edition, 2011, Published by Atria Books)

- Emotional Intelligence: Why It Can Matter More Than IQ by Daniel Goleman (1st Edition, 1995, Published by Bantam Books)

- Drive: The Surprising Truth About What Motivates Us by Daniel H. Pink (1st Edition, 2009, Published by Riverhead Books)

- Atomic Habits: An Easy & Proven Way to Build Good Habits & Break Bad Ones by James Clear (1st Edition, 2018, Published by Avery)

- The 7 Habits of Highly Effective People by Stephen R. Covey (1st Edition, 1989, Published by Free Press)

- The Inner Game of Tennis: The Classic Guide to the Mental Side of Peak Performance by W. Timothy Gallwey (1st Edition, 1974, Published by Random House Trade Paperbacks)

- Peak: Secrets from the New Science of Expertise by Anders Ericsson and Robert Pool (1st Edition, 2016, Published by Eamon Dolan/Houghton Mifflin Harcourt)

- Mastery by George Leonard (1st Edition, 1992, Published by Plume)

- Man's Search for Meaning by Viktor E. Frankl (1st English Edition, 1959, Published by Beacon Press)

- Grit: The Power of Passion and Perseverance by Angela Duckworth (1st Edition, 2016, Published by Scribner)

- The Power of Now: A Guide to Spiritual Enlightenment by Eckhart Tolle (1st Edition, 1997, Published by New World Library)

- Start with Why: How Great Leaders Inspire Everyone to Take Action by Simon Sinek (1st Edition, 2009, Published by Portfolio)

- The Untethered Soul: The Journey Beyond Yourself by Michael A. Singer (1st Edition, 2007, Published by New Harbinger Publications)

- The War of Art: Break Through the Blocks and Win Your Inner Creative Battles by Steven Pressfield (1st Edition, 2002, Published by Black Irish Entertainment)

- Mindfulness for Beginners: Reclaiming the Present Moment—and Your Life by Jon Kabat-Zinn (1st Edition, 2012, Published by Sounds True)

- The Leadership Challenge by James Kouzes and Barry Posner (6th Edition, 2017, Published by Wiley)

- True North by Bill George and Peter Sims (1st Edition, 2007, Published by Jossey-Bass)

- What Got You Here Won't Get You There by Marshall Goldsmith (1st Edition, 2007, Published by Hyperion)

- Meditations by Marcus Aurelius (Penguin Classics Edition, 2006, Published by Penguin Classics)

- The Analects by Confucius (Oxford World's Classics Edition, 2008, Published by Oxford University Press)

- Think and Grow Rich by Napoleon Hill (Revised Edition, 2005, Published by TarcherPerigee)

- High Output Management by Andrew Grove (Revised Edition, 1995, Published by Vintage)

- Freedom, Inc. by Brian M. Carney and Isaac Getz (1st Edition, 2009, Published by Crown Business)

- Who Says Elephants Can't Dance? by Louis V. Gerstner Jr. (1st Edition, 2002, Published by Harper Business)

- Coaching for Leadership by Marshall Goldsmith, Laurence Lyons, and Alyssa Freas (2nd Edition, 2006, Published by Jossey-Bass)

- The Art and Practice of Leadership Coaching by Howard Morgan, Phil Harkins, and Marshall Goldsmith (1st Edition, 2005, Published by Wiley)

- Ignited Minds: Unleashing the Power Within India by A.P.J. Abdul Kalam (1st Edition, 2002, Published by Penguin Books India)

- Dear England: Lessons on Leadership by Gareth Southgate (1st Edition, 2022, Published by Hutchinson Heinemann

9 79 8 8 9 9 9 6 1 7 9 9 7